Parents, Professionals and Mentally Handicapped People

APPROACHES TO PARNTERSHIP

Edited by
PETER MITTLER and HELEN McCONACHIE

CROOM HELM
London & Sydney

BROOKLINE BOOKS
Cambridge, Massachusetts

© 1983 Peter Mittler and Helen McConachie
Croom Helm Ltd, Provident House, Burrell Row,
Beckenham, Kent BR3 1AT

Croom Helm Australia Pty Ltd, Suite 4, 6th Floor,
64-76 Kippax Street, Surry Hills, NSW 2010, Australia

First paperback edition 1984
Reprinted 1986

British Library Cataloguing in Publication Data

Parents, professionals and mentally handicapped
   people.
   1. Mentally handicapped services – Congresses
   I. Mittler, Peter II. McConachie, Helen
   362.3'8   HV3004

   ISBN 0-7099-1750-3
   ISBN 0-7099-1797-X

Published in the USA and dependencies,
Central and South America by
Brookline Books, PO Box 1046,
Cambridge, MA. 02238

Library of Congress Cataloging in Publication Data
Main entry under title:

Parents, professionals and mentally handicapped people.

   Papers from a seminar held at the University of
Manchester, 1981, which was sponsored by the Bishop
Bekkers Foundation, Utrecht, and jointly organised
by the Bishop Bekkers Institute and the Hester Adrian
Research Centre, in association with the International
League of Societies for Persons with Mental Handicap.
   Bibliography: p.
   Includes index.
   1. Mentally handicapped – Family relationships –
Congresses. 2 Mentally handicapped – Europe – Family
relationships – Congresses. 3. Mentally handicapped –
Services for – Europe – Congresses. I. Mittler, Peter J.
II. McConachie, Helen. III. Bishop Bekkers Institute.
IV. Hester Adrian Research Centre. V. International
League of Societies for Persons with Mental Handicap.
HV3004.P37   1984   362.3'8   84-23751
ISBN 0-914797-12-3

Printed and bound in Great Britain by
Biddles Ltd, Guildford and King's Lynn

CONTENTS

SECTION FOUR: THE SCHOOL YEARS

SECTION FIVE: ADOLESCENCE AND ADULTHOOD

SECTION SIX: DISCUSSION AND FOLLOW-UP

TABLES AND FIGURES

This book is affectionately dedicated to Dorothy Jeffree on the occasion of her retirement from the Hester Adrian Research Centre, in recognition of her outstanding work in promoting partnership between parents, professionals and mentally handicapped people.

ACKNOWLEDGEMENTS

The editors wish to thank Beryl Sweeney and Norma
Bewley for their careful typing. We are very grateful to the National Council for Special Education
for permission to adapt Chapter 1 of this volume
from the pamphlet *Partnership with Parents* (Peter
Mittler and Helle Mittler, 1982) in the series
'Developing Horizons in Special Education', and
also to Ballière Tindall (Publishers) for permission
to reproduce Figure 5.1 from *Tredgold's Mental Retardation, 12th Edition* (Edited by M. Craft).

On behalf of all the participants, we thank the
Bishop Bekkers Foundation, Holland for creating the
opportunity to meet together in the European
Seminar, on whose proceedings this volume is based.

SECTION ONE: BACKGROUND

INTRODUCTION

Peter Mittler and Helen McConachie

This book is based on a European Seminar on the theme of 'Approaches to Parental Involvement' which was held at the University of Manchester in the autumn of 1981. It was sponsored by the Bishop Bekkers Foundation in Utrecht, and jointly organised by the Bishop Bekkers Institute and the Hester Adrian Research Centre in association with the International League of Societies for Persons with Mental Handicap.

The idea for a European Seminar arose from Dr. Sandor Nemeth and Enno Felix of the BBI which, in addition to its research and development work in the Netherlands, is now stimulating international studies designed to advance knowledge and understanding of the needs of mentally handicapped people. In May 1980 the Institute organised a workshop on the needs of young mentally handicapped children in developing countries which, with the support of UNICEF, Rehabilitation International and other organisations, has now developed into a major international study involving 13 developing countries in different parts of the world.

Closer collaboration between professionals and parents of mentally handicapped people was chosen as the theme of the seminar because it was felt to be one of the most significant developments in the field of mental handicap, and one in which much could be gained by the exchange of experiences and constructive suggestions for change among people from different countries. Over and above this, however, we wanted the seminar to lead to new developments in each country represented. To this end, we suggested that participants from each country should identify one or two ways in which they could use what they learned in the seminar in order to introduce or stimulate some degree

3

of change in their own communities.

With this end in view, two participants came to the seminar from each of nine European countries - generally one parent and one professional. The parents were nominated by the national parent societies, who were mostly members of the International League of Societies for Persons with Mental Handicap (ILSMH). In general, it was the parent who then nominated a professional 'partner', mostly teachers and social workers but also a psychiatrist and a physiotherapist. There were 23 participants from Austria, Belgium, Denmark, England, France, West Germany, Netherlands, Norway and Sweden. The Royal Society for Mentally Handicapped Children and Adults (MENCAP) was represented by Pauline Fairbrother (vice-chairperson), James Ross (director of Welfare Services) and John Chillag, chairperson of MENCAP's International Committee, and also of the European Committee of ILSMH.

Eleven papers were specifically written for the seminar and were circulated to all participants in advance. With the exception of a contribution from Canada, all the papers were prepared in Britain, six of these by members of research teams based in the Hester Adrian Research Centre (HARC) and the other five by parents and professionals from other areas.

Staff of HARC have for the past 11 years been involved in a variety of different approaches to working with parents (briefly summarised in *Parents' Voice*, vol. 29, pp.14-15, 1979). In 1970 and 1971 Cliff Cunningham and Dorothy Jeffree directed a series of informal evening workshops in which parents of pre-school mentally handicapped children were helped to assess the developmental level of their children and on this basis to help them to reach the next stage in their development. This led in 1973 to a four year research project in which Dorothy Jeffree and Roy McConkey developed a series of measures to help parents to assess their preschool child's current abilities and also devised a large number of simple teaching games which were incorporated in a series of books published by Souvenir Press (eg. *Let Me Speak, Let Me Play, Teaching the Handicapped Child*). Cliff Cunningham's home visiting programme to Down's syndrome infants and their parents also began in 1973 and still continues. The Anson House Preschool Project was launched in 1975 and has developed influential models of practice in relation to the integration of handicapped and non-handicapped children and also in

4

respect of parental involvement. In 1977 Dorothy
Jeffree and Sally Cheseldine began the Parents and
their Handicapped Teenagers project by conducting a
survey of over 200 mentally handicapped school
leavers and their families in Greater Manchester;
they then developed a variety of approaches designed
to help these young people to extend the range of
both their leisure skills and their social interactions, partly through parental involvement.

These and other HARC projects reflect a variety
of different approaches to working with parents and
also reflect the exploration over the past ten years
of a variety of patterns of partnership. The
European seminar helped to widen our horizons and
has stimulated new developments.

The chapters that follow are based on edited
and adapted versions of the papers which were
presented at the seminar. In addition, we have
summarised the discussions following the presentation of each paper or group of papers; these were
led by teams from six of the countries, each of
which had made a particularly close study of the
papers before coming to Manchester, often in association with other colleagues in their own areas. We
have also prepared summaries of the accounts given
by participants of the situation concerning
relationships between parents and professionals in
their own countries or in their own immediate
localities. We also prepared edited versions of the
discussions which follow the papers.

The book is introduced by an 'overview' chapter
by Peter and Helle Mittler which tries to provide
definitions and a rationale for partnership between
parents and professionals, and which gives a number
of examples of specific ways in which such a
partnership can be realised at various stages of a
child's development. Particular attention is given
to the needs of parents of adolescents and young
adults. The following two chapters (Phillipa
Russell and James Ross) are by parents in positions
of leadership in voluntary organisations, the first
summarising parents' needs and the second illustrating one way in which parents have helped and
supported each other.

The next four chapters illustrate a variety of
approaches to partnership in the early years of
childhood. Dana Brynelsen describes a government-
supported home visiting programme for developmentally delayed children in British Columbia.
Cliff Cunningham reports on a home visiting project
for families of Down's syndrome children in the

first two years of life, starting as young as six
weeks. Sally Beveridge describes a university-based
integrated facility for mentally handicapped and
normally developing pre-school children, where
parents are fully involved in all decision-making
concerning the child's individual programme and
attempts are made to understand and meet the needs
of the child in the wider context of the family.
Helen McConachie's chapter discusses how these and
other families of young handicapped children
perceive their roles as parents and siblings and how
widely individual families differ in their organization of daily life at home.

Relationships between parents and teachers of
school age children are then explored in three contrasting chapters. Barbara Smith literally provides
an A-Z of the various elements of partnership
between teachers and parents. Shirley Rheubottom's
chapter illustrates some of the difficulties of
developing such a partnership when the authorities
provide a transport service which unwittingly
distances parent and teacher, and the child from
other children. Jill Gardner provides a detailed
account of how one school gradually modified its
relationships with parents in a series of workshops
in which parents were helped to become proficient in
specific teaching skills within the context of
curriculum objectives set by the school.

Relationships between professionals and parents
develop new dimensions and new problems as children
become adolescents and young adults. Dorothy
Jeffree and Sally Cheseldine illustrate some of
these in the context of a survey of the social
abilities and leisure interests of a group of young
people about to leave special schools, which highlighted the vital importance of parents and teachers
sharing their knowledge and skills at this crucial
time. Pauline Fairbrother takes this a step further
by considering some of the basic questions facing
young adults and their families, including those
concerned with the development of adult sexuality
and the need to prepare adults for separation from
their parents and for their eventual death.

The last section of the book looks to the
future. First, Helen McConachie summarises reports
from European participants concerning relationships
between parents and professionals in their countries
which indicate clearly that, in some countries, at
least, particularly the Netherlands and Sweden,
parents have consciously decided against close
partnership, preferring to leave teaching to

teachers and to be free to concentrate on their role as parents. Other countries report a range of relationships, some involving open conflicts and some working painfully towards collaboration. For a British audience, it was particularly interesting to hear accounts of teachers employed in schools established by parent organizations and supported from public funds.

Finally, Peter Mittler summarises possibilities for progress. Some of these were drawn from the plans prepared by participants themselves during the course of the seminar, in fulfillment of the aim of 'putting the seminar to work' by developing an action plan for implementation in their own communities. Others arose from the papers and from discussions following the papers.

We are publishing this book because we learned a great deal from the seminar. It was refreshing to meet people from other countries and to be able to share ideas and experiences in small groups. We learned that although we have a great deal in common in terms of many of the basic questions which confront anyone working and living with mentally handicapped people, there are also many major differences in attitudes and approaches – to being a parent, to being a professional and to the range of possible relationships between the two. The fact that parents and professionals came 'in pairs' meant that at least some of them had already established some kind of working relationship before they arrived. But many of them found that hearing about the rich variety of possible relationships caused them to re-examine their own and to listen with special interest to accounts which differed radically from their own experience.

There is clearly no prescription for partnership, just as there is no prescription for how to be a parent or a teacher. Although some professionals are aware of how much there is to gain by working in closer collaboration with parents, parents in their turn should not feel forced to collaborate and should have the right to 'opt out'. Just as children are seen as unique individuals, so parents must also be seen as individuals with unique personalities and needs. But for those who are prepared to explore what is involved in working together, there is much to be learned from the experience of others. We hope that this book will make a contribution to the development of partnership and to meeting the needs of children and adults who are mentally handicapped.

7

Chapter 1

PARTNERSHIP WITH PARENTS: AN OVERVIEW

Peter and Helle Mittler

INTRODUCTION

The development of better working relationships
between parents and professionals constitutes one of
the most significant developments in the field of
special education during the past decade. But
although a whole series of reports from government,
professional and parents' bodies endorse the principle, we have remarkably little information on actual
practice. Despite the positive climate of opinion
on the desirability of closer partnership between
parents and professionals, there is still considerable uncertainty about what to do and how to start.
    This chapter explores some of the elements in-
volved and provides examples of ways in which
partnership has been realised. An attempt will be
made to define and provide a rationale for partnership, and to illustrate different patterns of
collaboration. Examples will be given of relevant
service provision at various stages of the child's
development, including infancy, the pre-school,
school and school-leaving period. A more detailed
account will be given of special issues arising from
collaboration between professionals and parents of
adolescents and young adults, since these have received relatively little attention in the literature
so far. Finally we will attempt a summary of some
of the essential elements of partnership in the
light of our discussion of current practice.

APPROACHES TO PARTNERSHIP

We begin by drawing a distinction between parental
involvement and partnership. Parents may be productively involved in the work of professionals and
collaborate with schools and other institutions but

this may fall a long way short of partnership. We
can think of partnership as an ideal, a goal towards
which we should be working but one which is not
necessarily achieved in practice, even when parents
and professionals seem to be working well together.

Three main phases can be detected in the
relationship of professionals and parents of handicapped children. For many years parents received
little help from professionals and were left largely
unsupported. Such advice as they received tended to
be negative and rarely included practical suggestions on what they could do to help their child at
home. Indeed, parents were at one time frequently
advised to place the child in residential care.

The second phase, called the 'transplant' phase
by Jeffree (1980) and beginning towards the end of
the 1960s, took the form of training parents to use
some of the techniques restricted to professionals
and regarding them as 'co-therapists' or co-teachers.
Many parents were quick to learn these techniques
and put them to good use with their children;
research workers began to investigate the most
effective methods of training parents and enlisting
their help in carrying out programmes devised by
professionals (O'Dell, 1974). Professionals largely
worked on the assumption that they knew best what
the child should learn and therefore what the parents should do at home. It is not surprising that
some parents rejected such a one-way approach and
resented the implicit assumption that professionals
knew what was best for their child.

We are now entering on a third phase which has
been characterised as the 'consumer model'. This is
summarised by Cunningham as follows:

> In the consumer model we ...... aim to augment
> parenting skills ...... and do not try to
> change the consumer (parent) into a profess-
> ional teacher; we do not attempt to 'trans-
> plant' professional skills into the home so
> that professional therapies per se are main-
> tained and extended via the parent. To do
> this is to risk 'rejection'. Instead, we
> offer parents what we feel is the necessary
> information for them to live with and help
> their child with Down's syndrome. They then
> select from this according to their current
> needs and in their own time.

> (Chapter 5, this volume)

9

The consumer model starts with the parents' natural style of interacting with their child and takes account of the needs, resources and uniqueness of each individual family. It rests on the assumption that:

> .. further progress in developing services for young handicapped children is crucially dependent on understanding, and respecting, the range of different ways in which families think and live their lives. Approaches based merely on educational technology will fail to meet a child's or a family's needs, just as institutional answers failed previously.
>
> (McConachie, Chapter 7, this volume)

Partnership involves a full sharing of knowledge, skills and experiences. A commitment to partnership rests on the assumption that children will learn and develop better if parents and professionals are working together on a basis of equality than if either is working in isolation. One of the foundations of partnership between parents and professionals lies in the recogniton of how much they have in common and how much they have to learn from one another. In fact, it is not as easy to make a sharp distinction between them as commonsense might at first suggest. Professionals increasingly recognise that there is a parenting component to their work, and that a degree of emotional involvement is essential. They must consider the needs of the whole child and not just the need to learn; they must build on their relationship with the child in order to teach. Similarly, parents are learning some of the technical skills of teaching, such as breaking a task down into small steps, using prompting, fading and reward techniques and so on.

Perhaps we have all become a little intoxicated in the past ten years by the success with which many parents have responded to the opportunities provided by professionals to share in the task of working with their own child. It certainly is extraordinary that it has taken so long for professionals to become aware of the many ways in which parents can be actively enlisted in day to day work with their child - so much so that the professionals now write of parents, with some surprise, as 'the only true experts', and 'the best resources we have'. Perhaps the shortage of skilled staff and the sudden drying up of public funds has caused them to see the light. It may also be due in part to a growing confidence among the professionals themselves, brought about by new developments in the technology of teaching which not only lend themselves to communication to parents but which lose much of their force if they are not shared with parents.

There is no doubt that many of the skills traditionally reserved for professionals can be learned by parents and that there is a sense in which professionals need to learn to share some of their skills with parents. But this is not necessarily a reflection of partnership, though it is undoubtedly a worthwhile and effective form of collaboration and parental involvement. Partnership involves a two way process of joint assessment and decision making in which parents and professionals come together right from the start.

Partnership can take many forms but it must by definition be on a basis of equality, in which each side has areas of knowledge and skill that it contributes to the joint task of working with the child. For example,

. it is not partnership when professionals unilaterally make their own assessments and decisions about what and how to teach the child and then ask the parents to co-operate in teaching the child or in keeping records to see whether he or she uses at home the skills that have been taught in school;
. it is not partnership when parents are shown how to carry out certain physical exercises without being given any intelligible explanations about the reasons why these particular exercises are necessary;
. it is not partnership when parents are not consulted about their own resources or abilities to collaborate even with teaching schemes that they themselves have helped to devise.

Partnership calls for an exploration of the needs of the families, of their feelings about their own competence and their own emotional and social resources as a family. Parents of handicapped people *have no common characteristics*; they come from all sections of society and represent the whole range of individual differences and personality. Profession-

als will therefore need to enlarge their own understanding of the tremendous variety of needs and the
infinite range of personalities which they will encounter in parents. They will need to strike a balance between helping parents to learn some of the
skills of professionals while at the same time helping them to retain their own sense of identity as
parents and as individuals.

Not all parents want to be involved in depth
and detail in the day to day task of teaching their
child, and even those who want to be involved may be
prevented from doing so by real practical obstacles
such as time, gross overcrowding, severe social or
marital problems or sheer exhaustion. If we are
serious about helping parents to choose, we must
allow them to choose not to be involved at the level
of detailed collaboration which some professionals
are now offering. After all, the level of work and
commitment to partnership with professionals is
still new in many places and quite unfamiliar to
some. Many parents still regard - or need to
regard - professionals as people with special training in working with handicapped children and as
possessors of all kinds of specialised techniques
which require three or more years training to
acquire. Having waited for several years for their
child to enter school, they need to believe that the
child is passing into the care of highly trained and
skilled professionals. It is therefore something of
a shock when they realise that teachers, like themselves, are often floundering and overwhelmed; they
may be unprepared for the opportunities for day to
day participation in assessing the child's needs and
in implementing daily programmes of collaborative
work.

A recent review by Turnbull and Turnbull
(1982), themselves both parents and professionals,
questions the extent to which parents really wish to
be involved in decision making and in joint teaching
with professionals. They review a number of studies
which reflect parents' frequently expressed wish to
be able to 'live their own lives'; to this end, what
they value most is competent teachers. When asked
to describe an ideal nursery school, only a few parents spontaneously mentioned parent involvement of
any kind as an essential component of the programme.
Furthermore, a number of studies cast doubt on the
actual quality of parents' participation in the
decision making process which is now a legal re-
quirement as a consequence of US Public Law 94-142.
In a survey of 2,300 parents from 438 school dist-

ricts in the USA, just over half the parents reported that their child's individual educational programme had been completed *before* the IEP meeting.
Other studies reviewed by the Turnbulls indicate
that teachers monopolised the conversation and that
parents' contributions were largely confined to personal and family issues and were not about educational matters such as assessment, curriculum and
placement.

The Turnbulls note the paradox that while
special education has made progress in knowledge of
how to meet the individual needs of children, it has
not yet reached the stage where it allows for a
sufficiently wide range of variation in the individuality of parents. This means that parents
should feel free to choose not to be involved with a
school programme.

> Rather than mandating that all parents be
> equal participants with the school personnel
> to make decisions jointly, public policy
> should tolerate a range of parent involvement
> choices and options, matched to the needs and
> interests of the parent.

A RATIONALE FOR PARTNERSHIP

A case for the development of a closer partnership
between parents and professionals might include the
following considerations (Mittler, 1979).
   1.   Growth and learning in children can only
be understood in relation to the various environments in which the child is living. These include
his or her immediate family, peers, schools, local
community and the wider society. The study of child
development calls for an examination of ways in
which the child interacts with, affects and learns
from these various environmental influences. We can
neither study nor teach the child in isolation.
   2.   Teachers and parents have similar goals,
particularly for the more severely handicapped.
Thus, both teachers and parents will be concerned
with ways of teaching the child self-care and social
independence, including self-feeding, dressing and
toileting, as well as early cognitive skills, sym-
bolic and representational play and learning to
understand and produce language. Social and emotional development are equally the concern of both
teachers and parents.
   3.   Studies contrasting the relative influence
of home and school on children's intellectual and

13

educational achievements strongly suggest that the
influence of the home is comparatively greater in
the early years and that children who come from
homes where the parents take an active interest in
the child's education tend to have higher school
attainments. These studies have for the most part
been carried out on normal children but there is
evidence that this relationship is likely to be even
stronger in handicapped children.

4.   Parents need to be aware of the precise
teaching methods and strategies being used by teachers and other professionals to achieve any particular teaching goal. It is important for parents and
teachers to adopt a reasonably consistent approach
in helping children to learn to feed or dress themselves, in encouraging the use of longer sentences
or in dealing with behaviour difficulties. Such
methods need to be discussed and agreed between
teachers and parents so that at the very least each
is familiar with the approach being taken by the
other.

5.   Mentally handicapped children have been
shown to have particular difficulties in general-
ising their learning experiences and to use in one
setting skills which they have learned in another.
Special measures are needed to overcome this def-
icit, including carefully planned programmes to
teach generalisation across settings.

6.   Knowledge and experience of normal children and ordinary parental intuition, while undoubtedly valuable, are not necessarily adequate to
assist the development of a handicapped child. It
is not enough for professionals to advise parents
to treat their handicapped child as they would any
other child. Such advice is well meaning but does
not go far enough in preparing parents for some of
the specific difficulties which they will experience
in meeting the needs of children whose development
is not proceeding normally or where there are severe
abnormalities and disorders of development or behaviour.

In the first place, the age of the handicapped
child is not always an adequate guide for the parent. Not only is the child likely to be developing
much more slowly than normal, but some areas of development may be proceeding more slowly than others.
It is important for the parent to be aware of the
significance of such uneven development, particularly, for example, in the area of speech and language development where underfunctioning is common.
Some parents are easily discouraged by lack of pro-

gress and need to appreciate the significance of even the smallest step in development and the means by which the child can be helped to attain it.

Furthermore, there is sometimes a risk that the child remains for too long at a particular stage of development because it is assumed that this is part of the handicap. Parents and teachers need to work together to plan the next developmental step and to remain alert to signs from the child of readiness to respond to teaching designed to help in the acquisition of new skills. When development takes place in 'slow motion' or when it is distorted by severe handicaps, it is particularly important to maintain a regime of demand and expectation and not to assume that all difficulties and problems are due to the handicap when they may to some extent spring from under-estimation of what can be expected of the child or from teaching goals that are no longer developmentally appropriate.

THE NEEDS AND STRENGTHS OF FAMILIES

It is all too easy to generalise about 'the needs of families' and to overlook the enormous range of individual differences. These will differ as much as, if not more than, the needs of any other families. We should also beware of drawing too sharp a distinction between parents of handicapped and non-handicapped people. For example, in studying the families of cerebral palsied children, Hewett (1970) concluded that "families meet the day to day problems that handicap creates with patterns of behaviour that in many respects deviate little from the norms derived from studying the families of normal children. They have more similarities with ordinary families than differences from them" (page 194). Most parents of handicapped people have also had several other normal children, and will, therefore, have considerable experience not only of child-rearing, but also of helping their older children to achieve independence. It surely makes sense to harness the experience and expertise of parents in bringing up their own children and in knowing the needs and strengths of their handicapped child.

To stress the essential individuality and normality of the families is not to deny the range and severity of the problems they face; rather it is to counter the assumptions and stereotypes which have so often been used by professionals and researchers about the underlying social pathologies to be found in the families. The danger lies in the consequent lack of appropriate action by professionals in response to families' needs. For example, parents seeking help at an early stage report being labelled 'overanxious' and denied credit for close observation of their child (e.g. Schaefer, 1979). Families seeking residential care for their handicapped member may be investigated for 'guilt' and 'rejection'; those not seeking relief may be labelled 'overprotective'. The behaviour of the families may be interpreted as abnormal whatever they do. Such negative stereotyped judgements are a poor basis for partnership (Mittler, Cheseldine and McConachie, 1981).

We need more information on how the family as a whole perceive their needs and what kind of demands are made on other members of the family both by the needs of the child and the expectations of professionals. The emotional reactions and practical realities of all the individual members of the family will determine the nature and degree of any possible partnership between the family and professionals. While the training and experience of social workers lays particular emphasis on the skills of working with the family as a whole, all professionals working with families will need to be aware of the normality of negative feelings and of the problems of balancing the needs of the handicapped person with those of other members of the family and household.

We should also note that whatever we might say about whole families, many mothers are in fact looking after handicapped children largely on their own and with little help or support from other family members or from the surrounding community (Wilkin, 1979). In addition, many children now live with only one parent, generally the mother. Unsupported mothers have special problems; although special financial incentives in the form of grants are available, these are rarely adequate to provide help with the day to day task of looking after a home and caring for and working with a handicapped child. Furthermore, some mothers would prefer to work at least part-time, just like mothers of other children, and do not wish to be tied to the home or to a programme of intensive care, however well thought out. Here again, we need to find the means of allowing mothers to express their own preferences, and to choose between rationally presented alternatives.

Many people are also acting as parent substitutes: in particular foster parents, staff of residential care establishments, including hospitals, as well as children's hostels or group homes. Residential care workers are currently discussing the extent to which they should in fact see themselves as substitute parents; doubts are being expressed about the possibility or even the desirability of professional staff acting as parent substitutes at all.

It seems essential that residential care staff should become as skilled as parents have shown themselves to be in working in partnership with other professionals to achieve developmental goals and objectives for the children in their care. This means that residential care workers should be encouraged to work in partnership with schools, with assessment and development centres and clinics, with parents themselves, and with any other agencies whose job it is to assess and draw up developmental plans for handicapped children. It is ironic that professional residential care staff rarely seem to take part in the process of assessment and programme planning, when many parents have demonstrated their willingness and ability to contribute their expert knowledge of the child by acting to all interests and purposes as members of the assessment team. It might be argued that professional staff should expect to be involved in both assessment and programme planning, and that they should be trained to acquire the necessary skills to do so.

In addition to partnership between professionals and parents in relation to their own child, we should also emphasise the growing participation by parents in policy formation at local, national and international levels. Parents are increasingly participating in decision making affecting the planning, development and operation of services. At local level, for example, more parent representatives will in future be acting as school governors, as members of community health councils and as members of joint care planning teams which have been established since 1976 to work for more effective collaboration between health and local authorities. Of course, there are still many parts of the country where parents are excluded from such bodies as a matter of policy but the movement for participation is growing.

At national level, parent representatives have worked effectively on a number of influential government advisory bodies - for example, on the Warnock Committee and the National Development Group for the Mentally Handicapped; they also take part in visits to field authorities by the Development Team for Mental Handicap. At the international level, the International League of Societies for Persons with Mental Handicap - a federation of 85 parent and professional societies in 65 countries - was not only responsible for the drafting of the UN Declaration of Rights of the Mentally Handicapped in 1971 but has since published detailed guidelines on how these rights can be implemented in services (ILSMH, 1978). It is also very active in working with the UN international agencies, such as WHO, UNICEF, UNESCO and ILO.

EXPRESSIONS OF PARENT-PROFESSIONAL COLLABORATION

Collaboration with parents is, then, one of the hallmarks of a well trained professional. Sheltering behind the walls of the organisation is a sign of professional insecurity, an indication that they are unsure of what they are doing or where they are going and are unable to share their concerns with those who care most about the handicapped person.

We can now consider a number of examples of collaboration between professionals and parents. Many of these examples are already in operation or are accepted in principle. Some are blocked for financial or administrative reasons; others cannot be implemented because of local attitudes and practices. Few call for significant new expenditure but all demand a commitment to working in closer partnership with parents (see also Pugh (1981) for other examples).

At Birth or Early Identification

Recent events have underlined the importance of ensuring that each maternity unit should develop procedures for the communication of the diagnosis of handicap to parents and should consider how this should best be handled. Although it is impossible to offer guidelines which would have general validity, there is ample evidence to indicate that the manner in which the diagnosis of handicap is first communicated to parents is of such profound importance for the development of the relationship between parent and child and between parents and professionals that it deserves the most serious study at local level. Current evidence suggests that this matter is still all too often handled with an absence of sensitivity to parents' feelings.

The balance of evidence from several surveys

indicates that the majority of parents want to be
informed of the diagnosis within the first 48 hours,
in the presence of both parents and of the child but
not in front of other hospital staff or students.
They also want access to accurate information and
opportunities to ask questions at subsequent meetings with the doctor. Above all, the parents want
practical support and guidance after leaving hospital (Spain and Wigley, 1975; Cunningham and Sloper,
1977).
     However well the early communication of handi-
cap is handled, it is essential to provide several
opportunities for parents to discuss their reactions
and to ask questions at leisure. Parents should
also be given a leaflet which briefly lists the
names and addresses of the main statutory and voluntary agencies that may be able to help. Parents
will not necessarily wish to avail themselves of the
offer of help at this stage but the opportunity to
do so at a later stage should be made available by
providing the relevant information in written form
to enable them to do so if they wish. Many parents
also welcome a written explanation of their child's
diagnosis and a factual statement of its possible
implications, together with some indication of the
forms of help that can be offered by the hospital.
In an increasing number of areas, an experienced
parent makes contact with the new parents, sometimes
accompanied by a health visitor or social worker.
     Hospital staff are not always well informed
about community support services for parents or
children. For example, they may be unaware of parents' self help groups, of 'parent to parent' programmes, of fostering, adoption and respite care
schemes developed by social services departments or
voluntary organisations. Nor are they necessarily
aware of the rapid developments which have taken
place in schools and in the development of methods
of teaching even the most severely handicapped children. As a result, an unduly gloomy prognosis may be
given which does not necessarily match up with the
development of services to young handicapped children and their families.

Children under Five
The 1981 Education Act marks a distinct advance in
recognising the importance of parents' access to information and services right from the start. Amongst
its most important provisions are the following:
     1.   Local Education Authorities are given the

powers to assess the special educational needs of
children under two, if the parents agree, and are
required to make such an assessment if the parents
request it (Section 6).

    2.   Health Authorities have a duty to inform
both the LEA and the parents of any children under
the age of five who are likely to have special educational needs. They must also provide opportunities to discuss with parents any decision to notify
the LEA, though parents cannot prevent this (Section
10).

    3.   Health Authorities also have a duty to in-
form parents of the name of the appropriate voluntary organisation that may be able to help them
(Section 10).

    Where children with special needs are attending
integrated forms of provision, it is particularly
important to ensure that the needs of their parents
are not overlooked. Many children are attending
ordinary pre-school services, such as nursery
schools and classes and playgroups but this does not
mean that parents are given opportunities to participate on a basis of equality and partnership in
the making of decisions about their child's day to
day programme of activities.

    Whenever possible one person should provide a
'single point of contact' for families, to act as
their source of support and, where necessary, of
advocacy to help to ensure that decisions taken by
service agencies are implemented and regularly reviewed. Services for the family should be mediated
by this person, to avoid duplication and the risk of
contradictory advice and misinterpretation. In a
sense, he or she acts as a co-ordinator and communi-
cator between professionals, as well as providing
support for the family. They should also mediate
between the family and professionals - for example,
in helping the family to express their dissatisfaction with the programmes being developed for their
child or in indicating that the pressure either on
the child to learn or on the family to participate
may be imposing excessive strain.

    A home-visiting service at the earliest poss-
ible moment should always be available. It is not
enough to ask parents to bring their baby to a paediatric or 'well baby' clinic. Many parents do not
feel sufficiently at ease in these situations to
enter into terms of equality with professionals.
Parents who brought their children to such centres,
often with considerable inconvenience to themselves
and distress to their children, have frequently ex-

pressed disappointment at the outcome. Although the child was generally expertly assessed, sometimes by multidisciplinary teams including not only doctors but psychologists, speech and physiotherapists and perhaps an educationalist or social worker, it was relatively rare for the parents to be given any advice or assistance on how they themselves could actively work with their child at home to further his or her development. They might be given general advice, along the lines of 'treat your child as normally as possible' or 'talk to him and play with him as much as you can' and told to come back in so many months so that the specialists could monitor the child's development. But they were not necessarily shown particular and specific approaches that might be helpful - for example, methods of holding and carrying a child with cerebral palsy, how to overcome feeding problems presented by a severely handicapped child, by a child with Down's syndrome who was exceptionally slow to feed, perhaps due to a large tongue or weak musculature, or how to help a child to learn to communicate.

Examples of a home visiting service for parents of preschool children can be found in the Portage programmes, developed initially in rural areas in the USA but now successfully replicated in the UK (Revill and Blunden, 1980). The model here is one in which a home visitor (who can be trained in as little as a week) visits families once a week in order to work out short term goals for the child and to introduce specific structured methods which the parents can use to try to help the child to reach such goals within one or two weeks. (See Chapter 4, this volume.)

Regular visits to the home also provide opportunities for the parent to raise wider issues beyond the immediate training programme - for example, problems or anxieties about future school placement, entitlements to allowances and benefits or questions concerned with the needs of other members of the family, particularly siblings. While the home visitor will be able to provide a considerable amount of support to the family in raising and discussing these issues, she or he will need to have sufficient knowledge of other agencies to know whether outside help should be sought. (See Chapter 5, this volume, and Cunningham and Sloper, 1978.) Even so, it is dangerous to assume that it will always be possible for parents to adopt a teaching role with their child. Discussions of a frank and open nature about what is appropriate and possible for each family is essential if we are to avoid the risk of imposing both practical and emotional burdens on families.

Partnership between Home and School
The range of relationships between parents and teachers is very wide. It can extend, at one extreme, from merely formal communication about dates of terms to open access to all reports and records on their child, to participation of parents in classroom teaching, discussions of school policy and curriculum and selection of teachers as members of school governing boards.

Many schools are now re-examining their practice, just as many parents are pressing for a greater degree of participation in the development of plans and programmes for their own child. In particular, parents who have had positive and successful experiences of collaboration with professionals before their child went to school represent a new generation of articulate, well informed and highly skilled parents. Once their child moves into full-time special education, they tend to ask questions about the school's policy for partnership with parents. "How are we going to work together in assessing my child's strengths, weaknesses and needs? When do we discuss selection of priorities for teaching and what kind of communication link are we going to set up to keep each other informed?"

Although there are a growing number of published reports of specific projects, we are short of factual information on the nature and extent of home-school links either nationally or regionally. One of the few exceptions is a survey of all special schools in Manchester undertaken by the Manchester School Psychological and Child Guidance Service in which one of us (HM) has been involved. A detailed questionnaire was developed which formed the basis of a semi-structured interview with headteachers and other staff of all the 28 special schools in the City. The results of the survey have been reported elsewhere (H. Mittler, 1982). Here we shall illustrate a number of ways in which home-school links are being developed, using as a starting point some items from the questionnaire and suggestions made by a number of writers. (See also Chapters 8 and 10, this volume.)

The Manchester questionnaire explored home-school links at three stages – when children first enter the school, while they are at school, and at the time of preparation for leaving. It also in-

22

vited suggestions from headteachers on ways in which parents can and do contribute to the life of the school and asked for examples of successful and less successful attempts to involve parents. As a result of this exercise, some headteachers approached parents about their own experience of collaboration with schools and invited suggestions from them on how home-school links could be improved. One new headteacher designed her own 36 item questionnaire, personally visited all the families of children in her school and is modifying school practice in the light of parents' responses (Boucher, 1981).

Entry into School
1.   Home visits *Does a member of the school staff visit the family at home before the child starts school?*
Such visits enable the head or class teacher to get to know the whole family not just the mother, and to see the child in the home setting. They can help teachers to learn something of the child's behaviour at home, and to begin to build up a picture of strengths and needs, as well as the priorities of the family. An initial visit can also help to identify the best ways for the child to start school - e.g. by periods of part-time attendance, the extent to which a parent should stay with the child, any special difficulties about eating, toileting, medical problems and transport.
        One of the aims of a home visit is to begin to discuss with the family ways in which home and school can establish a working relationship. This will obviously take time to negotiate and will depend on the resources and priorities of the family but visits to the home can begin to lay the foundations for a realistic discussion of what will and will not be possible. This is also a good opportunity to make it clear that parents are welcome at school.
2.   Assessment. The 1981 Education Act formalises the rights of parents to be involved in decisions concerning their child's special educational needs. These rights are summarised in DES Circular 8/81 but further regulations and guidance are promised. Amongst the changes in the new Act are the following:

    1.   LEA's must notify parents of their inten-
          tion to make an assessment and provide in-
          formation about assessment and procedures.
          They must also notify parents of the
          results of the assessment. Parents must
          be given the name of an officer from whom

23

they can obtain further information and
be informed about their rights of appeal
to the Secretary of State.

2.   Parents must receive a draft of the LEA's
     statement of special educational needs and
     have a right to an interview with an
     officer of the LEA and with anyone who
     gave advice to the LEA about their child's
     statement of needs. The LEA must consider
     any representations made by parents.

3.   Parents have the right of appeal to a
     local appeal committee against special
     educational provision specified in a
     statement. Although the appeal committee
     can refer an appeal for the reconsider-
     ation of the LEA, they do not have the
     power to overrule the LEA. In this case,
     or if the appeal committee agree with the
     LEA's judgement, the parents can appeal to
     the Secretary of State if they are not
     satisfied with the LEA's decision. He or
     she has the power to confirm or amend the
     statement or to direct the LEA to cease to
     maintain the statement.

4.   LEA's have a duty to comply with requests
     for assessments made by parents, 'unless
     it is in their opinion unreasonable'.
     Parents may appeal to the Secretary of
     State if they feel aggrieved by the LEA's
     decision not to make an assessment.

5.   Parents are required to present the child
     for any examination felt necessary to
     enable the Secretary of State to determine
     issues arising from the provisions of the
     Act.

Once the child is in school, collaboration
between parents and teachers is a matter of good
practice rather than legislation. The question can
therefore be put as follows:
*How are the parents involved in the assessment of their
child's skills, abilities and needs?*
The answer to this question will depend on the kind
of assessment procedures used in the school. Some
schools use published developmental checklists,
others have developed their own checklists. In
either case, it is worth considering ways in which
parents can provide information based on their own
expert knowledge of the child's behaviour. Some
schools go through a checklist with the parents item
by item, others leave a copy of the list with the

parents and ask them to fill it in (perhaps each parent doing so independently); others leave the parents to study the questionnaire and then go over it with them either at home or at school. Discrepancies between the assessments of parents and teachers can form a productive starting point for discussion, since it is not uncommon for certain behaviours to be more in evidence in one setting than another; for example, a child may put on his own shoes at home and not at school, or vice versa. Several studies have shown that parents' and teachers' assessments correspond fairly closely when they use the same instruments.

Do parents see records or have an opportunity to comment on the observations of teachers towards the end of the initial period of assessment and before their implications for further teaching are considered by the school?

Once the school has completed its initial assessment, perhaps sometime during the first term, parents should be given an opportunity to discuss the interim findings, to contribute their own observations and to comment on anything which they feel might give a misleading impression of their child's behaviour. Where there is genuine disagreement about some aspect of a child's behaviour, the parents' observations should be recorded and noted, with their knowledge.

For involvement of parents in the initial process of observation and assessment and in the resulting formulation of the child's programme is of the first importance. Parents should have the opportunity to identify and discuss their priorities for the child and to share with school staff the methods that they have found helpful and unhelpful in their own experience of the child at home. This is also a good time to discuss ways in which teachers and parents are going to continue to communicate and to keep each other informed about the child's progress and further needs. It is this initial period that lays down the foundations for later collaboration and trust. It is only if parents know and understand what their child is learning and doing at school that they can support and work productively with teachers.

During School Years

Collaboration between parents and teachers can take a very wide variety of forms during the child's years in school. The nature and quality of collaboration will vary with the changing needs of the child, the parents and the teachers. Relationships between home and school must therefore be flexible and must be able to respond to changing circumstances and the different responses of different families. There is clearly no set formula for partnership.

The questions and suggestions that follow merely represent some examples of current practice. We are not suggesting that all of them should apply in every school and for all children. But we do suggest that each school should consciously think out its policies and practices in relation to the development of partnership with parents. (See Chapter 8, this volume, for further examples.)

1.   Access to school staff. Many headteachers say that 'parents are welcome in my school at any time'. What does this mean in practice? Can they go straight to the child's teacher or are they expected to talk to the headteacher first? What about access to other school staff? Are they clear about procedures for contacting staff? Should they telephone for an appointment first? What facilities are there for parents while they are waiting to see a member of staff? Many parents find it difficult or even stressful to stand or sit about with nothing to do and this can discourage them from visiting the school.

2.   School meetings. Most schools arrange meetings of parents for a wide variety of purposes. Nearly all parents can visit schools at set times to look at displays of childrens' work and attend Christmas plays but these are really open days rather than meetings called for specific purposes - e.g. to discuss children's work and progress, sometimes following the preparation of the school report.

Meetings are held to provide opportunities for parents to meet visiting specialists such as physiotherapists, speech therapists, psychologists or doctors, not only to talk about their child but also to learn more about the work of these specialists and how they relate to teachers. Some schools also hold meetings to discuss important educational issues, such as possible changes in the policy of the school, aspects of the curriculum, methods of teaching, changes in services or legislation, new developments in services for adolescents or adults.

In addition to meetings for parents as a whole, some schools make it possible for small groups of parents to meet either informally or for a particular purpose. For example, some schools have a special parents' 'den' where they can meet at any time, make hot drinks and simply chat, and where meetings can be held to discuss particular issues. The actual physical arrangements for parents to wait are important if parents are to feel both comfortable and welcome when they visit the school.

3. <u>Review meetings</u>. Many schools now hold regular meetings to review the progress of each child and some invite parents to attend either the whole or part of such a meeting. Such meetings can be particularly productive where schools have developed a detailed curriculum plan with recording systems which enable both teachers and parents to provide information on the child's progress in reaching specific goals. Furthermore, the 1981 Education Act gives parents the right to take part in annual meetings to review the child's progress.

4. <u>Sharing success</u>. Some teachers invite parents into school to see the child at various stages of a programme designed to teach a specific skill. The parent is involved in planning and, if possible, carries on some of the teaching at home. Emphasis on achievements rather than problems can provide a good foundation for partnership between parent, professional and child.

5. <u>Asking the parents</u>. There are many ways in which schools can approach individual parents directly. Most commonly, they may make a special point of discussing a particular problem presented by the child and working out ways in which they can jointly work towards a solution. This can be done by inviting the parents into the school, by a visit to the home or by a combination of the two.

Quite apart from questions concerned with an individual child, teachers may find it helpful to discuss a range of general issues with individual parents. These might concern questions of school policy, organisation or curriculum, or a change which is under consideration but which has not yet been decided. Some schools have also taken the initiative in asking parents about their preferences for receiving reports, information from the school, social and informal meetings that would interest them, contacts with school and visiting staff and with other parents. Parents are more likely to feel involved in the work of the school as a whole if staff take them into their confidence about wider questions of policy.

It is also worth asking whether enough opportunities are available for parents to offer any special interests or skills to the school. Some schools wait for the initiative to be taken by the parents, others ask parents directly or make suggestions based on their own knowledge of parents' special interests. The range of possibilities among any group of parents must be very wide - it can include participating in extra-curricular activities, swimming, school visits or a particular skill or interest, such as cooking or carpentry, drama or other hobbies.

Residential Schools
Where a child is attending a residential school, partnership between parents and school staff presents obvious difficulties. Despite the special challenges involved, there is scope for considerable progress.

The number of children and families involved is not considerable. According to the most recent DES statistics relating to the year 1979 (DES, 1981), around one sixth of all pupils receiving special education in 1979 were in some form of residential school (not counting hospital schools). The majority of pupils in maintained and non-maintained residential schools were classified as ESNM (6165), followed by maladjusted (3951), and by either delicate or physically handicapped or both (3708). Comparable figures for independent schools are not available, though it is likely that many of the pupils with special educational needs would be classified as maladjusted.

The number of children in residential schools must be falling rapidly as a consequence of the financial problems facing local authorities. Many LEA's are either closing or reducing the numbers of children in residential schools for which they have a direct responsibility or are no longer able to pay the fees of children attending schools run by other LEA's or by private or voluntary organisations.

The withdrawal of children from residential schools clearly poses special problems of relationships with parents, particularly where the LEA proposes to return the child to the parental home. If the staff of the residential school and of the placing LEA have worked closely with the parents throughout the child's stay in the school, the foundations for effecting a smooth return to the family home or to a substitute home may well have been laid. Where this has not happened, the upheaval resulting from the closure of a residential school can be deeply harmful both to the child and the family and can adversely affect the development of both.

There should be clearly agreed procedures with-

in the LEA and between its officers and the parents
about how links between home and school are to be
established and maintained. Clearly, the needs of
families and children will vary widely, and will
also change significantly over time, so that detailed guidelines would not be appropriate. But whether
one LEA is involved, whether the placing LEA needs
to relate to another LEA in which the residential
school is situated, or to the staff of a non-maintained or independent school, the questions that
need to be asked are essentially similar. We will
list merely a few of the more obvious ones here,
since most of the issues already discussed in relation to day special schools and classes apply in
varying measures to residential schools also.

1. *How far do parents have the information on the
   range of possible schools at the time when the
   issue of boarding education is first raised?*

2. *Do all parents have an opportunity to visit
   possible schools? Who goes with them - a professional person responsible for the placement
   such as a social worker or educational psychologist or advisor?*

3. *How far are decisions on the choice of school
   in the hands of administrative staff? In that
   case, what opportunities are there for parents
   to discuss choice of schools with them?*

4. *When parents visit the school to discuss possible placement, do they meet the whole range of
   staff or only the headteacher?*

5. *If the child's admission to school is likely,
   does a member of the school staff visit the
   family at home? If so, do they also liaise with
   staff of the child's previous school and the
   agencies responsible for the placement - e.g.
   school psychological or child guidance service?*

6. *Once the child is in school, what kind of
   communication links are envisaged between home
   and school?*

7. *Is there a step by step plan either to return
   the child to his family or to make alternative
   arrangements (e.g. fostering, hostel)? In the
   latter case, how are the parents informed of a
   decision to seek alternative forms of care?*

8. *While the child is in residential school, who
   works with the family - is it local staff (e.g.
   school psychological, child guidance, social
   services) or staff of the residential school or
   both? What happens in school holidays?*

9. *How do those responsible for the placement*

> decision monitor the child's progress and the
> appropriateness of their recommendations and
> choice of school?

10. *How does the placing and paying LEA satisfy it-*
    self that the school is meeting the needs of the
    children they have placed there? Do they reg-
    ularly visit the school or do they ask an officer
    of the LEA in which the school is situated to do
    so? Who visits - psychologist, teacher, social
    worker, administrator?

11. *Within any one residential school, what arrange-*
    ments have been made to develop effective com-
    munication concerning the needs of the child and
    how these will be met jointly between teaching
    and residential care staff? Are all school staff
    responsible to the headteacher or are residential
    care staff responsible to someone else, either
    inside or outside the school? To what extent do
    residential care staff help to share in decision
    making and planning - e.g. through case confer-
    ences and review meetings?

Most of the questions we have raised could also
be asked in those situations where children attend a
day school but are living in a hostel or small group
home. This is not uncommon in the case of ESNS
schools; children may be living in a hostel attached
to or close to the school, sometimes for five days,
sometimes for the whole week. In this situation,
the three-way relationship between parents, school
and residential care staff can become quite complex
and requires very careful handling.

Preparation for Leaving School
Although much has been written about the need for
careful and detailed assessment of the abilities
and needs of school leavers, we have little information about the involvement of parents in the process of assessment and decision making involved.
As we discuss this matter in detail below, we will
merely list a number of questions at this stage.
How far are parents involved in the planning and actual imp-
lementation of the school's curriculum for leavers?
Since parents will in many cases assume complete
responsibility for the care of the young person, it
is obviously essential to learn about their own concerns and priorities and to work for the fullest
possible partnership at this critical time.
Are parents involved in the assessment process?
In order to build up a comprehensive profile of all
the young person's abilities it is essential to draw

on the parents' knowledge of what he or she can do
at home. In a study of 214 mentally handicapped
school leavers. Cheseldine and Jeffree (1982)
showed that the Pathways to Independence Checklist
was realiably used by most parents, even though very
few had previously been given opportunities to complete a developmental checklist on their child.
Do teachers visit the family at home?
Home visits to both parents (and to other members of
the family living in the household) are particularly
important at this time not only to elicit the parents' knowledge of what their child can do but also
to learn about their own priorities, needs and resources.
*Do parents attend any case conferences held to discuss their
child's future?*
Not all schools hold case conferences and parents
are not necessarily invited to attend those that are
held. Sometimes they are only invited in on a
'token basis' once the decisions have been made.
*Do parents have opportunities to talk individually to profess-
ionals involved in the assessment process or in the provision
of future services?*
These might include the educational psychologist,
careers officers, social worker, adult training
centre manager, staff of further education college
or one of the courses run by the Manpower Services
Commission, doctors, speech therapists or physiotherapists.
*How much of a say does the young person have in the process of
decision making and what happens where the opinion of the
young person and those of the parnets are clearly at variance?
Are there parent workshops and discussion groups specifically
for parents and school leavers?*
Some schools have held such workshops with the
specific aim of developing a consistent approach to
helping pupils acquire community living skills and
of ensuring that skills that are learned in one
setting, whether at home or school, are not only
used in the other but also in 'real' situations in
the community. Such joint approaches have been used
to help young people to use public transport, self
service cafes, sport and recreational facilities.
In addition to specific training objectives, workshops and discussion groups have also been held to
explore questions concerned with personal and sexual
relationships, family problems and disagreements
between the young person and family or teachers.
*How much do parents know and see of the self-help and inde-
pendence skills that their child is being taught at school?
What steps have to be taken to link such teaching with what*

the parents are doing at home?

PARENTS OF ADOLESCENTS AND YOUNG ADULTS[1]

The period of school leaving marks a critical point
in the life of the family as well as that of the
adolescent. But although there is now a considerable literature about parents of younger handicapped
children, very little is known about families of
handicapped adolescents and young adults. How far
do such families have special and distinctive needs?
To what extent do the roles of parents of handicapped adolescents differ from the role of parents
of younger children, both those who are handicapped
and those who are not? What kind of services do
families need to help them to fulfil their role?

Some Service Needs of Parents
The time of school leaving provides an opportunity
to take stock not only of the needs of the young
person but also those of the family. Families
should feel that there is time and opportunity to
discuss any aspects of their family life which concerns their son or daughter either now or in the
future. Such discussions need not be limited to the
immediate questions arising from school leaving and
placement into adult services. Both parents and
professionals are increasingly expressing the wish
to move away from a crisis-orientated service towards one which anticipates needs and tries to plan
constructively to meet them. For example, parents
should be given the opportunity to discuss questions
concerned with residential care long before there is
a direct need for it.

Information. First and foremost, parents need information on the range of provision which is available
or planned in their locality. In interviews with
parents in one area where services were well developed, many parents were badly informed about day or
residential services for adolescents and adults.
Very few had visited the Adult Training Centres
which their children would almost certainly be
attending in the coming months (Cheseldine and
Jeffree, 1982). They were also poorly informed
about facilities for short-term and longer-term residential care in their localities. Lack of information was more common among parents who were not
members of parents' societies or who did receive
the parent journals in which such issues are regularly discussed.

32

A number of authorities have been producing short information leaflets on local services. These generally contain addresses and telephone numbers of key organisations and individuals as well as useful information on where to get advice or help to meet particular needs. These leaflets are often aimed at parents of younger children; there is a case for an information sheet written especially for parents of young people approaching school leaving age. This might include information on the following:

. local provision for assessment of young people approaching school leaving age - e.g. which professions should be routinely involved in assessment and decision-making and which others are available for consultation if the need should arise;

. procedures for parents to be involved in the process of assessment and decision-making; how and when they should be consulted; how they can obtain the information or advice which they feel to be necessary and whom to contact if they are dissatisfied;

. the range of alternative provision which is available locally - e.g. day services, further education colleges, work experience courses, sheltered employment, vocational training. This should include the names of key individuals in these organisations who can advise parents and who might be able to arrange for preliminary visits to the agency;

. the range of residential services - both long term and short term - should also be summarised in such a leaflet, together with some indication on how parents can visit facilities informally;

. information on welfare rights for which the young person and the family are eligible;

. in addition to listing services for handicapped people, such leaflets should also include information on all relevant resources available to the rest of the community and to young people in particular - e.g. careers advice, work training, further education facilities, evening classes and the whole range of leisure, sport and recreational facilities in the area.

Anticipating needs for residential and support services
Information leaflets may provide the basis for an informed discussion between parents and professionals on the availability of local resources. For

example, parents often express the need not only to be told about the local services that are available or planned but also to have the opportunity to discuss the advantages of the various alternatives in relation to the needs of their son or daughter and of the family as a whole.

Discussion about the range of alternatives may also provide opportunities for families to express more general feelings about their attitudes and needs. To this end, it is obviously desirable that there are opportunities to relate to a single individual, preferably someone with experience of working with families.

For example, a quick and superficial visit to the family may well result in a report that the family are unwilling to consider residential care. But several visits and the development of a more open and trusting relationship may help the parents to speak more freely about the problems in continuing to provide 24 hour care and may make them less hesitant to express their wish to think about residential care outside the home.

Similarly, some parents may refer to arrangements that have been made for an older brother or sister to make a home for the handicapped youngster when the parents are no longer able to do so. This was mentioned quite frequently in interviews, particularly when many of the leavers are the youngest of a large family, with many brothers and sisters now married (Cheseldine and Jeffree, 1982). But parents may be reluctant to rely on their own children to take over care, though there is evidence that older siblings no longer living at home tend to give considerable help and are willing to take over. Bayley (1973) found that among mentally handicapped adults living in the community, 85 per cent of those who could be living with a sibling (i.e. both parents dead) were doing so, though of those in hospital, half had been admitted immediately after the death of a parent. But such an arrangement is not necessarily entered into willingly by the older brother or sister or their spouse; it may be made in order to reassure worried parents that the handicapped youngster will be taken care of when the time comes. Furthermore, circumstances can change, particularly in a growing family. For these and other reasons, it is important for the professional not simply to record that family arrangements have been made but to explore the situation in some depth and detail with the parents and the younger family involved.

34

In interviews in the Greater Manchester area, we found few families of school leavers who were well-informed about the residential services which were available in their area. Many still assumed that the long-stay mental handicap hospital was the only alternative to remaining at home and were unaware of existing and planned local authority provision for hostels and group homes. The movement towards the use of ordinary housing for handicapped people, although increasingly influential in professional circles, has not made the same impact on individual families.

Using ordinary housing. Many parents expect to continue to provide a home for their handicapped son or daughter indefinitely, until they are no longer able to do so by reason of age, incapacity or death. The notion that young people might be given opportunities to live away from their families *before* there is a crisis has as yet made relatively little headway. This is partly due to the shortage of provision in the community but is also related to the narrow range of alternative accommodation which has until recently been considered appropriate. This may change, now that more consideration is being given to the use of ordinary housing and evidence is beginning to be published indicating that even severely handicapped people can live in ordinary houses.

Providing ordinary or adapted housing in the local community means that people can live in small units with as much staffing and support as their individual needs require. Some will require only a very occasional visit from a social worker, health visitor or voluntary worker; other houses may contain three to five more dependent people who will need to have staff living in the house with them; in other cases, professional staff live in a nearby house but are available when needed. The emphasis in such schemes is on providing a wide range of residential accommodation to meet the wide range of need of individuals.

From the parents' point of view, such arrangements provide ideal opportunities to help their sons and daughters to learn to live more independently. At the same time they can prepare themselves to accept that although they will eventually need to live away from home, such a home need not be a distant hospital or institution but a house not very different from their own.

Whether or not the young person is in regular

35

contact with professionals, parents can be given the means to try to develop active teaching methods which are designed to help the young person learn new skills and to become more independent. Whelan and Speake (1979) have written a handbook specifically for parents of mentally handicapped adolescents. Beginning with a *Scale for Assessing Coping Skills*, parents are helped to complete a simple checklist of the young person's abilities in the areas of self-help (personal, domestic, community) and interpersonal skills (e.g. conversation, friendship, sexual knowledge and behaviour). Detailed suggestions are then made for ways in which parents can design and carry out a teaching programme to help the young person achieve specific skills. Such an approach can also form the basis of structured workshops in which groups of parents and professionals meet regularly in order to define short-term goals and agree on methods of reaching them.

Because parents and professionals may not have the same goals, it is important to provide opportunities for a free discussion to identify expectation of the level of independence that may be achieved since these may differ widely in both groups. Just as several professionals working with the same adolescent may have different expectations of the final outcome, so different members of the same family may vary considerably in their estimate of the extent to which the young person can learn the skills to live successfully in the community. It may therefore be helpful to explore these questions through discussion. It is clearly dangerous to press ahead with carefully structured training programmes to teach social independence when one or both parents may have misgivings about whether such a programme is justified. They may also be anxious about the risks involved in undertaking it. Questions concerned with sexuality represent the most obvious examples where full discussion about goals and philosophies is important. Similarly, parents and professionals may have different perceptions about the extent to which a particular youngster is 'ready' to start a course of social independence training - e.g. in learning to use public transport, go to a supermarket or a disco unaccompanied, go on holiday with a group of friends etc.

Special Problems of Partnership?
Are there distinctive problems about developing partnership between parents of adolescents and adults and the staff who work with them?

Even where parents and professionals are apparently agreed on the overall programmes for social independence training, difficult issues arise when it comes to discussing the nature and degree of parental participation in such programmes. Although there is now a strong body of evidence which testifies to the effectiveness of internsive parental involvement where teaching programmes with younger children are concerned, is it right to extrapolate these to parents of adolescents and young adults? How appropriate is such detailed involvement from a normalisation point of view? Is it appropriate that parents should know exactly what their son or daughter is doing in the course of their day to day social education or training programmes? Even very much younger children like to maintain separate identities between home and school and tend to fend off well meaning enquiries from parents about what they have been doing in school. It could be argued that even where such enquiries are not apparently resented and even where parents and professionals are working well together to achieve goals that are in the long-term interest of the adolescent, such a close involvement on the part of parents may in fact reinforce rather than diminish dependency.

These issues about goals and philosophies are not widely discussed in the literature, nor, we suspect, do they receive as much consideration as they should at the level of the individual family when professionals are beginning to draw up training programmes for handicapped young people. (See chapters 11 and 12, this volume.) Professionals may themselves need help in facing these issues; for example, group discussion, possibly accompanied by role play, may help staff to face some of the delicate and complex issues involved. Clearly, no two families have the same needs but certain general strategies can be discussed within a group. For example, some parental involvement programmes may begin with a fairly intensive and detailed level of training by parents but in the context of a clearly worked out plan to reduce the amount of parental involvement on a step-by-step basis. This can be done more easily with some programmes than others - e.g. in teaching a young person to travel to a day centre by public transport, the programme would probably consist of gradually 'distancing' the parent from the young person. Similarly, the amount and intensity of supervision in teaching a young person to wash their hair can also be slowly but systematically withdrawn.

37

Now that parents are being asked to enter into detailed and often day-to-day working partnerships with professional staff in teaching their son or daughter to acquire specific skills, it is particularly important to provide opportunities for them to express their feelings about any difficulties they may be experiencing in working in a teaching role. Some parents quite understandably find such work both demanding and stressful but may find it hard to admit to this, for fear of being thought unco-operative or not 'good parents'.

Preparation for adulthood also involves preparation for loss and separation. One of the greatest anxieties that parents face - even from the earliest days - is how their handicapped son or daughter will manage when parents are too old or too ill and when they die. These issues are often pushed aside 'taking each day as it comes'. But parents' and professionals' co-operation can be most valuable and mutually supportive in the joint task of helping the handicapped person and family to prepare for separation, both temporary and permanent. One of the most insightful and thought-provoking accounts of the meaning of the death of a parent to a mentally handicapped adult can be found in a work of fiction - *Walter*, by David Cook (Penguin Books, 1980).

CONCLUSIONS: THE ESSENCE OF PARTNERSHIP

Partnership between parents and professionals is an easily accepted principle but the constructive relationship it represents is much more difficult to achieve. It calls for considerable thought and effort on both sides.

What, then, are some of the essential elements that we look for in partnership?
1. *Mutual respect and recognition of the essential equality between parents and professionals*. Each has a deep interest and concern for the child. Each wants the best possible future for the child and works towards this in their own way. The parent is more deeply and intensely involved, more 'partial', as Elizabeth Newson puts it. Most parents have a life long commitment to the child and their responsibility lasts for 24 hours a day, during holidays and sickness. Professionals have, on the whole, a more finite commitment. Their work may be more specialisted in nature - concerned with the education in a broad sense, speech and language, mobility, vocational training and so on. They may change jobs or work

with another group of children.

Nevertheless, the roles of parent and professional in the field of handicap are more than usually
interactive and complementary. The warm and affect-
ionate care of the parent and the physical help a
parent offers will need to be maintained when children are aware from their parents; parenting needs to
be carried on by professionals. Similarly, teaching
to minimise the handicap needs to be carried on by
the parents at home to a greater degree than when no
handicap exists. This is particularly true of mentally handicapped children who need help to generalise the skills they have learned from one setting
to another.

2. *Sharing of information and skills.* Parents have
known and cared for their child since birth. They
know intimately the child's idiosyncratic responses
over a wide range of activities - eating, sleeping,
elimination, playing, recognition of people, responses to sound, sights, likes, dislikes, fears.
All parents will have experience of having helped
their child to develop certain skills and will have
gained valuable insights from their efforts. The
parents will also know the social and physical
environment in which the child lives and will continue to develop.

Professionals, for their part, have a background of knowledge derived both from their theoretical training and from the experience they have
accumulated in working with a large number of handicapped children and their families. They will have
learnt from their failures as well as their successes. Their experience helps them to acquire a
range of methods and techniques to observe and
assess strengths and needs and to help children to
acquire skills and to increase independence.

It is vital for parents and professionals to
share skills and information with each other, and
to do so in an open, honest way which includes a
sharing of each others' limitations in knowledge
and expertise. This is not to deny that each has
their own area of authority. This too needs mutual
recognition and, hopefully, leads to the development of a common language and understanding without
which little can be achieved together.

3. *Sharing of feelings.* Partnership can only be
arrived at through a process of sharing. While
practical skills and decisions may be the outcome
of this process, the feeling element is at least
equally important.

Traditionally, parents and professionals have

been wary of one another. They have come together with preconceived assumptions and ideas about each other and there is often an element of rivalry in their contacts. Inevitably, they lack confidence in how to approach one another: professionals rarely have preparation or training in ways of relating to parents. Parents often remember their own negative experiences of school and these experiences are re-activated when they meet teachers and other professionals.

Professionals can begin to meet parents on a personal level by being open about their own feelings. Sharing their initial reactions to handicap and early difficulties and failures may make parents more comfortable in expressing their own doubts and worries. Similarly, professionals and parents can help each other through difficult periods when little progress is being made and it is only too easy to be discouraged. Sharing of feelings with the knowledge that progress often comes in spurts and after a fallow period can bring comfort to both.

The sharing of positive feelings of warmth and enjoyment of the child may be even more important. Success and achievement, however small, are even more previous when so much effort has gone into helping the child to take even a very small step forward in development. The sharing of a sense of satisfaction and joy that the effort has been worth-while is of inestimable value to the child, to the parents and to the parent-professional bond.

But such a two way process of support is only possible on the basis of a genuine two way flow of communication and some element of joint undertakings and activities.

4. *Sharing the process of decision making*. Parents have not always played an active part in the process of assessment, planning and decision making. The initiative has lain largely with professionals who may only have informed parents of the outcome or provided them with an opportunity to agree or dis-agree. But parents have increasingly asserted their wish to be consulted and their right to be more in-volved is now reflected in legislation.

The most obvious areas for joint decision con-cern the nature, type and degree of collaboration between parents and professionals. This involves discussion of methods of communication - telephone, written form, notebooks or visits either in school or to the home; frequency of contact, parents' in-terests in different aspects of the life of the school; the practicalities of time and family commitments. It involves discussion of parents' special skills and interests which they might be encouraged to share with children staff and other parents. They will have valuable and constructive suggestions to make and will in any case enjoy being asked.

Professionals can usefully ask parents actively and directly about their preferences for collaboration. They may need to do so at regular intervals, as circumstances and needs change. They must also accept parents' wishes to opt out and not be involved in detailed programmes of teaching.

5. *Recognition of the individuality of families and the uniqueness of the handicapped child*. Many recipients of professional services have complained bitterly about the generalised judgements of professionals. Obvious examples include the concepts of guilt and over-protection on the one hand and rejection on the other; that a handicapped child means a handicapped family and that all parents must be helped to 'accept' that their child is handicapped. These generalisations and stereotypes need to be constantly questioned; if professionals want to establish comfortable and productive relationships with parents, they will need to explore with each family afresh what the situation means to them and how each family can 'learn to live with' the handicapping condition of one member.

Flexibility of approach is fundamental to partnership. If partnership is not working, the onus is first on professionals to ask themselves how they can more effectively meet the needs of parents and how they can discuss problems on an open and equal basis. Partnership between parents and professionals is justified by the needs of the child, the parents and professionals. Each depends on the knowledge, skills and experience of the other if the needs of the child are to be fully met.

NOTES

1. The section entitled 'Parents of Adolescents and Young Adults' was adapted from a paper *Roles and Needs of Parents of Handicapped Adolescents*, by Peter Mittler, Sally Cheseldine and Helen McConachie in response to a commission from the OECD study on The Handicapped Adolescent. We are grateful for permission to make use of this material (see Mittler, Cheseldine and McConachie, 1981, for the full version).

REFERENCES

Bayley, M. (1973) <u>Mental Handicap and Community
    Care</u>. London: Routledge and Kegan Paul
Boucher, J. (1981) Parents as partners. Talk to DES
    course 'Applications of Warnock', University of
    Manchester, November 1981
Cheseldine, S. and Jeffree, D. (1982) Mentally
    handicapped adolescents: A survey of abilities.
    <u>Special Education: Forward Trends</u> (research
    supplement), <u>9</u>, 19-23
Cook, D. (1980) <u>Walter</u>. London: Penguin Books
Cunningham, C. and Sloper, P. (1977) Parents of
    Down's syndrome babies: their early needs.
    <u>Child: Care, Health and Development</u>, <u>3</u>, 325-347
Cunningham, C. and Sloper, P. (1978) <u>Helping Your
    Handicapped Baby</u>. London: Souvenir Press
Department of Education and Science (1981) <u>Stat-
    istics of Education</u> (1979) Vol. 1: Schools.
    London: HMSO
Hewett, S. (1970) <u>The Family and the Handicapped
    Child</u>. London: Allen and Unwin
International League of Societies for Persons with
    Mental Handicap (1978) <u>Step by Step: Implemen-
    tation of the Rights of Mentally Handicapped
    Persons</u>. Vienna: Lebenshilfe and ILSMH
Jeffree, D. (1980) Personal communication
Mittler, H. (1982) Collaboration between parents
    and special schools: a local survey. Paper
    given to Division of Educational and Child
    Psychology, University of York, January 1982
Mittler, P. (1979) Parents as partners in the edu-
    cation of their handicapped children. Paper
    commissioned by UNESCO, ED/79/conf. 606/7
    Paris: UNESCO
Mittler, P., Cheseldine, S. and McConachie, H.
    (1981) <u>Roles and Needs of Parents of Handi-
    capped Adolescents</u>. Paris: Organisation for
    Economic Cooperation and Development (CERI)
O'Dell, S. (1974) Training parents in behavior
    modification: a review. <u>Psychological Bull-
    etin</u>, <u>81</u>, 418-433
Pugh, G. (1981) <u>Parents as Partners: Intervention
    Schemes and Group Work with Families of Handi-
    capped Children</u>. London: National Children's
    Bureau
Revill, S. and Blunden, R. (1980) <u>A Manual for Imp-
    lementing a Portage Home Training Service for
    Developmentally Handicapped Preschool Children</u>.
    Windsor, Berks.: National Foundation for Edu-
    cational Research

Schafer, N. (1979) Does She Know She's There?
    London: Futura
Spain, B. and Wigley, G. (eds.) (1975) Right from
    the Start: Services for the Preschool Mentally
    Handicapped Child. London: MENCAP
Turnbull, A.P. and Turnbull, H.R. (1982) Parent in-
    volvement in the education of handicapped
    children: a critique. Mental Retardation, 20,
    115-122
Whelan, E. and Speake, B. (1979) Learning to Cope.
    London: Souvenir Press
Wilkin, D. (1979) Caring for the Mentally Handi-
    capped Child. London: Croom Helm

SECTION TWO: MEETING PARENTS' NEEDS

Chapter 2

THE PARENTS' PERSPECTIVE OF FAMILY NEEDS AND HOW TO MEET THEM

Philippa Russell

THE NEW PARTNERSHIP

In the course of the last decade, many studies have been published about the needs of children and their families. Families of handicapped children have been the focus of three major British government reports (DHSS, 1976; 1979; DES, 1978) of increasing numbers of research studies and policy statements and of countless professional workers in the statutory and voluntary services.

In many respects, families do receive more help than they used to. Not only have DHSS benefits and the Family Fund (Joseph Rowntree Trust) provided practical help, but increasing awareness of the needs of families and of the value of parental involvement in professional programmes has led to a new dialogue. But it is also possible that the reinforcement of parental confidence and competence may be threatening to some professionals. The new philosophy of shared care carries responsibilities; it also confers benefits and new strengths. The emphasis on support from professionals to parents confirms the Court Report's conclusion that, "We have found no better way to raise a child than to reinforce the abilities of his parents to do so".

But this philosophy also imposes fresh challenges on professionals and may require new initiatives in working with families of handicapped children. For despite the initiatives of the last ten years, the birth of a handicapped child still constitutes a family crisis and calls for complex services for both child and parents. Additionally, the move to 'normalisation' and 'integration', focussing quite properly on the needs of the mentally handicapped as people with rights, can impose heavy new responsibilities on parents whose dual roles as caretakers and enablers may at times be confusing and contradictory.

PARENTS' NEEDS

The movement towards early intervention programmes for young mentally handicapped children has perhaps distracted some professional awareness from the fundamental, problematic, and even destructive personal problems which can accompany any disability in the family. Partnership with parents presupposes mutual professional and parental adaptation to the child's disability (as well as an optimistic and realistic appraisal of capacity for future development). Unfortunately some parents are initially themselves too stressed to be able to work effectively with their own children, so that support and counselling may be critical to the future success of any programme.

It is no accident that pregnant women are said to be 'expectant': they are expectant of a healthy normal baby who will fulfil at least some of their hopes for future family life. If the child is handicapped, there may be a great gulf between the dream and the reality. Many parents cannot handle the initial trauma and may go through a period of aggressive and irrational behaviour. Cunningham (1979a) described this aptly as "a model of psychic crisis at the disclosure of handicap", and noted that if parents did not receive adequate professional support in this critical period then the shock reaction could be perpetuated through many months or even years. (See Chapter 5, this volume.) On the other hand, the provision of appropriate information, counselling and active involvement in the care of the child could lead to adaptation and orientation. It should be added that, whilst many parents are optimistically told to 'accept' their handicapped child, few can do so except in a fatalistic and usually unproductive way. Whilst the *child* may indeed be accepted, few parents will accept a *disability* and a constructive emphasis on adaptation and orientation is more productive and realistic.

Recent developments in services, including home teaching and home visiting programmes (Pugh, 1981) and family support centres (Pugh and Russell, 1976) have demonstrated how these early needs may be met. The availability of services is also important since many families may conceal distress and ambivalence beneath a superficial shell of competence. Brimblecombe (1976) and others have well documented

the widely expressed parental needs for accurate
information, practical help and positive guidance on
how to help their child. But because services for
families with handicapped children are often frag-
mented, professionals may be unaware of pressures
from within the family, and of the often differing
expectations of family members.

Studies of the psychological and emotional
impact of a handicapped child on the family have all
tended to emphasise the potentially damaging impact
of such a child on family life. An investigation of
30 families with a Down's syndrome child found that
33 per cent of the mothers suffered from clinical
depression in the first 18 months of their child's
life, and emotional and sexual problems were common
amongst both mothers and fathers (Gath, 1978).
Wilkin (1979) found that 72 per cent of the mothers
in his study reported problems with 'mental health'
and noted the sense of isolation experienced by many
families, 90 per cent having no free time at all at
weekends and most experiencing a reduction in
ordinary social and leisure experience compared to
friends with non-handicapped children.

Similar observations have been made with regard
to an increase in the rate of divorce and separation
after the birth of a baby nursed in a special care
unit (Leiderman, 1976). In this case, as with
handicap, parents also have to face changed expectations and unanticipated immediate role restructuring. Without recognition of the difficulties
implicit in such restructuring, the family unit will
be vulnerable. Similarly there is some evidence
(Leiderman, 1976; Gath, 1978) that parents were *more*
depressed a year after the birth of their handicapped child - which could be related to falling off
of early support services and home visits about this
time reported by Cunningham and Sloper (1977). All
studies clearly demonstrated the importance of
including fathers in any intervention programme and
in recognising depression and anxiety before
starting any programmes with the child.

Although it is commonly said that the clearly
identified stresses found in families with handicapped children are likely to precipitate marital
breakdown and divorce, the evidence is unclear. As
we live in an age of increased divorce rates across
the population as a whole, it is extremely difficult
to differentiate between other existing problems and
those arising from the presence of a handicapped
child. Lansdown (1981) suggested that, whereas the
additional problems of having a handicapped child

could exacerbate existing difficulties in a poor relationship, the shared concerns might actually strengthen the marriage in a good relationship. In any event it is important to question studies which assume a pathological model of the family when there is a handicapped child. As Hewett (1970) noted, "The general tendency to characterise parents of handicapped children as guilt ridden, anxiety laden, over protective and rejecting beings is unfortunate. ... Their common characteristics appear much more to be the need for money, services and information. Counselling without these latter is of little value". Whilst it would be unrealistic to minimise the trauma of disability in the family and the necessity to restructure some family roles in the light of the new responsibility, adverse effects upon families are not inevitable, and may be prevented by appropriate services.

CHANGING NEEDS, CHANGING SERVICES

Parents invariably emphasise the need for *practical* information, support and advice. Studies by Hewett (1970), Bayley (1973), Carr (1974), and Wilkin (1979) have all highlighted the practical day-to-day problems encountered by families and the need to develop services to solve them. The same studies also emphasised the need to provide a flexible continuum of provision, pointing out that whereas all families of young children will experience management and care tasks which are demanding due to the children's dependency, such dependency diminishes over time in 'ordinary' families. In the case of a handicapped child becoming an adolescent and young adult, the care and expectations have a different quality, and the maturation of siblings, together with the desire of the parents for greater freedom, may all impose new strains. In such circumstances, the parents' quality of life and personal relationships will be less dependent upon sympathy and counselling (though both are important) than upon active involvement in planning for their child's future, education in the developmental process and how to enhance it and practical help to minimise the inevitable care tasks in the home.

In the early days, parents may be very demanding of professional time. They will need not only verbal advice but practical demonstration of skills by which they can control and help their child. A report on the Honeylands Home Visiting Programme (Devon) observed that, "Some parents have been very slow to accept that they can actually bring about progress in their child by working with him" (Rubissow, Jones, Brimblecombe and Morgan, 1979). The experience of the first year of the project also suggested that, "Because we have encountered parents' participation in observation and goal setting, we have somewhat deliberately created a tension of expectation in the parents which is trickier to work in than a customary clinic visit where the child is removed from the parents' arms for treatment and then returned".

Helping families to help themselves must take into account individual family dynamics. Brazelton (1979) suggested that the success of any intervention programme should be measured not only by the child's development but by "increased family comfort, decrease in the divorce rate, lower incidence of behaviour problems in siblings......perhaps by pretty soft signs but they may be a lot more important as measures of effectiveness of intervention than is a rise in IQ or increased motor capacity on the part of the child". Brazelton described working with the family as the "soft work" and queried how many professionals were willing and able to relate their professional demands to family needs.

Some parents, who have been late in accepting a permanent handicap, may still cherish hopes of a 'cure' so that disappointment and accompanying depression can occur many months after the child's birth. Equally, the availability of a multidisciplinary service is only helpful if the family have their key worker or 'named person' who will ensure that they do have access to the team and fully understand the nature of the advice and recommendations made by it. Helping a parent to feel more confident in order to become more competent may be difficult. Parents' groups may be an invaluable way of establishing not only solidarity but a real recognition that a parent is a person with difficulties and not a failure. With the nature of families changing - young and isolated parents in a mobile society facing particular problems in developing appropriate parenting skills - such groups are an obvious way of creating a network of carers for vulnerable families. Also they may enable parents to admit to hostile or aggressive feelings which are often a normal early reaction to the discovery of a handicapping condition but which will be superseded by more positive feeling if information and support are provided.

Handicap is usually a chronic condition which

will last for the child's whole life. During this
time, parents will themselves change, and so will
their needs. Behaviour problems and physical
burdens of care which are acceptable in a baby or
toddler may become disastrous when the child is a
young adult. Equally, parents have been encouraged
to work with their handicapped child, to have higher
aspirations and, indeed, to expect quality services
as of right. When the handicapped child becomes
the handicapped school leaver, there is likely to
be a conflict between the anticipated and the actual
level of service. Similarly, families will age and
their life styles may alter. Professionals must be
ready to provide a continuum of service which can
meet these changing needs. Many families will
experience critical periods of care when a high
level of intervention is required.

PARENTS AS EDUCATORS

The new move towards the perception of parents as
co-workers and educators has important implications
not only for parents' self image but for their
child's progress and maturation. Newson (1976)
commented when considering parents as a resource in
diagnosis and assessment that:

> We should start from the basic assumption that
> parents in fact have information to impart;
> that parents are experts on their own
> children. This is not to say that they know
> of their children in any systematic or inte-
> grated form; one cannot ask the parents to
> bring along......an ordered case history of
> the child....but the fact that their knowledge
> may be diffuse and unstructured does not
> matter as long as it is available. It is the
> professional's job to make it available.
> Structuring can come later.

Beginning in the USA in the 1950's and 60's,
the development of early intervention and home
teaching programmes has offered major initiatives
in helping parents work with professionals in a
structured way. The idea of a constructive
partnership utilising a systematic teaching
approach makes sound common sense for parents.
Hopefully linked to a system of 'shared care' such
as that offered at Honeylands or the KIDS Family
Centre (Russell, 1981), home teaching programmes
give parents skill to utilise that expertise

52

recognised by Newson but often dissipated or wasted without appropriate professional support. Since handicap is not an anticipated family disaster (unlike old age, illness or redundancy) parents will be required to develop new skills precisely at the chronological time when they are most vulnerable and confused. Whilst the Honeylands Home Visiting Programme clearly indicated that parents' general needs must be recognised first before they can most effectively carry out home teaching, the great value of early parental involvement programmes lies in the assumption that parents can not only merely monitor the development of their child but that they can also share in goal setting and in devising the means to achieve these goals.

Early intervention programmes teach success. They provide ongoing contact with an involved and informed professional and they are largely *home based*. Whilst there are problems for some professionals in working on a domiciliary basis - Sandow and Clarke (1978) describe in their Hull programme the diffi- culties in working in a small room "surrounded by three generations of a mutually hostile family, in an atmosphere composed of equal parts cigarette smoke, sweat and old chip papers" - the home is where the child spends a large part of the time, and the nature and quality of the home environment will affect that child's development. The balance of any home intervention programme can be determined by what is possible within a particular family and the level of commitment can be matched to what is actu- ally feasible. Additionally, the practical needs of the family can be observed. Washing machines or tumble driers purchased through the Family Fund may be critical to the success of any programme, if they can give the mother *time*. Places for siblings in play groups or other pre-school facilities; advice on practical aids and adaptations; transport for hospital or other clinical visits may all reduce pressure on time and remove additional stress. Since most of us who are parents wish to appear com- petent, it may take the objective eye of a profess- ional to observe what the practical needs really are and to seek to alleviate them. Similarly, parents can talk to a regular professional on sensitive personal areas which they might hesitate to share with a 'one-off' team visit or a busy hospital doctor.

53

WORKING WITH PARENTS

Early intervention programmes tend to fall into two
main categories. Parent Workshops (using scarce
professional skills very effectively but perhaps
making strenuous demands upon some parents) and Home
Teaching Programmes all have the common denominator
of helping parents help their child. Behavioural
techniques were initially used to help children with
abnormal behaviour but the same principles were soon
applied to children with mental handicap. Behavioural techniques may work in a variety of ways, not
only by directly modifying unacceptable behaviour
but by teaching new skills which obviate the necessity for the undesirable behaviour. As Cunningham
(1975) pointed out, the priorities for parents of
mentally handicapped children are not necessarily
the same as those for parents of behaviour disturbed
children, since the former are more concerned with
long-term objectives and sustained treatment and
cannot be assured that after 'treatment' their
problems will go away. However, the behavioural
approach can work extremely well if a suitable
detailed programme is developed with long-term
support from professionals and clear-cut objectives
for the parents to work towards.
    Teaching methods vary between the different
schemes and the tightness of structure must vary
according to the group teaching situation of a
workshop or the one-to-one of a programme in the
home. The main objective of such programmes for
parents is the creation of an environment in which
learning can take place. The 'cook book' approach
will seldom work, for parents need to understand
the principles and concepts of the approaches so
that they can in turn intuitively use the skills
which they are acquiring. As one psychologist put
it to a parent workshop, what happens out of the
teaching situation is as important for parents as
what happens in it. In any event, any good intervention programme must teach parents to succeed.
If the child is severely handicapped and gains will
be slow and painful, then the parents will need
support. Short-term and long-term goals are
critical and the development of developmental
checklists such as the Portage Guide and the Parent
Involvement Project's charts can enable parents to
understand how to break tasks down into basic
stages (Bluma, Shearer, Frohman and Hilliard, 1976;
Jeffree and McConkey, 1976).
    The majority of home intervention projects

involve weekly visits by a home visitor (who may be
drawn from a range of disciplines or even a trained
volunteer) backed up by a team of professionals.
The purpose of the visits is to develop a tailor-
made programme with the parents to use in their own
home and to place such programmes in the context of
a wider spectrum of help and advice from community
services. Some other approaches have, however, also
been developed. The Honeylands Home Visiting Programme uses home visitors as soon as any child in
the catchment area is identified as having a developmental problem. In these very early days, the
home visitor is likely to offer family-centred
rather than child-centred support, although the two
are closely related. Such services, working right
from the start, have as a primary objective the
alleviation of family stress and the establishment
of good and positive relationships with available
services. The Haringey 'FISH' Project involved
social workers, using a behavioural approach, to
work more specifically with the problems of having a
mentally handicapped person in the family, including
problem-solving through simple programmes and behavioural methods (Kiernan, 1982). Since social
workers are sometimes criticised for their 'tea and
sympathy' approach - usually a misunderstanding of
the nature of social work involvement - the behavioural approach offers a new and more constructive
approach to social work in families with a handicapped child. But, whilst making social work more
acceptable to the parents, it also makes new
demands upon social workers who may be generic in
training and have to master new skills in order to
be effective.

The parent workshop approach can also be highly
successful with parents and, when based on a school,
can be a powerful agent for linking objectives
between parents and teachers (Pugh, 1981; see
Chapter 10, this volume). There has been a suggestion that the workshop approach may succeed better
with more articulate parents who can utilise the
limited time most effectively. However, Cunningham
(1979b) noted that, "The socio-economic and educational level of the parent is not generally correl-
ated with their ability to learn and apply techniques for training and stimulating their child".
Workshops like the Kith and Kids 'Two to One'
(using volunteers under psychologists' supervision
to work with handicapped children over a period of
two weeks) very effectively demonstrate that anybody can work well with handicapped children pro-

provided the professional support is good and the
objectives clear (Collins and Collins, 1975). The
Wessex Portage Project also showed that anyone from
a professional or voluntary agency could be trained
in the skills required and methods used by the home
teacher, although - as with any job - certain background experiences will be advantageous (Smith,
Kushlick and Glossop, 1977; Pugh, 1981). As the
Honeylands Home Visiting Programme also found,
because tact, sympathy, care as well as positive
thinking are all necessary when working with vulnerable families, some home teachers (or workshop
organisers) will be better than others.

Potential difficulties
The concept of the 'difficult' or 'hard to reach'
parent is widely perpetuated. But, from the parents' point of view, many so-called maladaptive
responses to having a handicapped child are almost
inevitable in view of the problems faced and the
frequent lack of cohesion in bringing services together. Genuine barriers to progress may lie not
only in early bad experiences (in which parents may
have inadvertently reinforced bad behaviour patterns
in their child) but in some cases with the parents'
loss of confidence in themselves. Parents who perceive themselves as inadequate may be demanding of
professional time and may also be highly dependent
on the 'good professional'. Such parents may literally ask their paediatrician if their child can
watch television or play with certain toys in a
frantic effort to do the right thing. Such parents
desperately need consistent help and guidance; to
be successful a home intervention programme must be
tactfully structured to restore their damaged self-
image and identify their strengths. Additionally,
it should be remembered that because handicap
affects whole families as well as parents, home
intervention should take account of extended family
members and their often contradictory and firmly
held views on how the handicapped child should be
handled.

PARENTS' GROUPS

The development of voluntary organisations has led
to important initiatives in enabling parents to help
themselves - and each other. A well-run and sensi-
tively directed group can do much to reduce stress
and it can also provide the peer group which so
many parents desperately lack when their child is

handicapped. Parents' groups are not necessarily
the same as voluntary organisations, since some
specialist groups, like those established at Health
Service Child Development Units, may meet the needs
of specific groups of parents utilising the same
services at a particular time. Some groups, like
the Southend Scheme (Pugh and Russell, 1977), link
professional and parental help from the earliest
diagnosis and provide not only instant visits and
counselling but introduction into a group of similar
parents. Some like Contact a Family aim to involve
all family members and develop group dynamics to
suit the locality and the parents involved. Again,
many national organisations like MENCAP have a network of local groups which can provide a variety of
parent resources. The importance of the parent
group lies in the increased comfort, solidarity,
practical advice and general support which it can
offer. Many parents of handicapped children are
isolated and lonely. Groups - like Kith and Kids -
can also help them identify their own needs and
literally begin to plan and to influence local
service developments in a positive and informed way.
However, parent groups can only help those who find
them and professionals need to be sensitive to the
local 'grapevine' and ensure that the shy or isolated parent is not missed out.

FIT FOR THE FUTURE? - THE NEW PARTNERSHIP IN ACTION

The concept of parents as partners is gaining
credence. However, such a philosophy of shared care
and active partnership poses a number of difficulties in implementation. The fundamental problem
lies in the creation of a genuine dialogue between
the professional agency and the family. Professionals may find themselves threatened by the
necessary blurring of accepted professional identities. Parents, anxiously seeking diagnosis, may by
implication expect cure and have unrealistically
high expectations of any programmes. Similarly,
some families may be difficult to work with. The
environment may be unsatisfactory, the parents dis-
tressed and oppressed by poor housing, marital
stress or other factors not directly related to the
presenting problem of handicap. Parents may also
expect immediate results. If early success is
achieved, but the child's development then levels
out, the parents may feel that they are to blame for
the delay. If they were able to facilitate early
success, they may feel by implication blamed for any

later failure. Alternatively, some parents will demonstrate exceptional skills in working with their child. Such progress may unconsciously threaten the teacher or professional. In difficult circumstances, it may also be tempting for the professional to overstep the mark and become a 'friend'. But criticism may be unacceptable from a friend and the professional relationship may be threatened and distorted.

Such dilemmas are not insoluble. They are, indeed, hallmarks of success in a system which is flexible to individual needs and where professionals will continually reappraise their method of work. In the end, the relationship between parents and professionals must be enriched by closer cooperation. The acceptance of the philosophy of parental involvement is seldom openly questioned; but the nature of the partnership is one which needs further debate and which must, indeed, reflect the very individual needs and abilities of parents and professionals within the context of their local services.

REFERENCES

Bayley, M. (1973) Mental Handicap and Community Care. London: Routledge and Kegan Paul
Bluma, S., Shearer, M., Frohman, A. and Hilliard, J. (1976) Portage Guide to Early Education. Windsor, Berks: NFER
Brazelton, T. (1970) Case finding, screening, diagnosis and tracking: discussant's comments. In T. Tjossem (ed.) Intervention Strategies for High Risk Infants and Young Children. Baltimore: University Park Press
Brimblecombe, F. (1976) Paediatricians and parents as partners. In The Early Management of Handicapping Disorders. Amsterdam: Associated Scientific Publishers
Carr, J. (1974) The effect of the severely subnormal on their families. In A.M. Clarke and A.D.B. Clarke (eds.) Mental Deficiency: The Changing Outlook, 3rd edition. London: Methuen
Collins, M. and Collins, D. (1976) Kith and Kids. London: Souvenir Press
Cunningham, C. (1975) Parents as therapists and educators. In C.C. Kiernan and F.P. Woodford (eds.) Behaviour Modification with the Severely Retarded. Study Group 8, IRMMH. Amsterdam: Associated Scientific Publishers
Cunningham, C. (1979a) Parent counselling. In M.

Craft (ed.) <u>Tredgold's Mental Retardation</u>, 12th
edition. London: Ballière Tindall

Cunningham, C. (1979b) Early stimulation of the
mentally handicapped child. In M. Craft (ed.)
<u>Tredgold's Mental Retardation</u>, 12th edition.
London: Ballière Tindall

Cunningham, C. and Sloper, P. (1977) Down's
syndrome infants: a positive approach to parent
and professional collaboration. <u>Health
Visitor</u>, <u>50</u> (2), 32-37

Department of Education and Science (1978) <u>Special
Educational Needs</u>. Report of the Warnock Committee of Enquiry into the Education of Handicapped Children and Young People. Cmnd 7212.
London: HMSO

Department of Health and Social Security (1976) <u>Fit
for the Future</u>. Report of the Court Committee
of Enquiry into Child Health Services. Cmnd
6684. London: HMSO

Department of Health and Social Security (1979)
<u>Report of the Jay Committee of Enquiry into
Mental Handicap Nursing and Care</u>. Cmnd 7468.
London: HMSO

Gath, A. (1978) <u>Down's Syndrome and the Family</u>.
London: Academic Press

Hewett, S. (1970) <u>The Family and the Handicapped
Child</u>. London: Allen and Unwin

Jeffree, D.M. and McConkey, R. (1976) <u>P.I.P.
Developmental Charts</u>. Sevenoaks, Kent: Hodder
and Stoughton

Kiernan, C.C. (1982) <u>Family Involvement with
Services in Haringey</u>. Final Report to DHSS.
London: Thomas Coram Research Unit, Institute
of Education

Lansdown, R. (1981) <u>More than Sympathy</u>. London:
Tavistock Press

Leiderman, P.H. (1974) Mother at risk. In E.J.
Anthony and C. Koupernick (eds.) <u>The Child in
His Family</u>. New York: Wiley

Newson, E. (1976) Parents as a resource in diagnosis and assessment. In <u>The Early Management
of Handicapping Disorders</u>. Amsterdam:
Associated Scientific Publishers

Pugh, G. (1981) <u>Parents as Partners</u>. London:
National Children's Bureau

Pugh, G. and Russell, P. (1976) <u>Shared Care: Support
for Families with Handicapped Children</u>.
London: National Children's Bureau

Rubissow, J., Jones, J., Brimblecombe, F. and
Morgan, D. (1979) Handicapped children and
their families: their use of available serv-

ices and their unmet needs. In <u>Mixed Communi</u>
<u>cations: Problems and Progress in Medical Care</u>,
No. 12 Nuffield Provincial Hospitals Trust.
London: Oxford University Press
Russell, P. (1981) KIDS - a family support centre.
<u>Concern</u> (National Children's Bureau), no. 38
(Winter 1980/81)
Sandow, S. and Clarke, A.D.B. (1978) Home inter-
vention with parents of severely subnormal
children: an interim report. <u>Child: Care</u>,
<u>Health and Development</u>, <u>4</u>, 29-39
Smith, J., Kushlick, A. and Glossop, C. (1977) <u>The</u>
<u>Wessex Portage Project</u>: <u>A home teaching service</u>
<u>for families with a pre-school mentally handi-</u>
<u>capped child</u>. Winchester: Health Care Evalu-
ation Research Team
Wilkin, D. (1979) <u>Caring for the Mentally Handi-</u>
<u>capped Child</u>. London: Croom Helm

DISCUSSION

In introducing the discussion of her paper, Philippa
Russell again stressed the diversity of needs in
families of mentally handicapped people. Coming to
terms with a child's handicap will proceed at different rates for different family members, and grandparents, for example, often exert a considerable
influence, which may not be considered sufficiently
by professionals.

Secondly, she made the point that, although
professionals should certainly try to make parents
feel competent in the education of their child,
they should beware of thinking of parents as 'professional parents'. If they do, parents may well
feel that it is their responsibility, or in their
power, to develop their child's abilities at a
constant and high rate. Such expectations are
bound to give rise to disappointment and feelings
of failure. Professionals need to help parents to
be both optimistic and realistic, and to allow
parents just to be parents.

Finally, Philippa Russell pointed out that co-
operation between parents and professionals may be
very threatening to professionals. The reasons why
partnership may not be achieved need to be explored - the possibly conflicting views of parents,
professionals and children are a complicated field.

In general discussion, the main topic was
'non-motivated parents', ie. parents who do not
join parents' groups and associations and who de-
cline cooperation with professionals. Labelling of

this type was argued against forcefully by several participants, who pointed out that parents will have good reasons for not joining in. For example, they may have serious personal problems (which are not necessarily connected with the child's handicap), or both parents may be employed, and have large family commitments. They may not get what they want from the service offered and the professionals may not have considered basic necessities such as transport and child-minding. The parents may have real mis-understandings about the handicap; for example, they may see assessment as the child failing a test, after which nothing can be done. Or they may feel strongly that they want to be part of 'normal' society. It was pointed out that in seeking to 'normalize' the children, we expect the parents to be different, ie. collaborating in special pro-grammes, etc. Parents may want a service which enables them to get on with leading their own lives, and also to keep their child.

The other side of the problem is that parents who do join in may be reacting to felt pressure, and avoiding being labelled as 'problems' of one kind or another. Professionals still tend to set up serv-ices without adequately consulting parents as to what would make most sense and be of greatest bene-fit to them.

Chapter 3

MEETING PARENTS' NEEDS: THE ROLE OF THE VOLUNTARY
ORGANISATION

James Ross

There is a strong tradition of 'voluntary' effort in
Britain. Ministers of successive governments have
acknowledged the enormous contribution which the
voluntary agencies make within the total provision
of services. Pioneer workers, such as Dr. Barnardo
and Lord Shaftesbury who rescued unwanted and
neglected children from the streets of London and
other cities more than a century ago, laid foundations in Britain and in other countries for the
health, education and social services which have
developed so rapidly over the last three decades.
But men and women of vision have frequently been
ridiculed for relentlessly defending the needs of
the socially, physically or mentally handicapped.
Even in the 1980's society continues to disregard
certain minority groups and areas of need.

CURRENT ROLES AND RESPONSIBILITIES

The roles and responsibilities of the voluntary
agencies today fall into four main categories:

  . to recognise special needs in our society;
  . to pioneer services by a process of research
    and example;
  . to present to government the established facts
    which clearly define the problems and the
    needs;
  . to lobby for public and government recognition
    of the responsibility to provide services.

In terms of the first role, there are those who
argue that the increase in statutory provision for
those in need of special services is diminishing the
responsibilities of the voluntary movement. In fact
the opposite is the case. Growth in the standard

of living and the enormous development of scientific and technical skills have created a materialist- ically rich and complicated society. Such progress has presented increasingly difficult problems of expectations and standards. Voluntary organisations are an essential part of a monitoring process which alerts the social conscience to the casualties of change and development; voluntary organisations identify the responsibilities of society. For example, they stimulated the debate about the res- ponse of government to the suffering of drug- damaged children and their families.

Secondly, voluntary agencies establish services as a temporary measure to relieve suffering and deprivation as far as possible. One advantage of a voluntary agency is its independence, which allows for a quick response and direct appeals for support. An essential part of this process is research: the collection, examination and exploration of the essential components of the problem. The widest implications of meeting special needs must be prop- erly analysed for a meaningful programme to be developed.

Thirdly, it is the voluntary organisations' responsibility to represent people's needs by a clear identification of the facts. The processes of identification and collation of information are slow and demanding because those with the most serious problems are scattered in the community. They may not know of the existence of others in a similar position, nor of the organisations who may be able to help. They are frequently isolated by the problems. It is not hard to recognise, for example, the enormous difficulties of the families who struggle to look after a severely multiply handicapped child or adult at home, but it is extremely difficult to establish and assess the total problem. Neither the voluntary organisations nor central government really knows the extent of the needs.

For example, there are few really good ex- amples of special care provision in special schools or Adult Training Centres, not because teachers do not care or are not convinced that more effort would be beneficial but because we are not sure what to do. Much more research is needed into methods of education and stimulation of profoundly retarded multiply handicapped people. One role of the voluntary agencies is to ensure that they are fairly represented in the claims upon national and local resources in providing for such needs.

Fourthly, a determined and articulate campaign is organised to influence the policy and programmes of government. The British democratic system depends to a large extent on lobbying by 'pressure groups'. The process is rarely sensational: policy is ultimately determined by consultation, working parties, evidence to Government Committees and Royal Commissions, and more often than not through the interest of a Member of Parliament who is able to gain the support of colleagues.

In recent years, voluntary organisations have had an increasing burden of campaigning to have legislation implemented: people in need are frequently not receiving services to which they are already legally entitled. Campaigning for the implementation of rights is one of the most disturbing responsibilities of the voluntary agencies today.

MENCAP

The Royal Society for Mentally Handicapped Children and Adults (MENCAP) has 40,000 members in 500 local societies served by 12 Regional Offices. It is a registered charity, supported largely by voluntary contributions. The primary objective of the Society is to secure for mentally handicapped people provision commensurate with their needs. To this end, the Society aims to increase public knowledge and awareness of the problems faced by mentally handicapped people and their families, and thus to create a sympathetic climate of public opinion as a necessary prerequisite of their acceptance into the community. Provision includes:

- support and help for the parents of mentally handicapped people through a network of Local Societies and Regional Offices in all parts of the country;
- funds and support for research into various aspects of mental handicap;
- books and literature, and the quarterly *Journal of Mental Deficiency Research* for professionals and research workers, and *Parents Voice* for parents and general readers;
- specialist advisory and information services for the lay public and for professional workers on all aspects of mental handicap;
- an ongoing programme to facilitate the sharing of knowledge on all aspects of mental handicap by means of symposia, conferences and information exchange sessions.

The Society developed from groups of parents of mentally handicapped children meeting together and supporting each other, trying to relieve both emotional and practical problems. Parents have responded magnificently to the challenges. Finding the energy after coping all day, and maybe several hours during the previous night, to turn out for a meeting to share with others who themselves may also be worn out by the sheer physical demands of coping with the everyday chores, takes a lot of determination and loyalty. One young mother summed it up recently:

> I seem to find new energy from the realisation that at last I can talk and relax with other parents who know what it is like. Most of the time I feel other people don't understand how guilty or angry and bitterly disappointed my husband and I feel. The people from the Town Hall, like the social worker and health visitor, don't seem to understand at all. Our doctor, when we go to see him seems to be more embarrassed than we are. Most of the time we have to put on an act of acceptance and it is difficult to relax or be natural. I don't know what I would do, or that I could cope, without the precious few hours once or twice a week when I meet other parents at our local society.

It may seem hard for some to realise that within the welfare state system many of the fundamental needs of parents are not and perhaps cannot be met by medicine, education, psychology or the social sciences. This is not to say that such expertise is unimportant, or not needed; but the services cannot stand on their own. Parents have proved from long and bitter experience that the parent-to-parent service of their local group is vital to the success of all the other elements which contribute to a responsive and caring service of practical value to families with a mentally handicapped member.

VOLUNTARY WELFARE VISITORS

In 1974, MENCAP established a Voluntary Welfare Visitors scheme, with the aim of ensuring that families have as much information and advice as is necessary to obtain the best services available in their area. Each local society selects a team of parents who are prepared to attend a training course and also to make a special study of the rights of mentally handicapped people and their families, in addition to compiling detailed information about all the services and facilities available in the local area which may be of help. The detail of this comprehensive source of reference is vitally important because the primary function of the Voluntary Welfare Visitor is to direct parents to the right kind of help and to avoid the unnecessary stress of being passed from one person or department to another. The Voluntary Welfare Visitor supplies the names of the professionals responsible for providing the service and often accompanies the parents, if they so wish, on their initial enquiries. The main advantage is that parents in each local society know they have another parent to whom they can turn for help and advice - a parent who has been selected and who has agreed to make his or her contribution to the self-help group as a 'specialist' in advice, support and direction. The Voluntary Welfare Visitor is a 'direction indicator' rather than a provider of services.

A second function of the Voluntary Welfare Visitor is to give moral support to parents, to give them the assurance that they are not alone, isolated or forgotten. This caring relationship is offered to families whether or not they are members of the local Society. Thirdly, there may be need for immediate practical help. This can range from advising a parent on how to complete an application for the Attendance Allowance to urgent problems where no other sources of help can be found at the time. For example, a Welfare Visitor may need to find immediate overnight accommodation for a mentally handicapped child or financial assistance from the local society welfare funds.

The Voluntary Welfare Visitor must foster a good working relationship with the various statutory and voluntary agencies. For example, some have established regular informal meetings with health visitors and social workers, by a monthly coffee morning or through a mother and baby group, when the professional workers are invited to call in for a short time. It is not unusual to find health and social services referring parents to MENCAP's Voluntary Welfare Visitors; the expertise of the parent visitor is increasingly being recognised by professionals.

All Voluntary Welfare Visitors are required to follow a 'code of practice' which has been compiled by MENCAP to help them in their work and also to avoid any misunderstanding about their role. It covers difficult areas such as confidentiality, areas of possible conflict with the statutory services, welfare funds, and reports.

The following guidelines show in greater detail how the MENCAP Voluntary Welfare Service operates.

1. The most important work of a Local Society is to be a good source of advice and help for parents of mentally handicapped people. The Local Society must be aware of the needs of its members and it is essential to ensure a well organised Welfare and Advisory Service is given the highest priority.

2. Each Local Society should have at least one Voluntary Welfare Visitor. According to the size of membership and the geographical area to be covered, it is often desirable to have a small team of such Visitors.

3. The Voluntary Welfare Visitor (VWV) is in a key position in the self-help philosophy of the Local Society. It is an important office which requires careful consideration by those responsible for the appointment. Obviously it is a position of trust and members must be able to share their problems or difficulties in complete confidence with the person or persons selected. The VWV may be recruited from the membership of the Local Society, or alternatively a suitable person or persons from elsewhere in the community may be invited to undertake this vital role. If it is necessary to appoint more than one VWV, it is important to designate one of them as responsible for co-ordinating the work and also for being responsible to the Executive Committee of the Local Society, as well as to liaise with the Regional Office when professional help and guidance is required from the Royal Society.

4. The VWV is an official (the same as the Chairperson, Secretary, Nominee member, Treasurer, etc) of the Local Society and must be accountable to the Local Society Executive Committee. Local Societies are advised to have a separate Welfare and Advisory Sub-Committee, and a Welfare Fund should be established to meet the out of pocket expenses of the VWV (e.g., training courses, conferences, reference books, travel, postage, telephone and stationery) and any exceptional needs of families which

cannot be met by statutory funding.

5. The role of the VWV is to give immediate help and support to parents who are in need, and to assure parents they are not alone, isolated or forgotten. The main concern should be to develop a caring relationship and a sympathetic understanding to which parents can turn whenever they feel the need for moral support, advice or practical assistance.

6. The Royal Society provides a full programme of support and training for Local Society Welfare and Advisory Services. Professional support is provided from the Regional Offices and VWVs should contact them whenever they require advice. The Directors of Regional Services and their staff provide the professional support, and the Central Office in London is able to give additional specialist advice and guidance. Training for VWVs is provided by a network of courses which are offered on a regular programme in London, and as the need arises in the regions. Training Courses will usually be organised in any part of the country if there are ten or more people prepared to attend.

7. The Training Courses have been carefully planned to meet the basic needs of the wide cross-section of VWVs and to help them understand the welfare state system, the statutory services and the rudiments of the legal rights of mentally handicapped people - children and adults. The syllabus is approved by the Royal Society's National Council and leads to official registration on the National Register for all VWVs who have satisfactorily completed both parts of the Training Courses and who continue to work by the 'Code of Good Practice' and the 'Basic Rules' taught as an essential part of the course syllabus.

8. It is recommended that all Local Societies do everything possible to encourage and make it possible for VWVs to attend the Training Courses. The Department of Health and Social Security and local authorities recognise the importance of the professional support and the training courses provided by the Royal Society. The credibility of this nationwide Welfare and Advisory Service

depends upon the maintenance of the highest
possible standards and it is therefore essential to ensure Local Societies affiliated
to the Royal Society are trained according
to the National Syllabus of Training
approved by the National Council. Only VWVs
who have completed the National Syllabus of
Training can be officially recognised and
placed on the National Register.

TRAINING AND SUPPORT OF VOLUNTARY WELFARE VISITORS

By 1981, there were 1500 Voluntary Welfare Visitors
working in the local societies. Each had attended
a comprehensive training programme to give them the
information and guidelines necessary to help other
parents. The training is divided into two courses.
The first covers the basic legal framework for
services, statutory rights, and an analysis of the
service providers. The second course includes the
Social Security system, the range of benefits,
allowances and services available together with a
detailed study of the role of the various professionals (e.g., social workers, health visitors,
teachers, etc.) in supporting mentally handicapped
people and their families.

Outline Syllabus for Part One

1. Introduction
   . The national scheme
   . The Welfare Visitor role
   . The Code of Good
        Practice -
        "Confidentiality"

2. Family Support
   . Advice and information
   . Counselling
   . The Code of Good
        Practice -
        "Keeping Records"

3. Important Legislation
   - session 1
   . The Education Acts 1970
        and 1981
   . Local Authority Social
        Services Act 1970
   . The Code of Good
        Practice -
        "Demarcation Lines"

4. Important Legislation
   - session 2
   . Chronically Sick and
        Disabled Persons Act
        1970
   . The Mental Health Acts
        1959 and 1982

	. The Code of Good Practice - "Authority and Action"
5. The Agencies	. Public and Statutory
	. Voluntary and Charitable
	. The Code of Good Practice - "Welfare Funds"
6. Local Welfare Services	. Family problems
	. Co-operation and Co-ordination
	. The Code of Good Practice - "Accountability and Reports"

Outline Syllabus for Part Two

1. Introduction	. Review of the services
	. The 'key' workers
	. Practical help series - The Local Society
2. Domiciliary Support	. The Health Visitor
	. The Social Worker
	. Practical help series - The Regional and National Organisation
3. Social Security	. The Social Security System
	. Social Security Benefits
	. Practical help series - Local guide and information
4. Education and Training	. The School Teacher
	. The Adult Training Centre
	. Practical help series - Leisure, Gateway Clubs, Holidays
5. Residential Care	. In the community
	. In the hospital
	. Practical help series - The Trusteeship Scheme
6. Specialist Advice and Support	. The Therapists
	. The Counselling and Advisory Agencies
	. Practical help series - Training and Employment

Part two of the course is open only to those who have completed part one. Each part of the training course covers six one-and-a-half-hour sessions as a minimum and those attending are requested to follow a basic reading list. The background reading is an important part of the total scheme because it provides information which it is not possible to cover in the formal sessions. In addition to the reading list, some basic reference books are recommended. Some of the sessions include a period of practical exercises to reinforce the instruction. Time is allowed for clarification, questions and discussion.

Regular seminars and meetings are held nationally and in the regions to support Voluntary Welfare Visitors and to provide them with up-to-date information on the development of services and changes in government benefits or policies. A Welfare and Rights Communications Pack, which ensures Visitors are well-informed on all matters concerning mentally handicapped people, is issued three times each year. National and international news, events and projects are included if they are of particular value to the work of Local Societies and parents. It is compiled especially for Voluntary Welfare Visitors but many professionals, local authorities, hospitals, colleges and other bodies find it a valuable reference resource.

CONCLUSION

This chapter has described the roles and responsibilities of voluntary agencies in the context of the present welfare state. One role in particular has been focussed on: the importance of ensuring that the delivery of services to mentally handicapped people and their families matches their entitlement and needs. Roles change as provision of services develops. Helping people to know their rights and what is available, or should be available, may be the major task of the voluntary organisations in the future. Of course, we have a long way to go before it will be the only task; but it is a serious mistake to secure statutory responsibility for services without carefully monitoring their implementation.

DISCUSSION

From discussion it seemed that in all the countries represented at the Seminar voluntary organisations have the same ultimate goal that society should take full responsibility for its handicapped members.

How far the voluntary organisations have travelled towards this goal depends both on the initiatives taken by parents and also on the political and social conditions in each country.

Erica Lund compared the situation in Sweden with that in Britain. She noted that the parallel body to MENCAP has the same number of members, even though Sweden has less than a sixth of the general population of England, Wales and Northern Ireland. (Scotland has a separate voluntary organisation.) The growth of organised parent groups in Sweden has taken place over a period of 25 years. In the beginning, they placed primary importance on gathering funds in order to be able to promote their own activities; professionals such as teachers in special education and psychologists were hired to lead these activities.

During the 1960's and the first half of the 1970's public agencies gradually assumed financial responsibility for various activities which had first been developed by parent groups, for example, nursery schools and summer camps. At the present time, voluntary organisations play an important role as pressure groups; but in terms of care, development and research, the contribution of statutory agencies has become dominant. In order to reach this level, voluntary groups have worked at intestigating needs, proposing improvements, and influencing both public opinion and political interests. The methods adopted reflect how voluntary groups now see their primary role. They go further than simply studying facts and information: through self-education in small groups they try to create conditions in which parents develop pride in being the parent of their handicapped child, and are more able to fulfil the task of providing the best possible social environment for the whole family.

James Ross commented further on the political role of the voluntary organisations, and mentioned that MENCAP now has an office in the House of Commons, where staff members monitor all political debates and can contact Members of Parliament whenever a debate concerns the rights of mentally handicapped people. It seems to be effective in directly influencing political decision-making.

Discussion then focussed on the topic of confidentiality. Parents from several countries expressed dissatisfaction at the lack of open access to files concerning their child. Confidentiality can also be a problem between professionals. For example, some felt that at the present time to open

up all records on a child's development could lead
to misunderstanding if parents cannot interpret the
wording of a letter or a report, or distress if the
terminology is cold and clinical. Some professionals have set up two sets of records, one open and
one closed, in an attempt to overcome these problems. It was forcefully argued that if a copy of
every document written about a child were given to
the parents, it would compel professionals to think
even more.carefully about what they write. Even if
the subject of confidentiality were to be regulated
by law, the implementation of rules would ultimately
depend on the willingness of professionals to allow
scrutiny of their own field of practice.

SECTION THREE: INFANCY AND EARLY CHILDHOOD

Chapter 4

INFANT DEVELOPMENT PROGRAMMES IN BRITISH COLUMBIA

Dana Brynelsen

INTRODUCTION

History
The first home-based Infant Development Programme in
British Columbia was started by a group of parents
of infants with developmental handicaps and professionals involved with services for these children in
Vancouver in 1972. With support and funding from
the Ministry of Human Resources, the provincial
goverment department responsible for funding family
support services, Infant programmes were then
developed elsewhere in British Columbia. A Provincial Steering Committee was appointed by the
Minister of Human Resources in 1975 to set terms of
reference for this new service as it expanded
through the province.
　　The terms of reference for the development and
operation of Infant Development Programmes were designed to encourage standard practices of service
delivery and are described in this chapter. They
were developed, however, with consideration for the
diverse circumstances of geography, population
cluster, climate and availability of specialized
resources in rural areas, which characterize this
large province. Therefore, in addition to standard
practices, there are also significant individual
differences among the programmes currently in operation. At present, 28 programmes serve an annual
population of approximately 1,500 infants and their
families. Since the programme's inception in 1972,
more than 4,000 infants and their families have received regular service from Infant Development Programmes.

Rationale

In common with similar services in the U.S.A. and elsewhere in Canada, Infant Development Programmes are based on the following theories:

1. Infancy is an important period of life; delays in development during this period may have long-lasting, cumulative effects on the patterns of development of any child, as well as on the patterns of interaction between the child and the family.
2. Intervention for children with developmental problems will be most effective if begun as early in the child's life as possible.
3. The family unit is the most crucial source of learning, developmental encouragement and emotional support available to the child.

The family thus becomes the primary focus of services for the Infant Development Programme and the home is the centre around which programming is built. While there is no question about the absolute necessity for good diagnostic services, medical treatment, genetic counsellors and other medical, social and educational agents, the focus of this programme is to provide early intervention in the home through and with the parents. The aims of the programme are to help parents make optimal use of available services, to enlarge their knowledge of those factors pertinent to the overall growth and development of their child and to learn skills which will enable them to encourage the development of their child.

Philosophy

The principles of 'normalisation' form the foundation for the development and operation of the Infant Development Programmes. Attempts are made to incorporate these principles at an individual level with families, at a community level with individual programmes and at a provincial level with policy making.

To illustrate this, we might encourage a family with a child who has a handicap to participate in a regular family recreation programme in the community, as opposed to recommending a segregated recreation programme serving only the child with the handicap. At a community level, we would request that the Infant Programme operate from the Public Health Office rather than from a specialized agency that serves only the handicapped. At a provincial level, we have worked with the government in developing community resources as alternatives to instituting resources for the family who has a child with a handicap.

POPULATION SERVED

Infant Development Programmes serve children from birth to three years, at which time they are eligible for pre-school. Children identified as developmentally delayed in one or more major skill areas, children with specific handicapping conditions such as Down's syndrome or physical handicap, and children at risk for delay, such as premature infants with low birth weight, are eligible for service. A special note of caution must be sounded, however, with regard to involvement of 'at risk', infants in a programme that serves children with handicaps. Infants at risk are defined as that population of infants who experience adverse prenatal, post-natal and/or socio-economic factors that are thought to contribute to developmental handicaps. Inclusion of at risk infants into programmes serving children with diagnosed handicaps must be done carefully. Parental expectations as to the developmental outcome of their infant appear to play an important role with regard to child development. Therefore, anxiety generated by a poor prognosis for development and subsequent referral to a programme serving infants with handicaps can be translated by the parents into lower expectations for normal developmental progress. This may contribute to developmental delay in a potentially normal infant (Kearsley, 1979).

It should also be noted that the programme accepts infants for whom no more appropriate service exists. For example, in large urban areas which have home-based programmes for hearing impaired infants, a hearing impaired infant would not be accepted unless another developmental problem was present. Hearing impaired infants are accepted into Infant Development Programmes in rural areas where more specialized service are not available. Cerebral palsy societies throughout British Columbia sponsor a variety of services for infants and children with cerebral palsy, as well as for children with other handicaps. Therefore, the Infant Development Programme serves very few children with cerebral palsy or other orthopaedic problems, as excellent resources are widely available to serve this population.

Table 4.1 gives a diagnostic breakdown of 738 infants who were receiving service from the Infant Development Programmes of British Columbia in May, 1981. It should be understood that the table

Table 4.1: Reasons for Infants Entering Infant Development Programmes

	No. of infants	Per cent of total
Developmental delay (more than one skill area)	208	28
Mental retardation (includes infants with Down's syndrome)	171	23
At risk	118	16
Developmental delay (one skill area)	102	14
Multiple handicaps	54	7
Sensory impairment (vision or hearing)	36	5
Cerebral palsy	25	3
Seizure disorder	12	2
Behaviour problem	12	2
Totals	738	100%

represents, in brief form, a compilation of the diagnostic information available for each child. Many children move into other diagnostic categories as they grow older. Some will cease to be 'labelled' when they catch up to the norm for their ages and are no longer in need of special services.

Population Trends Over Time
Statistics on 1,000 infants referred to Infant Development Programmes from 1973 to 1978 were compared to the caseload of May, 1981, and revealed a positive trend in terms of population served. In 1978, 60 per cent of infants who had received service had diagnosed handicaps and 40 per cent were developmentally delayed or at risk. Over time, as the programmes have gained acceptance by the medical community, other professionals and the public in general, the referral of infants with developmental delay or at risk for developmental delay has increased. At this time, 60 per cent of the popu-

lation in Infant Development Programmes is delayed or at risk and 40 per cent has diagnosed handicaps. This is encouraging because a significant number of children who are delayed may benefit from early intervention and will have a much greater chance of intensive medical investigation and referral to appropriate pre-schools if they are involved to intervention programmes early in life.

Another significant and positive trend is the age at referral. In the early years of the programme, the average age at referral, both for children with diagnosed handicaps and developmental delay, was 15 months. In 1981, 50 per cent of infants in Infant Development Programmes were referred under six months of age; 80 per cent were referred by 18 months.

REFERRALS TO INFANT DEVELOPMENT PROGRAMMES

To encourage early referrals, Infant Development Programmes have an open referral policy: parents as well as professionals may refer to the programme. An open referral policy, as compared to more traditional referral policies which require a physician's referral, was established for a number of reasons.

British Columbia does not have universal surveillance of the child population. Generally, a surveillance system ensures appropriate referral to social, educational, or medical services at the time that delay is evidence in an infant. Without such a system, however, referrals are not the mandated responsibility of any individual or agency. Therefore, it has been an unfortunate, documented fact that, in British Columbia, the suspicion of parents that, "Something is wrong with my child," has sometimes taken up to three years to confirm through medical diagnosis (Sheps and Robinson, 1979). If referral to the Infant Programme was dependent on a physician's confirmation of delay and referral, many of the early referrals we receive would not occur.

Some parents have described the period between suspicion of delay, confirmation of concern, and referral to a programme as being the most difficult period to cope with emotionally. From our experience, the longer this period continues the more difficult it is to intervene in effecting change in parental attitudes and in helping the parents to set realistic goals for their child's development. One key to this relates to how the parents perceive themselves in relation to the child's development. Studies elsewhere, as well as one study of 59 devel-

opmentally delayed infants in Infant Development
Programmes in this province, demonstrate that, generally, parents providing the optimal home environment were those who believed in their ability to influence their child's development and felt a personal sense of responsibility toward that development (Tolleson, 1978). The parent with prolonged,
unsuccessful caretaking experiences, which may
result from not understanding how best to meet the
baby's needs, may feel unable to influence the
child's development. That parent is at risk for
withdrawing more and more from normal parenting
practices. These pre-diagnostic experiences have
been significant factors in post-diagnostic decisions resulting in out-of-home care for many children in this province (Brynelsen, 1982).

To prevent further delay in terms of referral
and contact with the family, parental or professional referrals are taken by telephone by Infant
Development Programme staff. Information is collected which includes family history, diagnostic and
assessment information and professionals presently
involved. A home visit by an Infant Development
Programme staff member to the family is scheduled,
generally within two weeks of contact with the programme. Further information about the family, the
infant and the professionals involved is collected
at that time. Services provided by the Infant Development Programme are described and the family is
asked to identify those needs that they feel are
priorities for them (e.g., assistance in feeding)
and practical suggestions that may be of assistance
are made on the initial visit.

Contact with Other Community Professionals and Agencies
Professionals involved with the family are informed
in writing that the family has been referred. These
professionals generally include the family doctor,
paediatrician and public health nurse.[1] They are
encouraged to work closely with the family and
Infant Development Programme staff persons in
sharing relevant information and co-ordinating intervention strategies. However, time constraints
caused by heavy work loads contribute to less than
adequate information sharing and joint planning for
some families. As well, some professionals regard
some children (e.g., severely multiply handicapped
children) as less entitled to their time and efforts
than other children, and are not prepared to work
with other agencies on their behalf. Infant Development Programme staff do send regular six-month

reports on children to professionals involved with the family. These reports present a developmental profile, current programme strategies, goals and recommendations. This reduces the risk of conflicting advice if reciprocity of information sharing is not achieved. Case review committees, comprised of Infant Development Programme staff, a community physician, public health nurse and physiotherapist consultant, meet regularly to review new referrals and progress of children on the caseload. This also provides a medium for collaboration and coordination of services.

Referral Trends Over Time
When a programme starts in a community, the primary referral sources are public health nurses, who generate 80 per cent of referrals. Physician referrals constitute approximately five to ten per cent and parents five to ten per cent. Programmes which have operated for more than two years in a community have referral trends as described in Table 4.2.

Table 4.2: Referral Trends for Established Programmes

Referral source	Per cent of pop.
Public health nurses	40
Physician	31
Parent	10
Social services	7
Other agencies	7
Other I.D. Programmes	5
Total	100%

The increase in physician referrals is attributed to the following factors. Parents are encouraged to talk to the child's physician about their involvement in the programme and physicians receive copies of the six-month reports done by Infant Development Programme staff on infants. The physician representative on the Local Advisory Committee is responsible for educating his or her

colleagues regarding the importance of early diagnosis of developmental delay and early referral to
intervention programmes.

STRUCTURE OF INFANT DEVELOPMENT PROGRAMMES

Funding
All Infant Development Programmes receive 100 per
cent funding from the government. The programme
budgets comprise mainly salaries for Infant Development Programme staff and transportation (mileage)
costs, which include in-service training.

Administration
Infant Development Programmes are sponsored by a
variety of voluntary societies in British Columbia.
These societies include associations for the mentally handicapped, neurological societies and family
and children's services societies. The staff
reports to the executive director or board of the
voluntary society, but receive direction and support
from a Local Advisory Committee to the Infant Development Programme.

Local Advisory Committee
This committee of the board of the sponsoring
society serves as a voluntary (unpaid) multidisciplinary consultant body which gives direction and
support to Infant Development Programme staff.
Membership on each committee must include: parents
of developmentally delayed infants who are receiving
service or who have received service from the Infant
Development Programme; a public health nurse; a
physician; a Ministry of Human Resources social
worker and a physiotherapist. Other professionals,
such as psychologists, speech therapists and early
education specialists, if available in a community,
are encouraged to sit as members.
     The aim of the committee is to concern itself
with the development and continuity of programmes
and services for developmentally delayed infants and
their families in the geographical area covered by
the Infant Development Programme. The terms of reference include the following:

   . to be aware of the standards set by the
     Provincial Steering Committee and the Ministry
     of Human Resources and to assist the Infant
     Development Programme in meeting these stand-
     ards;
   . to provide consultation to the society in the

hiring and on-going monitoring of the Infant
Development Programme staff;
. to assist the staff in reaching the goals of
the Infant Development Programme;
. to encourage the development of quality
programmes for infants and to develop proposals
to overcome gaps or inadequacies in service for
developmentally delayed infants;
. to encourage parent-to-parent support;
. to foster good relationships between parents
receiving services and professionals;
. to facilitate the sharing of information in the
area of early intervention.

INFANT DEVELOPMENT PROGRAMME STAFF

Requirements
Staff of local Infant Development Programmes must
have professional training in a field or fields related to early childhood development (e.g. nursing,
therapy, early childhood education). Demonstrated
ability to work with infants and very young children
and their families, as well as other professionals,
is desirable. Organizational ability and the
ability to operate independently are essential.
    Individuals considered for the position of
Infant Development Programme worker must subscribe
to the following management principles:

. decisions are centred on the child and the
family;
. family members are the principal decision
makers and advocates for their child;
. a developmental disability may have lifelong
ramifications;
. a transdisciplinary approach is essential.

    Infant Development Programmes attempt to utilize
the transdisciplinary approach in service delivery.
"Transdisciplinary describes the ability of professionals to cross over and function effectively in
areas outside their primary specialization," which
facilitates coordination of service (Accardo and
Capute, 1980). It has become increasingly evident
that coordination of services for families who have
children with developmental problems can be as
important as availability of expert consultants. In
fact, lack of coordination of services has resulted
in out-of-home care for a number of children in the
province. Primary involvement of one person is an
essential ingredient in the transdisciplinary model.

The role of the primary person is gathering information from a variety of sources and translating it
into daily, practical use for the family (Bricker,
1976).

Role
The Infant Development Programme worker has a multi-
faceted job in the home-based programme. One major
aspect of the job involves working with the family
to develop an individualized programme for the
infant that will promote development in major skill
areas. To develop an individualized programme, the
worker ensures that:

- the infant is assessed on a regular basis
  by standardized assessment;
- input from parents and appropriate consulting
  professionals is actively pursued;
- resource materials and programmes of instruction relating to normal and atypical development
  are utilized.

Ongoing evaluation of short-term and long-term
goals and methods of attainment are worked out with
the family during the course of home visits, and the
programme is continually revised in consultation
with the family and consulting professionals to meet
the changing development and needs of the infant and
family.
Medical assessment throughout the infant's stay
in the programme is actively sought. At times,
limited resources in some rural areas make it difficult to obtain comprehensive assessment and diagnostic services, but the programme workers are aware
of the importance of sound diagnostic and treatment
procedures. Specialists, such as paediatric physiotherapists or speech therapists, are actively sought
out and referrals are made to these specialists when
available. The active participation of these specialists in planning the individual programme for
each child is encouraged by the staff.
The second major aspect of the job is that the
Infant Development Programme workers must provide
expertise on the resources available in the community for the family and the infant. Staff provide
the parents with information about various programmes, policies and services that may pertain to
the family's needs. In consultation with consulting
professionals, they also help the family learn more
about the handicapping condition. Opportunities are
available, informally or through Pilot Parents, to

meet other families who have a son or daughter with a similar handicap. For some families, this has been the most helpful service provided by the Programme. The Infant Development Programme workers help the family locate and utilize specialized services and information which may enhance their care of the atypical youngster.

Recruitment and maintenance of a qualified and competent staff has been pursued through a number of organizational methods.

1. Societies and Local Advisory Committees establish hiring committees comprised of parents and professionals to screen, select and hire staff and to monitor their performance.
2. Guidelines, job descriptions and relevant criteria to be considered when hiring are described.
3. All new staff members are provided with a practicum placement at the beginning of their employment; evaluations are made during that time and throughout an initial six-month probationary period by the Programme Supervisor, Local Advisory Committee and Provincial Advisor, if requested.

SERVICES PROVIDED BY INFANT DEVELOPMENT PROGRAMMES

All Infant Development Programmes in British Columbia must provide the following services:

1. Home visits will be made on a regular basis by professional staff to assist the family in planning learning activities and to utilize appropriate resources in the community.
2. Parents will be given the opportunity to meet other parents who are successfully coping with the problems of caring for a handicapped child.
3. Parents will be encouraged to attend workshops, lectures and parent meetings which will further their understanding and knowledge of child development.
4. A resource library and toys will be available for loan to the family.
5. The family will be inffrmed of alternatives open to their child as he or she grows older and will be encouraged to take part in any decision making process regarding education

or health services.

Other services may be provided by the Infant
Development Programme. These services might include
a group situation for infants, out-of-boundary services and providing practicum placements for
students.

THE ROLE OF THE PARENT IN INFANT DEVELOPMENT
PROGRAMMES

Infant Development Programmes are designed to
encourage the participation of parents in the home,
in the community and at a provincial level. The
open referral system enables parents to initiate
contact with this service. Parents work with Infant
Development Programme staff in planning activities
for their infant. Their priorities and needs and
those of their infant, as they perceive them, are
incorporated into the home programme.
Initially, parents may be unaware or uncertain
as to the importance of their contribution to
decisions on management issues made regarding their
child. This relates, in part, to traditional
parent-professional encounters where the professional instructs or delivers a service to the non-
professional who is usually in a passive, receiving
position. However, it is the responsibility of
Infant Development Programme staff involved to
encourage active participation of the parent at
whatever level seems appropriate and to whatever
degree the parent wishes to be involved.
Beyond the individual work with their infant,
parents are involved in planning and/or running
workshops for other parents. Parent to parent
support groups and individual counselling through
Pilot Parents are set up by, or liaise closely with,
parents involved in Infant Development Programmes.
At the organizational level, parents whose sons or
daughters are or were in Infant Development Programmes work with professionals in directing and
monitoring the programme in each community. Parents
are appointed by the Deputy Minister of Human
Resources to sit with other professionals on the
Provincial Steering Committee of the Infant Development Programme. At this level, they advise on the
implementation and operation of the programmes
throughout British Columbia.

CONCLUSIONS

Infant Development Programmes are a relatively new
model of service in British Columbia. Their expans-
ion throughout the province has not occurred without
some struggle or conflict with existing, more traditional services or approaches.
     There are a variety of specialized services for
children with developmental problems in British
Columbia. They range from institutions housing up
to 800 children and adults to segregated, special
pre-schools and schools. Efforts have been made by
these agencies to put the principles of normalisation and integration into practice but, in many
instances, change has been slow. Because many
families involved in Infant Development Programmes
require services from these agencies, close working
relationships are important. However, philosophical
differences have caused some conflict in the past.
In addition, Infant Development Programmes have been
criticized for adopting a transdisciplinary
approach; some professionals do not subscribe to the
sharing of skills or the relinquishment of traditional powers required in this approach.
     Within the programmes themselves, we have had
to look closely at our relationships with families
and our expectations for their involvement. Retrospectively, our initial efforts with families were
more instructive and directive than our approach
today. Like other professionals in the community,
we underestimated the contributions that families
made to the development of their children and we
overestimated our contributions. Our approach to
families has changed over the years and these
changes will continue as we learn - both parents and
professionals - how best we can share our skills and
work together more effectively.
     Although there have been no simple resolutions
to these problems, positive changes are occurring:
many agencies which were antagonistic are now referring children; more professionals are sharing
skills, if for no other reason than the current
economic climate, which inhibits growth; and research is providing us with a strong rationale and
the tools to enhance parent-professional working
relationships (eg. Bromwich, 1981).
     One major advantage these programmes have had,
in comparison with most services which operate in
British Columbia or elsewhere, is that from the
beginning there has been a sense of comradeship and
sharing among staff, parents and societies involved.

The programmes were fortunate that the provincial government appointed a Provincial Steering Committee early in the development of this service to ensure that standards were established and a spirit of co-operation generated. Early intervention through and with parents was and is such a new and challenging field that close, cooperative relationships are essential in the home, in the community and at the provincial level.

NOTES

1.   Editors' footnote: Public health nurses are the equivalent of Health Visitors in Britain.

REFERENCES

Accardo, P.J. and Capute, A.J. (1980) Paediatric Education and the Needs of Exceptional Children. Baltimore: University Park Press
Bricker, D. (1976) "Educational synthesizer". In Hey, Don't Forget About Me. Vancouver: Council for Exceptional Children
Bromwich, R.M. (1981) Working with Parents and Infants: An Interactional Approach. Baltimore: University Park Press
Brynelsen, D.L. (1982) Problems Experienced by Line Staff in the Management of Children with Multiple Handicaps. Vancouver: University of British Columbia Press. (In press)
Kearsley, R.B. (1979) Iatrogenic retardation: a syndrome of learned incompetence. In R.B. Kearsley and I.E. Sigel (eds.) Infants at Risk: Assessment of Cognitive Functioning. Hillsdale, N.J.: Lawrence Erlbaum Associates
Sheps, S.B. and Robinson, G.C. (1979) Children with Developmental Handicaps: Is There a Gap Between Suspicion and Referral? Vancouver: Department of Paediatrics, University of British Columbia
Tolleson, L. (1978) Parents' beliefs, attitudes and values and their relationship to home environment provided for developmentally delayed infants involved in a home-based intervention programme. Unpublished thesis, University of British Columbia

Chapter 5

EARLY SUPPORT AND INTERVENTION: THE HARC INFANT
PROGRAMME

Cliff Cunningham

BACKGROUND

The Hester Adrian Research Centre infant research
programme began in October 1973. It has focussed on
infants with Down's syndrome but has also included
25 infants with other mentally handicapping conditions. Initially we wrote to paediatricians out-
lining our research and requesting referrals of
those parents who were willing to co-operate. At
first referrals were rather sparse and confined to
particular doctors. However, as parents involved in
the research returned to their paediatricians with
positive statements, the referral rate increased
rapidly. This was aided considerably when we requested referrals from the health visiting service
and even more so when a health visitor was seconded
to the research team. Over 200 families with a
child with Down's syndrome have so far taken part in
the programme. The majority have been referred by
paediatricians and health visitors and about ten per
cent are self-referrals. We publicise as much as
possible that we are an open-referral system and
that any parents may refer themselves to us. This
is important as it assumes that parents have the
right to seek help for themselves and their infants
and that they do not require the permission of a
professional.
    From Spring 1974 until August 1980, all infants
with Down's syndrome born in Greater Manchester, and
whose natural or foster parents wished to be involved in the research, were included. Subsequent
enquiries of health visitors, developmental assessment clinics and pre-school and school facilities
have indicated that 85 to 90 per cent of infants
with the condition born in the area during this time
are in the sample. These, together with two dozen

or so families from neighbouring districts, make up
the total sample of infants.

BROAD AIMS AND ORIENTATION

The broad aim of our research is to investigate the
development of infants with Down's syndrome in order
to improve their early stimulation and care. Our
aim is not merely to develop and to assess the effi-
cacy of specific training activities for the infant.
We strongly believe that those engaged in early
intervention must seek to foster opportunities for
the family as a whole to flourish. Thus we are as
concerned with family dynamics, attitudes and
resources as we are with the developmental curriculum; and as concerned with the nature of the service provision as with experimental design. Whilst
we acknowledge that resource limitations make such
aims appear unrealistic, nevertheless we feel that
to concentrate purely on developmental training for
the infant is of limited value and may have harmful
consequences for the family in some circumstances.
Our conviction is based on the fact that mental
handicap presents a multi-variable set of problems
in relation to cause, consequence and treatments and
that considerable variations are found within the
range of individual children and their families.
Consequently, it is unlikely that a standard treatment can be specified which will be generally
applicable to all the children, parents or families.
Even where a system of treatments is designed, this
must include a great deal of flexibility to meet and
cope with the many changing variables. We also feel
that we lack sufficient knowledge of content and
method in early intervention to define with confidence - except in the broadest sense - specific
treatments and approaches. For example, as will be
discussed later, we would seriously question whether
infant training activities derived from current developmental tests are sufficient, or even valid, as
a base for the curriculum for many mentally handicapped children.

ORGANISATION AND METHODOLOGY

To meet these aims and to cope with this diversity,
we feel that the approach has to be longitudinal,
and responsive to growth and change in the child and
in the family over the years. It has to be concerned with the many variables that impinge on the situation and it must observe this in as natural a sett-

92

ing as possible, i.e. the home and the community.
For us, this comprises four stages:

1. We try initially to observe over a range of variables in as natural a setting as possible, with the purpose of identifying pertinent factors.

2. From these observations we formulate hypotheses for testing with an emphasis on experimental manipulation. Thus we apply the principle that in order to understand change or development, one needs to try to influence it, and then to evaluate its rate and direction. One important aspect of this is parent comment on the intervention we provide. Equally, we do not discourage parents seeking other available services, but instead monitor this as an important source of information.

3. From such experiments and observations, we attempt to formulate models to guide future research or practice, and to develop dissemination procedures. We would argue that researchers who advocate early intervention programmes must be accountable and must demonstrate both effectiveness and efficiency, with respect to short and long term gains, for parents, service agencies and, of course, the infants involved. Therefore:

4. We try to evaluate these action models in the field under existing conditions of service provision.

The core of our research is the 'cohort' of infants with Down's syndrome and their families and our research activities centre on a home-visiting programme that includes as a minimum:

1. One or more 'first' visits as soon as possible after the diagnosis has been disclosed.

2. Regular six weekly home visits from six weeks of age until 78 weeks of age, which incorporate assessment, support and advice on stimulation.

3. Home visits at 12 weekly intervals until two years. These maintain the support and advice but begin to 'wean' parents away from the programme and encourage them to seek out other support and advice services such as playgroups, opportunity groups or schools.

4. Home visits at six monthly intervals until five years of age. These essentially collect

follow-up data of mental development but also
provide, within the context of a one and a half
to three hour visit, some advice and guidance
in response to parent questions.

Throughout these five years all parents are
told repeatedly that we are available for consultation on any issue at any time. They initiate
these consultations by telephone or in writing. In
cases of bereavement we always try to maintain some
contact and carry out at least one home visit
approximately two to three weeks after the child's
death.

Our complement of staff has grown during the
programme and so the primary visitor, i.e. the one
who carries out the majority of home visits in the
first year or so, has varied since the research
began. The first 46 infants were visited alternatively by myself and another developmental psychologist; the next 55 families were visited by a health
visitor attached to the project. This was a repli-
cation study of our early intervention.

Since then we have had two postgraduate students carrying out investigations requiring one, two
or three weekly visiting. The core staff, however,
carry out all the six weekly visits and we have en-
deavoured to ensure continuity of visits to individual families by the primary visitor. This was
based on the assumption that it would be organis-
ationally simpler and more beneficial to the stimulation programme and to the parent if the same home
visitor carried out the visits. During recent
studies involving several home visitors, however, we
have noted that whereas the primary visitor felt all
was progressing well - as indicated by the general
comments and discussion during the visit - when a
'new' visitor made the visit some parents would reiterate their fears and concerns. In some cases,
this appeared to be no more than the parent 'making
conversation', assuming the visitor would be interested. In others, it was a definite need for parents, and we can only conclude that they assume
repetition of their worries to the familiar primary
visitor will be inappropriate. Also, the new
visitor would often raise some queries over the
stimulation programme, suggesting alternative
approaches or making novel observations. Thus we
are beginning to feel that the best home visitor
service is built around a team who have shared
skills and close communication. Each has a caseload and is the primary visitor, but visits by other

members are systematically built into the programme. This notion is similar to that of the 'named person' or 'key worker' but incorporates recognition of the importance of a team sharing common objectives and techniques but with varying skills and backgrounds.

With the exception of some specific experimental manipulation, all staff in our research who carry out home visits do use similar approaches and share the same philosophy. The importance of a consensus of method and philosophy must be emphasised. Conflicting advice from professionals usually causes parents a great deal of anxiety and can lead to disillusionment with or even rejection of service provisions.

HOME VISITING: PHILOSOPHY AND METHOD

The first tenet of our approach is to endeavour to set up an equal partnership with the parent. This is usually done in the 'first visits' when father is present. We state that as babies are all very individual and because parents have close and continued contact with the baby, it is they who will acquire the expert knowledge about their baby. We, on the other hand, have knowledge about Down's syndrome and development, and we have contact with many babies. This provides us with our expertise and credentials. Thus *together* we will try to ensure that the baby is given every opportunity to develop.

The second tenet is best exemplified by contrasting two polarised 'models': the 'consumer model' and the 'transplant model' (I am grateful to Dorothy Jeffree for this second tag). In the 'consumer model' it is held that:

1. Because each of us brings our own set of knowledge and abilities to new situations, parents are already likely to have some knowledge and skills which are required for the stimulation of their infant.
2. Because each family and parent will react differently to the birth of a handicapped baby - influenced by past experiences, present family circumstances, aspirations, values and attitudes - they will have different needs and requirements.
3. Whilst a large part of our 'sales offer' to parents concerns teaching and therapeutic techniques, parents are not professionals. For example, one can expect a professional to be reasonably objective and objectively

reasonable, ie. one can expect a professional
to make observations and decisions without too
many emotional overtones, and to use factual
knowledge in coming to a relatively realistic
solution. But being a parent means responding
to unreasonable demands (from the professional
viewpoint) from your child: this is one factor
that makes the relationship unique to the
child. Similarly, being the child's parent
gives you the socially legitimate right to make
unreasonable demands for your child.

In the 'consumer model' we do not try to change the
consumer (the parent) into a professional teacher;
we do not attempt to 'transplant' professional
skills into the home so that professional therapies
per se are maintained and extended via the parent.
To do this is to risk 'rejection' of the intervention. Instead we offer parents what we feel is
the necessary information for them to live with and
help their infant with Down's syndrome. They then
select from this according to their current needs
and in their own time.
    We believe that this approach compensates for
our lack of knowledge of the requirements of
families and the efficiency of techniques, and hopefully prevents our imposing too stressful a regime
on the family. In a sense, the approach is experimental rather than prescriptive and dogmatic. It
also implies that the families are responsible for
themselves and their children: the parent is responsible for acquiring the information needed.
    Thus the parent is the consumer and, like any
consumer, can accept or reject our 'goods'. In
such a model, consumer satisfaction becomes an
important variable to monitor, and has strongly
influenced our approach.
    We also hope that this model ensures we remain
firmly in the servicing and advisory role and do not
fall into the trap of 'professional authoritar-
ianism'. This can only lead either to parents rejecting our services or to their becoming too
dependent upon our services (Sandow and Clarke,
1978). Some years ago my attention was drawn to
that eminent developmental text 'House at Pooh
Corner' and the following passage:

    It was going to be one of Rabbit's busy days.
    As soon as he woke up he felt important, as
    if everything depended upon him. It was just
    the day for Organising Something, or for

Writing a Notice Signed Rabbit, or for Seeing
What Everybody Else Thought About It. It was
a perfect morning for hurrying round to see
Pooh, and saying "Very well, then, I'll tell
Piglet", and then going to Piglet and saying,
"Pooh thinks - but perhaps I'd better see Owl
first". It was a Captainish sort of day, when
everybody said, "Yes, Rabbit", and "No,
Rabbit", and waited until he had told them.

(From A.A. Milne, House at Pooh Corner,
Methuen, 1926)

Human experts and rabbits have much in common.
Firstly, they multiply at a prolific rate. Secondly, they are both highly susceptible to infection;
rabbits catch myxamatosis and experts catch expertosis. The symptoms are common to both: the head
swells and the patient goes blind. So as we visit
more families in the course of intervention programmes, we increase our confidence and expertise
and with this the risk of expertosis. Suddenly we
begin to pre-empt and short-cut parent questions.
We stop manifestly working through developmental
problems with parents, explaining our observations
and analyses as we go; instead, we recognise some
increasingly familiar cue and are likely to produce
an increasingly familiar recipe for action. But
this is in opposition to one of our basic aims. If
parents are to be independent, they need to be able
to do their own programming. Thus they need to
'consume' or 'internalise' the teaching approach
that we apply in developing training activities
(Cunningham and Jeffree, 1971). To do this it is
essential that the parent is constantly encouraged
to understand why the activity is important for the
child, to invent and augment the ideas of how it can
best be carried out and to observe for themselves
the progress being made from which to make their own
decisions for change. It is too easy and too comfortable to provide packaged recipes for action
which do not require parent involvement at this
level.
    We do not know which parental characteristics
are most essential to this increasing independence.
My impression is that parents generally can quickly
acquire and improve the major elements of the experimental teaching approach: objective observation,
task analysis, presentation procedures (both direct
as in behaviour modification or indirect as in play
therapy) and evaluation and reappraisal. We believe

that home visitors should consciously decrease their
input of these skills and encourage parents to take
over. What is more difficult is the content of the
stimulation. Parents generally do not have the
depth of developmental knowledge required to select
appropriate teaching goals. Reliance on simple
checklists may be a current practical necessity but
it is by no means sufficient; a far greater knowledge of early developmental processes is needed.
      What then do we do? We cannot give the parent
a crash course in development and education which
will suffice all needs throughout early childhood,
let alone later life, even if the knowledge were
readily available. Parents are going to require
continuing advice on the content of treatment and
management as the child grows and changes. Thus we
aim to prepare parents to seek out this advice by
increasing their confidence and skill in dealing
with professionals. This comes about through positive experiences gained with the home visiting team,
with increased use of a professional vocabulary and
concepts, and is aided by explanations of professional roles and expectations, and in some cases, our
direct intervention as mediators between parents an
other professions. Recently several professionals
and students who have had short attachments to the
programme have expressed surprise at the parents'
questions and dealings with them; as one social
worker put it, "They have obviously been well trained at coping with us". Schools are also beginning
to feel the challenge of such knowledgeable parents,
especially when closely questioned about objectives
and individual teaching programmes.
      We aim, then, to augment parenting skills and
not merely 'transplant' our own teaching and therapeutic values and techniques into the home. During
the course of this, we attempt to minimise stress
on the parent and family. Parents are often anxious that they are not doing enough or that they
are directly contributing to the handicap through
poor management. This is virtually inevitable,
given the underlying concept of behavioural and
stimulation programmes that control over environmental factors can have a great effect on the
child's level of functioning. We attempt to set up
a partnership with the parents based on mutual
respect for each others' expertise and skills and
try to avoid making assumptions and value judgements on what parents should and should not do.
Instead, we try to maintain the role of a consumer
service; the infant is their infant not ours. We

appreciate that parents should be as independent of
the services as possible in their teaching and
management, but equally we realise that they will
need the services to provide practical resources and
support and knowledge on many occasions throughout
the child's life.
   Thus we aim to provide:

. information and training on how parents can
  devise and carry out activities to aid the
  child's development;
. advice on the management of health difficulties
  which are likely to be associated with Down's
  syndrome, such as feeding, diet and respiratory
  problems;
. advice on management of behavioural difficulties when necessary;
. accurate information about Down's syndrome
  which includes the causes, risk rates, mortal-
  ity and short and long term prospects;
. information about local and national support
  services, both voluntary and statutory;
. advice on how to use the services, including
  preparing parents in advance with realistic
  expectations of service provisions;
. liaison between the parent and other services;
. last, but not least, we provide emotional
  support.

In relation to these goals, our intervention programme can be seen as having three phases. The
first centres on the 'first visits' and the parents
learning to "accept and come to terms with" the
handicap. This is followed by a phase which aims at
helping the parent to acquire and to develop the
knowledge and skills needed to organise and carry
out stimulation activities. The third phase, the
'weaning' phase, is near the end of the 18 months
to two years and aims to help parents move on to
other services.
   These natural phases in the programme reflect
the changing needs of the family following the
birth of an infant with Down's syndrome. In the
first year we have found three distinct phases
which are common to the majority of families -
particularly the mothers (Cunningham and Sloper,
1977). The first we tag the 'traumatic period' and
this usually lasts from a few days following the
disclosure to about 12 weeks. Our intervention at
this time accepts that many parents are likely to
have a *grief reaction* or *psychic crisis* to the disclosure

(see Figure 1).

We visit the family as often as required during this phase and spend the majority of our time explaining causes, consequences, treatment, and future possibilities. We always try to provide the parent with some practical activities and advice - usually on handling and strength exercises - as our experience suggests that this will help to speed up their passage through this period. As with grief reactions to bereavement, one should not try to deny, ignore or reduce this reaction, as it does appear important for many parents. During the early visits one needs to allow parents to reiterate fears and the intervener needs to be ready patiently to repeat points previously covered. My concern here is that whilst we appear to do this with most mothers during our regular visits, we usually only see those fathers whose work allows them to be at home and who are willing to meet us. I cannot discuss fathers to any great extent here but two points need to be considered. Firstly, my experience suggests that fathers are more likely to have difficulties in accepting the condition and secondly, many fathers seem to prefer discussing the problems of adjustment with a man during this first phase. I would also note that whilst we see both parents together at the first visit, it is often useful to see parents separately by discretely managing one's visiting, particularly if parents are still debating whether to take the baby home or not.

An essential point in this first period, which occurs in the adaptation or the orientation phase, is when the new infant begins to establish a behavioural interaction with the parent. We have carried out a number of studies in this area (Berger, 1981) and as a result we prepare the parents for the slower emergence of eye-gaze and smiling at about nine to 12 weeks. We also try to teach the parents how to improve the phasing of their behaviour to that of the infant: in most cases this requires parents to pause longer between emitting a signal and expecting the infant's reaction. This process can also be aided by telling parents just to imitate the infant's behaviours, thus ensuring that the parents give the infant time to respond, or to send out a behaviour to which parents then immediately respond. As yet we are unable to provide objective evidence that these interventions are necessary or useful, but anecdotally there are many supportive cases. For example, whilst counselling the parents of an 18 week old infant with Down's syndrome who

Figure 5.1: Model of Psychic Crisis at Disclosure of Handicap

PARENT IS TOLD	PSYCHIC CRISIS	Manifestations		Needs
	SHOCK PHASE	Emotional disorganisation confusion, paralysis of actions, disbelief, irrationality	Can last from 2 minutes to several days.	Sympathy and emotional support
Frequent oscillation between phases	REACTION PHASE	Expression of: sorrow, grief, disappointment, anxiety, aggression, denial, guilt, failure, defence mechanisms	A process of reintegration through discussion.	Listen to parent. Catharsis through talking out. Sympathy but honesty. Facts on cause
	ADAPTATION PHASE	Realistic appraisal: parents ask 'What can be done?' This is a *signal of readiness* to proceed with 'How can we help?'		Reliable and accurate information on medical and educational treatment and future
	ORIENTATION PHASE	Parents begin to organise, seek help and information, plan for future		Provision of regular help and guidance in treatment
	CRISIS OVER			Appropriate provision of services

From: Cunningham, C.C. (1979) Parent counselling. In: Tredgold's Mental Retardation, 12th Edition. Edited by Craft, M. London: Ballière Tindall had not received any support or advice, I explained the slower maturation of the nervous system, the slower processing abilities and the slower rates of transmission along the nerves. This, I argued, meant that we should alter our natural interactive phasing and slow it down. I then gave the infant to mother and asked her to imitate the baby, to wait longer for responses and generally "switch to second gear" (I had mentioned she seemed to be in overdrive most of the time, probably because she was so anxious to help the baby). Within a minute or so, she had begun to elicit consistent smiling and vocalisations from the infant. She hugged the baby to her breast and beamed at her husband. (I assume this is what is meant by bonding.)

Our observations indicate that this first stage is coming to an end when the parent begins to get more satisfying interactions with the baby, due largely to the developmental changes in the infant, and it is often signalled by parents referring to the baby by name rather than by 'the baby' (Cunningham and Sloper, 1977).

However, in most cases there is a functional acceptance of the condition at this time; the parent is ready to face most days and challenges and is ready to learn how to help the infant. I do not know whether parents ever totally accept the condition - or whether they should (Cunningham, 1982).

The next period (three to 10 months) we tag the 'euphoric phase'. Parents (mothers) often begin to tell us that "the baby is as quick as my others" or that "he's just as quick as next door's baby". They say that he or she is really like any baby, not what they expected. "Perhaps she will be a 'bright one'." This is the period when the parents appear to be most open to learning the new observational and analytical skills of the intervention.

A typical visit during this period begins with an assessment of the infant's developmental level. We use the Bayley Scales of Infant Development (Bayley, 1969) as this provides us with standardised data for research purposes. From an intervention viewpoint, a reasonably detailed checklist is sufficient. It will pin-point the infants' current level of development and those behaviours which might reasonably be expected to develop next. We insist that parents observe these assessments. I cannot stress sufficiently that these 'checklist' assessments act purely to focus attention on the developmental areas and create a set of initial situations within which to interact with the child.

They do not constitute the sole means of identifying behavioural goals. From these assessments, we set up a number of possible training methods in discussion with the parent, taking care to explain the developmental significance of the selected behaviours across different aspects of development.

For example, the baby who can sit up not only can use his or her hands to play and to explore and has a wider range of visual opportunities, but is more likely to engage in social interactions. Similarly, we explain that putting cubes in cups or boxes serves to extend the infant's span of attention as well as to open up new games and motor activities to facilitate these behaviours and explore how these work with the infant. This usually acts as a demonstration and during it we note the effect of using prompts, rewards, cueing and phasing. On many occasions we then ask the parent to try it out and can correct the parent's behaviour. (It must be noted that these are guidelines and not every guideline is automatically applied to every behaviour or every parent every time.)

In our first group of 46 infants we did not provide written instructions for these activities, but parents were encouraged to take notes. Occasionally they would request a written explanation for fathers, and as memory aids for themselves. The parents who did this however were less than five per cent of the sample. In the next group of parents, the health visitor wrote down detailed explanations of the behavioural goals and how to carry them out for all visits. However when next visited, many of the parents could not find the notes easily and most admitted that they seldom referred to them.

Recent groups have been given more detailed, typed booklets of activities and these are referred to during visits; parents are also given recording sheets to note when and how often they carried out an activity. We are currently assessing the effect of this more structured and organised approach but our impression is that no significant effects are reflected in the developmental scores of the different groups at 18 months to two years. Certainly no significant developmental differences were found between the mental ages of the first and second groups.

We try to inform parents of management and training techniques as part of the immediate stimulation activities and we explain the significance of developmental processes of the selected behaviours. We also discuss attitudes and philosophies of child rearing. We do not impose a strict training regime of so many minutes a day, or a set number of training sessions on the parent (except in some recent experimental manipulations). Instead, we try to emphasise that they can do much of the necessary stimulation during their every-day interactions with the infant. In other words we avoid centering all the mother's or family's activities on the stimulation programme and instead try to emphasise the use of the ideas or skills within the daily regime. Hopefully, this maintains the balance within the family and avoids, to some extent, a sudden concentration of effort on the infant at the expense of other family members and activities.

Following the 'assessment and training' part of the visit we relax with the parent, usually over a cup of tea, and talk about various matters. We see this as an essential part of the intervention but we do not formalise it to the parent. The purpose of our visit is the 'assessment and training', not counselling for stress or problems. This comes about in a more indirect manner. Wherever possible, we avoid direct questions about likely difficulties unless the problem has been voiced and discussed previously. I clearly remember the consensus of outrage of a group of parents when one noted that the opening remark of a social worker was, "Well, what problems have you got?". Why, they asked, do so many people think you have to have problems just because the child has a handicapping condition. We always try to answer all questions honestly. If information is not known we frankly admit it but also say that we will try to find out.

We are also very sensitive about ending our visits. We try not to stay too long as there are enough disruptions to family routines at this time. Usually visits last from one and a half to three hours. Care is also taken not to appear to hurry away from the visit as our experience has indicated that the issue which is really worrying the parent is often raised as one is about to leave.

This visit pattern is fairly typical throughout the two years, but varies with the changes in the parent. As noted earlier, we aim to withdraw more and more from talking about 'how to teach' the baby as parents increase their skills. However, in the early visits we try very hard not to make the parents feel incompetent at coping with their baby. A major worry of all new parents of a handicapped child is, "Will we cope?". The home intervener must give the parent confidence to cope, not prove how

good the intervener is with the infant at the
expense of the parent. Thus there are no obvious
cut-offs or changes in our parent training, just a
series of subtle adaptations. By seven to 12
months, most parents will quite suddenly 'see' the
handicap. Their baby will be next to another; and
they will compare and 'see' the delay. This is
usually a gross motor activity, like sitting. At
this stage, one needs again to be ready to discuss
worries about the future. It is not as manifestly
traumatic as the initial phase and is often overlooked.

I must also note that around this fourth
quarter of the first year, the babies often begin
to develop more independence and are less willing
to be taught. It is no longer easy to physically
prompt a hand movement, as they begin to resist.
If they wish to get on their feet and bounce about,
it is difficult, and possibly not appropriate, to
make them sit and post shapes. We try to meet this
by again explaining the importance of emotional
development, self-initiated activities, exploration
and independence, and to begin to help parents
organise play situations which will aid development.
Indeed, we strongly encourage the parent shifting
to more indirect teaching approaches at this stage.
This appears to meet the developmental demands of
the infant and to reduce stress on the parent.

The beginnings of the toddler stage (18 months
to two years) brings further increased independence
as well as a new factor - mobility. We now find
ourselves advising parents on behavioural management
techniques. This stage often leads into the discussion of facilities such as playgroups, nurseries
and so on.

CONTENT OF THE DEVELOPMENTAL ACTIVITIES

The details of our curriculum have been published
elsewhere (Cunningham and Sloper, 1978). The main
feature of our approach is that we take the view
that the child's development is the result of
interactions between maturational processes and the
environment and that this can be influenced by
specific deficiencies. These deficiencies can
arise in the sensory systems, e.g. vision, hearing,
etc.; or at the cognitive level in impaired learning and information processing. Thus the role of
the intervener is to try to weigh up these influences for each set of developmental activities and
to seek appropriate treatments.

We view development, particularly in the child
with Down's syndrome, as taking the form of a series
of spurts and plateaux in which there are times when
the child is more likely to be sensitive to and
react to intervention than others. These times
normally coincide with a spurt forward in development. The plateaux coincide with either maturational waiting periods or consolidation periods of newly
acquired skills; that is, the infant rehearses and
adapts a skill across a range of environmental situations. We view development as having both vertical
and horizontal components and hence, intervention
need not, and possibly should not, be a continuous
process.

This is important for parents. For example, in
our first group of families we often found parents
becoming very disillusioned and self-blaming when
little progress was seen to occur in the child.
Lack of progress was seen even after we had broken
down the tasks into minute steps, tried different
teaching strategies and so on. We began to analyse
our developmental profiles of the children and found
that there were some regularly occurring 'plateaux'.
One, for example, is around six to seven months when
the child moves from simple play - sucking, banging,
pushing and throwing all objects - to relational
play where the child begins to use objects together
or in a functional manner, e.g. taking out and
putting into cups. We surmised that this was a consolidation period when the child needed to spend
time rehearsing simple play skills, or alternatively
that cognitive development had not progressed sufficiently to allow the next move forward. At this
time mothers are advised on tasks which extend the
skills sideways (i.e. horizontal) rather than seek
to establish the next step up the developmental
ladder. During these periods, we encourage mothers
to carry out 'probes' on new behaviour so that at
the first glimmer that a spurt might be about to
take place, she can begin to organise the activities
to encourage the development.

Our experience is that parents are very relieved to understand that it is not their poor
teaching or lack of effort that is causing the
apparent halt in development, but the child's own
maturational programme.

Similarly, we emphasise that mentally handicapped babies are born with great innate variations
in ability and personality. Thus not all parents
can have the brightest Down's syndrome baby. I
find that parents, though disappointed, are comfort-

ed by this. Unfortunately, many early intervention
programmes have published results in high euphoria
which, when diluted through various dissemination
and media channels, have proclaimed that great benefits for potentially severely mentally handicapped
infants will result from early structured stimulation. Kysela (1974), as only one example, emphasised the comparability of motor co-ordination and
communication skills of Down's syndrome children to
the attainments expected of any child of the same
chronological age, when reporting on his visit to
the Washington Down's Syndrome Programme. Clunies-
Ross (1979) refers to the same programme and reports
that at five years of age the children are achieving
95 per cent of tasks expected of normal children of
the same age. Whilst this is true for a small minority, our results strongly indicate a tremendous
range of ability regardless of the early intervention provided. We have children with measured
intelligence in the normal range (i.e. mental ages
of four to five) at five years, and others who have
been given as much care and help who have mental
ages of 12 to 18 months. Thus we must not lose
sight of the nature of the handicap in our desire
to help. There are limits to what can be achieved
and whilst we must continually test these limits we
must, at the same time, maintain a realistic
picture for parents.

CONCLUSION

I have tried to emphasise that great individual
differences are found in mentally handicapped children, even those with a similar condition like Down's
syndrome. Great individual differences are also
found in mothers, in fathers, in families; in homes
and in communities; in individuals' resources,
abilities, attitudes and interests. Thus, whatever
we do, our approach has to be flexible, tolerant
and open to change. Providing we do this, there
can be little doubt that early intervention is of
great importance to the family and to the mentally
handicapped infant.

REFERENCES

Bayley, N. (1969) Bayley Scales of Infant Develop-
    ment. New York: The Psychological Corporation
Berger, J. (1981) Early development of social sig-
    nalling, attentional and communicative behav-
    iours in Down's syndrome and non-handicapped

infants. Unpublished Ph.D. thesis, University
of Manchester

Clunies-Ross, C.G. (1979) Accelerating the development of Down's syndrome infants and young
children. Journal of Special Education, 13,
169-177

Cunningham, C.C. (1979) Early stimulation of the
mentally handicapped child. In M. Craft (ed.)
Tredgold's Mental Retardation, 12th Edition.
London: Ballière Tindall

Cunningham, C.C. (1982) Down's Syndrome: An Introduction for Parents. London: Souvenir Press

Cunningham, C.C. and Jeffree, D.M. (1971) Working
with Parents: Developing a Workshop Course for
Parents of Young Mentally Handicapped Children.
Manchester: The National Society for Mentally
Handicapped Children (North West Region)

Cunningham, C.C. and Sloper, P. (1977) Down's syndrome: a positive approach to parent and professional collaboration. Health Visitor, 50,
32-37

Cunningham, C.C. and Sloper, P. (1978) Helping Your
Handicapped Baby. London: Souvenir Press

Kysela, G.M. (1974) Early childhood education for
children with Down's syndrome. Mental Retardation Bulletin, 2, 58-63

Sandow, S. and Clarke, A.D.B. (1978) Home intervention with parents of severely subnormal,
pre-school children: an interim report. Child:
Care, Health and Development, 4, 29-39

DISCUSSION

Because of their similar subjects, papers four and
five were discussed together. Dana Brynelsen gave
some extra examples of the practical implementation
of the philosophy behind the British Columbia Infant
Development Programmes. Group meetings include
mothers' and toddlers' groups once or twice weekly,
evening classes (e.g. on language development) and
parents' meetings for mutual support. She also
described the involvement of "pilot-parents", who
themselves have a handicapped child, and who undertake to visit the parents of a newly-diagnosed
handicapped child who say they would welcome such
contact. Several participants expressed enthusiasm
for such a service, suggesting that, for example, it
can help fathers to adjust more quickly, and
counteract a family's feelings of isolation. However, a number of caveats were mentioned. It must
not be forgotten that the parents usually first have

thought the child was normal, and that it takes time
to accept the new identity of 'parent of a handicapped child'. The parents may feel under pressure
to accept the services offered, and may rather need
to be protected from too many visitors at this early
stage. There may be a problem, particularly when
the diagnosis is uncertain, of parents seeing the
pilot-parent's child as the model for their own
child's future development.

Cliff Cunningham commented that about half of
the parents in the HARC Infant Project did not want
(or retrospectively would not have wanted) to meet
other parents at an early stage. Philippa Russell
made the point that families have changing needs, as
well as differing needs, and that at some times they
may want special services, and at other times to
concentrate on ordinary things. It was also noted
that 'adjusting to the child's handicap' should not
ideally be such an enormous and traumatic step.
Society has the responsibility of accepting and not
devaluing handicapped people.

Cliff Cunningham commented further on some of
the ways in which relationships between parents and
professionals may become estranged. He suggested
that, as well as our recognizing the responsibilities of professionals, parents too have some
responsibility and must be expected to be sympathetic in their dealings with professionals. In
turn, professionals must make clear that they are
not in a hurry when visiting parents, and ensure
that parents know they can always get in touch. The
HARC Infant Project staff give parents their home
phone numbers, and find that it certainly does build
up parents' confidence yet leads only to infrequent
calls.

Discussion then centred on fostering and
respite care. Dana Brynelsen noted that five to ten
per cent of participants in the B.C. Infant Development Programmes are not the natural parents of the
child, i.e. foster parents in most cases. Cliff
Cunningham estimated that in ten to fifteen per cent
of cases known to his research, the natural parents
had not taken the Down's syndrome baby home with
them from hospital. Many do eventually take the
baby home; the project had a number of such cases
which clearly showed that counselling about the
causes and future development, and the promise of a
regular home visiting service which would provide
guidance and support were influential in helping the
parents decide. The time parents took to make the
decision was also reduced. In several cases, after

a three-to-four hour counselling session when questions were answered, the parents went to collect the baby within 24 hours. However, not all parents do this - with or without counselling - and about ten per cent of the sample are fostered. The foster parents are then involved in the early intervention programmes.

Despite active participation in an intervention programme and good relationships with professionals, some families find the child brings many pressures on them. But they may recoil from the notion of sharing the care with others. In the HARC Infant Project, the staff have begun to encourage parents to consider the use of shared care as a *positive* resource. It is emphasised that the notion of independence and being as 'normal' as possible will mean that the child will eventually leave home and live in the community or a sheltered environment. Thus they need, like any child, to get used to this. Staying overnight with a friend or relative, school trips etc. are all part of this process. In some cases where parents find it particularly difficult, they may be too tired to realise that they are getting close to a crisis. Hence the regular use of shared care, either with relatives or short term fostering (e.g. occasional weekends with another family) will give parents a chance to consider how things are. In this sense, respite or shared care becomes a positive aspect of intervention for both parents and children, and not a desperate result of what the parent sees as his or her own failure.

Chapter 6

DEVELOPING PARTNERSHIP: THE ANSON HOUSE PRESCHOOL PROJECT

Sally Beveridge

INTRODUCTION

The Anson House Preschool Project is one of a number of projects at the Hester Adrian Research Centre, University of Manchester. It began in 1975 as a service and research project concerned with pre-school mentally handicapped children and their families. It is funded primarily by Dr. Barnardo's, with additional support from Manchester Education Committee, and since 1981, from Manchester Area Health Authority. Initially the project team consisted of psychologists and teachers: over time the need for multidisciplinary service provision became apparent, and the current team comprises two teachers, a nursery nurse, three psychologists and a social worker. In addition, regular input is made to the project by a speech therapist and physiotherapist, and close links have been established with a range of specialist services within the community.

Since 1977 a special feature of the project has been the integration of children of widely differing developmental abilities within the classroom group. The development of classroom provision for groups of preschool children ranging from those who are profoundly retarded and multiply handicapped, through those with less severe handicap, to children who show no developmental delay has been described by Gunstone, Hogg, Sebba, Warner and Almond (1982). Children who attend the project are drawn from the City of Manchester, and are referred by a range of professionals including preschool teachers, paediatricians, health visitors and social workers, or families may refer themselves. Currently twelve children, eight of whom are handicapped and four non-handicapped, attend Anson House on four mornings

a week. One parent of each child (usually the
mother) is asked to attend one session per week so
that we can work together with the children. In
practice most parents attend more frequently, many
attending almost as often as their children.

The model of parent involvement in Anson House
has gradually been developed through the experience
of working together practically with the parents and
their children who have participated in the project.
This paper will summarize the changes which have
taken place in our approach to parental involvement
over time, the current model and the day-to-day
service provision. Finally new directions in the
work to be undertaken at Anson House are raised.

THE STARTING POINT (1975-1977)

When the Anson House Preschool Project started in
1975 there was already wide recognition that in
order for early intervention schemes to be really
effective, professionals needed to involve the parents as fully as possible. Bronfenbrenner (1976),
in his influential review of Head Start programmes,
noted that it was only when parents had been actively involved that there was evidence of lasting
intervention effects. With the benefit of hind-
sight, his findings concur with common sense: for
most young children the parents remain the primary
caretakers and the home is their primary environment. No matter how intensive professional intervention may be, it is clear that the family home
environment is of vital importance to the child's
development. Moreover, it has been demonstrated
that parents could be effective teachers of their
own children (e.g. O'Dell, 1974; Cunningham, 1975).

The project at Anson House therefore started
with the explicit aim of providing educational
intervention for preschool mentally handicapped
children both directly, through programmed work in
a classroom context, and indirectly, through parent-
teaching work. We knew that we could not hope to
achieve very much, particularly given our limited
contact time with the children, unless we developed
a consistent approach between home and Anson House:
in other words, we as professionals needed parental
cooperation in order to put our own intervention
schemes into most effective practice.

From the outset then, parents were asked to
participate in the project by attending at least one
session per week, so that discussion of their children and the educational programmes that had been de-

112

vised, as well as joint observation and assessment
of their children could take place. The first formal
parent-teaching courses began in 1977.

THE CHANGING FRAMEWORK (1977-1980)

Through the experience of working practically together with the parents and their children, we became aware of the necessity of meeting a wide range
of parents' needs. This led to changes both in our
theoretical approach to intervention, and in the
practicalities of the project's day-to-day service
provision. At a theoretical level, we moved increasingly towards an ecological approach to intervention (Hogg, 1979). This position makes explicit
the importance of taking full account of all the
social settings in which an individual participates.
Most obvious of these for the children at Anson
House is the home, but other settings include playgroups, schools and hospitals. In practical terms,
the appointment of a social worker to join the project team enabled closer and more effective links to
be established, not only between Anson House and
home but also with community services.
     Thus, from an initial focus on the child as
client, we were moving towards service provision for
the families of the children, including social work
intervention and community liaison as well as parent-
teaching work. At the same time, integration of the
children's classroom provision began to be matched
by integration of the service to families; accordingly, the same service was offered to the families
of both handicapped and non-handicapped children who
attended the project.
     By this stage, parents were seen by the project
staff not just as recipients of professional help
and advice but also as full partners in the intervention process. This partnership emphasised the
need to bring together parents' in-depth knowledge
and intimate relationship with their own children
with the project staff's broader perspective e.g. of
child development and educational methods, in order
to best facilitate the children's development.

PARENTS AS PART OF THE MULTIDISCIPLINARY TEAM (1980+)

As the project's multidisciplinary approach to
intervention became established, it was increasingly
felt that the parents should be fully and explicitly
involved as members of the multidisciplinary team.
This resulted in an attempt to define and clarify

with the parents not only their role as they saw it
but also the roles of the other members of the team
in sharing responsibility for the children's development.

If we place too much emphasis on the parents'
expertise with their own children without relating
it to the complementary expertise of others involved
in early childhood development, we run the risk of
placing an extreme burden on parents' shoulders by
making them feel solely responsible for their
child's progress. Thus we have a strong responsibility in our work with parents not only to work together to foster their confidence in their expertise
and role as parents, but also to make clear exactly
what the roles of the many different 'helping' professions are.

DAY-TO-DAY PARENTAL INVOLVEMENT IN ANSON HOUSE

When their children join the classroom group, parents have already gone through a process of gradual
introduction to the project. They will have visited
Anson House and seen the classroom in action, and
met parents and staff. They will also have been
visited by certain of the project staff at home.
The social worker makes initial contact with a
family and continues home visits until the child
joins the project; in her visits she gives information about the project, carries out a social work
assessment, and coordinates transport arrangements.
A project teacher and psychologist also visit the
family in order to discuss the child's development
with the parents, and to explore what their priorities for educational intervention for their child
are. A play-based assessment of the child also
takes place during this visit.

The first months of participation in the project constitute a settling-in phase for both children and parents. Because of the general availability of staff and parents in Anson House, there
is opportunity for a great deal of informal discussion as well as for formal meetings which are
arranged in order to introduce parents to staff
roles and routines within the project.

From this point, and throughout a family's
participation in the project, daily contact takes
place between parents and classroom staff on all
those occasions when a parent attends Anson House;
fortnightly meetings are timetabled with speech and
physiotherapist where appropriate. The social
worker is available in the building for both in-

dividual and group discussion, as well as maintaining home visits with each family. Each child is
also assigned as the administrative responsibility
of one of the psychologists. Administrative responsibility incorporates:

1. Anson House administration: responsibility
   for explaining and discussing assessments
   of their child with the parents; responsibility for co-ordinating the decision-
   making procedure e.g. in termly case
   conferences; development and monitoring of
   individual educational programmes both in
   Anson House and at home.
2. Outside administration: responsibility for
   liaison with other educational agencies
   and hospitals with whom families have contact; responsibility for liaison concerning
   such contacts with the project social
   worker.

The regular meetings which are timetabled
between parents and the psychologist with administrative responsibility include parent-teaching
sessions.
Two of the major aims of our service for parents are to increase parents' confidence in their
own expertise and knowledge of their children and to
increase their information about what it is that
different professionals have to offer, and about how
the service provision within the community is organised. We are concerned that there should be a
smooth transition to community provision for all
families when they leave Anson House. Thus, parental involvement in the project begins with intensive support and help where needed, which is gradually faded in intensity as parents feel more confident. By the time a child and family leave the
project, they will already have been linked with
certain key workers, such as staff of their local
school and social services department. For example,
they will have visited and have had introductory
meetings with teachers in the school to which their
child is moving, and the staff of the school will
have visited Anson House. Joint observation of the
child, and discussion of assessment and programme
records takes place at Anson House with parents and
local authority staff, who are then invited to
participate in the final project case conference.
A continuing transitional service is offered to
the parents over the following term after they have

left Anson House. This includes liaison with the
schools and social services department by project
teachers and social worker, and monthly visits at
home by the psychologist with administrative
responsibility for the family in order to follow
through on parent-teaching work.

THE CURRENT SERVICE MODEL

The current service model incorporates social work
intervention, liaison with community networks and
resources, and parental involvement in educational
intervention. This model is influenced by the recognition of certain parental and staff needs.

Parental Needs
Parents of mentally handicapped children have been
described as a group under pressure, who share certain needs, anxieties and difficulties. The picture
of common needs which emerges from research studies
includes:

- the need to understand the nature of their
  child's handicap more fully;
- the need to know what to expect in the future,
  not only in terms of their child's development
  but also in relation to community provision;
- the need for information about aids and
  appliances which are available, and the allowances and services to which they are entitled;
- the need for introduction to the relevant
  representatives of voluntary and statutory
  agencies within the community;
- the need to know what they can do to best
  facilitate their child's development.

In developing the framework for our service
provision, we have been concerned to respond to
these expressed needs of parents of mentally handicapped children as a group, while yet remaining
aware of the differences in needs between individual
parents - differences which relate not only to their
preschool handicapped child, but also to a wider
family and social environment in which they live.
At the same time, and of particular importance to
us, has been the aim of developing a model of equal
relevance for all the parents involved in Anson
House, whether or not their children are handicapped. While recognising the special needs of
families with handicapped children, we have
attempted to develop an appreciation of the common

needs shared by all families of preschool children.

Staff Needs
Anson House staff have identified needs for collaboration with parents in the following areas.

1.   <u>Assessment of the children</u>.   If we did not have
access to the parents' wealth of information about
their own children, any attempt to draw up an
accurate picture of each child's strengths and weaknesses in different areas of development would be
difficult and time-consuming.   Moreover, a comprehensive assessment requires us to take account of
the experiences of those who know the child best and
who know how the child typically behaves in a range
of different contexts.

2.   <u>Educational planning and intervention</u>.   For
most of the children, their family home is their
primary environment, and one therefore in which
learning must take place.   We cannot assume that
skills learned in one context are automatically
generalised to others, either home to Anson House
or Anson House to home.   We therefore need to try to
ensure that, together with the parents, we develop a
consistency of approach and a common set of priorities and goals.

3.   <u>Social work intervention</u>.   In order to involve
parents effectively in the project, we must take
account of the pressures and stresses within individual families.   We need to know how the home-
school liaison, mediated by social work involvement,
can help towards a better understanding of the
family's needs by Anson House staff.

The Model for Parental Involvement
The current model incorporates five major areas:
social work support; exchange of information; parent participation; developing parent-child relations; liaison between the children and their
families and community resources.

1.   <u>Social work support</u>.   For many parents Anson
House is their first encounter with a social worker.
Some parents have not heard of social workers, and
others are often left wondering about the aim and
purpose of their visits.   The Anson House social
worker discusses with the families attending the
project whether or not they need any of the following
services to assist them with the care of their child

at home:

1. Provision of information about the availability of national and local services for
   mentally handicapped and preschool children and their families.
2. Advice about the use of services e.g.
   criteria for eligibility, organisational
   functioning in terms of identifying who
   needs to be contacted to ensure effective
   service delivery.
3. Liaison on their behalf with statutory
   and voluntary agencies.
4. Opportunities to clarify and resolve areas
   of difficulty and stress created by the
   child within the family.

2. Exchange of information. Three broad areas can
be described:

1. Information about the project - its philosophy, organisation, and goals.
2. Information about child development, the
   relationship between delayed and non-
   delayed patterns of development, and
   principles of early education.
3. Information about local authority and
   voluntary organisation provision within
   the community.

3. Parent participation within the team. Three
possible levels of involvement in their child's
education may be described:

1. In assessment: parents are always involved in any assessments carried out in
   the project. The purpose of the assessment is discussed beforehand, and the
   meaning of the results afterwards. Parents have continuing access to the individual file in which their child's
   assessment and programme records are
   kept. They are also consulted before
   any such information is passed on to
   outside agencies.
2. In the decision-making process: case conferences are held each term, involving
   both parents, in which the establishment
   of priorities for educational intervention, and the planning of individual
   programme work, are discussed and re-

viewed, and decisions made.
3.   In the observation and teaching of their
      child: one parent from each family is
      asked to participate in a formal parent-
      teaching course. Parents meet individ-
      ually with one of the project psycholo-
      gists on a weekly basis. Together they
      select a task which the parent works on
      at home with his or her child. Each week
      the parent and child demonstrate how the
      teaching task is progressing, and the
      psychologist discusses the use of a range
      of teaching techniques with the parent.

4.   Developing parent-child relationships. In the
past years of the project, new parents frequently
expressed a lack of confidence that they were "doing
the right things" with their young mentally handicapped child. Through the parent-teaching work,
parents are made aware of the strategies they are
already using in interaction with their child, and
are also introduced to other teaching techniques and
strategies and to individualised programmes for
their own child. The emphasis is on developing consistency and confidence in their own approach.
      Through social work intervention, confidence in
the parents' abilities or competence and reassurance
concerning parent-child relationships are discussed
individually within the home setting and informal
group discussion at Anson House.

5.   Liaison between families and community networks
and resources. Because of the complexity surrounding the provision of services, part of the social
work task is to act as locator of resources within
the community and as interpreter of parents' needs
to other community networks and resources. The
roles of mediator with unresponsive or poorly functioning networks and of advocate ensuring families
receive services for which they are eligible play an
important part in the project.

      The model outlined here is used as a framework
of service provision for all the parents attending
Anson House, whether or not their child is handicapped. The different components of the service
have been fully described in Beveridge, Flanagan,
McConachie and Sebba (1982).

WHERE NEXT?

A major area of concern underlying the development
of parental involvement in Anson House relates to
how one may best tailor the service provided to fit
the needs of individual parents and of the wider
family.
     Taking parent-teaching work as an example, a
study was undertaken during the first phase of the
project to explore differences in parents' natural
styles of interacting with and teaching their own
children. Some parents are naturally more directive
than others in their approach, and prefer to intervene actively and to prompt their child's activities. Others are less directive and prefer to set
up activities and then sit back to see what their
child will do. We have attempted to respect the
parents' preferred style of interaction, and take
account of these and other differences between parents in developing an individualised approach to
parent-teaching work. However, we are aware of a
large number of differences between families that
have not been taken into account in this work so
far.
     Where social work intervention and liaison with
community networks at Anson House is based on
assessment of family needs, the parent-teaching work
undertaken so far has been restricted to one parent,
usually the mother. The importance of taking
account of the structures and routines of family
life, and the involvement of other family members
than the mother in caring for the child are elabor-
ated by McConachie (Chapter 7, this volume). Future
studies in Anson House will seek to explore the
following questions: Do parents see teaching as part
of their role as parents? Do other family members
than the mothers spend time playing with and teaching the children? Does our emphasis on parent-
teaching sessions with the child disrupt the established family routine? How can we fit our intervention to meet the needs of an individual family?

REFERENCES

Beveridge, S., Flanagan, R., McConachie, H. and
     Sebba, J. (1982) Parental Involvement in Anson
     House. Anson House Preschool Project Paper 3.
     Barkingside: Barnardo's
Bronfenbrenner, U. (1976) Is early intervention
     effective?: facts and principles of early
     intervention - a summary. In A.M. Clarke and

A.D.B. Clarke (eds.) Early Experience: Myth
and Evidence. London: Open Books
Cunningham, C.C. (1975) Parents as therapists and
educators. In C.C. Kiernan and F.P. Woodford
(eds.) Behaviour Modification with the Severely
Retarded. Study Group 8, IRMMH. Amsterdam:
Associated Scientific Publishers
Gunstone, C., Hogg, J., Sebba, J., Warner, J. and
Almond, S. (1982) Classroom Provision and Org-
anisation for Integrated Preschool Children.
Anson House Preschool Project Paper 2.
Barkingside: Barnardo's
Hogg, J. (ed.)(1979) Anson House Preschool Project:
The First Two Years. Barkingside: Barnardo's
O'Dell, S. (1974) Training parents in behavior
modification: a review. Psychological Bulle-
tin, 81, 418-433

DISCUSSION

Sally Beveridge drew out for discussion the two
major principles which underlie parent-professional
partnership in the Anson House Preschool Project:

- . that any service provision for young children
  is best conceived within an ecological framework;
- . that partnership between parents and professionals implies parental involvement as members
  in a multidisciplinary team.

The ecological approach to service provision leads
to the recognition that we need to take account of
all of a child's relationships and environments in
developing our services. First, and most important, we have to consider the most influential setting which is the home and family. This does not
mean simply that we should involve the child's parents and family in the intervention that we have
designed, but that as far as possible this involvement should be sensitive both to the priorities of
needs within the family, and also to the structure
of the child and the family's home life. Next, we
need to take account of other important influences
on the child and family, e.g. paediatric specialists, hospital social workers, health visitors and
preschool teachers. It is vital that effective
links are established with all professionals who are
involved with a family, so that the particular
expertise which can be offered by one professional
is neither duplicated by nor confounded by the input

of another, and that families do not feel over-whelmed by a multiplicity of information and advice.

Partnership of parents in a multidisciplinary team involves a conscious acceptance and valuing of what parents have to offer and of what they see as their role as parents. Similarly, it means that we need to make explicit the roles of all the other members of the team, by formulating the extent and boundaries of expertise as well as overlap between roles. This helps parents to ask pertinent questions and to learn who can offer which services, and how to use these services. The aim is that par-ents will have the ability, the information and most importantly the confidence to meet and work with a wide range of professionals in other settings.

From the detailed questions put to Sally Beveridge, and to Rita Flanagan the project social worker, it was clear that the Anson House Preschool Project aroused a great deal of interest from both parents and professionals participating in the seminar. Further description was given of the stages of careful introduction to the project before a family decides they want to participate. There-after, parents are welcome to attend Anson House as often as they wish (in addition to the agreed one session per week) and have the opportunity for con-tact with other parents in the communal sitting room; contacts with the other children in the class-room group; and consulting the social worker, who is always available in the building for individual advice, group discussion or an informal chat over coffee. Parents describe this informal contact with other parents and with the social worker as an in-valuable source of support.

Sally Beveridge also explained further the composition of the classroom group. The staff en-deavour to compose the group of 12 children in such a way that they represent a developmental continuum, but this rule is not applied dogmatically. If possible, any child referred when there is a vacancy will be taken. The non-handicapped children in the group may be siblings of the handicapped children, or may have been referred to the project by a social worker or health visitor. Often parents of non-handicapped children refer themselves, having heard about the project from other parents or contacts within the community, and wanting their children to benefit from mixing in an integrated group.

One further topic of discussion concerned record-keeping. At Anson House, parents have open access to the files of their own child. All reports are written primarily for the parents, who receive the first copy and are asked to correct this if necessary. If the staff receive confidential information from other professionals, they ask for permission to share it with the parents.

Further discussion arose from the observation, expressed particularly by the Dutch and Swedish participants, that parents in Britain seem to be much keener to be involved with professionals than those in other countries. It may be that different approaches work in different places, and that we then need to look at what doesn't suit individuals in each system. Peter Mittler emphasised the need for a range of choice of services. He pointed out the problem that the more professionals find working with parents successful and beneficial to the child, the more they are tempted to produce a model and to try and apply this in every case. Research has shown that generally collaboration between parents and professionals in educational programmes will enhance a child's development. However, collaboration must not be forced on parents: those who want to opt out of partnership with professionals are to be respected in this choice. Generalizations on what is best for families with handicapped children and what they need should be avoided, not only by workers in the field but also on the level of planning of statutory services. In future, we should work towards the individualization of our services and remain very conscious that the element of choice be preserved.

Chapter 7

FATHERS, MOTHERS, SIBLINGS: HOW DO THEY SEE
THEMSELVES?

Helen McConachie

As has been described in the previous chapter, the
model of parental involvement developed at the Anson
House Preschool Project is one of partnership and
aims for maximum flexibility. When the parents are
involved in teaching their own children at home, the
approach takes into account individual differences
in parents' interaction styles, and individual
children's particular learning difficulties and
abilities.

On reflection, and in conversation with parents, we become aware of a number of aspects of
bringing up a young child which had not necessarily
been taken account of in the parent teaching work at
Anson House. We lacked consistent information about
the home life of the children attending the project:
how activities fitted into the daily routine, how
much fathers and other children were involved in
child care, what aspects of their child's upbringing
parents saw as the most vital, and so on. Through
the social worker, we would have information about
any problems arising at home, and therefore for any
particular family we could ensure that pressures
were not increased by our expectations of involving
the parent in teaching. However, we wanted to look
beyond the level of 'problems', and to compare
families on more fundamental characteristics. It
seemed very likely that there were differences within and between families of potential relevance to
the degree of success of their involvement in teaching their children.

This chapter concentrates on families of young
children, and on the role of parents as teachers, a
role which parents of mentally handicapped children
are increasingly expected to adopt. However, there
are many varied and shifting interpretations of what
is meant by 'teaching', by 'learning' and by 'parent-

ing'. We may need to consider more throughly what
it is to be a parent of any child, and from that
gain a clearer perspective of how, where and when
teaching may be an appropriate part of a parent's
role.

Many professionals seem to find it easier to
have a model parent in mind - one who sees her or
his handicapped child as a special responsibility
and a special challenge, who gives a lot of individual attention to the child and who is eager and
organised to do special teaching or play sessions.
Yet many parents first and foremost see a little
girl or boy in front of them, a child who wants to
have fun and to play and to be mischievous. They
may expect their child to learn just by being in
different situations and therefore feel that they
are teaching by providing opportunities for the
child. They may feel uncomfortable with a
'didactic' model of parenting or primary concentration on the child as 'handicapped'.

The first section of the chapter will discuss
how parents of young mentally handicapped children
see themselves and their role in bringing up their
children. The following sections explore what is
known about some family members who have received
comparatively little attention - fathers, sisters
and brothers. The basic argument underlying the
discussion is that further progress in developing
services for young mentally handicapped children is
crucially dependent on understanding, and respect-
ing, the range of different ways in which families
think and live their lives. Approaches based merely
on educational technology will fail to meet a
child's or a family's needs, just as institutional
answers failed previously.

HOW PARENTS SEE THEIR ROLE

In talking to parents of young mentally handicapped
children, it is clear that they have a range of
different philosophies both about how to bring up
their children in general, and about how to bring up
their handicapped child. Some see their primary
role as creating a warm, stable environment for the
child; others stress helping the child to learn the
skills required for independence. Some find parent-
hood arduous, others find it enjoyable, and the
feelings may change with different periods of the
child's development. In some countries nowadays,
parents may have been surrounded by exhortation and
advice on playing with their child, from the moment

125

the handicap is known, through television programmes, popular literature, home visitors, etc.
Some have even been told the unfounded myth that
their child will stop learning at five years old,
and so they must teach everything they can quickly.
The pressure can be quite a burden; it can take the
fun out of playing with the child, and watching his
or her development.

Professional workers need to keep in mind that
parents have a lifelong commitment to their child.
Thus, they are building a relationship and an interaction which will need to change and grow with the
child, and to remain appropriate not only when the
child is very young, but also during the school
years, and eventually when he or she attempts to
establish adult independence.

Most parents want advice on practical handling
of their child, and find positive activitiy one of
the ways in which they come to terms with the
child's handicap. However, advice needs to be based
on a full knowledge of the parents' own ideas and
desires. There are many difficulties in gathering
such information in a way which does not distort it.
For example, it is unlikely to be a sufficient evaluation to ask parents for their views only at the
end of an intervention programme in which they have
been involved. The statements will be a reaction to
what has been offered, and will not tease out what
else parents might have wanted. If they have been
offered a chance to learn about educational goals
and techniques, they may feel diffident about expressing their own view of their child's needs. One
parent who had been involved in Anson House explained her reaction to involvement in teaching: "A
parent working with a child is not the same as a
teacher teaching. As a parent you are also wanting
to develop other things, for example, exercising
choice; therefore you are not as strict as a
teacher".

In research at Anson House, we have attempted
to explore how parents view bringing up their child,
in a way that will let them speak for themselves,
and yet will also allow for comparisons to be made
between parents, and over time. We will also
attempt to relate parents' views to observed differences in interaction style and to differences or
similarities between fathers and mothers.

Parents were asked to think about a number of
everyday situations which involve themselves and
their children, such as getting the child dressed,
going shopping together, looking at books, etc.

They were then asked to rate each situation on
questions such as how enjoyable the situation was
for them, how much attention the child required or
whether discipline was important to them. The overriding concerns of each parent can be pulled out
from the structure of the ratings. For example, one
parent saw the most important things for her as
being that she and her child should have fun together and communicate well. One situation in which
her child insisted on being independent was in playing with toys. It seems likely that conflicts might
arise if this parent were involved in a parent
teaching programme and was expected to have regular
structured sessions with her child (for example,
working on shapes or colours). The child might resist working with her; and she might not wish to
jeopardize their fun together by being more controlling than usual, even if she agreed with the
overall aims of the programme. Another parent
grouped together the ideas of teaching, treating the
child as 'handicapped' (rather than as normal), and
"I get harassed". She seemed enthusiastic about
participating in teaching her child, but in subsequent discussion of the ratings realised the
ambivalence in her feelings which might have less-
ened her involvement.

Eliciting parents' ideas about everyday situations can help to identify potential conflicts at
the time of offering a teaching course. The process will also begin to establish shared meanings
of concepts and will lessen miscommunication
between parents and professionals. However, there
will be many layers of ideas and concerns not
tapped by a concentration on everyday situations.
For example, parents look ahead, and worry about
how to prepare their children and themselves for
the time of entry to school. They may be aware
constantly of the conflict between their child's
special needs, and how to 'normalise' their own and
their child's lives. Professional staff may seem
to assume that the central business of life is
bringing up children, and to be interested in parents only as members of a special group, 'parents
of handicapped children'. Voysey (1975) has
suggested there is an implicit official morality of
child-rearing and of family life which affects how
parents and professionals communicate, and how
parents see themselves (eg. "coping splendidly",
"self-sacrificing", "just as normal", "changing
society's attitudes", etc.). Such complexities may
affect crucially the long-term effectiveness of

programmes offered by professionals, if time to
listen and responses to differing family needs are
not built in to the structure of the programme from
the beginning.

FATHERS

Very little has been written specifically about
fathers of handicapped children in comparison with
the voluminous literature on mothers, or about
families, often derived solely from mothers' reports
(McConachie, 1982). Likewise, there has been relatively little research interest in the father's role
in child care, except in relation to the topic of
father-absence. And yet it has long been established that young children may form strong bonds
with several people. Schaffer and Emerson (1964)
showed that relationships with fathers, grandparents
and siblings begin early in life; in about a third
of the infants studied, the primary attachment was
observed and reported to be to the father rather
than to the mother. As roles in child-care have
changed (in Western society), it has become more expected that fathers will be involved in child care.
The extent to which this actually happens remains
unclear; or rather, studies show that mothers are
still responsible for the majority of child care.
Researchers have often used inadequate definitions
of 'father participation'. For example, Newson and
Newson (1968) concluded that 51 per cent of fathers
of four year old children in Nottingham had a 'high
level of participation' in child care. But the only
questions asked were general ones, such as "How much
does your husband have to do with ...?" Fathers
themselves were not interviewed. The answers will
tend to reflect feelings and values rather than
quantitative data. Oakley (1974) gave a more precise definition (though still relative to the rest
of her sample of fathers) and rated only 25 per cent
'highly participant'. The same contrasts in researchers' definitions are apparent in studies of
the families of handicapped children: Hewett (1970)
and Carr (1975) stressed fathers' participation, and
Wilkin (1979) the lack of it.
     In some ways, we might expect the pressures on
fathers of handicapped children to tend to decrease
their involvement. For example, they may feel left
out of the processes of getting and giving information, through being at work during the child's
probably numerous clinic appointments, or visits by
educational home visitors. They have less chance to

talk about their feelings and may not easily meet
other parents in the same position. They may feel
incompetent with this child who is 'different' and
so tend to give up. They may feel bitterly disappointed that their ambitions for their child will
not be realised.

It certainly would seem desirable to promote
consistency in handling the handicapped child, and
to help both parents to feel more confident. Yet it
would be irresponsible for professionals to issue a
blanket exhortation for fathers to be more involved
with their handicapped child. It is likely that the
primary effect would be to *increase* the burden on
mothers, through feeling that it is their failure if
the father is not involved. We need more background
information on what fathers of handicapped children
do at present, so that we can plan any involvement
on a sound basis.

I have made a study of children's home routines
and of which parent is involved in giving them
attention. Nineteen families were involved in the
research, each of which included a child who had
been identified as developmentally delayed or mentally handicapped, but not multiply handicapped. The
children ranged in age between twenty and forty-
five months. Parents were interviewed together, and
recounted in great detail everything the child had
done, and with whom the child had been, for two days
including one day when one or both parents had been
at work, and one day when they hadn't. Therefore,
for many families, the interview took place on a
Monday evening. Care was taken to avoid days which
had been particularly unusual (e.g. birthdays, illness). Four levels of interaction were defined:
'concentrated', 'continuous', 'available' and
'separate', (cf. Douglas, Lawson, Cooper and Cooper,
1968) and rated for the parents. (Other family
members' interaction levels with the child were not
established fully.)

In terms of the amount of time each parent was
available to the child, fathers' working hours outside the home meant that their weekday time was much
less than mothers', except for one unemployed
father. However, it was on average over a quarter
of the child's day (median 28 per cent, range 1 hr.
30 mins. to 10 hrs. 25 mins. for employed fathers).
Thus, fathers were perhaps potentially more available to the children than one commonly thinks is the
case.

In research on parent-child interaction it is
often noted that the *amount* of time a parent is

available may be quite unrelated to the *quality* of
how the time is spent with the child. This observation was confirmed in the present study, in that
the overall amount of time a parent was available to
the child did not predict how much time he or she
spent in 'concentrated' interaction. This level was
rated when parent and child were sharing the activity and giving it their full attention, often with
physical contact involved (e.g. reading books,
dressing). The definition includes the minimum conditions for the kind of structured teaching a parent
might undertake in a programme, though this is not
meant to imply that teaching in any formal sense was
taking place in time so rated. It was observed that
some parents who had relatively little time with the
child spent a large proportion of it in concentrated
interaction, and vice versa. Mothers still overall
had more concentrated interaction than fathers, even
when fathers' lesser time available is taken into
account. On the whole, fathers gave concentrated
attention to the child during play activities and
mothers gave concentrated attention during caretaking activities.

It was striking how widely fathers differed in
the extent of their interaction and involvement with
their children. One reason for this was suggested
by the finding that those fathers who were most involved tended to be the ones whose children could
use words, rather than still being at the stage of
using sounds or gestures. This observation suggests
that fathers may become discouraged, for example,
through not understanding the child's attempts at
communication, rather than not really being interested in playing with the child. Therefore, guidance at the right time might help some fathers to
become more involved with their children early on.

There were clearly differing patterns of co-
operation between parents. As a definition of
'participation in child care', the amount of both
'concentrated' and 'continuous' interaction time was
looked at, therefore including all time when the
parent was at least partly responsible for the
child, and communicating frequently (e.g. mealtimes,
shopping). Of the nineteen families, one father was
the child's primary caretaker, and two more seemed
to take over from the mother at the weekend. Five
couples shared time and responsibility for the child
at the weekend. In eleven families the mother was
always the primary caretaker. Therefore, in some
families it seems an obvious step to involve fathers
as well as mothers in planned programmes. In other

130

families, we may need to proceed more carefully. The present routine will have its own momentum, which we might threaten by suggesting unrealistic changes. Yet we should keep in mind the potential benefits to both father and mother of fuller information and a more equal sharing of the care of their child.

Once again, flexibility in service provision will be a key factor. Change might begin with case conferences being held in the evenings or in families' homes. Fathers may need professionals to make a special point of their participation being important. For example, they may have perceived their role as beginning when the child is older, and being concerned primarily with discipline and activities outside the home. Yet, with encouragement, they may be able to take time off work to attend particular meetings and workshops. There are cultural differences in how fathers will be involved with professionals. Already, in the case of Asian families, it is often fathers rather than mothers who have detailed contact with services (Beveridge, Flanagan, McConachie and Sebba, 1982). To develop ways in which services can be organised, on a basis of partnership, and sensitive to the needs of all the members of the family, will require imagination and commitment.

BROTHERS AND SISTERS

As well as parents, siblings can often be very significant figures in a young child's life. Studies of the families of mentally handicapped people have tended either to omit or to make only passing reference to the siblings. In the past, parents may have been advised to institutionalize a mentally handicapped child "for the sake of the normal children". However, those studies which are available have drawn a variety of conclusions as to the effects upon brothers and sisters of living with a handicapped child. Some studies have suggested that many siblings feel jealous, embarrassed or aggressive toward the handicapped child (e.g. Kew, 1975) and that older siblings, especially girls, have to undertake a heavy burden of housework (e.g. Gath, 1974). However, the way in which many studies have been conducted have left them difficult to interpret. For example, few studies have actually asked siblings themselves; and few have included a comparison group of siblings whose brother or sister is not handicapped.

131

When siblings are asked directly, the reported
incidence and severity of problems seems low.
Relationships with parents, and with the handicapped
child, are mostly satisfactory and warm. Grossman
(1972) interviewed college-age siblings, and found
"a surprising number of brothers and sisters of retarded children who appeared to us to have benefited
in some way from the experience of growing up with a
handicapped sibling". We asked siblings (aged eight
to fifteen years) who were living at home with a
younger brother or sister about their everyday activities and attitudes, and found only one aspect
which siblings of mentally handicapped children reported significantly more than did a matched group
of siblings of non-handicapped children. That was
the extent to which the younger child was a disrupt-
ion, not leaving them alone when they were busy, and
tending to wake them up at night. Siblings reported
often playing with and helping the younger child and
several mentioned buying little presents for him or
her. The teenage siblings were rather more negative
in their attitudes (whether the child was handicapped or not) and seemed to be reacting as any
teenager might to a bothersome younger sister or
brother (McConachie and Domb, 1982). It might be
suggested that siblings will react more strongly
when the handicapped child is older and 'childish'
behaviour is less acceptable. However, Gath (1973)
did not find any difference in psychological disturbance between those siblings who were born before
the handicapped (Down's syndrome) child and those
siblings who were born after.
    The researchers who have reported a general
level of negative reactions in siblings seem to have
started with the assumption that there will be harmful effects and so find what they are looking for.
Parents, too, may find it difficult to interpret
unhappiness or disobedience in a sibling, and may
wrongly ascribe its cause to the presence of the
handicapped child. They may forget how ordinary it
is for siblings to squabble.
    In effect, parents often try very hard to make
sure that the siblings do not 'lose out' because of
the handicapped child. Fuchs (1974) interviewed
mothers, and found that many organised the family
routine carefully to reduce any potential adverse
impact on siblings. For example, they would ensure
the handicapped child did not interfere with home
work. She found six (out of twenty-five) families
which did not have deliberate organisation and in
five of these tension was noted between the sib-

lings and the handicapped child. Thus it is important not just to look at siblings in isolation but to study the family system and routines in order to elucidate how they are currently balanced to favour all the children in the family.

Background information of this type would seem essential in considering whether or not siblings could be drawn into programmes to help the young child. There are few reports of sibling groups in the literature. Weinrott (1974) described a summer training camp for teenage siblings, where they followed a behaviour modification course, and then applied their new knowledge at home with the mentally handicapped member of the family. The aim of the programme was not that siblings should spend more time concentrating on the handicapped child but that the time that they already did spend should be as helpful as possible. Therefore, the siblings learned strategies for minimizing disruptive incidents and ways to help their brothers or sisters to become more independent. Hart and Walters (1981) have described a British workshop for siblings which also included information on behaviour management and teaching skills. Other sibling groups meet in Liverpool and in Swansea, and a newsletter for siblings ('*Sibs*') started in 1980.

However, given the research findings outlined above, it would seem that any aim to provide services, such as therapeutic discussion groups, for all siblings would be misplaced. It is undoubtedly true that some siblings find living with a handicapped child hard (as, for example, Fairbrother (1980) described in welcoming *Sibs* newsletter). We need to look in greater depth at what difficulties these siblings have faced, and what help they might welcome. Those who do want to take part in activities connected with their mentally handicapped sister or brother possibly will gain most from goal-directed activities, such as teaching new skills, acting as advocates for their brother or sister or participating in their own siblings' organisations.

CONCLUSIONS

In this chapter a number of themes have been outlined of relevance to families' involvement in programmes for young mentally handicapped children. The child's activities and routines at home require consideration in order to ensure generalization and maintenance of new learning. It is suggested that programmes which respect the current organization at

133

home will be more successfully taken up than those which unwittingly demand changes in routine or ignore current family structures of child-care. Likewise, parents have views on bringing up children which are not happened on by chance, but have been worked out through considerable experience. Professional workers need to keep in mind that they can potentially do harm as well as good in intervening with a family.

All this is not to say that we just need to leave things to families' good sense. A handicapped child does have special needs and parents usually do ask for practical guidance. But there is a need for flexibility in responding to an individual family's current viewpoint and practices if parental involvement is to be a real partnership.

There are many difficulties to be overcome in making partnership a reality. Professional workers do not necessarily adjust well to being 'equal partners'. It is often still the case that parents are told what the child's programme should be, without involvement in decision making, even if they are to be the main agents of carrying out the programme. Once a programme has been entered into by parents, they may feel they have no alternative but to drop out, if it fails to take account of their present situation. For example, a service geared to practical teaching might not offer the time and sensitivity to talk through complex emotions or overriding practical difficulties at home. No one type of service, be it a home advisory service, a toy library, a parent workshop or an integrated nursery, is able to meet the needs of all families. The important thing is not the invention of new structures of services but rather flexibility in responding to each individual family over time. And that requires professionals to really listen to parents and siblings. Partnership remains the goal to guide our efforts.

REFERENCES

Beveridge, S., Flanagan, R., McConachie, H. and Sebba, J. (1982) Parental Involvement in Anson House. Anson House Preschool Project Paper 3. Barkingside: Barnardo's

Carr, J. (1975) Young Children with Down's Syndrome. London: Butterworth

Douglas, J.W.B., Lawson, A., Cooper, J.E. & Cooper, E. (1968) Family interaction and the activities of young children. Journal of Child

Psychology and Psychiatry, 9, 157-171
Fairbrother, P. (1980) Siblings. Parents' Voice, 30, 22
Fuchs, J. (1974) The impact of mentally handicapped children on family routine, with particular reference to siblings. Unpublished Masters Thesis, University of London
Gath, A. (1973) The school age siblings of mongol children. British Journal of Psychiatry, 123, 161-167
Gath, A. (1974) Sibling reactions to mental handicap: a comparison of the brothers and sisters of mongol children, Journal of Child Psychology and Psychiatry, 15, 187-198
Grossman, F.K. (1972) Brothers and Sisters of Retarded Children: an Exploratory Study. New York: Syracuse University Press
Hart, D. and Walters, J. (1981) A group work project with siblings of mentally handicapped children. Association for Child Psychology and Psychiatry News, no. 8, 6-9
Hewett, S. (1970) The Family and the Handicapped Child. London: Allen and Unwin
Kew, S. (1975) Handicap and Family Crisis. London: Pitman Press
McConachie, H. (1982) Fathers of mentally handicapped children. In N. Beail and J. McGuire (eds.) Fathers: Psychological Perspectives. London: Junction Books
McConachie, H. and Domb, H. (1982) An interview study of the siblings of mentally handicapped children. Unpublished manuscript, Hester Adrian Research Centre, Manchester
Newson, J. & Newson, E. (1968) Four Years Old in an Urban Community. London: Allen and Unwin
Oakley, A. (1974) The Sociology of Housework. London: Robertson
Schaffer, H.R. & Emerson, P.E. (1964) The development of social attachments in infancy. Monographs of the Society for Research in Child Development, 29 (3, Serial no. 94)
Voysey, M. (1975) A Constant Burden: The Reconstitution of Family Life. London: Routledge and Kegan Paul
Weinrott, M. (1974) A training program in behavior modification for siblings of the retarded. American Journal of Orthopsychiatry, 44, 362-375
Wilkin, D. (1979) Caring for the Mentally Handicapped Child. London: Croom Helm

DISCUSSION

In introducing her paper, Helen McConachie raised
the question of the purposes of conducting research
into the relationship between parents and professionals. Two considerations had informed the theme
of her paper. Firstly, she stressed that we need to
be careful of what we mean by the word 'family'.
Very often the word has been used loosely and has
meant, both for services and research, simply
'mother'. In order to take account of how a child
experiences the world, we need to focus on what
actually happens at home, rather than what we suppose to happen or what happens in a clinic or school.
        Secondly, she emphasised that adequate evalu-
ation of early intervention must include more sensitive criteria than numbers of children seen, or
numbers of skills gained on a checklist. We must
take account of long term outcomes and of less
easily quantifiable factors such as parents' confidence, and the level of stress in family life.
        Because of these two considerations, her paper
had included more in the way of description of
research methods and an outline of some research
results than did most of the other papers. She
wanted to demonstrate that it may be possible to
quantify aspects of family life and parents' perceptions of bringing up children, in ways which do
not unduly constrain and distort what actually
happens. Collection of this type of objective and
complex information should precede the design of
a structure for collaboration between parents and
professionals.
        Mariet van Hattum from the Netherlands had pre-
pared a detailed consideration of the themes of the
paper. She agreed with the observation that not all
parents will want to work with their child as a
'teacher'. The relationship between parent and
child differs fundamentally from the relationship
between a teacher and child: for one thing, it is
lifelong. Children occupy a central place in a
teacher's work, and the teacher has chosen to do
this job. However, should we take for granted that
the child will have a central place in the parents'
life? And parents have not chosen to have a handicapped child. Notwithstanding the respect paid to
parents' life-styles and wishes in the paper, it
gave the impression of professionals' standards pre-
dominating.
        Similarly, in considering siblings, profession-
als will often seem to focus on the handicapped

child as the centre of the family. A brief interview will not be able to bring out the character of
the complex ways in which siblings may feel. Where
siblings suffer, it may be that they suffer especially because of their parents' sadness and over-
burdening, and not directly because of the handicapped child. Also, the ambivalence which all parents feel about their children may be divided in a
family with a handicapped child. The handicapped
child may cause much stress, and the other children
be seen as easy, or feel they should not cause any
trouble. On the other hand, a handicapped child's
passivity may be seen as easy, and the normally
vital child seen as a nuisance.

We can regard it as very positive when siblings
want to be involved in caring for their handicapped
brother or sister. But it also has a dangerous side
to it. The siblings have experiences and opportunities open to them which the handicapped child does
not have, and they may feel 'survivors' guilt'
because of this. Often siblings enter careers connected with caring for handicapped people. But does
this choice really suit their personality, or do
they single out this occupation in order not to feel
a burden of guilt?

In general discussion, the consensus seemed to
be that siblings may be prevented from having problems if other parents and professionals succeed in
making their parents aware that the normally developing children are just as important as the mentally handicapped child and that they should be careful not to give them a feeling of being left out.

Cliff Cunningham raised the question of whether
we can perhaps create problems by looking for them.
How much should we prepare people for possible problems? The dilemma for professionals may be whether
to offer help, information and counselling, or to
wait until parents ask for it. The discussion again
highlighted the notion that the needs of families
with a mentally handicapped member change over time.
From the very beginning families should have access
to help, either statutory or voluntary, in a flexible system which enables them to utilize these resources if and whenever they choose to do so.

SECTION FOUR: THE SCHOOL YEARS

Chapter 8

COLLABORATION BETWEEN PARENTS AND TEACHERS OF
SCHOOL-AGE CHILDREN

Barbara Smith

> ....the successful education of children
> with special educational needs is dependent
> upon the full involvement of their parents
>
> Warnock (1978)

The insistence that parental involvement is a vital
component in the educative process if handicapped
children are to develop to their fullest potential
is at the heart of the Report "Special Educational
Needs" prepared by the Warnock Committee on educational provision for all handicapped children. Such
involvement is referred to as a partnership between
parents and professionals. It is this concept of
partnership to which I am utterly committed in my
dual role, both as mother of a severely mentally
handicapped adolescent son and as a teacher of mentally handicapped pupils at an ESNS school.
    Just over ten years ago it would have been sur-
prising if parents of mentally handicapped children
in this country realised that there was a contribution they could make to furthering their children's educational development, for our society did-
not consider them to be educable. Prior to the Education (Handicapped Children) Act 1970, those children ascertained as mentally handicapped were segregated from the educational system. As a parent, I
received a formal letter from my local education
committee before my son's fifth birthday telling me
that he was "suffering from such a disability of
mind as to make him unsuitable from education at
school" and that the decision would be recorded,
after which it wouldn't be possible for him to be
admitted to any school in the authority or be sent
to any other school. However, April 1971 saw the
transfer of responsibility for mentally handicapped

children to the Education Service, with some 24,000
children in Junior Training Centres, 8,000 children
then in hospitals and an uncertain number at home or
in private institutions at last entitled to receive
special education.

It was at this time that Cunningham and Jeffree
undertook their first two pioneer workshops with
highly motivated, self-selected groups of parents of
young children, and showed that active involvement
of parents in the education of their mentally handicapped children was both feasible and fruitful
(Cunningham and Jeffree, 1971, 1975). These workshops must be of historical significance in the
development of parental involvement and have been
followed by many others in different parts of the
country.

What follows aims to be a fairly comprehensive
yet brief overview of current practice in collaboration between parents and teachers of school-age
children, from which models for future development
may be drawn.

AN A - Z OF PARENT/TEACHER COLLABORATION

A   ASSESSMENT

Differing types of assessment take place throughout
the school-life of a mentally handicapped child.
These may occur formally or informally.

1.   Assessment along with discovery and
diagnosis are contributing stages of the three-fold
process whereby a child is 'ascertained' as being in
need of special educational treatment and upon which
subsequent school placement is based. Up to now,
the necessary paperwork procedure (S.E. forms) has
not allowed for the parents to give any written
statement about their child's needs, although an
Educational Psychologist or previous Head Teacher
may incorporate this. As a result of the 1981
Education Act new procedures are being introduced
which will give parents a somewhat greater share in
assessment.

2.   On-going educational assessment should be
the basis for curriculum planning in school and,
some would argue, for the total management of the
child. This may be undertaken by the school without
reference to the parents or may be a joint undertaking.

I myself have had experience as a teacher of
older pupils in working with their parents in the
joint completion of the *Pathways to Independence*

Checklists compiled by Jeffree and Cheseldine (1982).
The parents and I have then jointly agreed suitable
curriculum objectives based on emergent strengths
and weaknesses which we have considered to have
particular relevance.

3.   Assessments by visiting specialists or
professional workers may concern the general condition of the child, specific sensory defects or
behavioural problems. Some schools invite parents
into the school for every such assessment, whether
routine or otherwise, believing it to be the right
of parents to have the opportunity to attend, whereas other schools may only invite parents in for selected assessments.

4.   Assessment relating to the post-school
placement of all young people will occur towards the
end of their special schooldays and will usually involve the pupil and parent and a number of other interested professional workers (eg. careers officer,
educational psychologist, doctor, social worker and
teacher), as aspirations and abilities are considered in relation to possible placement. In my
experience, this assessment is a real point of interest amongst parents; their involvement is vital
in promoting successful transition from school to
post-school life.

B   BOOKLET

Increasing numbers of special schools are producing
a booklet about the school. In many cases this is
specifically produced for parents and prospective
parents. It may include illustrations and will give
basic information which may be of a very practical
nature but may also include details relating to the
aims and organisation of the school and curriculum
content.

C   CASE CONFERENCES

These are normally formal meetings called for a
specific reason to enable a number of people working
with a child or young person to share assessments
and experiences and to make treatment and placement
recommendations. Parents may or may not be invited
to the case conferences depending on the reason for
which they are called.

In my experience it is customary for inclusion
of parents to be the norm - except when there has
been a very specific reason for exclusion.

D   DIARIES

Diaries or home-school notebooks exist in a great many schools for the purpose of written communication between home and school. In some schools they travel to and from home daily, either in the charge of the pupils (who may be trained to accept that responsibility) or in the care of a transport escort who accompanies the children. In other schools the book may be sent on a more intermittent basis.

In my experience diaries seem to be used in three ways: for general items of information (eg. "Hello, my name's Barbara Smith and I'm the new teacher.."); for more specific instruction (eg."... his calipers seem to be rubbing his leg, will you look at them in school today and see what you think?"); and for active collaboration on a joint teaching venture (eg. in a programme on undressing skills, a parental comment one morning was, "Only help last night was shoe-lace, which she pulled into knot, and unfastening her bra - the other's not like that, she can do it herself. I'll get her another like that one then she'll be able to manage it on her own all the time.").

E   EQUIPMENT

Equipment in the form of books, toys and specific teaching material may be sent home on a daily or longer term basis. This may be selected by pupil, parent or teacher and may be for a very general reason (eg. pupil may choose a favourite toy or book) or for a very specific reason (eg. "4 sets of that word lotto game, so that the whole family can play together with him after tea.").

I have found it necessary to make very careful selection of equipment to ensure that vital classroom materials are available when needed in school. As pupils have proved their reliability to return things daily and without damage, so they have progressed to the more 'vital' things. I have found that the use of a clearly marked bag travelling daily between home and school has enabled this borrowing facility to be extended to younger or more severely handicapped children.

F   FORMAL RECORDING SYSTEM

Most schools have some formal system for recording documentation about pupils. Frequently the infor-

144

mation involved falls into one of two categories, either that which results from professional consultation and may be of a sensitive nature and passed in confidence, and that which is of a more factual nature, relating to the child, and family, progress and attendance. In my experience the former information has been on restricted access, whereas the second type of recording has usually been readily available for parents and all professionals working with the child.

There would appear to be some quite distinctive methods of recording this second type of information. Some schools use a tick chart system, some a termly or yearly record book in which they note progress. Other establishments, however, use a more comprehensive record showing details of assessments, current objectives and evaluation. My own records have tended to be of the latter kind and I have made use of them with parents in discussion about their child's work and progress.

It is my personal belief that all documentation about pupils should be available to their parents and that this would aid contributors, from whatever discipline, in their pursuit of objectivity with such reports.

G   GOVERNORS

The inclusion of parents on to the Governing Bodies of schools is relatively new in some areas and is by no means accepted universally as yet. Some consider that parent governors represent a formal means of collective co-operation between parents and school.

H   HOMEWORK

Homework activities can provide a useful means of joint involvement and may occur for a number of different reasons.
1.   They may relate to a joint teaching programme (eg. in an agreed pre-writing programme, a pupil is closely supervised by a parent at home going over lightly pencilled motor patterns with a felt tip marker).
2.   They may relate to the request of a parent or suggestion from the teacher to give the child a useful activity at home - eg. a pupil living in high-rise flats in an inner city area, and who goes out from home very rarely, was given a holiday workbook compiled by the teacher for her to

145

use over the holidays. Not only was all the work completed but the family had found the activity so useful that further work was prepared by a brother.

   3.   Finally, it may be that pupils want to take home a homework book or activity because they are aware that there are others doing such a thing and want to be like them.

I   INFORMATION

Basic information will include notification of school openings and closures for the year, general letters from the Head Teacher relating to special events or changes at the school. This kind of information may not be individually addressed but may be give to transport escorts to give to each parent. However, such a system might run into difficulties unless very tightly organised by the school to ensure a system of cover for children who are absent or who are not met by a parent from the transport. A second form of information is that which is personally addressed and may include a child's annual report or personal letter to a Parent-Teacher Association Committee member. It seems that this type of information is not 'at risk' in the same way.

J   JOINT INVOLVEMENT

The joint involvement of parents and professionals will vary considerably in the level of intensity.

   1.   At a general level there will be those parents who have some knowledge of their child's progress and what is going on rather generally in school and are keen to co-operate in a simple venture. For example, when it was known that we were involved in watching the series of "Let's Go" TV programmes for mentally handicapped young people and adults, one father watched the repeat programmes at home with his child and the series gave rise to some useful communication.

   2.   At a more intense level will be the joint involvement where parent and teacher have agreed together a suitable target, have developed some breakdown into steps of the target behaviour, work with the child towards it, and exchange information regarding progress. For example, such a programme arose in the case of an eleven year old pupil of mine who was having great problems in fastening his rather small coat! After collaboration between his mum and myself, the proposed new coat was bought

146

with a specially selected large zip. A joint
teaching programme was evolved, using a backward-
training procedure, and the pupil managed to un-
fasten the zip within twenty-four hours and to
fasten it in just under a week.

3.   There will be those parents who do not
wish to engage in any form of joint involvement
with the school. I believe that this is a right
which parents have and which should be recognised
by professionals.

K   KITCHEN FACILITIES

The availability of some form of kitchen facilities
(ie. independent provision for making a drink and
washing up) along with a parents' room to act as an
informal meeting place or 'parents' den' is a relatively new innovation. However, some schools are
providing such a facility if space permits.

It is my belief that for parents to have their
own base in school is of the utmost importance, as
long as they know that they do still have easy
access to the classrooms and teachers.

L   LEND-A-HAND

The 'lend-a-hand' involvement of parents has been
continuing in many schools for a long time. In
this venture parents may volunteer their services
or expertise in order to help the school.

In my own experience, I have found it most
valuable to have regular parent volunteers to help
with weekly riding sessions, to have a fathers'
working party make or repair items of equipment,
and to have parents with specific expertise who
have shared this by working in with the pupils.

M   MEETINGS

Meetings in schools have occurred for many years.
They often fall into one of two categories: those
which are for all parents (eg. an informative
evening when the welfare rights officer comes and
is willing to answer questions) and those which are
'class' meetings where parents whose children are
all in the same class are invited into school together to meet with one another and the class
teacher in an informal way or for a specific
purpose (eg. to hear about short term care facilities from the Senior Social Worker responsible).

147

N   NEEDS OF PARENTS

That collaborative ventures should arise from an
awareness of the needs of parents is a fundamental
principle. Warnock (1978) sees these as being
three-fold, the need for information, advice and
practical help. That of *information* relates to diagnosis, prognosis and the availability of services;
that of *advice* is considered by many to be the two-
way process in conjunction with the professional
which encourages the parent to play a fuller role
in the child's education; that of *practical help*
relates to the acquisition of allowances, aids and
relief (through use of formalised or informal care
facilities).

O   OPENING EVENING OR DAYS

The Open Evening or Open Day would seem to be quite
a tradition in many special schools. In some cases,
it provides little more than the opportunity for
parents to walk round the school, note the attractive displays and have a chat with staff. However,
there are those where it is held shortly after reports have been sent out to parents, and it is held
specifically to afford parents the formal opportunity of coming into school to discuss their
children's work and progress with the class teacher
and visiting specialists.

P   PARENT-TEACHER ASSOCIATION

Attitudes toward Parent-Teacher Associations tend
to be polarised. Some decry them completely whilst
others consider them to be a vital part of school
life. The objectives of such associations may vary,
although most seem to draw their activities from
fund-raising, social or informative events. In my
own experience, I feel that much valuable contact
has been encouraged through parents and professionals working together in the organisation and
running of family social events where teachers are
clearly not perceived as the experts.

Q   QUESTIONNAIRES

There are some schools where due consideration is
given to the views of parents in relation to the
school curriculum and joint involvement. The information is gathered by means of the school sending out a questionnaire to the parents who are then

asked to complete it.

Recently I have had experience of such involvement. Seventy five per cent of parents completed the questionnaire. When asked about their aims for their children, Self Help Skills were thought to be very important, closely followed by Language and Communication (both with ratings of over 80 per cent). Independence came next, closely followed by Appropriate Behaviours (both with ratings of over 60 per cent). In relation to advice, 75 per cent of parents who completed the questionnaires wanted advice and 44 per cent wanted specific advice. Of those who wanted advice, 44 per cent said they would like it given at home, 12 per cent said definitely not at home, 30 per cent said they would like it at school, 14 per cent said definitely not at school; however, the most requested method for advice was the Diary or Home-School Notebook with 56 per cent asking for this and only 10 per cent not wanting it. Of those who wanted advice in school, twice as many as those who said they would like to be involved in a workshop approach said they would like to receive individual advice.

Such findings were valuable for a number of reasons: firstly, it was rewarding to the school staff to have such a high proportion of questionnaires returned, and secondly, the responses helped the school in determining its future parental involvement policy and in staff discussions relating to curriculum priority areas.

R   REPORTS

It would seem that most schools record the progress of their children at least on a yearly basis. An increasing number of schools now send out annual reports to parents. In some cases this is then followed by an opportunity for dialogue. I believe it is the right of every parent to receive an annual report and consider that any schools not providing parents with one are failing in their responsibility.

S   SENIOR PUPILS' PARENTS' GROUP

Some schools have been aware of the problems faced by senior pupils in their transition from school to post-school life, but there has been an increasing awareness of the parents' role in this transition and of their preparation for it.

A social worker and I have been jointly responsible for the formation and running of a Senior Pupils' Parents' Group where post-school opportunities have been investigated by means of talks (some illustrated), discussions and visits. Experts were invited to give information, and subsequently the relevance and application to individual needs were considered and developed more informally.

T   TELEPHONE CONTACT

Telephone contact, where parents have a 'phone, may be used either to supplement or take the place of home-school diaries.
I have found this approach to be most valuable where parents are not fully literate, but have also used it to give support and encouragement relating to joint programme implementation. There have been rare occasions when I have felt my right to privacy has been impinged upon once a parent knows my 'phone number. However, as a parent, I have greatly valued being able to relieve my own son's frustration at his inability to communicate something 'vital' about his day at school by a short 'phone call to his teacher.

U   USEFUL LITERATURE

Leaflets and booklets relating to local provision of services and welfare rights for the handicapped are made available to parents in some schools. The parents' den, if provided, is an obvious place for these to be displayed, along with any books that are specifically written for parents.

V   VISITS

Parents' visits into school have been encountered for many years but of more recent origin is the visiting of teachers to see parents of their pupils in their own home, either in the daytime or evening. The visit of parents into school may be at a pre-arranged time for a specific purpose, but many feel it important for parents to have informal access to the school at any time. Such access may pose problems for both parents and teachers alike. The teachers may not be able to make themselves available at short notice, and the parents might have to be left waiting about, unless there is a parents' den where they can feel at home.

W   WORKSHOPS

A number of schools have used developments of the
workshop model pioneered by Cunningham and Jeffree
(1975) as a means of joint collaboration, with
parents being helped to assess their children's
abilities, select learning objectives, break these
down into steps, work with their children and evaluate progress. In some cases other professionals
(eg. psychologists and speech therapists) have co-
llaborated with school staff in such ventures.
    In working with parents of older children, I
have adapted the workshop model and tend to use the
principles on a much more individualistic and informal basis although I believe that the topic 'Use
of Leisure' could well prove to be of interest to
enough parents of older pupils to make a more traditional workshop viable.
    I have known one teacher of profoundly handi-
capped children helping his parents increase their
effectiveness by putting volunteers through a
shortened course in behaviour modification based on
a course he had himself undertaken.

X   XMAS ACTIVITIES

Xmas activities (eg. Nativity play, pantomime or
concert), Harvest Services, Sports Days and other
social events are held in many schools and seem to
be important to a wide range of parents who appear
to enjoy the participation of their children in
these more 'normal' school events.

Y   YOUTH ACTIVITIES

Some schools run regular Youth Clubs for their
pupils and may involve parents in helping with this
activity. Others may run a Duke of Edinburgh Award
Scheme where collaboration with parents is an important factor. Another vital "youth activity" has
been the occasional 'minding service' arranged in
school for pupils whose parents are then able to
attend some school function.

Z   ZEAL

Success or failure of collaboration may well be related to the extent of the ZEAL (hearty and per-
sistent endeavours) of professionals for parental
involvement!

REFERENCES

Cunningham, Ç.C. and Jeffree, D.M. (1971) <u>Working with Parents: Developing a Workshop Course for Parents of Young Mentally Handicapped Children</u>. Manchester: National Society for Mentally Handicapped Children (N.W. Region)

Cunningham, C.C. and Jeffree, D.M. (1975) The organisation and structure of workshops for parents of mentally handicapped children. <u>Bulletin of the British Psychological Society</u>, <u>28</u>, 405-411

Jeffree, D.M. and Cheseldine, S. (1982) <u>Pathways to Independence</u>. Sevenoaks, Kent: Hodder and Stoughton

Warnock, H.M. (1978) <u>Special Educational Needs. Report of the Committee of Enquiry into the Education of Handicapped Children and Young People</u>. Cmnd. 7212. London: HMSO

Chapter 9

"HANDICAPPED CHILD - TAXI"

Shirley Rheubottom

A taxi or bus service to school is one of the more
mundane and simple measures of support for parents
of handicapped children given by local authorities,
but has broader implications for families and consequences far beyond giving relief and help with
transport. What is very important for parents is
how the taxi service affects the kind of involvement
in the school and in their child's education that
would be expected, routine and unquestioned, from a
parent of an ordinary young child. The threat of
losing this involvement has highlighted its importance for some parents and brought into focus the
reasons they wish to collect and fetch their child
from school. These reasons will be explored below
and consideration will be given to ways in which a
transport service can be modified or made more
flexible to take them into account, as well as ways
in which other forms of parent involvement could
compensate.

THE RESEARCH INTERVIEWS

This chapter arises from a series of ethnographic
interviews with parents of children who have at one
time attended the Anson House Preschool Project and
have now entered state schools full time. By way
of introduction, I shall discuss a few selective
aspects of ethnographic interviewing, a methodolog-
ical tool widely used in sociological and social
anthropological research. It should be noted that
ethnographic interviewing has many things in common
with other forms of interviewing, i.e. those known
as in-depth, thematic, conversational, psycho-
analytic, counselling and non-directive interviews,
to give a few examples. However, I shall point out
some of the distinctive features of the ethnographic

interview. More detailed accounts can be found in Paul (1953) and Spradley (1979).

First and foremost the ethnographic interview is a strategy for getting people to talk about what they know. It is an attempt to understand how other people see their experience and to obtain a description of it from their point of view. Ethnography means learning from people and that to learn from people, one must be taught by them; consequently, the researcher must become the student. It is assumed that the researcher has a naive ignorance about what the informant (parent) knows and has experienced. The researcher asks very brief orienting questions, which may be asked over and over in slightly different contexts with frequent requests for clarification, e.g. "tell me about...", "describe...", "what is the difference between...", "give me an example...". The parent talks about activities and events that make up his or her lifestyle and by doing so defines what is important for the researcher to find out. The principle that the researcher is there to learn guides the questioning within the limits of the focus of the research. In the ethnographic interview, the parent teaches the researcher and thence a wider audience. This gives dignity, respect and importance to what the parent has to say: the parent becomes the expert.

The ethnographic interview, unlike ordinary conversation, is very one-sided, i.e., the informant does most of the talking. The researcher limits her or himself primarily to questions or statements to guide the parent, and then comments or makes restatements to encourage the informant to continue, to give some approval for the direction being taken, and to indicate attentiveness and interest as well as placing value on what is being said. This approach could as easily be used to establish the view of professionals or of one professional group about another. It happens that in this paper the view of the parents focussed on educational officials. It must be recognized that while professionals' views are often heard and represented, it is relatively rarely that the position of parents is presented from their point of view. Frequently, professionals have presented what parents' roles and contributions ought to be within the conceptual framework of their own disciplines and professional outlook.

MAKING THE CHILD DIFFERENT

Parents have reported that they are informed by
school officials or by the educational psychologist
that their handicapped child will be collected in a
taxi when the child reaches school intake age and is
offered a place in some form of Local Authority
special provision. Some Local Authorities are more
assertive than others in insisting or implying that
all children use the transport service. For many
parents, this assistance is most appreciated since
it relieves some stress and strain and creates no
additional problems for the family. For others, who
may also welcome this assistance, it has broader implications which are not so positive and far out-
weigh any benefits.

One such implication is that parents who aspire
to having their child treated in as many ways as
possible as any ordinary child find that using a
taxi service is another means of differentiating
their child and family from the norm. This differ-
entiation - some prefer to call it discrimination -
extends to the family, the neighbourhood and the
school. This is especially so for children who are
moderately handicapped, have non-handicapped siblings, and whose placements may be in diagnostic
units or special ESNM units attached to ordinary infant schools. In addition many parents have, up to
this point in the child's life, been able to arrange
for a place in an ordinary playgroup. They report
the influence these experiences have had on their
expectations and hopes for finding other integrated
settings for their child.

An illustrative case was reported by a parent
whose handicapped child attends a special unit in
the same infant school where her non-handicapped
sibling attends a nursery class. These parents had
been planning to take both children to school in the
family car. One of the reasons for selecting this
school was that it was nearby and it would be feasible for both parents to share this responsibility.
However, when admission to the school was settled,
they were surprised to find out that :

> They just assumed, well the psychologist
> assumed that Dorothy would go in the taxi, so
> she would be like the other children in the
> unit - not like the other children in the
> school - the other children in the unit.

155

This special unit is attached to an ordinary infant
school for the explicit purpose of promoting the
integrated education of handicapped children.
Before rejecting the taxi service, the parents tried
to effect a compromise whereby the non-handicapped
sibling could ride in the taxi as well.

> We have never been able to get John in
> officially....He goes to the same school now
> and they wouldn't give him a place in the
> taxi.

But conditions for financial support restrict use of
the taxi to handicapped children. Therefore, the
handicapped child was being set apart not only from
other children in the school but also from other
children in the family. Previously these two children had both attended an integrated nursery classroom, and would have continued to go to school together if both were non-handicapped. The parents
were concerned that the handicapped child should
develop and maintain ties and friendships with other
children in the neighbourhood and school. Although
they could appreciate the teacher's rationale for
wishing the handicapped child to have an informal
opportunity to associate and develop friendships
with the children in the unit, they were equally
concerned about her exclusive association, or "being
lumped together", with other children who had behaviour problems or were handicapped. In the first instance, the use of the taxi interfered unnecessarily
with the relationship with the sibling as they
wished it to develop, and in the second it pushed
the handicapped child into an additional segregated
setting for other than academic reasons. In fact,
it would deprive her of an integrated experience
well within her capacity to manage.
    The parent explained how this differentiation
extended into the family in another way. Parents
were expected to collect and fetch the non-handicapped child, but were unable to do the same with
the handicapped child if the taxi were used. As the
mother put it:

> Then there was no provision for me to go in
> the taxi because there was no way that they
> could bring me home.

Thus it prevented them having the same kind of informal contact with their handicapped child's
teacher that they had with their non-handicapped

child's teacher. This leads to a chain of events
which could unwittingly contribute to the isolation
of the family from the handicapped child and the
child from the family, a division contrary to
current trends toward integration and community-
based care.

Another example was reported by a parent whose
friend had a handicapped child attending a special
school.

> ...but there again as my friend pointed out,
> she drove her other child to school and it was
> the same journey more or less, so why couldn't
> she drive Gordon to school? Because a normal
> child you would have taken to school, you
> wouldn't put on a bus. The only place where
> he was actually being different in normal
> everyday life would have been if he had been
> put on the bus. It made him different from
> other children in this neighbourhood. Whereas
> if he went to school in the car he was just
> the same as all the other children.

Again the effect is that the child is made different, quite unnecessarily, from his or her own
family and neighbourhood.

Labelling is a problem which parents face
regularly especially with children whose medical
diagnosis is Down's syndrome and whose physical
features reflect this. This is a problem they meet
in the school and in the community, and one which
using the taxi service exacerbates. More importantly, however, is how the use of a taxi service
labels a child within the family, and brings the
family to discriminate against one of its own
members - the handicapped child.

One parent described how the educational
psychologist made a concerted effort to 'wean' her
child from her by asking the child's teacher to see
to it:

> ...that Mrs. Bales lets the child go by taxi,
> she shouldn't take her to school by car.

To which the teacher responded:

> Look, what is wrong with taking a child to
> school by car? I took my child to school
> until she was eleven or twelve.

Earlier the parent had told the psychologist:

No, she won't go by taxi...I shall expect to
take her...I feel it is perfectly reasonable
to take a five year old to school. Why should
she go by taxi?

The parent in anger summed up her view of this
episode:

Handicapped child equals taxi!

INTERACTION BETWEEN PARENTS AND TEACHERS

While the issue of integration was not of central
concern to all families interviewed (irrespective of
the nature or degree of the child's handicap), informal interaction with the teacher was of general
concern. It is easy to have this kind of contact
while collecting and fetching the child; in cases
where the child does go by taxi, some parents and
teachers have found other means of achieving regular
informal contact, e.g. the telephone, school-home
notebooks, escorts, and invitations to come at any
time to the school. They emphasize communication is
the key to this informal interaction with the
teacher. Often the communication centres on information about the child's physical needs, e.g. feeding, toileting, sleep and also general mood. But
these exchanges also extend to academic skills which
traditionally have been the exclusive domain of
educationalists. Exchanging information on items of
mutual concern, not exclusively the domain of either
parents or teachers, provides continuity from one
setting to another, i.e. from home to school and
back home again.

And you know I'd go and they would say he has
had two dinners today, you know, roast beef
and Yorkshire pudding...that was a big problem with Paul, his eating, and I got very
full reports on what he had or had not had.

The problem of communication not only applies
to children living at home but also to those attending residential schools who return home at holidays.
In one instance the Local Education Authority would
have paid for a taxi, driver and escort for a full
day to make the 400 miles round trip. The parent
refused the offer, accepting petrol money instead
and arranging for a friend to accompany her. Since
the Local Authority paid for escort and driver only
when they had to provide transport, it saved them a

substantial sum. The parent was aware how tiring and inconvenient the trip was for her and what additional strains it put on the family, but explained its importance:

> I felt if I go down to the school, you can talk to the teachers yourself and the people there and find out what is going on. And they'll say what they are up to and what they are doing with Pauline. So that when she comes home I can try and keep her more or less in the same routine.

When returning after the holiday respite at home, she described her discussion with the staff:

> Usually when I get down, I'll say, oh she did this or she didn't do that. She's been dirty or she's been a little devil this time or she's been playing up or...she actually stayed dry all night...I usually tell them anything that she's done that she doesn't usually do. And of course we tell them the funny incidents...it will remind them of something that she's done while she's been there and they say, "yes," and so we get the feedback that way.

It is possible that while this exchange may have little to do with formal education or parent involvement, it assumes greater importance when a child is away from home for substantial periods of time. It validates the parent's earlier decision to place the child in a residential setting. This parent was reassured by what she saw.

> You walk in there and there is an atmosphere in the house...now it doesn't matter how many of the children are in...it is so nice to just sit there. You feel so relaxed. It is so calming...I think many a time then, "It's no wonder Pauline does so well for them because there is no rigid atmosphere."

Contact appears to be critical in the transition period from being at home to starting school for the first time. Parents seek continuity generally, but probably more so with a handicapped child who is often more dependent upon an adult. The child may also be less able to communicate his or her own needs or what has happened during the day. As one parent expressed it:

> I actually took her the first day...with
> another mum in the taxi. We both took them
> there and settled them down...you feel a bit
> more confident you know, just taking them
> that first day.

This parent continued to have daily communication
through the other mother who was official escort for
both children, thus maintaining communication without actually collecting and fetching the child herself.

> Everyday I have a report. We have had terrible
> problems with Sam feeding. Everyday I like to
> know whether he has eaten any dinner..if he
> starts fussing around with his tea at night and
> I know he has had a big lunch, then I don't
> push it too hard, but if I know that he has not
> eaten anything..then I have to be sure that he
> gets a decent tea.

The mother who escorts converses daily with the
teacher in the classroom and in addition serves as a
volunteer dinner lady observing the feeding herself,
if not actually feeding Sam. Sam's mother, who
stated she did not want to be directly involved,
clearly wished to maintain access to information.
  Other parents who wish to be actively involved
in doing school work at home find exchange of information essential.

> And then when he was learning to read and
> write, I heard what he was doing...I found it
> was very helpful to be able to reinforce.
> When he came home and was trying to do some-
> thing, at least I knew what he was trying to
> do.

Recalling joint work on toileting, one parent
argued how exchanging information on the child's
progress helped.

> The ideal - I liked to come in just two
> mornings a week - 'cause it was nice to just
> chat about what (they) had been doing in
> classroom, but the other useful thing was
> (their) notebook, that was very good
> actually...that was sufficient then to keep
> tabs on what she was doing and to be involved..

This parent found a combination of collecting and

fetching the child and a home-school notebook to be
a satisfactory communication arrangement.

Another aspect of collecting and fetching the
child that this parent values is the opportunity to
build a relationship with the teacher, who initially
refused to give the parent work to do with the child
at home. The teacher gradually relented and the
parent attributes this in part to the daily contact
they had.

> ...that is a good chance of talking with the
> teacher and that's when she was asking about
> the grading and that's when you get most of
> the information....on a day-to-day basis.
> It is very useful to pick him up.

Information gathering of other kinds may take
place through informal meetings at the classroom
door. It may be the only opportunity parents have
to meet the other children in the classroom and to
gain some perspective on their own child's development and abilities. It gives parents a chance to
assess their role in the care and education of their
child and its impact on their lives.

> I mean we have only got to look around other
> handicapped children to realise that Sam is
> one of the worst handicapped...we have such
> a hectic time with him...I would go so far
> as to say Sam is about probably the most
> awkward, time-consuming child; that isn't
> just me saying it, I mean that is the teachers
> ...I mean I look at other kids and think "God,
> I could look after two of those as well as
> Sam and it probably wouldn't put me out one
> tiny bit."

It made her feel that the job she was doing was
indeed difficult and that realistically she was not
a 'fussing, nagging mother'. While this parent does
not collect and fetch the child, close contact is
maintained with the school. The teacher telephones
if any problems arise and the parent said she can be
at the school in seven minutes with ease. The
school has made it clear that parents are welcome to
visit, and that no appointment is necessary. As
this parent viewed it, she could just 'breeze in'
and was certain to be made to feel welcome.

Parents say that they acquire skills in an in-
cidental manner, impossible to learn under more
formal conditions. For example, one parent observed

a teacher dealing with a behaviour problem, a method
that she decided to try at home. Her description of
the incident reveals its impact.

> And she just got hold of Joan's hand, gently,
> firmly, she didn't grab her...and she said, "I
> think, Joan...it would be a good idea if you
> went up to your room and had a look at some of
> your books." And as she was saying it, she was
> walking her to the door...up she went and we
> never heard another muff out of her..."Yeah,"
> I thought, "yeah, I'm going to try that with
> Pauline when I get home."

This parent was extremely pleased to have achieved
the same result, successfully with her own child, a
major step forward from her point of view.
    Parents reported learning about appropriate
educational material through contact with school,
enabling them to make wiser choices in gifts and
toys for their child.

> I know I got some smashing ideas from the
> classroom..with books and everything. And I
> went and bought these books and things like
> that, that I thought she would be able to do.

Finally, a parent noted how collecting and
fetching her child is the only opportunity she has
to meet other parents in the school. Through these
brief casual meetings, she has learned that they
have some mutual concerns and has been prompted to
think about what might be accomplished if parents
met regularly as a group. In her own words:

> It would be more useful to get to know the
> parents, 'cause I only know the parents...
> to speak to casually when I actually pick
> them up...I think we could give a concerted
> push if you like...in things like bringing
> your work home and also this business of
> transport 'cause I felt I was a lone voice
> until I realised that there were other
> mothers who felt the same way as I did.
> And also we would like to get to know the
> other parents of those people who go in the
> taxis. I find it useful talking to parents,
> other mothers in MENCAP say, just talking
> over difficulties at home and things like
> that..how they cope....swapping ideas and
> tips. I think that would be even more useful

where there are similar ages and the same
classroom situation.

Thus, this informal short meeting of parents at the
classroom door has stimulated thought about the
worth of a more systematic approach to discussion
with other parents.

CONCLUSION

While a transport service is often a valuable source
of support, its use has implications broader than
relieving stress, some of which parents perceive as
disadvantageous to the child and family. Two areas
that they claim to be primarily affected are integration and parent involvement. While collecting
and fetching a child has hardly been viewed as an
integral part of 'parent-involvement', as defined by
professionals, it is clearly valued by parents
because it permits regular unconstrained communication with the teacher and the school.
    If present policy continues to move towards
integration and parent involvement, then the practical implications for policy regarding a transport
service are that it must be administered flexibly in
response to individual families. Where children do
use taxis, more thought needs to be given to finding
means to ensure that regular informal access to the
teacher and school is available to parents. Some
successful alternatives have been mentioned but
others could be explored.

REFERENCES

Paul, D. (1953) Interview techniques and field re-
        lationships. In A.L. Kroeber (ed.) Anthro-
        pology Today: An Encyclopedia Inventory.
        Chicago: University of Chicago Press
Spradley, P. (1979) The Ethnographic Interview.
        New York: Holt, Rinehart and Winston

DISCUSSION

Papers eight and nine were discussed together.
Barbara Smith stressed that professionals bear the
primary responsibility for the creation of good
parent-professional relations. Her reasons included
the fact that professionals are more likely to be in
touch with recent changes in the techniques and
attitudes of service-providers than parents,
particularly those of older mentally handicapped

163

children, and therefore that it is the responsibility of professionals to discuss these with parents. Many parents do not know, for example, that they have a legal right to be present when their child is examined by a doctor or a psychologist. She also felt that, as well as talking with parents about their practical and emotional needs, discussing 'professional' issues will contribute to the development of a trusting relationship. However, it is important to be careful about the language used in talking with parents and writing reports on the child, so that parents feel confident and fully understand. She urged that much greater attention should be paid to these aspects of co-operation with parents in the training of teachers.

Christoph Hublow from Germany, who is also a teacher, said that both the preceding papers had asked the right question: "Why should parents *not* be involved?" He wanted more practical discussion and guidelines on how exactly to best involve parents in assessments and case-conferences, and help parents understand the scientific background of special education. It became clear in discussion that schools vary widely in how parents and teachers collaborate in practice. There were also national differences in expectations about the proper content of education (see Chapter 13). There is an enormous gulf to bridge if parents think education is about reading, writing and arithmetic, while teachers think in terms of helping the child to acquire practical skills and ways of communicating with others; or the other way round. Considerable obstacles to partnership can arise from the preconceptions parents and teachers have about each other's roles.

Mariet van Hattum commented that in Holland home-school notebooks are commonly used in describing to parents what the child has done in school during the day. But the drawbacks of such a system include its formality, and the families' lack of contact with each other. She herself experienced the 'special little bus' which took her daughter to school as a source of humiliation (ie. arising from her own feelings) rather than of discrimination (arising from the world outside), and other parents had told her they had similar difficult feelings. Special transport seems to emphasise the inevitability of the handicap. She suggested that there was probably no real solution to the problem, as it was having a handicapped child which hurt parents, rather than any one particular aspect of the whole.

Many participants considered that relationships between parents and teachers would be greatly improved in future with the advent of early intervention. In some parts of Britain, the main regular contact which families with a mentally handicapped baby experience is with some kind of peripatetic teacher, for example, in the Portage Projects. Apart from the benefits to the child's development, this collaboration also helps parents to get used and to expect to work with professionals.

Chapter 10

SCHOOL-BASED PARENT INVOLVEMENT: A PSYCHOLOGIST'S VIEW

Jill Gardner

It has often been argued that the education of handicapped children is a highly skilled task which should only be carried out by specially trained staff. While I would agree that there are many good reasons why special school staff should be highly trained, I do not feel that this need in any way exclude parents from the educational process, since there are many ways in which the active inclusion of parents can greatly enhance the educational opportunities of children with special needs.

Of the total time available for teaching the handicapped child during his or her lifetime, a relatively short period of time will be spent in school. This, coupled with the need to ensure generalisation of skills learned in school to other settings, provides a strong motive for schools to involve parents as active participants in the learning process. A policy of parental involvement should also ensure that families become more aware of their children's capabilities, and in taking a positive approach towards their children, will be less likely to find themselves coping alone with possibly increasingly disruptive behaviour problems.

School-based parental involvement also encourages parents to help each other, eg. by forming self-help groups, thus reducing the likelihood of the social isolation of families with a handicapped child. These self-supporting groups can also be used by other professionals as a vehicle for more general discussion with parents who experience common worries and problems concerned with the medical aspects of handicap, the services available to them in the community and so on. Above all, parent involvement can ensure that teachers and parents work together on an equal footing for the benefit of the children, thus breaking down long-established

barriers between those who are trained to teach
handicapped children and those who live with them.

Awareness of the importance of parental involvement in teaching their children has led to the
development of a variety of well-documentated projects which differ widely in purpose and organisation. Reviews of these projects can be found elsewhere, so I shall now consider just a few examples,
before discussing the ways in which the skills of
teachers and the school curriculum can be used in
parental involvement.

INDIVIDUAL THERAPIST/FAMILY INVOLVEMENT

Many individual studies of 'parents as therapists'
have been documented which illustrate the effectiveness of parent training by another professional in
the management of problem behaviours or in the training of new skills (e.g. Sandow and Clarke, 1978).
Traditionally, this model of parental involvement is
not school-based, but involves the therapist (often a
psychologist) in setting up a teaching or management
programme which is put into action between therapy
sessions by the parents. Using this individual
model to teach new skills, staff involved in the
Portage Projects (Shearer and Shearer, 1972) have
been able to demonstrate a rapid increase in the
acquisition of new skills in pre-school handicapped
children who were taught at home by their parents,
with assistance and regular visits from specially
trained home teachers.

The model of individual parent/therapist involvement has two main advantages but several disadvantages. The advantages are that the parent is
actively included in the training of the child
and that the model has a built-in evaluation system
in that the success or failure of intervention is
directly measured in terms of the child's performance. The disadvantages of this approach are that
it is extremely costly in terms of therapist time;
it lacks planned involvement of other family members,
which is potentially undermining both to the 'main
parent' and to the others; there is potential dependency on the therapist in weekly visiting, with the
danger of reducing parent confidence; the parents
are not given an opportunity to form self-supporting
groups; and there is no planned link between programmes used for the child in school and at home.

It is worth noting here that the Portage Project
in particular was designed to meet the needs of
families with pre-school handicapped children who had

no access to pre-school facilities and who were living in a large geographical area, so that there was no opportunity for the disadvantages inherent in this model to be overcome.

GROUP THERAPIST/FAMILY INVOLVEMENT

Many of the disadvantages of individual parent support can be overcome where parents are brought together in groups to discuss their special children's problems and/or to be given practical advice by a therapist. This group parental involvement model has been used in a variety of settings, for example, as part of a research facility (Cunningham and Jeffree, 1971); as an evening course at an Adult Education Centre (Cummings, 1975); and as part of a school-based facility (Bevington, Gardner and Cocks, 1981). In this wide variety of settings, parents can not only receive guidance in the management of their children in a way which is an efficient use of therapist time, but they can also form self-supporting social groups. Though these groups are advantageous in many ways, it becomes much more difficult to evaluate their effectiveness. The advantages of forming a self-help group would be difficult to measure, and since the children are not directly involved in the group, methods need to be found to measure the effect of therapist/parent interaction in terms of changes in child behaviour.

These difficulties of evaluation may in part explain the paucity of data collected during parent involvement projects. Burden (1978) aimed to measure changes in maternal attitudes during such intervention, and in several studies reports are given of parents' subjective views of the helpfulness of parent workshop course (eg. Cummings, 1975). Rarely does there seem to be any attempt to evaluate changes in parents' knowledge or use of teaching techniques, except by the use of anecdotal evidence.

EVALUATION OF LOCAL PARENT WORKSHOPS

During our involvement with local authority schools for the severely mentally handicapped (ESNS), we have developed a number of parent workshops which were jointly planned by psychologists and teachers, and held in schools. Since we were at that time new to this field of work ourselves, we felt that it would be very important to find out how well we were communicating our ideas and skills to parents, so that we could modify our course for the future.

Evaluation should form an integral part of course planning, rather than an 'optional extra' tacked on to the last session. In other words, before one can find out what effects have been produced, it is vital to list the effects which are being sought, and to plan teaching strategies accordingly. Since we had, in teaching children, evaluated the effectiveness of our teaching in terms of specific skills learned by them, we felt that we should follow the same procedure when teaching parents.

Our original study is documented in detail elsewhere (Bevington, et al., 1978). In summary, we started by writing general aims for our workshop, which were derived from specific needs outlined to us by parents in an initial interview. From these general aims, we listed a number of targets which we felt it would be important for parents to master in order for their general needs to be met. Originally these specific targets were written in terms of the parents' ability to use teaching techniques in simulated teaching situations and their ability to answer correctly questions designed to test their theoretical knowledge of the areas covered. Less emphasis was placed upon their attempts to teach new skills to their children at home. We later realised that this was a mistake.

Having devised specific targets, we were then in a position to plan our teaching methods: that is, we could decide how many sessions to run, how to present the material and so on. We were also able to collect specific information from parents so that we could find out to what extent they had in fact learned the skills which we had set out to teach.

The information gained was encouraging, since many of the parents had in fact mastered the pre-set targets. We were also encouraged by parents' regular attendance and their positive comments. At the end of the course, we again visited the families at home to try to find out what effect, if any, the course had had on their attempts to teach their children at home. It became very clear that we had not developed any reliable means of gathering evidence of behaviour change on the part of the parents, and that a change in 'verbal behaviour' (i.e. what parents' can say, write, etc) as a result of the course was no guarantee whatever of parental behaviour change in the home.

EFFECTS ON PARENTS' SKILLS

Our subsequent projects therefore have had a different emphasis. We have recently been much more concerned with planning, teaching, and evaluating effective means of teaching parents practical skills, and have de-emphasised the need for verbalisation of theoretical information.

In our most recent study, parents were invited to join the workshop and were told specifically that the group was designed to assist them in teaching skills to their children. The parents who volunteered were visited at home and asked to demonstrate for us a short teaching session with their child. During this initial observation we were able to record, for example :

- the task chosen by the parent (eg. toilet training, colour discrimination, self-help skills);
- the way in which instructions were given by the parent;
- the ways in which the parent reacted when the child succeeded at the task;
- the ways in which parents tried to give children extra help if the task was proving too difficult; and so on.

All of these observations were measured against the skills which we planned to teach the parents by the end of the workshop. Thus, we now had some objective data on parents' teaching skills.

From these observations we were able to construct a list of targets for the parents; in other words, we were able to specify those skills which we were planning to teach parents during the course of the sessions. From these targets we were then able to plan our teaching methods as before. Since we were emphasising parents' abilities to use the teaching techniques in practice with their children, we tried to ensure that sufficient time was given for parents to learn these new practical skills, by showing videotaped demonstrations, organising discussions and group practical sessions.

Half of the families who attended the workshops were also visited at home in between sessions so that parents could practise their teaching skills at home with supervision from ourselves. The skill areas covered during the sessions included :

- gaining the child's attention and co-operation;

- ensuring that the child was given consistent and simple task instructions;
- techniques to be used when the child failed on the task, e.g. the use of prompts;
- the assessment and use of rewards;
- training of the child to imitate;
- planning programmes by breaking tasks down into simple steps;
- recording progress.

It was felt that these skills were essential for parents to have mastered if they were to be successful in teaching their children at home.

At the end of the course, parents were again asked to complete questionnaires, which gave us information both on their views about the usefulness of the course, and some indication of their ability to verbalise their knowledge of the teaching techniques we had covered. Knowing now that this was important but insufficient information, we again visited families at home and made observations on a single teaching session which the parents conducted with their own children.

In summary, our results once again indicated significant and positive change in parents' verbal behaviour (i.e. what they could say, write, etc, about the teaching techniques). However, we also found a marked discrepancy between the actual teaching abilities of those parents who had been given guided practice sessions at home and those who had only attended the course without any extra support. Those parents who had been given an opportunity to practise their skills with constructive feedback from ourselves were much more able to conduct a teaching session which more nearly resembled the list of skills involved which we had originally devised. These results are not very surprising in retrospect, but they do illustrate once again the importance both of careful planning and of evaluation of expected post-course outcomes.

Despite the fact that we felt that we had started to make some progress in terms of our increased efficiency as parent trainers, we were confronted with another problem. While many parents could, under optimum conditions, exhibit proficient teaching skills, we also discovered that parents were not teaching their children either often enough or for long enough, and were finding it difficult to keep careful records. In other words, parents now *had* improved teaching skills, but were not *utilising* them to greatest effect.

What reasons could we find for this? Obviously,
motivation to help their children was not in doubt,
since they had volunteered for the course, had
attended regularly, and were still regular visitors
to formal and informal gatherings held at school.
The problem seemed to stem not from a lack of enthusiasm but from a lack of specific direction. Although parents now had teaching skills, they were
often unsure which task to choose, and after the
course ended there was no planned follow-up to give
further guidance or suggest teaching areas to them.

USING THE SCHOOL CURRICULUM

The problems which parents experience in choosing
appropriate tasks and in keeping careful records of
their children's progress can be overcome if the
school has developed a structured curriculum. In
using a behavioural curriculum model, teachers in
the school will have selected appropriate teaching
targets for each child. They will have done this by
first assessing each child's skill levels, using the
curriculum as an assessment procedure. By breaking
down each target skill into a step by step programme, they will then be able to select an appropriate teaching step. By using record forms, they
will have an accurate record of the child's progress.
    Because this detailed information is already
available in school, there is no need for parents
either to choose a teaching target in an arbitrary
fashion or for them to be given a separate observation schedule (such as a developmental checklist)
to help them in their teaching. Instead, teachers
will be able to tell the parents exactly what the
child has learned in school and precisely which
targets are currently being taught. In this way
parents can either assist school staff by sharing
the teaching of the weekly target or targets, or by
assisting the generalisation process through teaching targets already learned in school, under the
different conditions of home, or in other settings.
    There may still be concern in teachers' minds
that parents may try to teach skills by using different instructions or different materials to those
used in school. Using a behavioural curriculum,
these problems can be avoided: firstly by ensuring
that the teaching skills taught to parents in the
group match up as far as possible with those used by
teachers in school; secondly, targets and steps in
the school curriculum are very clearly specified,

with the instructions to be given and materials to be used written into the programme. This not only means that different teachers are more likely to teach these skills in the same way, but it also assists parents, and gives them very precise quidelines.

Record-keeping by parents is also facilitated since it is an integral part of the programme, and separate different record forms do not need to be produced for use by parents: rather it would be preferable if they were given duplicates of the class teachers' record forms for their use at home.

Perhaps the greatest advantage of using the school curriculum in this way is the effect that this has on parent motivation. Instead of home and school working separately with each child, parents and teachers can more easily work together to achieve the same result. The fact that parents are thus seen working alongside the teacher has enormous benefits for all concerned. The parent knows that after a period of teaching the child at home, there will be detailed information to bring back to school in the form of data on the record form. Parents and teachers can then enjoy a much more useful discussion on the child's learning, problems arising from the use of the programme, and so on. When a target is achieved, parents will know that they will again be involved in working with the teacher on the selection of the next appropriate teaching target. Thus, the emphasis of parent involvement groups can shift away from a series of lectures or discussions, towards a permanent collaboration, which should be maintained until the child leaves school.

In terms of practical arrangements, there are a variety of ways in which this ideal situation could be achieved. This will depend upon the number of families interested in working in this way, and the availability of staff either during or after school time. One possible means of organising such a venture might be to run a short series of weekly workshops after school to cover aspects relating to parents' acquisition of teaching skills. Thereafter meetings could be held less often - say once a month - at which parents could discuss progress, and be given new targets to work on where appropriate.

CONCLUSION

This chapter discusses the contribution which parents can make to the education of their children and suggests some ways in which schools might involve

parents in the teaching process. Parental involvement requires careful planning if it is to be successful. A school which uses a behavioural model
for curriculum planning has readily available a
number of resources which can be utilised by parents
to the greater advantage of the children. This also
ensures that a more meaningful evaluation of parental involvement can be carried out, since measures of
changes in child behaviour are being collected con-
tinuously both at home and at school.

REFERENCES

Bevington, P., Gardner, J.M. and Cocks, R.P. (1978)
    An approach to the planning and evaluation of
    a parental involvement course. Child: Care,
    Health and Development, 4, 217-227
Burden, R.L. (1978) An approach to the evaluation of
    early intervention projects with mothers of
    severely handicapped children: the attitude
    dimension. Child: Care, Health and Development,
    4, 171-181
Cocks, R.P. and Gardner, J.M. (1978) Parent work-
    shops. Apex, 6 (2), 18-19
Cummings, P. (1975) You and your handicapped child.
    Unpublished paper, School Psychological Serv-
    ice, Birmingham.
Cunningham, C.C. and Jeffree, D.M. (1971) Working
    with Parents: Developing a Workshop Course for
    Parents of Young Mentally Handicapped Children.
    Manchester: National Society for Mentally
    Handicapped Children
Sandow, S. and Clarke, A.D.B. (1978) Home inter-
    vention with parents of severely subnormal,
    pre-school children: an interim report. Child:
    Care, Health and Development, 4, 29-39
Shearer, M.S. and Shearer, D.E. (1972) The Portage
    Project - a model for early childhood edu-
    cation. Exceptional Children, 39, 201-207

DISCUSSION

As a preliminary to discussion, Jill Gardner gave a
description of two series of workshops in which she
had been involved, of a very different kind from
those described in her paper. One was for a group
of Asian mothers, initiated by the school because
the contact with this group was felt to be insufficient. The families were invited for a series of
six visits to the school. They were shown the kind
of tasks that their children were doing in school

and were involved in helping their children at meal-time and in play sessions. A member of staff of the local authority Social Services Department also talked to the parents about their rights and where to go for help and information locally. The other workshop was for parents of school-leavers and aimed at providing information and discussion about subsequent provision such as Adult Training Centres and hostels.

Christopher Hublow questioned whether teaching was a task which parents should take on, and stressed the need to remain *parents* who try to provide at home a loving, natural family setting for all their children, and by doing so balance the handicapped child's systematic training at school. He suggested that teaching might create distance and emotional disturbance between parent and child. He also questioned the behavioural curriculum model, suggesting it was too narrow a framework for all of education. For example, how could parents be helped to find interesting and challenging leisure events and social activities for their children?

Jill Gardner replied to the concern about emotional distance being created between parent and child by emphasising that parents had been given very pessimistic prognoses in the past, with concentration on what the child could not do. Therefore, an accent on the positive, and on what parents *can* do to help, fosters confidence in the parents and brings them closer to the child as they experience success in teaching.

Cliff Cunningham also pointed out that learning about teaching skills would not only have the aim of helping parents with their child, but would also tend to increase their understanding of the work of teachers, thus making a dialogue easier.

SECTION FIVE: ADOLESCENCE AND ADULTHOOD

Chapter 11

WORKING WITH PARENTS OF ADOLESCENTS: THE WORK OF THE
PATH PROJECT

Dorothy Jeffree and Sally Cheseldine

The approach to parental involvement discussed in
this chapter arises out of a four year research project, Parents and Their Handicapped Teenagers, concerned particularly with the leisure time activities
of these young people. It explores their knowledge
of and participation in various pastimes, their
patterns of friendship and levels of socialization,
as well as the concerns of their parents.

WHY PARENTS?

At an age when mentally handicapped teenagers are
being helped to become increasingly independent, why
do we work with parents?

1. Parents or parent substitutes have the
    greatest individual effect on any child's
    development.
2. The time any child or young person spends
    at home is greater than the time spent at
    school.
3. At a time of transition on leaving school,
    when teenagers are faced with an environ-
    mental change, a change from familiar
    personnel, a break from friends and a new
    regime, parents form the only stable link.
4. Parents remain the decision makers and a
    young person's future will largely depend
    upon the parents' continued ability to
    cope, e.g. whether or not they ask for
    residential care for the young person.
5. Parents of today's adolescents have re-
    ceived very little help in the past but
    may need special advice and assistance at
    this critical time.

WHY ADOLESCENTS?

Families may be faced with critical decisions throughout their child's life. Why have we chosen to concentrate on the period of adolescence?

1. Leaving school is a critical period for any adolescent who has to cope with physical, mental, emotional and environmental change. Without help, mentally handicapped young people may be ill-equipped or unready to make this step and their lives may become more restricted, rather than less restricted as in the case of a non-handicapped teenager.

2. Although there is increasing help for pre-school and school age mentally handicapped children, what about those who were born too soon to benefit from these changes? Changes are only just beginning to take place in provision for adolescents and adults. It is never too late to learn and mentally handicapped individuals, deprived of early stimulation and training, have been able to benefit from structured programmes later in life (Clarke and Clarke, 1976).

3. At adolescence many mentally handicapped teenagers are only just reaching the developmental level of normal children starting school (Marshall, 1967). At a time when they could benefit from educational, social and recreational programmes they may be least likely to have the opportunity to do so.

WHY LEISURE?

At a time when human worth is usually equated with socio-economic status at work, why do we choose to concentrate on leisure?

1. "The normalizing potential of recreation is yet to be realized ... unfortunately mentally retarded adults who are proficient at their jobs may fail to adjust to community life because they are not aware of recreational resources available to them, or have not learnt how to use them" (Luckey and Shapiro, 1974).

2. All school leavers now have more time on

their hands, often being unable to get
work. This has nearly always been the
case for mentally handicapped people.
3. Many parents of the handicapped speak of
their isolation within the community.
This may be even greater for handicapped
people themselves. Properly programmed
leisure activities have great potential
for integration.
4. The importance of play in the social,
emotional and intellectual development of
children is not in doubt. For mentally
handicapped people, this period of childhood play may need to be extended and
accepted until they are ready to partake
in the leisure time activities of their
normal peers

A SURVEY OF SCHOOL LEAVERS

Although the abilities of children leaving Junior
Training Centres in the 1960's were charted by
Marshall (1967), there is scant information on the
abilities of children currently leaving ESNS schools
and even less on their home situation. For this
reason a survey of all the known ESNS school leavers
in the Greater Manchester Area (214), 87 per cent of
total, was carried out by the PATH Project (see
Cheseldine and Jeffree (1982) for a full report).
    The homes were visited and the informants were
the parents supplemented by information from the
young people themselves. A checklist of self-help
skills - *Pathways to Independence* (Jeffree and
Cheseldine, 1982) - was prepared and each teenager's
present status in ten areas of self-help was
charted. In addition a semi-structured interview
was carried out and the parents reported on their
son or daughter's leisure time activities and
friendship pattern, as well as being given an
opportunity to identify problems and difficulties
and to make suggestions. Some of the findings will
be reported in the context of the main discussion.

The Home
The majority of ESNS children live at home, only
9.5 per cent of the 214 teenagers being in residential care. However, when children leave school
and become adults, the parents themselves are also
growing older and their continued ability to cope
becomes problematic. When their children leave
school, parents become increasingly concerned with

what is going to happen when they die. Many feel
that it would be unfair to pass on the burden of
responsibility to siblings who have their own lives
to lead.

In our survey 83 per cent of the fathers were
over 40 and seven per cent over 60 (Cheseldine and
Jeffree, 1981b). We note that the years between 16
and 20 are the peak period for admission to mental
handicap hospitals (National Development Group,
1978).

Planning for the Future
Individually and communally it is important not to
be put off doing anything about the future until a
crisis occurs but to plan in good time. Nationally,
as the National Development Group (1978) suggest, we
need to develop community services to prevent inappropriate hospital admission. Individually there
is also much that can be done to prepare young
people to live more independently (Mittler,
Cheseldine and McConachie, 1981). Information
gleaned from the parents in our survey has highlighted some important areas of concern where
ideally action should be taken before the young
people leave school.

Pathways to Independence
A minority of mentally handicapped adults do become
sufficiently independent of their families to be
able to lead relatively autonomous lives in the
community. If we mapped out the pathways that lead
to this degree of independence, their number could
perhaps be greatly increased. We should also consider the obstacles that lie in the way of independence and how far along the road each individual
has already come.

Hannam (1980) suggests that sometimes the mentally handicapped are less dependent when away from
their homes and can do things which parents thought
were quite beyond them. In this context, we need to
provide opportunities for them to practise the
skills they already possess as well as helping them
to develop new skills in priority areas.

Our survey suggests that most parents have done
a very good job in ensuring that their son/daughters
are reasonably independent within the home environment. Their achievement must not be underestimated, for it is often quicker to do things for
others than to teach them to help themselves. Most
of the young people in our survey needed no assistance in eating and drinking (77 per cent) or toilet-

ing (58 per cent). They also helped with the household chores and over 50 per cent could set and clear the table, about a third were able to wash and dry dishes on their own and put them away and 46 per cent could make their own beds.

Having started on the path towards independence, we need to consider some of the priority areas in which extra help may be needed. For instance, for an independent existence a young person needs to be able to prepare a simple meal. But although most of the young people in our survey were able to prepare a cold drink (77 per cent) and many a hot drink (51 per cent), only three per cent could prepare a simple meal on their own.

We found that most of the young people went shopping 'en famille', though a few were sent on errands to nearby local shops. However, very few went further afield on their own and only two per cent were reported as able to use public transport independently, even on a familiar route. One of the difficulties seemed to be in the handling of money – and here there seemed to be a lack of opportunity as well as of skill. We found that many of the young people were never given pocket money of their own to handle and that money was handed over to them only for specific purchases. Only six per cent of the young people could combine coins and notes to a specific value.

Many schools are well aware of these priority areas and have instituted training programmes to ensure that initial disabilities do not become lasting handicaps. However, unless these skills are also practised at home, their work may be in vain. How this might be achieved will be discussed later.

Integration
The importance of peer group friendships can hardly be overemphasized, for even amongst the handicapped themselves, two friends will have complementary skills and disabilities and can often accomplish far more than either could achieve on their own.

Many parents were concerned about their child's isolation from the local community of peers. They reported that when the children were younger they were accepted by the other small children and played with them amicably, but as they grew older the gap widened and the other local children 'didn't want to know'. The situation was exacerbated by the handicapped teenager's increasing self-consciousness. The young people who were the most fully accepted were often those who had attended normal schools and

183

retained their school friends or who lived in more
impoverished inner city areas.

In this context we found that, although the
majority of young people had one or more specific
friends at school and their parents often knew of
them, yet only a quarter ever visited their school
friends out of school hours. In some cases, the
parents had overlooked the importance of such
friendships but the geographical distances involved
made visiting impracticable and lack of independent
mobility on the teenagers' part made this even more
difficult. The parents themselves contributed an
interesting point. They pointed out that they did
not know the parents of their handicapped children's
school friends very well. It was different with
their normal children; contact with other parents
was made early on at the nursery or infant school
gate and family visits followed naturally.

The Forgotten Hours
We know that a mentally handicapped young person
spends more hours at home than anywhere else, in
spite of the increase in special holidays, expeditions and clubs which give their parents a welcome
relief. The parents themselves are very well aware
of these 'forgotten hours' of weekends, long
holidays and evenings. The way in which these hours
are filled, in frustration or lethargy or constructively, may have a direct bearing on the families'
continued ability to cope. However, little information has been available as to how they were spent.
Such thoughts prompted us to include in our survey
information from the parents on the teenagers'
leisure time pursuits when at home (Cheseldine and
Jeffree, 1981).

Nash (1953) has suggested a hierarchy of
leisure pursuits. The lowest level of this hierarchy is spectator activities, through activities
with greater involvement and those with increased
socialization, to highly creative activities. A
handicapped person may remain at the lowest level of
this hierarchy without specific intervention. As
Bates and Renzaglia (1979) remarked, "The constructive use of leisure time depends to a great extent
upon the skills and interests an individual has
acquired and these skills and interests develop as
the result of planned, systematic experience with
specific activities". Katz and Yekutiel (1974) add,
"Handicapped individuals often spend long periods of
time engaged in passive activities like watching
television because they have not acquired the skills

184

for engaging in a greater diversity of leisure time activities". Although the situation had been reported in America, very little was known about mentally handicapped teenagers' use of leisure in England and no systematic attempt had been made to help teenagers to acquire the skills necessary for a greater diversity of leisure time occupation.

The Handicapped Teenagers' Use of Leisure Time
The parents or guardians listed their son or daughter's leisure time occupations in a semi-structured interview. The four most frequently mentioned occupations were listening to tapes of records (89 per cent), watching TV (87 per cent) or going shopping (70 per cent). The shopping mainly consisted of expeditions with other members of the family. A hobby such as painting or drawing was mentioned by 31 per cent and knitting or sewing by 12 per cent. It can be seen that the most frequently mentioned activities are comparatively passive and do not require much personal involvement or interaction with other people.

Did these activities arise from choice or because without the necessary skills or friends there were few alternatives available? A partial answer to this question could be gained by planning systematic programmes to train a variety of alternative leisure time activities and seeing how the young people chose to occupy themselves after they had acquired these skills. In order to put this to the test, we carried out several pilot studies in which we observed the young people in free choice situations and recorded what they did. We then trained them individually on a programmed series of table games of chance and observed their behaviour when these games also were available. The observation sessions were carried out both at school and at home. Once they had acquired the skills to engage in new activities, there was a significant difference in the pupils' behaviour. In a free choice situation both at school and at home, there was a decrease in solitary activities and an increase in skilled interactive pursuits. At home, before the introduction of the games, 56 per cent of the reported activities were solitary but after the introduction of the games this dropped to 39 per cent. Once the skills had been acquired, the handicapped teenagers were able to play with others on equal terms.

"The school is obviously the greatest help the
parents receive. What is less satisfactory than the
progress the school has achieved with the child,
continues to be the quality of communication with
the school." (Hannam, 1980)

Our experience also suggests that the quality
of communication between home and school is less
than satisfactory. This was our conclusion in spite
of the fact that parents were loyal and appreciative
of what the schools were doing and most schools had
some form of Parent Teacher Association. However
only a minority of parents attend the meetings.
Possible reasons for this non-attendance will obviously vary from school to school; one of the most
obvious is the distance of home from school and
transport difficulties. Pupils are transported to
school by taxis or special buses but parents find it
difficult to make their own way to school,
especially when both are working. There is no easy
solution to this problem, though one school has
used the school minibus to pick up parents for
evening meetings which then have very high rates of
attendance. More important still, to what extent
do these meetings meet the parents' real needs?
Very few parents suggested that they did not. A few
mentioned a somewhat excessive emphasis on fund
raising.

We were particularly concerned about how little
some of the parents seemed to know of what went on
in school, and conversely, how little the teachers
knew of what went on at home, though home and
school activities should have been complementary.
For example, one mother did not allow her son near
the cooker in the kitchen and said he could not make
hot drinks or toast and then added the comment, "I
think he does it at school, but I am not sure". As
Hannam (1980) remarked, "Surely the school and
parents must aim at approaching the problem of
education jointly rather than separately". Careful
planning and preparation will be needed in order for
this to come about. One way in which this has been
done successfully in this country is through parent
workshops (Cunningham and Jeffree, 1971).

WORKSHOPS

Some schools have started workshops for parents of
their top classes. In these workshops, parents and
teachers work together as equals. Other profess-

ionals such as speech therapists, physiotherapists and psychologists are invited for some of the sessions. In preparation for the workshop, both parents and teachers complete the Pathways to Independence checklist independently for each pupil (Jeffree and Cheseldine, 1982). The first session is given over to the discussion of any discrepancies which appear in the two versions of the checklist and the reasons for these differences, e.g. behaviour at school and at home is often different, one place provides opportunities that the other does not, parents have knowledge of early development which the teachers have not, misunderstandings may arise in the interpretation of some items, both parties may have a tendency to over- or under-estimate the pupils. Frank discussion of these differences prepares the way for the planning and implementation of joint programmes.

We also found that many parents were very vague about provision for school leavers, although their children were due to leave school shortly. Staff from Adult Training Centres, and Colleges of Further Education can be invited to the workshop sessions to fill this gap and alleviate some parental anxiety.

Hannam (1980) has said, "Parents have to fight for their rights - the initiative comes from them". He also suggests that working class families are often less successful in getting help than middle class families. The workshop experience gives these parents increased self-confidence and a realisation that they have an important contribution to make.

Perhaps one of the biggest contributions the workshops have to make is providing a venue in which parents can get to know one another better. The outcome of one workshop was the sharing of leisure time activities. One parent who was very well provided with leisure time facilities threw these open to her daughter's friends and to other normal teenagers, which was a start towards further integration.

QUESTIONS FOR THE FUTURE

In this chapter we have posed questions for the future on the issues of parent-professional collaboration and on recreation and leisure for the mentally handicapped school leaver. In conclusion we will select a few of the leading questions which call for immediate attention.

1. *Are we satisfied with the present level of parent/ professional involvement and, if not, what can be done to improve matters?*

Parents of mentally handicapped children are only too ready to shoulder responsibility for their child; the majority of these children live at home, where they spend more time than anywhere else and are included in most family activities and outings and holidays. This means that parents continually live with their anxieties about the future which they are usually powerless to alleviate.

Professionals could do much to reduce these anxieties. There is an obvious need for an extension of educational, recreational and residential provision, and also, with help, many more young people could become less of a burden to their families, more independent and integrated into the community. However, unilateral training in independent living skills which are never practised at home is unlikely to be effective. Parents and professionals need to work together to plan and implement programmes.

Professionals may justifiably answer that opportunities already exist for discussions with parents but they are not taken up by the majority of parents. This dilemma raises a number of important issues:

. is the right kind of help being offered?
. have parents been consulted on the time and place of meeting?
. is transport available?
. is provision made for the rest of the family?
. are parents given prior information on what is being offered?
. are parents treated as fellow professionals?

Where efforts have been made to answer these questions parent participation has increased.

2. *Should we be giving greater consideration to ways of providing satisfying alternatives to paid employment, that is "significant living without work"* (Warnock, 1978)? We live in a society which still adheres to the work ethic but is developing in such a way as to reduce employment possibilities, especially for the mentally handicapped. The functions which paid employment fulfils have been summarised by Tizard and Anderson (1978) as giving the individual a sense of identity, a feeling of contributing to society, financial independence, an opportunity for social contacts and a structure to the day. They go on to suggest alternative ways in which these functions can be fulfilled for the physically and mentally handicapped school leaver who is unable to gain paid

employment. In this chapter we have suggested ways in which leisure time activities can fulfil some of these functions, especially in giving the individual opportunities for social contacts, a structure to the day and a feeling of personal identity through the exercise of choice.

There are signs that recreation and leisure are beginning to be taken seriously. Recently an O.E.C.D conference was given over to the topic of "The education and social integration of handicapped children through recreational activities" and follow-up seminars are taking place in the participating countries. Although much of the emphasis of this conference was on organised outdoor activities for the physically disabled (horse riding, swimming etc.) one of the key issues which arose from the conference was the need for *early* induction into the use of leisure (Neale, 1982). This is particularly important when we are considering mentally handicapped people.

How can we ensure that every individual is given a start, how ever low down on the hierarchy of leisure activities? What is the first step towards socialisation through recreation, which can eventually lead to integration into the community and use of community facilities? As most of leisure time is spent at home, how can we involve the family in taking that first step? Finally, to what extent is systematic teaching being used to facilitate recreational skills in schools?

REFERENCES

Bates, P. & Renzaglia, A. (1979) Community based recreation programs. In P. Wehman (ed.) Recreation Programming for Developmentally Disabled Persons. Baltimore: University Park Press

Cheseldine, S.E. & Jeffree, D.M. (1981) Mentally handicapped adolescents: their use of leisure. Journal of Mental Deficiency Research, 25, 49-59

Cheseldine, S.E. & Jeffree, D.M. (1982) Mentally handicapped adolescents: a survey of abilities. Special Education: Forward Trends (research supplement), 9, 19-23

Clarke, A.M. & Clark, A.D.B. (1976) Early Experience: Myth and Evidence. London: Open Books

Cunningham, C.C. & Jeffree, D.M. (1971) Working with Parents: Developing a Workshop Course for

Parents of Young Mentally Handicapped Children.
Manchester: National Society for Mentally
Handicapped Children (North-West Region).
(5th edition, 1979)

Hannam, C. (1980) Parents and Mentally Handicapped
Children, 2nd edition. Harmondsworth: Penguin

Jeffree, D.M. & Cheseldine, S.E. (1982) Pathways to
Independence: a Checklist of Self-Help Activities. London: Hodder & Stoughton

Katz, S. & Yekutiel, E. (1974) Leisure time problems
of mentally retarded graduates of training programmes. Mental Retardation, 12, 54-57

Luckey, R.E. & Shapiro, I.G. (1974) Recreation: an
essential aspect of habilitative programming.
Mental Retardation, 12, 33-45

Marshall, A. (1967) The Abilities and Attainments of
Children Leaving Junior Training Centres.
London: National Association for Mental Health

Mittler, P., Cheseldine, S. and McConachie, H.
(1981) Roles and Needs of Parents of Handicapped Adolescents. Paris: Organisation for
Economic Cooperation and Development (CERI)

National Development Group (1977) Helping Mentally
Handicapped School Leavers. London: DHSS

National Development Group (1978) Helping Mentally
Handicapped People in Hospital. London: DHSS

Nash, J.B. (1953) Philosophy of Recreation and
Leisure. Dubuque, Iowa: William C. Brown

Neale, M.D. (1982) An overview and summary of proceedings. In The Education and Social Integration of Handicapped Children through Recreational Activities, Report of an International
Seminar. Paris: Organisation for Economic Co-
operation and Development

Tizard, J. and Anderson, E. (1978) The Education of
the Handicapped Adolescent: an Interim Report
of the First Phase of the Project. Paris:
Organisation for Economic Cooperation and
Development

Warnock, H.M. (1978) Special Educational Needs.
Report of the Committee of Enquiry into the
Education of Handicapped Children and Young
People. Cmnd. 7212. London: HMSO

DISCUSSION

In opening the discussion of their paper, Dorothy
Jeffree and Sally Cheseldine mentioned that all the
parents they had met in the course of their
research had been very polite and helpful and
willing to answer their questions. They understood

that the investigation might further the improvement
of services for mentally handicapped young people.
However, many voiced feelings of disappointment that
this attention from professionals came too late.

The parents of this generation did not have the
chance to benefit from the kind of services which
currently offer help as early as possible. They did
not have the chance to get used to working with professionals. Possibly as a result of this, many did
not make use of opportunities that were available to
them; for example, few of the parents in the survey
ever attended meetings of the Parent Teacher Association of their child's school.

Even though the actual number of severely ment-
all handicapped school-leavers is small (estimated
at 4 or 5 per 100,000 total population per year)
preparation and planning for this critical period
are very unsatisfactory. We still do not often
arrange multidisciplinary assessments and plans for
the teenagers' future after leaving school. In
order to meet their needs better, families must have
information about the options which are open, perhaps through 'Careers Conventions' and 'Leisure Conventions', bringing together teachers, staff of
adult services and of colleges of further education,
social workers, parents and the mentally handicapped
adolescents themselves.

Dorothy Jeffree emphasised the importance for
the good practice of professionals of learning from
collaboration with parents. Yet this must be temp-
ered with common sense: 'making relationships with
parents' obviously takes time because making
relationships with people takes time. Professionals
must also learn to judge when they are adding unduly
to the pressures on parents, by raising expectations
of the parental role.

Professionals will sometimes be faced with the
problem of conveying to parents their assessment
that the adolescent is being kept more dependent
than necessary by the parents' handling. Parents
may not feel able to provide opportunities for the
young person to practice skills of independence and
self-reliance. Such pressures may result in residential placement for the young person, because the
family feels they cannot cope any longer, rather
than the move being undertaken in a positive framework. In discussion, the consensus was that it
should be possible to avoid problems of conflicting
interests and views if appropriate steps are taken
long before the situation arises. Such action
would include the fuller provision of information,

and opportunities to discuss issues with other parents and with professionals.

Chapter 12
NEEDS OF PARENTS OF ADULTS
Pauline Fairbrother

The 35 year old son of a member of my local MENCAP
society died recently. Many parents of my generation, and many mentally handicapped people also,
attended the funeral. Everyone, of course, was very
sad, not only for the death of Peter, but for his
parents in their obvious grief. But the thing that
struck me most forcibly was what many parents said
to me. They said how sad it was "...but...he's
safe. At least John and Pat haven't got to worry
about what will happen to Peter when they are gone."
There was even a touch of envy in their voices.
What a terrible indictment of a society that drives
parents to wish that they outlive their son or
daughter! We know that we can fight for their
rights and protect them whilst we are alive, but we
have no guarantee of what is going to happen to our
children when we are no longer here.

THE FUTURE

When my daughter Diana was born 31 years ago, what
was going to happen to their mentally handicapped
child when they were dead was the greatest worry of
all parents. It is still our greatest worry today
and our biggest unsolved problem.
       Parents have, in the UK, tried to help them-
selves. They have tried to make their son or
daughter financially secure through Trusteeship and
Trust schemes, but even some of these are threatened
by recent government legislation. By far the best
guarantee is MENCAP'S Homes Foundation, which enables parents to leave property and money and form
Housing Associations that attract government and
local authority funds and guarantee a place to live
and people who care for their children[1]. This has
the weakness that it ultimately depends to a large

extent on money being available from national and
local government sources; even then, it can only
bring security to a fairly small proportion of mentally handicapped people.

So, this most agonising problem depends always
on the support of professionals and legislators,
public money and the concern and encouragement of
the man and woman in the street.

Many countries, including the UK, have Advocacy
schemes. Advocates are trained to guard the rights
and the quality of life of those individual mentally
handicapped people who are without families. But
these advocates are volunteers, with all the disadvantages of volunteers. They cannot be ordered to
do something, many drop out for personal reasons and
we can't get enough of them to meet the need.

So none of these many schemes, good as they
are, can fully relieve parents' anxieties about the
future. Only two things can do that:

1.   Existing services for education, training
      and therapy must be so good that their son
      or daughter is stretched to the limit.
2.   That there is sufficient residential pro-
      vision to guarantee the most suitable
      accommodation for their son or daughter
      when it is wanted.

CHANGING POLICIES

By the time their son or daughter has reached adulthood, not only have parents gone through their early
struggles but they have had to face the hard facts
of life of adulthood: the sort of work that most
mentally handicapped people are allowed to do; the
fact that their son or daughter is never going to be
completely independent; that they themselves will
never know the fully independent life that most parents of grown-up children enjoy; that their son or
daughter will probably never marry and that there
will be no grandchildren. These are painful things
to come to terms with. But just to come to terms
with these problems is not enough: it is the point
where working together really starts. We all need
to examine our attitudes, explore new ways of looking at things and maybe change our philosophy more
quickly. If parents and professionals do this together, we may speed up the whole process of change.

It is not easy to drop one's natural protectiveness once a handicapped child grows into an adult.
We never completely achieve it; but then we continue

to feel some elements of protectiveness towards our normal sons and daughters once they too are adults. Nevertheless, to a greater or lesser degree, we do manage to accept their adulthood and their need for some independence. But we are thrown back to our protective role if either the possibility for their development as adults is thwarted because of attitudes or lack of training or facilities, or if we feel that they are being pushed into situations for which we believe they are not ready. If they are not able to continue their education into adulthood, if they are not able to find work in the community, if the only place for them to lead independent lives is in a subnormality hospital or an institutional hostel, then we are back fighting for them, protecting them from a hostile world which rejects them.

What areas do parents and professionals need to explore?

The Value of Work

Firstly, we must talk about work. We live in a society that values paid work. We value academic achievement, monetary success and status. Work fulfilment, developing the human being into a happy, well adjusted, sociable person is only an afterthought. Maybe we should start viewing work for mentally handicapped people in this way. As education for fulfilled adulthood involves the whole life and not just the hours spent at a training centre or workshop, parents and professionals must truly be partners once the philosophy is agreed upon.

Teaching Programmes

How much should parents be involved in training programmes whether they be physical, educational or training towards independence? I believe that they should only be involved if they are happy and comfortable in that involvement. They should be involved in decisions on setting goals and they should be made aware of the methods of teaching involved.

If speech therapy is being given, then the family must know how and what is being taught so that they can encourage better communication in their everyday family life. This does not mean that they should feel obliged to sit down every day for half an hour doing what the speech therapist does. If crossing roads is the skill being taught, then the families can encourage them to try out this task whenever they have occasion to cross a road. This way of co-operating will not only give the mentally

handicapped person confidence, but it will give confidence to the rest of the family that he or she is
capable of mastering these skills. By giving
encouragement, parents must reinforce the training
or teaching programme in everyday life. We must not
strive so hard with parents to make them into
teachers and therapists that they have no time left
to be the one thing that they are most valuable at
doing, being parents.

Given real co-operation, with parents feeling
comfortable and valued and equal members of the
team, then goals that are set, targets that are
aimed for must come as the result of honest discussion where in the end everyone agrees that those
goals are attainable. No parent wants to see their
offspring pushed into a situation that they feel
they cannot handle. Too often decisions are made
and training is carried on without any consultation
with the parents and quite often the parents are
left in complete ignorance of what is happening.
The parents, when they are told, may have no information which can give them confidence in their son's
or daughter's capability to achieve the goals set.
This not only makes it more difficult for the mentally handicapped person to achieve success, but also
it leaves the parents feeling helpless and frightened at the situation which is apparently out of their
control. Decisions and programme planning must be
arrived at and agreed on together.

Independence for Parents
In the past, the situation of parents and professionals preparing mentally handicapped people to lead
independent lives has rarely arisen; if parents did
keep their mentally handicapped son or daughter at
home, they usually stayed there until the parents
became incapable of caring for them or one or both
parents died. But for at least the last 20 years
there has been a growing feeling amongst parents
that they have rights. One of these rights is their
right to lead lives independent of their children
once they have become adults.

Life becomes very restricted if you have a
mentally handicapped adult relative at home with you.
Your social life shrivels, friends stop inviting you
to visit them. Your holidays are restricted to
those suitable for your relative and your financial
situation is probably affected. Mothers find difficulty in going out to work, because problems arise
when their child is ill, or needs to go to the
doctor, the dentist, the chiropodist, the hairdresser

and the clothes shops. Life is different from the
life enjoyed by your contemporaries. All this would
possibly be acceptable if it truly helped the mentally handicapped person, but they know their lives
are restricted also. They can not go out on their
own, they are lonely. Normality for both parents
and offspring is leaving the family home, seeking
independence, on reaching adulthood. Parents'
rights and the rights of mentally handicapped people
do not conflict; they are in harmony.

I remember many years ago speaking to a group
of parents about the fact that parents had rights
too. An elderly mother of an adult mentally handicapped daughter came up to me, put her arms around
me and started to cry. "Thank you", she said, "for
saying out aloud what I had always felt, but was always guilty about having such selfish thoughts."
That guilt should not be allowed to develop; however,
it is often fed by well-meaning professionals and
legislators. Recently, I had a letter from my
Member of Parliament replying to a letter from me on
the plight of mentally handicapped people in hospitals. He felt that the solution lay in the hands of
parents: they should visit their children more
often; they should have them home. That was adding
guilt upon guilt - and this was from a responsible
law maker.

The Rights of Adults
I talked earlier of the rights of mentally handicapped people and parents being in harmony. But
sometimes the fact that they are really similar is
not recognised by parents because the parents have
not understood, for a variety of reasons, that they
should be part of the team. The only right that
they are interested in is the right to protect their
mentally handicapped son or daughter. As a result
of this attitude the mentally handicapped person's
rights may be being denied. This situation must
obviously not be allowed to continue and the rights
of the mentally handicapped person must take priority and be jealously guarded. But it must always be
recognised that the reasons behind the attitude of
the parents are rarely selfish or deliberately ob-
structive. Their attitudes have grown out of love
for their son or daughter. It is quite likely that
professionals have not approached them in the right
way, and have not taken their feelings and anxieties into account. We must never give up seeking
their co-operation and approval and support, even if
for the moment, decisions have to be taken contrary

to the wishes of the parents. But we must be absolutely sure, before such a drastic step is taken,
that if we did not take that step more harm would be
done to the mentally handicapped person concerned
than the harm that will be done by flouting the
parents' wishes.

Sexual Needs
It is time for us to talk together about the sexual
needs of mentally handicapped people. Parents have
many anxieties about these needs. But because both
parents and professionals are human beings with
sexual experiences and sexual attitudes, good and
bad, discussions on this subject should be on a
truly equal basis. It will not be productive if
professionals call a meeting of parents to discuss
the parents' attitudes, and intend just to help the
parents. Professional attitudes needs to be examined also.
        Discussions on sexual attitudes and needs have
to be planned carefully. Small groups in relaxing
surroundings are essential. I believe that the best
person to lead the discussion is a parent, preferably a mother, because a parent can say things to
both parents and professionals that will not be rejected by either on the grounds of, "What does he/
she know about it?" I also believe that a parent
can talk about sex with more warmth and humour. A
professional, because of his or her profession, has
to view it more clinically and with less humour.
Sexual intercourse is only a part of our sexual
needs. We should discuss what we believe are the
sexual needs of severely mentally handicapped people
whom we know and the relationships which they form.
Perhaps we can then modify or better still banish
some of our fears that every kiss and cuddle will
inevitably lead to bed and sexual intercourse.
        Do we allow relationships to develop or do we
intervene because, in our judgement, they are unsuitable relationships, or we are worried because of
what they might lead to? Remember that we are talking about people who, because of the severity of
their handicap, are never alone. They are never
allowed to pursue close personal relationships, because they need to be alone with the other person
for this relationship to flourish. How often are
they allowed to learn how to relate to other people,
to make mistakes and to learn from them? How often
have we said on seeing two people petting," I know
that it is nice, but not on the coach (or at the club
or in the workshop). It is not socially acceptable"

(or words to that effect)? Do we ever ask ourselves where and when it *is* socially acceptable? What are people's sexual rights?

We need to discuss marriage between severely mentally handicapped people and their having children. Have they ever been exposed to the reality of a baby or have they a starry-eyed view on babies? If they are not, in our opinion, capable of independent living and the responsibilities of marriage, are they then to be excluded from loving, intimate relationships?

Finally, we must discuss how we should help mentally handicapped people understand their bodies, their emotions and their relationships.

Helping mentally handicapped people understand and develop their sexuality should be a joint programme. Parents and professionals have distinctive and separate roles to fulfill, but these roles will only be fulfilled if they are carefully worked for together.

Death and Bereavement
One further thing that we need to talk about together and help each other about is death. We handle it very badly with mentally handicapped people. We don't prepare them for the death of people whom they love. We shut them out from mourning because we think we are protecting them from hurt. Very often, with the sudden death of a parent comes, for the first time, removal to an institution or hostel, a strange place with strange people.

The subject of death can, like sex, be very painful to talk about. In discussing both topics it is necessary to look at our own feelings first and then to look at the problem in relation to mentally handicapped people.

Preparing mentally handicapped people for the death of their parents must mean preparing them for living an independent life. To lead an independent life they must have training, they must have a fulfilling occupation, they must be able to satisfy their sexual needs and, most important, they must have a suitable place to live.

That brings me back to where I started. The overwhelming need of parents is for a guarantee of security for their sons or daughters. Until parents have that guarantee they will go on wishing to outlive their mentally handicapped son or daughter.

CONCLUSION

Parents need to feel that all they have learned from
having a mentally handicapped son or daughter, all
the years of experience, all the years of achieving
professionalism have not been wasted, that they are
recognised and used. Parents, particularly of adult
mentally handicapped people, have a lot to offer, on
equal terms with other professionals. Frequently
only lip service is paid to the parents' role in the
team. I recently heard a paediatrician stating that
when parents are invited to talk about their child
with the professional team, the team, after discussing the case in private, should break up into standing, chatting groups before the parents are invited
it. In this way the parents will not come into an
already-seated group and will feel more at ease as
they all take their seats together. Why was all
this necessary? Why were they discussing the child
without the parents being present? That is giving
the lie to their stated belief that parents are an
important, some say the most important, part of the
team.
      Parents and professionals can only give
strength to each other through mutual respect and a
spirit of true equality.

NOTES

      1.   Information on all these schemes can be
obtained from MENCAP, 123 Golden Lane, London
EClY ORT.

DISCUSSION

In discussion, Pauline Fairbrother reaffirmed the
potential value of the experience and skills of parents of adult mentally handicapped people both for
professionals and for parents of younger children.
Many parents want to share their experiences and to
feel that their knowledge can be used in planning
services, in solving practical problems and in
giving emotional support to others. Sharing the
information they have gathered can benefit themselves too, feeling that they are contributing to
today's better services rather than feeling bitter
that they did not have such provision when their own
child was growing up.
      There was considerable discussion of the diffi-
culties in realising a 'normal' life-style for mentally handicapped adults. Pauline Fairbrother felt

that the concept of 'normalisation' required much greater discussion than at present between professionals and parents in order to avoid the adoption of inappropriate aims. For example, 'normalisation' should not result in highly abnormal pressures on parents and siblings, nor should the handicapped person be made unhappy.

Mentally handicapped people have, as any other adults do, a right to independence and privacy; a right to choose eg. what to wear or where to go on holiday; and a need to be away from their parents at least some of the time. But on the other hand, they need help to achieve these things. In many cases, the skills required to cope with the everyday demands of living in the community can be taught, if there is cooperation between parents and professionals and if a relatively consistent environment is provided in which to exercise these skills.

However, parents very often are uneasy about the idea of their son or daughter living away from home. Philippa Russell pointed out that it will mean a change in, and perhaps a loss, of close relationships for both the handicapped person and the other members of the family. Henri Bissonnier raised the question of how the relationship between the family and residential care staff (of whatever level of supervisory responsibility) is managed, and how the responsibilities of the family are conceptualised in the case of an adult mentally handicapped person.

Parents' reluctance to 'put their child away' may arise from a lack of suitable alternative provision, from a lack of information about alternatives (eg. hostels, group homes), or from a deeply felt moral obligation to care for the handicapped person for as long as possible. The phrase 'putting him/her away' is still often used by parents in discussing the subject. Dorothy Jeffree stated that most parents of teenagers interviewed by the PATH project also rejected short-term care, even if offered simply as preparation for a future time when the parents would no longer be alive. Some parents except or have arranged that another of their children will take over the care of the mentally handicapped person, although the sibling may have promised while not really welcoming the responsibilities.

Ensuring that families have information about alternatives, and real choice, will greatly improve the chances of mentally handicapped people being able to live as fully in accordance with their potentialities as possible.

SECTION SIX: DISCUSSION AND FOLLOW-UP

Chapter 13

EXAMPLES OF PARTNERSHIP IN EUROPE

Helen McConachie

LANGUAGE AND PERSPECTIVES

Fundamental to the rationale for the European
Seminar was the appreciation that participants from
different countries would approach our discussion
from a variety of perspectives. In learning of
others' experiences, we would be enabled to see our
own more clearly. Our discussion revealed interesting differences in past and current relationships
between professionals and parents of handicapped
children and several participants wrote vivid
accounts of their experiences. This chapter is
drawn from those experiences.

Gugu Kristoffersen from *Denmark* directly tackled the
issues underlying how differing experiences are described, ie. how we perceive our experiences and how
we describe them through the imperfect medium of
language. An appreciation of such issues helps to
clarify some of the ways in which parents and professionals may fail to communicate even when
attempting to do so.

"When preparing myself for the seminar I had
piles of books and articles around me, and I thought
to myself how much has been written and discussed,
and how experts of various kinds have shared their
information.

The very first seminar I attended ten years
ago was the International League of Societies for
the Mentally Handicapped Seminar in Copenhagen on
"Cooperation between parents and staff". Another
report arrived just days ago, a UNESCO report on
Early Detection, Intervention and Education. In the years
in between, transdisciplinary initiatives have produced hundreds of pages of *words, words, words*. I
thought to myself, will *we* manage to boil down our
experiences to a few crystal clear sentences, worth

passing on to politicians, parents, care-workers, the public - and will one or two ideas inspire researchers?

We parents need research badly: sometimes statistics can persuade politicians. When mothers are actively speaking or writing, their messages are seen through a stereotype of the mother-child bond that to most people will mean not only love, but mercy and overprotection. What do professionals think of parents? I think an investigation would show a colourful picture and, I am sad to say, not a very true picture. An active parent is often not listened to, dismissed with 'She is not typical!' I would like to see some research in this area.

As family patterns and constellations change, it is important for us to be particularly open to what is happening in society. *The last to enjoy progress in a society are handicapped persons.* One present trend is that women want to 'realize themselves' - maybe fewer mothers want to stay at home. Also the economic situation is such that the family cannot exist on one person's salary. We need to discuss these issues when considering home-visiting services.

Another trend in society is that fathers are being drawn into the lives of little children much more than before. It is generally accepted that fathers are present at the birth of their children, that they take part to a greater extent in the changing of nappies, playing, feeding etc. This trend is a good trend which will benefit handicapped children also - and mothers.

Some even suggest that this trend will make itself felt in political decisions in times to come; in questions about war and peace; in higher priorities for families with children, for kids on bicycles in comparison with motorways, etc.

I would like to explore the problem of language. We use a lot of words, but are we talking about the same things? We must choose our words and make sure we are being understood. For example, how do we pass on research results in plain language to those who need the information? We must make 'translations', rewrite and perhaps rediscover. Researchers need a dialogue with parents who can contribute greatly with examples from their experience, etc. Both parties will understand more.

Personally, I feel torn between my usual colourful subjective way of expressing myself as a mother, and the dull, cool, objective way I struggle to learn and use for reports as a student of education.

An even greater language problem is that of professional *secrecy*. If we do not share information, we cannot cooperate. If the care-worker knows everything about me, and I know nothing about him or her, it will never be a genuine, relaxed cooperation. Parents are sensitive to professional jealousy. Professionals have their different roles, but parents have no uniform, no set role. They are problem-solvers, and so are part parents, and part social workers, care-workers, physiotherapists, speech therapists. Thus, they have difficulty in understanding the fencing-in of little parts of the problem.

As a practical example of exploring roles and language, I have often asked for parent instructors at training-colleges for care-workers - not just a parent asked to give a lecture once a year on a certain topic, but parents' perspectives reflected in every part of the curriculum.

Also, in Denmark, there is a growing awareness of the problems of guest workers' families. How can we identify children who need help early? How do we overcome language and religious barriers, ignorance, discrimination? Practical, social and cultural problems piled on top of each other.

When looking at early stimulation, it is important to see the first two or three years in perspective. They are part of the whole, crucial not only for the child but also for the lifelong attitudes of the parents and for any later co-operation with the services. For fifteen years I have been tackling problems essential to the understanding of early stimulation: *early* stimulation of parents, of children, of staff; *eternal* stimulation of politicians and the public."

EARLY INTERVENTION

Our discussion in the seminar of what kinds of early help are most appropriate for children and for families was furthered by hearing about a *Belgian* example of close cooperation between parents and a professional. *Lucienne van Loon* described the centre for early support to families with preschool mentally handicapped children in which she works with *Claudine van Malderen*, who also attended the Seminar.

"In contrast to most of the existing services, our centre was started by parents, all members of the National Association for the Mentally Handicapped, who already met as a self-support group. Although we largely succeeded in helping parents,

we gradually became aware that to attempt to meet
all needs, we had to engage a professional
(Claudine van Malderen, a 'pedagogue'). Unfortunately, being the first ones to start a service
centre in this way has meant that, up to now, we
have not had any government funds, and we work on a
voluntary basis. However, in the near future,
similar service centres will be set up all over the
country, and recent contact with the government has
led us to hope that they will be state-aided.

We started our centre four years ago, and
during that period well over seventy families have
attended. Our team is composed of the pedagogue and
a so-called 'key-parent'. The reason why we included a parent in the team is that no one can
sympathize with parents of a handicapped child as
well as another parent of a handicapped child. We
have had the same griefs, the same disappointments,
the same guilt feelings, the same negative feelings
towards our child. I can assure you that it gives
great relief to talk freely with a fellow parent
about those emotions and to realize at the same time
that you are not the only one to have them. In
addition, the newly affected parents can learn from
the key-parent's experiences with her own child and
especially that, although life with a handicapped
child has problems, these are not so insuperable as
it seems at first.

The early intervention we provide aims to meet
the specific needs of each family. Therefore, we
offer several kinds of help:

- emotional support;
- realistic and genuine information about the
  handicap;
- documentation;
- information about other existing services;
- early intervention programmes;
- educational advice;
- information about social rights and help in
  getting allowances.

Thus, we offer a choice of services for the parents,
the handicapped child and the siblings, but we never
force them to make use of any of them. Our experience has shown that each family has its specific
needs, expectations and problems and does not
necessarily make use of all the offered services.

When families visit the centre, the key-parent
welcomes them and makes them feel at ease as much as
possible and also tries to be a link between them.

while they all chat together and drink a cup of
coffee, each family in its turn visits the pedagogue
in a separate consulting-room. Ms van Malderen
evaluates the child's development, using standardized tests. The parents have a great deal to contribute to making the assessment, by giving information about their child. According to the results,
Ms van Malderen explains what is to be expected as
the next step forward in the child's total development and she demonstrates how the parents can
stimulate the child by playing adapted games. At
the same time she stresses the meaning and the
importance of the games, so that the parents are
motivated to play at home with the child. She also
writes down notes so that the parents can easily
remember what was suggested. We feel it is very
valuable in encouraging positive attitudes in the
parents for the professional to play in an enthusiastic way with the child. During the consultation,
which usually lasts between one and one and a half
hours Ms van Malderen will also invite the parents
to talk about other problems, for example, difficulties with siblings.

Our first aim is that parents should be reassured that they can cope with the education of
their handicapped child. The interval between consultations is fixed in such a way that each time
parents can see progress in development of the
child. Apart from the consultations, the parents
are always welcome to drop in for a chat, and they
can also ring us at any time. After the child has
gone to school, parents can still call upon us whenever they need to.

We have chosen to have a team of one professional and one key-parent for each family in order to
create a confidential relationship which will help
to establish a clear view of the family's special
needs and problems. The importance of the key-
parent is evidenced in the kinds of questions parents ask her; meeting other parents increases
"comfort, solidarity, practical advice and general
support" (Russell, Chapter 2, this volume). Besides
the working of the centre, the association provides
parent contacts in organizing play-groups for the
children, discussion groups, conferences with a
guest speaker, etc.

We are well aware that we cannot solve all the
problems. When specific therapies are indicated, we
introduce the parents to professionals of another
discipline. By preference we suggest professionals
who accept the parents as co-educators."

STRUCTURE OF SERVICES

The Belgian parents' group had challenged the usual
structure of services by being the ones to hire the
professional worker. Other ways in which parents
have influenced services into becoming more responsive to individual families' situations were described by *Erica Lund* and *Henrik Pelling* from *Sweden*.

"Parents' organizations have influenced the
creation of new forms of cooperation between professionals and parents. The earlier form of centering attention around mothers has been widened to include fathers. Very often this type of cooperation
can be created when both parents, and to a certain
degree even brothers and sisters, take part in receiving information after the handicap has first
been diagnosed. When the first crisis has become a
general concern for *all* family members, it will be
easier for every one to participate in caring for
the handicapped child. A division of labour where
the mother mainly takes care of the handicapped
child, and the father concentrates on helping the
brothers and sisters, can naturally function well
in many cases, but the model can show itself to be
weak, since the mother is a bit too alone in her
involvement in a very difficult task.

Every individual and every family is unique,
and therefore it is important that contacts be
limited to a few professionals who get to know the
family well. Organized parent groups for different
types of handicap have together influenced the coordination of the various facilities of the society.
A special organization entitled 'child habilitation'
is being developed at present for this purpose. In
this organization each family will have a 'contact' person whose main role will be to support the
family, coordinate resources, and help as an inter-
mediary, in terms of information from different experts. This 'contact' person can belong to any of
several occupational groups: physical therapists,
psychologists, social workers, for example. In this
way it will be easier for the specialists to concentrate on their own tasks, be it speech therapy,
medical help etc. The 'contact' person will be able
to help the specialists cooperate among themselves,
as it is he or she who is most able to survey the
individual family's needs and resources."

PARENTAL RELUCTANCE?

The description of the Belgian parents' group

aroused great interest, particularly as several seminar participants cited 'parental reluctance' as an obstacle in the way of creating partnership. For example, *Bob van Zijderveld* described the situation in the *Netherlands*.

"In preparation for the seminar, two meetings were held of a small group of parents and professionals. Our impression is that in Holland parents do not often become involved in systematic educational programmes. Dutch families seem to be concerned in the first place with providing their children with security and a warm emotional climate in the home and family (ideally, that is!). They are not very eager to become involved in the education of their children in day-centres, kindergartens and schools. For example, a mother told a social worker she was afraid to answer the telephone, because it might be the day-centre asking her to join a coffee-morning. Apparently, parents often do not like the confrontation with other handicapped children, and see their own situation as unique.

It is our experience that parents in Holland are less interested than parents in Britain and some other countries in contributing directly to what they consider to be the field of professionals: they leave to the professionals responsibility for the development of educational programmes. They expect the experts to know the solution to any problem, to train the child and to work systematically on its psychological education."

The Dutch description of parental lack of involvement in educational programmes was couched mainly in terms of parents' personal emotional feelings. However *Sonja Barthel*, a teacher from *West Germany*, saw the issue more in terms of traditional attitudes toward the teacher's role.

"For parents, professionals generally signify 'authority'. When they were children the teacher was a person to be obeyed and never contradicted. The expectations parents have of a teacher's role are generally associated with 'performance' or 'achievement'. Can this attitude be changed? Do teachers always want to be looked on as an authority? Do they make excessive demands on their pupils?

In my experience, it is not the teachers who do this, but the parents! The majority of parents are of the opinion that their child should have at least as good a life as they do, that their sort of standard of living can only be reached by way of a good education, and that this can only be obtained with the aid of the teacher. In principle, parents by-pass the abilities and needs of the child when they take this attitude."

Christoph Hublow, also from *West Germany*, balanced this description by stressing the influence of teachers' traditional attitudes towards parents that teachers have the answer to every question whether or not they have been asked. He also expanded the point about the nature of parental expectations of 'a good education'.

"German parents generally tend to put very great emphasis on their children's learning the '3 Rs', whereas they do not fully acknowledge the value of practical skills. In the case of severely handicapped children, who are really unable to learn any abstract skills, cooperation between teachers and parents may become very difficult."

He also raised the point that many parents - perhaps tending to be the younger, more progressive ones - are now reluctant to cooperate with special schools, "despite the fact that these schools were founded and established according to and because of parents' wishes and concepts, 10 or 20 years ago. They argue that special schools hinder the process of social integration of handicapped children, and are convinced that their children could learn more if they were allowed to go to normal schools. Many of them refer to the Italian school-system "(which become fully integrated in 1975).

Thus, rather than parents being 'reluctant', they may in fact be asserting a different viewpoint from professionals on their children's education. The *Swedish* participants also challenged professional assumptions that parents should be heavily involved in their children's education.

"Voluntary organizations in Sweden have succeeded in making society responsible for support and aid, which for each handicapped child should mean that he or she receives the greatest opportunity possible to be integrated into normal life. In practical terms, this means integration in schools, integration in ordinary living areas, supplemented with the necessary supervision, and adoption of places of work for the handicapped. When these measures are taken, there is a less negative influence on the social life of the family with a handicapped child.

One important thing is that direct parental assistance in treatment or training programmes in nursery schools, regular schools, boarding schools etc. is no longer necessary. Instead, parents have the freedom to choose how much time they wish to spend on their child's training programme and day-care. In essence, the parents' responsibility for training of new abilities has now been transferred to professionals. The parents' task is to provide the best possible environment in a socially intact family, in which the handicapped child can best use his or her new abilities."

Several of the themes described above as contributing to difficulties in the relationship between parents and teachers - parents' seeing education as solely the responsibility of teachers, fear of challenging authority, placing high value on academic skills - were clearly illustrated in the history of a *German* working partnership presented by *Sonja Barthel and Renate Börner*, from which extracts are given below.

PARENT AND TEACHER

Renate Börner's son, Andreas, contracted a virus in-infection at the age of 15 months and suffered brain damage as a result.

"From the beginning I took part in physical and speech training exercises with Andreas and found out myself how severe his handicap was and what an effort he had to make. When he entered the preliminary class of the special school for educationally subnormal children, I was very disappointed with the type of education he received. In the class 25 children, ranging from those with mild to those with severe learning difficulties, were given two hours of instruction daily. The teaching involved only academic skills. The children had to sit at desks and write out numbers and letters of the alphabet. It was frightful. One girl with Down's syndrome copied out English texts, although she could neither talk nor recognise any of the letters. Some of the children were hyperactive, and for them having to sit still was next to impossible. Every one of the children showed uneasiness, evidenced in such behaviours as burying their heads in their arms or hanging on the doorpost so as not to have to enter the classroom.

The teacher was quite unable to meet our queries and reservations with understanding. He perceived our concerns as an attack on his authority. As a group of those united by the same fate, we parents eventually found the strength to do something about the unsatisfactory conditions.

Together with some of the staff from the local

Teacher Training College, we founded an action group to set up a remedial facility, and had 24 children tested to assess their mental handicap, and to establish their claim to a different form of schooling. By 1972 we had reached our goal and 55 children entered the new facility. During the time in which the facility was being built, we had worked out a conceptual basis for the children's instruction with the college staff, teachers and 'educators'. ('Educators' have trained to work in kindergartens; in special schools they generally teach social, musical and practical skills.)

As a result of the good liaison within the group, the discussions, the frankly stated opinions and the bad experience with schooling which lay behind us, we decided that no academic skills would initially be taught in the day facility, although some parents found this decision difficult to accept. My son had been attending a Rudolf Steiner boarding school in southern Germany, and I participated in the life of his school and the instruction there for two or three days every four weeks. However, after some years, he increasingly expressed the desire to live at home with his brothers and sisters. As we missed him just as much, we decided to bring him home again, where he joined Frau Barthel's class."

Sonja Barthel gave us an account of her experiences as a teacher up to this time. She had taught in a school for educationally subnormal children, and then moved to the school for mentally handicapped children. As a trained teacher, she came under pressure from parents' expectations that their children would acquire academic skills.

"As I had never worked with children with an IQ under 60 before, I took over the parents' expectations and tried to build up a system which would allow the children to recognise words and letters and to understand and reproduce them. Slowly and with a good deal of effort some of the children did manage to recognise letters of the alphabet. However, as progress was so slow, the parents made it clear to me that the children should also have homework. Although I did not think it was necessary, as the children were at school from 8 a.m. until 3 p.m., and often had an hour's travelling time, I did give them homework. Interest in learning new things dropped off considerably in some children, until I found out that the parents were treating their handicapped children as they did their other children; for instance, pages of work

which had been completed would be torn up and had to
be written or painted again, because they were not
'neat' or 'tidy' enough.

In the meantime, however, I had begun to have
insight into the ability of each child in my class.
I began discussions with the parents, and, unfortunately, I found myself in the same frustrating
position as that in which I had been with the parents in other schools. Only a few of them were able
to see me as an equal partner. The image of the
teacher which they had assumed in their childhood
prevented them from seeing me as anything other than
an 'authority'. The meetings usually ended with the
parents' accepting my observations and suggestions
without comment, although I noticed that there were
things that they were not really happy about. Many
of them considered that their children had a greater
ability to learn than I described. To a certain extent they were right, for each child in my class had
practical abilities and could in some way or other
be approached by way of musical activities. Many a
child who could hardly speak could find his or her
way around the town and the shops, and enjoyed
weaving, painting or handicrafts. My aim was to
foster these abilities, but, sadly, this was not
enough for many parents; the 'tools of culture'
were more important to them.

I then had a piece of luck in that the child
of one of the founders of our institution joined my
class. The broadmindedness of Andreas's mother,
who accepts her son's handicap, and recognises his
limits, helped the other parents in the class to
see their children as they are and not as they
would like them to be. Frau Börner encouraged parents to visit the classes and take part in educational walks, etc. This means that the parents experience their child in the community with the
others in the class, and, as a result, they are
much more able to accept his or her capabilities.

It was natural for Frau Börner and me to
discuss everything we noticed about Andreas,
whether it was positive or negative. Together we
tried to find ways to build up the positive aspects
and minimise the negative ones."

Renate Börner then described the next stages
in the life of the school.

"In our class group of mothers (fathers
usually were occupied elsewhere), teacher and educators, there was a frank and friendly atmosphere.
In some groups, however, the atmosphere was no
longer good, because the teachers had assumed too

great an influence.

This started to develop in 1976, when it became obligatory for mentally handicapped children to attend school. (In the West German federal system, different parts of the country organize school-systems differently, and brought in a compulsory education law at different times.) The teachers, who had previously been paid by the Ministry for Social Affairs, took a second examination after some time, and were then employed by the Ministry of Education as teachers in special schools for the mentally handicapped. We wished to see a continuation of our model, drawn from experience, that teachers and educators have equally important roles to play in the training of the children.

Sadly, the new kind of school, which is, by law, more tightly organised than before, led to the teachers gaining the upper hand. There was no more equality; the educators increasingly took on the role of assistants. As a result the parents fell back into their usual behaviour towards school - the teacher is an authority, only addressed when problems crop up, one does not dare to discuss anything, because the teacher, being an expert, knows everything better anyway. The frank and easy 'general assembly' was replaced by the School Conference. As a result, the parents were intimidated and conversations at an equal level were no longer possible.

Frequently the newly arrived teachers did not understand how easily parents of handicapped children, living, as they often do, in permanently overtaxing conditions, can be made to feel unsure of themselves and also feel guilty when the children do not meet the demands made on them.

In summary, it can be said that cooperation between parents and professionals has become more difficult to implement since the new school system was introduced.

If more favourable conditions, such as those Andreas enjoyed, are to be maintained, teachers must recognise that parents of handicapped children need more time and understanding than others do. It is important actually to include them in the instruction the child receives in practical, social and musical skills. This is certainly unusual and requires many meetings with parents, not just the conventional single parents' visit in the year. It means being able to listen, and to take up and work on the observations made by parents and educators. It is only when teachers learn these - at present unconventional - forms of interaction, and when parents grow to understand that, owing to their daily experience with their children, they are themselves experts and certainly have a right to participate equally in the 'schooling' of their children, that a genuine partnership between parents and professionals can result."

Another team of parent and teacher, *Berit Rohmen and Kari Storemyr*, came from *Norway*. They described the ways in which parental involvement in special schools is formally structured there.

"Cooperation between teachers and parents in liaison committees is authorized by law, and every school must establish such a committee. It includes two parents, two teachers, the headteacher, one pupil, one member of the non-teaching staff and one member appointed by the community education authority. The committee's work includes advice and recommendations on the school budget, on educational subjects and on other matters concerning the school society. A subcommittee consisting of three members elected amongst the parents is responsible for arranging meetings, leisure activities like skiing, and other events and projects of a social and informative character."

Kari Storemyr, a teacher in a 60-pupil school, then described how she works with the parents of her pupils.

"I have to arrange two group meetings a year with parents of children in my class. These are usually in the evening and we talk about the curriculum for the year and about the class in general. Twice a year I write reports to the parents about the child, where the main content is the child's progress and social functioning at school. The form of record is the same which we use in school in order to follow up the child.

Twice a year we also arrange case conferences, where the whole staff of professionals is assembled. Parents are not allowed to take part in the conferences, and they do not receive a record of them. However, parents have questioned this, and we are currently discussing including the parents, which I hope will happen soon.

One hour a week is set aside for conferring with parents about matters of mutual concern. I also contact parents regularly by telephone, letters, visits, home-school notebooks and homework.

During each year, I have two meetings at school with each set of parents to discuss the child's work and progress. I feel that I am succeeding in my efforts to build a relationship of trust with most of the parents. We are becoming friends and are able to communicate even if we have different opinions. But it depends, of course, on the parents being willing to collaborate. Collaboration is of great value when parent and teacher work on an equal footing, trying to stimulate the child from different angles.

In Norway, discussion similar to elsewhere is going on, around the argument that the education of handicapped children is highly skilled and has to be carried out by specially trained staff. I agree with this point of view, but stress that active inclusion of parents can enhance the educational opportunities of our children. I regard parent involvement as a necessary part of the total school situation."

Erica Lund and Henrik Pelling echoed their Scandinavian neighbours in stressing the value of parents' and teachers' differing roles, and suggested very positive reasons for this recent emphasis.

"Clearer roles, more detailed and defined, make professionals more aware that parents are specialists at taking care of their particular handicapped child in their family. The reason for more clearly defined roles amongst professional groups such as teachers in special education, physical therapists, psychologists and physicians is largely due to better education. When they are being trained for their respective occupations, they receive more information concerning handicaps, both theoretical and practical. Parents in organized parent groups, because they have received better help from professionals, have been able to place emphasis on the most important question concerning their roles - this question is: 'How can my family, in the best possible way, take care of all family members, including those who are handicapped?'"

ADOLESCENTS AND ADULTS

The two participants from *France, Henri Bissonnier* and *Yvonne de Laval,* made some observations about services after school-age for mentally handicapped people which suggested that immediate needs may have been met there more adequately than in many other countries. Mentally handicapped young people may attend Centres d'Aide par Travail (C.A.T.) which were set up as a preliminary step towards a sheltered workshop, but which do not themselves have a work output, nor do they include specific training. A

218

problem of transfer to sheltered workshops has
arisen in that there are now very few of the latter
for severely mentally handicapped people. Instituts
Medico-Professionels (I.M.Pro.) provide training in
fundamental skills for more able mentally handicapped people up to the age of about 20 years. They
are then expected to find work in ordinary jobs;
there is a legal quota system to aid handicapped
people in gaining employment in France. Other
possible avenues on leaving school include Occupational Homes, and weekly Boarding Schools for
severely mentally handicapped young people aged 16
to 21 years. All of these options give handicapped
adolescents opportunities to meet peers and to make
friends. In addition the Franco-American Volunteers
Association organizes integrated youth clubs and
sports activities.

A feature of these services is group discussion
between parents and staff, who aim to understand and
try to help with the particular problems of this age
group. For example, adolescence may be the time
when young people become acutely aware of their
handicap and its vocational consequences, and they
may need help to develop, retain and bolster their
sense of self-respect. In certain respects, they
will be truly adolescent, for example in developing
sexual interests, and yet at the same time remain
'childish' in cognitive levels and play interests.
Relations with brothers and sisters may become
strained, if they are younger and yet are allowed
greater independence.

As well as supportive discussion, families
will often welcome the opportunity for positive
activities. In France, groups of mentally handicapped adults and their families meet on Sundays
with young people and other families, meeting as
friends to do things together, not *for* the handicapped person.

In France, a greater proportion than in Britain
of mentally handicapped adults are in some kind of
residential accommodation, away from their families'
homes. Professor Bissonnier laid stress on the
problems of expecting siblings to look after a
mentally handicapped brother or sister. "This must
generally be considered as too heavy a burden for
them, particularly when the siblings marry and have
their own children. Furthermore, it is not always
suitable nor reasonable for a mentally handicapped
adult to belong, like a child, to an older or even a
younger brother or sister. 'Looking after' must
instead be understood as having the commitment to

protect and to defend the rights and interests of the handicapped person, not necessarily taking charge of him or her in their own home." The question then arises of how this commitment, and the relationship with care staff, can be best facilitated.

CONCLUSION

The contrasting viewpoints speak for themselves. A strong feeling emerged from the discussion that so many important questions were being raised by our comparing experiences and perspectives that such a Seminar should be perhaps only the first of many. We also realised that our knowledge of and ideas about partnership between professionals and parents of young children were greatly in advance of our understanding of the issues and our knowledge of current examples in the case of adolescents and adult mentally handicapped people. Our planning for the future is described in the next chapter.

REFERENCES

United Nations Educational Scientific and Cultural Organisation (1980) Handicapped Children: Early Detection, Intervention and Education. (ED/MD/63) Paris: UNESCO

Chapter 14

PLANNING FOR FUTURE DEVELOPMENTS

Peter Mittler

ACTION SEMINARS

A seminar or conference is only as good as the results that spring from it. But all too often, this
is left to chance on the assumption that ideas which
have been stimulated by what has been heard either
in the conference or - more often perhaps - in social encounters outside the formal sessions themselves, will somehow lead to new developments. On
this occasion, the seminar organisers made it clear
at the time when invitations were first issued that
participants would be asked to do everything possible to work for short term goals relevant to parent-
professional collaboration in their own countries,
and were asked to think from the outset about ways
in which they might contribute to this, either as
single individuals or in pairs. They were also asked to make suggestions for improvements in parent-
professional relationships, either in their own
country or elsewhere, whether or not these formed
part of their own personal plans.
     The notion of using conferences and seminars as
a catalyst for the development of a local initiative
is beginning to be considered at both national and
international levels. In contrast to meetings where
people come together mainly to listen to 'experts'
or to discuss amongst themselves, the conference is
deliberately organised and planned from the outset
in such a way that participants can plan some form
of implementation after they return to their own
communities.
     Such a model was used in a recent workshop org-
anised in Hong Kong by the International League of
Societies for Persons with Mental Handicap (ILSMH)
with support from the United Nations Fund created
within the framework of the International Year of

Disabled Persons. Thirteen countries from the Asian region were invited to nominate teams of three people - a parent of a mentally handicapped child, a teacher/educator and a community worker. An intensive five day workshop was held in which participants first shared ideas and experiences about their own situations but then worked almost entirely in small groups practising specific methods and techniques of assessment and individual programme planning relevant to teaching handicapped children basic skills, such as movement, activities for daily living and self-care, language and communication and socially appropriate behaviour. A prerequisite for being selected for the workshop was that each 'national team' undertook to develop a realistic goal plan which would lead to measurable improvements in some aspect of their local situation. These goal plans were listed and publicly discussed at the end of the workshop; the extent to which they are actually implemented is being investigated by an independent evaluator who will keep in touch with participants and will visit most of them in their own communities, with the help of funds specially provided for this purpose by the UN (see Mittler and Beasley, 1982, for a full report).

At national level in the U.K., the King's Fund and the Association of Professions for the Mentally Handicapped have held a number of 'action seminars', in which small groups come together to identify a problem, prepare and discuss an action plan for implementation in their own localities and then reconvene some months later in order to share ideas and experiences on their successes and failures. In this way, small teams from different parts of the country can benefit from one another's experiences. Such an approach may help to make conferences and seminars more productive and 'cost effective' at a time when the world-wide economic recession is making it increasingly difficult to organise and fund both international and national conferences.

Accordingly, the final session of the seminar was devoted to a general discussion in which participants briefly discussed their own plans and listed other suggestions which they wished to make. This chapter summarises the plans and the suggestions, but also extends the discussion by considering a number of wider issues concerned with the theme of partnership and lists a number of ways in which the relationships between parents and professionals can be enhanced, as well as some of the obstacles which may impede progress.

GOAL PLANS

Plans reported by participants took a variety of
forms, and were quite properly a reflection of individual needs and local priorities. What is possible
in one community is not necessarily realistic in
another. It was emphasised that the plans should be
capable of realisation in a short period of time and
that the degree to which the plans had been implemented should be objectively measurable. For example, plans to 'modify professional attitudes' cannot easily be judged in terms of outcome, unless
quite concrete or specific criteria for evaluation
can be specified - in which case it would surely be
better to select these as goal plans in the first
place.
    The basic ingredient of a 'goal plan' is that a
specific target for action should be identified, so
that it would be a relatively simple matter to
determine whether or not the target had been
attained. For example, several teams agreed to
write an article on what they had learned from the
seminar or to give talks to both parents and professional associations on a relevant subject. Here
again, as some participants found, it is one thing
to write an article, quite another to have it
accepted for publication.
    A second essential element of a goal plan is
that it should include an action plan setting out a
step-by-step programme on how the goal is to be
reached. If, for example, the goal is to form a
parent-teacher association at a school, the first
step for a parent might be to arrange an appointment
with the headteacher to discuss the subject. Some
tasks need only one step - e.g. making a telephone
call - others may require a number of steps, some of
which may in turn require breaking down into even
smaller steps if they cannot be achieved in one
operation.
    Another element of a goal plan involves the
drawing up of a list of 'strengths' - i.e. the resources which are already available. These might
include one or more like-minded people who can help
in reaching the desired outcome; it can include the
availability of existing policies - for example, a
school may already have formally adopted a policy of
working more closely with parents; but it can also
include one's own personal qualities, even one's
determination to secure a particular goal.
    There are obvious parallels between the drawing
up of an individual goal plan for a particular

223

handicapped student and the development of a goal
plan for the attainment of a particular objective
for a service or for part of a service. In each
case, there needs to be a clear statement of *who* will
do *what, when,* under what *circumstances* and with what
help, and with what *result* - i.e. how can it be known
for certain whether the goal has been achieved?
(For guidance on goal planning, see Georgiades and
Phillimore, 1975; Houts and Scott, 1975; Blunden and
Revill, 1980.)

Exploring and Meeting Local Needs
Many participants felt stimulated and encouraged to
explore ways in which better relationships between
parents and professionals could be developed in
their own local settings. One common way of initi-
ating discussions which was felt to be promising was
to call a meeting to report verbally on the seminar,
to translate or distribute at least some of the pre-
circulated papers, summarise the discussions and to
highlight particular points or examples of collaboration which might be taken up at local level.

     One deputy head teacher decided to call a ser-
ies of parents' meetings to share ideas on ways in
which parents might like to be more involved in the
life of the school; she noted that parents were
often more willing to help in 'normal' activities,
such as sports days, school outings, and to lend a
hand with skills they already had; moreover, some
parents needed help with transport and baby sitting.

     Another suggestion was that schools might
write down their present policies and practice with
respect to parent-professional relationships and
use this as a basis for discussion between parents
and school staff on how they could work more
productively together in the future.

     In Manchester, the School Psychological and
Child Guidance Service had just begun to develop a
questionnaire for each of the City's 28 special
schools in which many specific elements of collaboration were listed. The results of this questionnaire have now been analysed (Mittler, H., 1982)
and are being fed back to the schools, to the parents and to other organisations. It is of particular interest that administration of the questionnaire interview itself appeared to stimulate ideas
and innovations. For example, one head teacher of
a school for mentally handicapped children developed her own questionnaire for parents and visited
each family at home in order to discuss their own
views on ways in which parents and teachers could

work together more effectively and has since implemented several suggestions made by parents. Another
ran a series of evening discussions for teachers and
parents in all the City's special schools. In
addition, the University Centre for the In-service
Education of Teachers organised a series of evening
meetings on Partnership with Parents; these were
attended by teachers from a range of special schools
as well as a small number from ordinary schools. A
few parents also attended, some invited by teachers
in the schools attended by their child. Talks were
given by professionals from various disciplines and
by parents; evaluations at the end of the course indicated that several new initiatives in local
schools had arisen directly from suggestions made
during the course.

The Writing of Reports and Articles
A number of participants thought it would be useful
to write an article, either summarising the content
of the seminar or drawing out implications for
practice in their own country. As an example of the
seminar theme, it was also suggested that articles
could be written jointly by a parent and professional to appear in each others' journals; for
example, a joint article in a parents' journal or a
professional journal might have more impact than one
by either alone, even on the same theme. It was
noted that we would all benefit from changing our
reading and writing habits - 'we like to read what
we already know'.
    In addition to articles which might be written
arising directly from the seminar, it would also be
useful to write articles illustrating examples of
collaboration between professionals and parents,
either in their own country or locality or elsewhere. It was felt that while there was much talk
about partnership, too little was known about actual
practice. It was also important to reflect the wide
variety of practice which had been illustrated in
the seminar and which had surprised some of its members. For example, it was useful to be reminded
that despite the general agreements that partnership
was a desirable goal, a different view was reflected
by the Dutch and Swedish participants of preferring
to leave teaching to teachers.
    As a supplementary suggestion, it was also
pointed out that photographs, films and videotapes
illustrating parent-professional collaboration would
be a useful resource and could complement written
and spoken accounts of particular schemes.

225

Inviting Professionals to Parents' Meetings

Inviting professionals to parents' meetings was also commended. Parent groups could occasionally invite professionals to discuss aspects of their work at parents' meetings and to take part in discussion. For example, it was felt that some parents had incorrect or partially out-of-date views on the work of specific professional groups and perhaps tended to exaggerate their expertise and skills. Speech therapy was mentioned as a case in point: some parents still feel that speech therapists are qualified primarily to correct defects of articulation, whereas their role has greatly broadened during the past ten years. Not only are they concerned with all aspects of language and communication (including non-verbal methods such as signing and symbol systems), but also with pre-speech activities and even with methods of feeding children who cannot yet feed themselves and they are increasingly working through teachers and parents as intermediaries. In other words, they (like other specialists) are moving towards the model of a 'consultant' rather than exclusively as 'clinicians' working with individual children.

Similarly, it would be useful to be able to discuss ways in which the work of psychologists is moving away from individual intelligence testing towards the development of assessment of strengths and weaknesses and the designing of an individual programme for each child. Most important of all, parents would welcome opportunities to hear about developments in the education of mentally handicapped children - whether these concern content and curriculum or new methods of teaching.

Discussion also highlighted the importance of providing information about the range of services available to children at later stages of development; for example, the survey of families of mentally handicapped school leavers (Chapter 11) had shown that parents knew very little about the adult services to which their children were about to move or about ways in which these services had been developing in the recent past. In particular, few parents were aware of 'new thinking' on the provision of ordinary houses and on a wide range of alternatives for living, and most still assumed that the only alternative to living at home was a distant large institution (see Chapter 1).

Inviting Parents to Professionals' Meetings
Several participants also emphasised the value of
inviting parents to meetings of professionals. Very
few subjects were thought to be so technical or so
specialised as to be irrelevant to parents. In many
cases, it seemed, professionals organising seminars
and conferences had simply not thought of inviting
parents; it was not a question of deliberate exclusion. Parents themselves could suggest that it might
be helpful for invitations to be issued by writing
formally to organisers but sometimes the initiative
to invite parents came from a professional after a
friendly hint had been dropped by a parent. In the
U.K. the Association of Professions for the Mentally
Handicapped had been formed in 1973 with the express
purpose of bringing together in one organisation the
whole range of professional groups concerned with
mental handicap. After a few months, it was decided to include parents in the membership and they now
play a full and equal part both in national conferences and local meetings. Unfortunately, the title
of the Association still fails to reflect its membership.

Parents' Participation in Local and National Planning
Parents were increasingly being involved in membership of local planning or advisory committees and as
members of school boards. Parents are now legally
entitled to representation on school boards in some
countries (Norway and the U.K. were mentioned) and
are also playing an increasing part as members of
local committees planning the development of services for handicapped persons of all ages. Even so,
surveys have shown that this practice is still sometimes resisted. Participants felt that membership
of such key policy and planning bodies was essential; one national team decided that they would make
more determined attempts to secure parent representation on policy planning boards in their country.

Parents Contributing to the Training of Professionals
Several examples were given of ways in which parents
had contributed to the training of professionals and
further ways in which they might do so in the
future. Parent groups at local and national level
might make a formal approach to institutes of higher
education such as universities, polytechnics and
colleges, as well as to professional associations
involved in training, in order to enquire about the
extent to which the training of professionals includes some degree of awareness and preparation for

working with parents. It was generally agreed by
professionals that this subject had been barely
touched on either in their initial training or in
subsequent post-experience in-service courses,
despite the much greater degree of priority given to
the subject in current thinking.

Although it was not feasible to think in terms
of specific training courses to equip professionals
with the skills needed to work with parents, few
people felt confident or competent in this relatively new area and it was thought that many would
welcome courses in which people would at least share
their experiences and problems as well as their
successes. Examples were quoted of courses for
doctors, teachers and social workers to which parents had contributed by discussing not only their
own personal experiences but also their ideas and
those of relevant parent groups and organisations on
ways in which professionals could develop better
working relationships with parents. Parents are
sometimes in a better position to draw attention to
examples of good practice in different parts of the
country; their journals and special contacts provide relevant information of which professionals may
not necessarily be aware. One teacher who was in a
good position to influence his local teacher training curriculum proposed to draft a chapter on co-
operation between parents and professionals for the
consideration of the appropriate committee.

Joint Training of Parents and Professionals
Rapid development of new methods of teaching and
working with mentally handicapped people makes it
essential to provide short practical courses on
specific topics. Unfortunately, many of these
courses tend to be organised for one group of professionals, either by universities or by single
professional associations - e.g. those concerned
with the further training of doctors, teachers,
psychologists, social workers, therapists, etc. It
is increasingly recognised that much of this training could be given to multidisciplinary groups,
since few of these new developments are so specific
that they are relevant to only one profession.
Similarly, there is no reason why opportunities to
participate in such courses should not be thrown
open to parents. It may well be that only a small
number of parents would be interested or willing to
attend but it is possible that many more would do so
if direct encouragement was provided for them to do
so. This might be done by specific invitations to

the local parent organisations or by schools and other agencies ensuring that parents are informed about available courses. Ideally, however, a personal invitation by a professional to one or more parents is likely to help parents to feel 'comfortable' in attending meetings and courses where they are likely to be outnumbered by professionals and where some of the discussions may at first seem remote and technical. Parents may feel diffident about attending such meetings but it helps if they know other parents will attend or contribute as speakers.

University Extra-Mural Departments or Adult Education Colleges have an important role in the development of multidisciplinary courses which make a deliberate effort to include parents. Such colleges are 'neutral' ground - i.e. they are not obviously associated with a particular profession or discipline and they provide opportunities for the public at large to take courses in any subject of their choice (Mittler, 1979).

The University of Manchester's Department of Extra-Mural Studies has been organising such courses over a number of years in different parts of Greater Manchester covering ten local government districts. These courses are often held in a school but make every effort to recruit both parents and professionals from the whole district and not just those from the school where the course is based. The content of the courses includes a substantial practical element in which participants practise various teaching techniques, sometimes using 'role play' in which one person pretends to be a handicapped child with a specific learning difficulty while others act the role of 'teacher'. Use is also made of specially prepared video-recordings illustrating particular teaching and rehabilitative methods as examples of good practice. Participants are introduced to methods of assessment and recording, such as the use of developmental checklists, and ways in which these can be used to design an individual programme. Quite apart from the skill-based elements, such courses can also provide opportunities for a free discussion on wider-ranging topics. The important point is that parents and professionals attend as equals, not because one group has made a special effort to 'involve' or 'invite' the other.

PARENTS AS EMPLOYERS

The seminar reminded us that in a number of countries it is parents who employ professionals and who

229

determine how a service shall be run. This is the
case in countries where voluntary societies are
themselves the main providers of a service, and are
grant-aided for the purpose by government or from
public money - for example, in the Netherlands, in
Belgium, in New Zealand, in some of the Australian
states, and in several other countries. This is an
unusual situation for professionals in Britain where
the voluntary sector provides very few major services itself, but rather works as a pressure group to
increase the quality and quantity of public services.

Where parents are employers and policy makers,
the quality of the parent-professional partnership
assumes a somewhat different dimension. What
happens, for example, when the original generation
of 'pioneering parents' is succeeded by a new generation of parents with very different ideas on
priorities - for example concerning ordinary housing
and integrated education, in contrast to 'village
communities' and special schools? (See Roseneau and
Provencal (1981) for a sensitive discussion of parental misgivings about community services).

These questions are reflected in a recent com-
parative study of mental handicap services in a
number of different countries prepared by Heron and
Myers (1983) who contrast a variety of models of
service delivery - e.g. in large federal countries
such as U.S.A., Canada, Australia with smaller non-
federal countries such as New Zealand, Israel, the
Netherlands, Denmark, Sweden and the U.K. Their
account reflects rapidly changing philosophies
among the voluntary societies. Moreover, it describes increasingly complex relationships with
governments who provide funds but who are not necessarily in sympathy with the policies of the voluntary societies - which may be too conservative or
too radical for them.

PARENTS AS MONITORS OF THE QUALITY OF SERVICES

Parent movements are also beginning to play an increasing part in monitoring the quality of services
provided by professionals, and insisting that professionals should express a greater degree of
accountability. Parent groups have issued their
own 'standards documents', such as MENCAP's (1977)
Stamina documents (concerned with minimum standards
in schools, adult training centres and residential
services) and have also been trained to use existing
methods of evaluating the quality of services. Many

230

parent groups in North America have become proficient in the use of the 'Program Analysis of Service Systems' (PASS 111) (Wolfensberger and Glenn, 1975), a rigorous system of evaluation based on principles of normalisation. PASS is also now beginning to be used in Britain as one of a number of approaches to monitoring the quality of services. In parts of Canada, parents are encouraged by professionals themselves to monitor the quality of the programme being provided and to express both their satisfaction and dissatisfaction (Brynelsen, Gall and Sax, 1982).

PARTICIPATION AND DECISION MAKING BY MENTALLY HANDI-CAPPED PEOPLE

One further topic was thought to be of particular importance and merited extensive discussion. This concerned ways of helping mentally handicapped people themselves to express a much greater degree of choice, to have more opportunities to participate in decisions concerning the quality of services being provided for them and in plans concerning ways in which their needs were to be met in the future.

Brief references were made during the seminar to a number of developments in both practice and research which were potentially of great significance and which might prove as important and innovative in the 1980's as 'parental involvement' had been in some countries in the 1970s.

The Development and Rapid Growth in Some Countries of Self-Advocacy Movements
The most far-reaching of these was undoubtedly the American 'People First' movement which demonstrated beyond doubt that mentally handicapped people were able to speak forcefully about their situation and their needs, and to articulate their needs both among themselves and before parents and professionals (Williams and Shoultz, 1982). The People First Movement has now become a major organisation, with annual national and regional conferences, with teams of speakers who meet local policy makers and decision makers and who also attend professional conferences and present their point of view.

Groups of mentally handicapped people both from People First and from comparable organisations in other countries attended the 1982 World Congress of the International League of Societies for Persons with Mental Handicap in Nairobi where they had the choice of participating in main sessions as well as

organising sessions for themselves. A delegation of
three mentally handicapped people has also addressed
a meeting of the General Assembly of the United
Nations organisation in order to make a plea for a
greater degree of recognition of the needs of mentally handicapped people.

No Bar to Participation
These developments are by no means restricted to the
most able mentally handicapped people - i.e. those
who are in the 'mild' or 'educable' ranges of
ability. The self-advocacy movement makes every
effort to ensure that less able and more severely
impaired people are encouraged to participate, often
despite severe physical and communication handicaps.
The film 'People First' made in the early period of
the movement illustrated how moderately and severely
handicapped people could participate in meetings and
discussions in a variety of ways, not necessarily by
addressing a meeting, and appeared able to follow
the main points of a discussion and to express
choice in decision making.

Student Committees
A survey of Adult Training Centres by a HARC doct-
oral student, Bronach Crawley (1982) has established
that well over a quarter of Adult Training Centres
now have a 'student committee', with some form of
active participation and representation by mentally
handicapped people attending the Centres. One
Centre (Avro Centre, Southend) secured affiliation
of the Centre and its students to the National Union
of Students, thus potentially gaining the status and
concessionary privileges available to all other
registered students in the U.K.

Communicating Opinions
A number of research workers in HARC and elsewhere
are developing and evaluating a range of instruments
designed to help mentally handicapped people to express preference in a number of key areas - e.g.
choice of preferred job (*Illustrated Vocational
Inventory*, Whelan and Reiter, 1980; *Me at Work*, Whelan
and Speake, 1980); choice of leisure activities
(*Junior Interest Profile*, Jeffree and Cheseldine, 1982);
and evaluation of the quality of the residential
environment (Howie, Cuming and Raynes, 1982). Howie
also reviews a range of other client-centred instruments developed in various centres in Europe and
North America, as well as her own innovative studies
in New Zealand.

232

PARENTS, PROFESSIONALS AND MENTALLY HANDICAPPED PEOPLE

The rapid growth of self-advocacy in the last few years is not only of great interest in its own right. It also raises a number of important issues in relation both to the parent movement itself and to parent-professional partnership. What if the views of a mentally handicapped person are in conflict with those of the parents? If the views of professionals are in sympathy with those of the young person, whose rights are paramount - those of the parents who are still responsible for the 'care' of their son or daughter, the 'experts' who are paid to promote their interests and protect their rights, or the mentally handicapped people themselves, with their own rights and responsibilities as adult citizens? What about the adult in residential care whose parents still want a voice in the programme? And what happens when a mentally handicapped person expresses a point of view which is consistent with the wishes of neither the parents nor the professionals?

Conventional wisdom as well as established practice tend to suggest that mentally handicapped people, almost by definition, are unlikely to 'know their own minds', are 'easily swayed by their peers' or by 'what they have just seen on the television', and that they are 'unrealistic'. On the other hand, research findings consistently suggest that staff and parents frequently and massively under-estimate the abilities even of mentally handicapped people whom they know well. Indeed, it has been suggested that under-estimation of their abilities constitutes their most significant handicap, since it prevents staff from exposing them to the challenge of demand and opportunity to learn on the grounds that they are 'unlikely to be able to benefit'.

Perhaps the self-advocacy movement provides the most telling illustration of this theme, since many people still do not accept that mentally handicapped people should or can express a point of view about their own situation, or participate 'meaningfully' in decision making, even in areas which immediately affect their day-to-day lives. Similar doubts were at one time expressed about disabled people generally, though the 'consumerism' movement is now very strong amongst physically disabled adults, who constitute an extremely powerful and articulate lobby both at national and international levels, and whose advocacy sometimes takes the form of militant antiprofessionalism.

These issues are at the forefront of discussion at the beginning of the 1980s and are likely to remain prominent for many years to come. We are only now beginning to confront the adult status of mentally handicapped people and are at the threshold of considering how they can be helped to express choice and decision making in issues that deeply affect their lives. This will remain one of the most challenging tasks for partnership not only between parents and professionals but for both of them with mentally handicapped people themselves.

REFERENCES

Blunden, R. and Revill, S. (1980) A behavioural approach. In The Handicapped Person in the Community (Unit 5, Block 2). Milton Keynes: Open University Press

Brynelsen, D., Gall, R., and Sax, P. (1982) Parent-Professional Partnership Profile. Toronto: National Institute on Mental Retardation (in preparation)

Crawley, B. (1982) Self-advocacy in Britain. Paper presented to the 6th World Congress, International Association for the Scientific Study of Mental Deficiency, Toronto, Canada, August 25th, 1982

Georgiades, N. and Phillimore, M. (1975) The myth of the hero-innovator and alternative strategies for organisational change. In C.C. Kiernan and F.P. Woodford (eds.) Behaviour Modification with the Severely Retarded. Amsterdam: Associated Scientific Publishers

Heron, A. and Myers, M. (1983) Intellectual Impairment: the Battle against Handicap. New York and London: Academic Press (in press)

Houts, P.S. and Scott, R. (1975) Goal Planning with Developmentally Disabled Persons. Hershey Medical Centre: Pennsylvania State University

Howie, D., Cuming, J. and Raynes, N. (1982) Development of tools to facilitate participation by retarded persons in residential evaluation procedures. (in preparation)

Jeffree, D. and Cheseldine, S. (1982) Junior Interest Profile. Manchester: Hester Adrian Research Centre

Mittler, P. (1979) People not Patients: Problems and Policies in Mental Handicap. London: Methuen

Mittler, P. and Beasley, D. (1982) A Multi-National

Family Training Workshop. Report to UNESCO and
UN. Brussels: International League of Soc-
ieties for Persons with Mental Handicap
Rosenau, N. and Provencal, G. (1981) Community
placement and parental misgivings. Mental
Retardation, 31, 3-11
Royal Society for Mentally Handicapped Children and
Adults (1977) Minimum Standards for Local
Services. London: MENCAP
Whelan, E. and Reiter, S. (1980) Illustrated Vocat-
ional Inventory. Manchester: Copewell Publi-
cations (HARC)
Whelan, E. and Speake, B. (1980) Me at Work.
Manchester: Copewell Publications (HARC)
Williams, P. and Shoultz, B. (1982) We Can Speak for
Ourselves: Self-Advocacy by Mentally Handi-
capped People. London: Souvenir Press
Wolfensberger, W. and Glenn, L. (1975) Program
Analysis of Service Systems (PASS 3) Toronto
(York University): National Institute on Mental
Retardation

NOTES ON CONTRIBUTORS

Sally Beveridge

Director, Anson House Preschool Project, Hester
Adrian Research Centre, Manchester University

Dana Brynelsen

Provincial Advisor, Infant Development Programs,
Vancouver, British Columbia, Canada

Sally Cheseldine

Research Fellow, Parents and Their Handicapped
Teenagers Project, Hester Adrian Research Centre,
Manchester University

Cliff Cunningham

Director, Infant Project, Hester Adrian Research
Centre, Manchester University

Pauline Fairbrother

Vice-chairperson, Royal Society for Mentally Handicapped Children and Adults, London

Jill Gardner

Educational Psychologist, Education Department
Psychological Services, Walsall

237

Dorothy Jeffree

Director, Parents and their Handicapped Teenagers Project, Hester Adrian Research Centre, Manchester University

Helen McConachie

Honorary Research Fellow, Hester Adrian Research Centre, Manchester University

Helle Mittler

Senior Social Worker, School Psychological and Child Guidance Service, Manchester

Peter Mittler

Professor of Special Education, and Director, Hester Adrian Research Centre, Manchester University

Shirley Rheubottom

Honorary Research Fellow, Hester Adrian Research Centre, Manchester University

James Ross

Director of Welfare Services, Royal Society for Mentally Handicapped Children and Adults, London

Philippa Russell

Senior Officer, Voluntary Council for Handicapped Children, National Children's Bureau, London

LIST OF OTHER SEMINAR PARTICIPANTS

Austria

Megan Hayward, physiotherapist
Sigrun Scheirl, parent

Belgium

Lucienne van Loon, parent
Claudine van Malderen, teacher

Denmark

Jørgen Kristensen, teacher
Gugu Kristoffersen, parent

France

Henri Bissonnier, professor of special education
Yvonne de Laval, parent

Great Britain

John Chillag, parent
Rita Flanagan, social worker

Netherlands

Enno Felix, Bishop Bekkers Institute
Mariet van Hattum, parent
Ms L Klaus, observer
Sandor Németh, Bishop Bekkers Institute
Marian Verhaart-van Zijderveld, observer
Bob van Zijderveld, social worker

Norway

Berit Røhmen, parent
Kari Storemyr, teacher

Sweden

Erica Lund, parent
Henrik Pelling, psychiatrist

West Germany

Sonja Barthel, teacher
Renate Börner, parent
Christoph Hublow, teacher

INDEX

Praise for
A Boy Made of Blocks

'The publishing sensation of the year: a compelling,
uplifting and heart-rending debut novel'
MAIL ON SUNDAY

'Funny, expertly plotted and written with enormous heart'
GRAEME SIMSION

'A heart-warming and wise story ... I shed a
few tears but was left with a warm glow'
CATHY RENTZENBRINK

'Very funny, incredibly poignant and full of insight. Awesome'
JENNY COLGAN

'One of those wonderful books that makes
you laugh and cry at the same time'
GOOD HOUSEKEEPING

'Searingly honest and poignant ... tremendously
moving. A truly beautiful story'
HEAT

'*A Boy Made of Blocks* is constructed around not just a
great plot, but a rare sense of honesty and insight'
GUARDIAN

Praise for
Days of Wonder

'An enchanting story about family, friendship,
love and loss which manages to be both very
funny and intensely moving – a rare feat'
MIKE GAYLE

'Made me laugh and cry in turn'
GOOD HOUSEKEEPING

'So powerful, yet incredibly gentle and poignant.
Utterly and completely beautiful'
JOANNA CANNON

'A story of life, love and hope –
the perfect antidote to today's world. Phenomenal'
CLARE MACKINTOSH

'A lovely, funny and very moving novel'
SUN

'This is the most emotionally powerful book
we've read all year'
HEAT

'A heartwarming and magical story'
LIBBY PAGE

'Utterly enchanting ... a truly beautiful story'
RUTH HOGAN

The
Frequency of
US

KEITH STUART

SPHERE

First published in Great Britain by Sphere in 2021

1 3 5 7 9 10 8 6 4 2

Copyright © Keith Stuart 2021

The moral right of the author has been asserted.

A CIP catalogue record for this book
is available from the British Library.

Hardback ISBN 978-0-7515-7294-0
Trade Paperback ISBN 978-0-7515-7293-3

Typeset in Electra by M Rules
Printed and bound in Great Britain by Clays Ltd, Elcograf S.p.A.

Papers used by Sphere are from well-managed forests
and other responsible sources.

Sphere
An imprint of
Little, Brown Book Group
Carmelite House
50 Victoria Embankment
London EC4Y 0DZ

An Hachette UK Company
www.hachette.co.uk

www.littlebrown.co.uk

This book is dedicated to the memory of Jason Brookes, my first ever editor, who taught me that the secret to good writing is obsession and detail.

Who believes not only in our globe with its sun
    and moon, but in other globes with their suns
    and moons,
Who, constructing the house of himself or herself, not
    for a day but for all time, sees races, eras, dates,
    generations,
The past, the future, dwelling there, like space,
    inseparable together.

WALT WHITMAN, 'Kosmos'

Part One

DISAPPEARANCE

26 April 1942

The sirens woke Elsa but not me. I'd crawled into bed only an hour or so before, exhausted, bruised, desperate to blot out the memories of the previous day; the awful things I'd seen. She was shaking me, harder and harder, and even then sleep would not release me. Finally she shouted, 'Will! Will! Wake up! Will, darling!'

'What is it?' I groaned, turning away from her, pulling the blankets up and over my head. She switched on her bedside lamp.

'Will, we have to go.'

For several seconds, I still couldn't understand her, desperate to return to the peace of unconsciousness. But then I heard for myself. The ululating wail of the sirens, and beneath them a sound like rolling thunder coming in. The bombers. The bombers were back.

Elsa was up and out of bed, pulling on her thick dressing gown, bumping against furniture in the darkness, a growing frenzy of movement and panic. I sat up, rubbing my eyes, and for a few seconds I entertained the possibility that the planes would pass overhead, as they had every night before last, on their way to

3

Bristol. But just as I was about to reassure Elsa, we heard the high-pitched whistling sound of falling bombs, dozens of them – a horrible choir. Then multiple impacts, low and distant.

We looked at each other.

'I'll need to get dressed,' I said. 'I have to report in.'

'You can't, you were out all day yesterday. For God's sake, let someone else go.'

'It's my duty.'

As I dressed, Elsa peeled back the black curtain and looked out of the window. From here, we had a panoramic view over the city; it was one of the reasons my parents bought the house. How lovely, my mother often said, to see Bath laid out before us like a picture postcard. Last night, we'd seen a very different prospect, vast areas on fire, like some awful vision of the apocalypse.

'Will,' said Elsa. 'There's someone in your workshop.'

A cold chill went up my spine.

'What? Are you sure?'

My shirt still unbuttoned, I joined her at the window and looked out toward the end of the garden. Sure enough, there was light seeping from beneath the workshop door. A shadow moved inside.

'Looters?' said Elsa.

'Surely not. I'll go and see.'

'No, Will, we have to get to the cellar!'

There were more long droning whines, seemingly nearer now, and then three massive explosions that shook the whole house. Outside, someone very nearby was screaming. The sound jolted me back to yesterday; the houses on the Lower Bristol Road, all obliterated, like a row of grotesque blackened skeletons. Bodies in the soot.

'You go,' I said. 'I'll have a quick look, there's a lot of equipment in there that . . .'

4

'Oh forget your damn contraptions, Will, come with me. *Bitte!*'
'I'll only be a moment, darling. I promise.'

When I opened the back door and looked out beyond the garden, the horror of it all hit me again. The smoke billowing beneath the red glow of the flares; the rumble of falling masonry; a smell in the air like molten tar. From further down the hill the gut-wrenching sound of another explosion, then cries from God knows where. Another wave of bombers was coming in for its turn at the city, untroubled by the pathetic patter of distant anti-aircraft fire. Bath had no defences of its own. No one had expected this.

I felt a hand on my elbow. Elsa was behind me in the doorway. I turned and kissed her.

'Go to the cellar,' I said.

She looked at me desperately, but started stepping back toward the cellar door, and for a moment I thought of following her. Instead, I scrambled out toward the workshop. My father had built it many years ago; my brother and I helped him, carrying bricks along the garden in a rusty old wheelbarrow. There had once been an orchard down there, he told us. As I got closer to the door, I could hear someone speaking inside; instinctively, I looked around for a weapon, a spade or pitchfork, anything. But then as my senses gathered, I realised with a start that I recognised the voice. I wasn't sure whether to feel shocked or relieved. I opened the door very slowly.

The interior was mostly lost in shadow, but a single lamp illuminated the large work table in the centre of the room, crammed with half-built wirelesses, tools and components. At the rear, a window overlooking the city let in a little more light, revealing the metal shelves lining the walls, loaded with more tools and parts. My father had tinkered with his car in here, but for me it was always wireless sets; there were several models I had bought or scrounged from work, several more I had made myself. And there, sitting at the desk with his back to me, one hand desperately fumbling with the dials on my radio transmitter, was a small boy, dressed in striped pyjamas.

'David,' I said. I spoke quietly, calmly, so as not to startle the lad, but I was aware we had to get out. 'David, what on earth are you doing here?'

Before he could answer there was a series of blasts, not far from us, perhaps along the road toward Camden Crescent. The whole building shook, releasing a shower of dust from the low rafters.

'David,' I said again, gritting my teeth to stop myself from yelling.

'I'm calling Daddy,' he said. 'He'll rescue us.'

'I'm sure your father is on his way, but we have to get to safety. Does your mother know you're here? David, she must be frantic.' I was terrified she would be out looking for him, combing the streets while the bombs fell. Should I take him back to his own home? He lived only a few houses along from us, but it seemed a tremendous gamble.

'Come with me to our cellar, you'll be safe with us. I'm sure Elsa will sing to you. Some of the songs she has been teaching you on the piano, perhaps?'

He turned away from the transmitter and toward me.

'"The Grand Old Duke of York"?' he asked.

'Yes of course.'

'But my daddy . . .'

'Your daddy will know we are in trouble. He'll fly in his plane and he'll shoot the Germans down, I'm sure of it. But for now, we have to go.'

'But how will he know?'

'The RAF has lots of technology to let them know what is happening in the war. I'll tell you all about it inside.'

I wished I'd never taken him out to see the workshop; a few months ago he'd been over for his weekly music lesson, talking about his father and his Spitfire, and I'd told him about how pilots used radios to talk to each other. 'Come and see,' I had said. I showed him the transmitter and explained how it worked. He had asked, 'Could I talk to Papa on that?' Since then he'd been a regular companion, helping me to clean the sets, replace valves – I enjoyed his enthusiasm, it reminded me of myself at his age.

Through the grimy window I could see flames licking the skyline. Something vast was on fire down there – perhaps the whole city this time, perhaps everything. And then my eyes rose slowly, attracted by an all-too-familiar noise: high up, but caught unmistakably in the bright moonlight, there were three bombers, heading in our direction, stark and black like mythical beasts.

'Oh Jesus,' I whispered.

Without thinking I leapt forward and grabbed the boy, knocking the chair from under him. He screamed and grasped at the radio microphone, but I had him in my arms as the noise grew louder. This is it, I thought. We either dive under the work table or make a run for the house. I had seconds to choose.

The house.

David screamed and punched at me as I kicked open the workshop door. 'Here we go, old boy,' I said and I bolted out onto the path.

Almost immediately a gust of hot, smoky wind hit me, filling my lungs. The sky was molten, the glow of fire reflecting in the windows of the houses. I stopped for a moment, almost transfixed by the horror of it, but the planes were so close now, I had to be fast. It was a steep climb back up the garden to the house with David in my arms, and after all that had happened yesterday I was worn out, my muscles ached. There was a cacophony around me. The sound of throbbing engines filled my ears like blood.

About halfway across the garden, I saw a figure standing in the doorway to the kitchen. It took my eyes a few seconds to adjust, but it was Elsa and she was shouting something. I was about to yell that she should go to the cellar, but then I saw her look up and her face distorted into an expression of pure, undiluted terror. She covered her eyes with her hands and fell back into the kitchen as though she couldn't bear to see what was coming. I looked up too.

And it was the strangest thing.

All of a sudden, everything seemed to stop. The screams, the rumbling, the crashing. It was as though a great peace had descended. There was a blinding light seemingly focused on us from somewhere very high up, as though we had been picked out by a theatrical spotlight. I saw raindrops swirling in the vortex like jewels. I was enraptured, frozen to the spot. Through the light and the whirling rain I was aware of a strange whooshing sensation that seemed to herald something approaching very fast. And I knew. I knew in a second of calm clarity what it was and that it was too late now to do anything. I held the boy close to me and bent over him as though shielding him from a sudden storm.

'David,' I whispered. 'Hold tight, son.'

I'd been told that the survivors of the London Blitz had a saying: you don't hear the bomb that's coming for you. I was surprised, in those luminous seconds, to discover it was true.

8

28 April 1942

I woke with a jolt and for several seconds I couldn't take in where I was or what had happened. The objects around me were unrecognisable. What was the last thing I remembered? The bomb. The boy in my arms. There had been a bright light, then an unbearable pressure, as though we were being flung back by a crashing wave, then blackness. Afterwards, there were fragments of memories – lying in my garden, people gathered around, shouting. One man, his face was coated in soot, he looked half mad. He grabbed me by the arms and he said, 'You saw it, didn't you? You saw it!' . . . He was furious no one was listening to him. Then I was inside an ambulance. Then nothing for what felt like days.

'Mr Emerson?' A voice was calling my name. A figure approached me through the blur.

I groaned, 'Where am I? What happened?'

'You're in the Royal United Hospital in Bath. You've had a bump to your head.'

With this information, things swam into focus. I could recognise the chaotic activity of the ward: the rows of metal beds, nurses running, vast black blinds over the windows. My head felt like it had been split open, it was agony just to breathe. In the bed next to mine, a man was moaning weakly, his right arm and leg bandaged,

9

his face ludicrously swollen and blackened with bruises. The bed on the other side was empty, but the ruffled sheets were smeared with dry blood.

The nurse hovered back into my field of vision, her face gaunt and tired, but filled with a sort of determined kindness.

'You were brought in yesterday morning,' she said. 'An ARP warden found you lying in your garden, unconscious. We'll need to check you over when a doctor is free. How do you feel?'

'Pain. A lot of pain.'

'I can bring you some aspirin, but morphine is being rationed.'

She was about to race away to someone more deserving, but I grabbed her arm.

'My wife,' I said. 'She was in the house when we were hit.'

The nurse fixed me with a quizzical stare, and my stomach lurched at the thought that she was trying to summon the courage to give me terrible news.

'You were brought in alone. I'm sure she's safe. I can ask around for you. What's her name?'

'Her name is Elsa,' I said. 'Elsa Klein.'

'I'll have a look around,' she said. 'It's chaos, mind. The hospital has taken some damage – the gas is off, we had no water for a day, the wards are all full to bursting. But I will try.'

Later that day, the nurse returned. She gave me a pained smile.

'Mr Emerson, I've phoned the casualty report line and a colleague at St Martins, and there are no records of an Elsa Klein being brought in.'

I allowed myself a second of relief, but then, from her expression, I knew her report was not over.

'What is it?' I asked.

'It's just that, there's no record of anyone else living with you at that address. I spoke to one of your neighbours who was brought in yesterday evening. He told me ... he told me you live alone, Mr Emerson. You're not married.'

'I have to go,' I said, lifting myself up. The pain in my head was like a gunshot.

'You can't,' said the nurse. 'We need a doctor to see you. You might have a brain injury.'

I struggled to my feet. I was wearing starched pyjamas in a faded blue, like prison clothes. 'I have to find my wife,' I said. 'I'm fine. For God's sake, let me go.' The nurse looked around. They clearly needed beds – casualties were still being dug out of the wreckage and brought in by exhausted ambulancemen. 'I will see my own doctor as soon as possible. I've got to get out of here and find Elsa.'

In the end, another nurse came by and handed back my torn, dirty clothes. Disorientated and weak, I half walked, half staggered from the hospital. A bus pulled up outside and I boarded with a rabble of similarly tattered people. An elderly woman sat next to me, smartly dressed and shivering.

'The world's gone to Hell,' she said. And from then on, she said nothing.

There was little obvious damage as we drove down Coombe Hill in the afternoon sun, but then as we approached the city along Upper Bristol Street, the carnage became clear – rows of houses with their windows blown out, roofs collapsed, smoke pouring from the skeletal remains of a motor garage. Groups of workmen gathered at the sides of the road, shovelling rubble from one place to another. There were pieces of furniture lining the pavements, packed suitcases left abandoned, and over everything a grey haze drifted like some poisonous fog. The road was closed before the turning up to Queen Square because of a ruptured gas main, so we all had to get out and walk. We were like a weird huddle

11

of refugees, padding slowly and aimlessly along – but when we reached the square we all stopped together. The Francis Hotel had been hit, its grand Georgian façade ripped in half, a fissure running through it like a valley. You could see what was left of the bedrooms either side of the crater – the luxurious wallpaper, a nightgown hanging from the back of a door, a pristine bathroom sink with a washbag still perched by it. People who had never seen inside the building stood and gawped. A man was having his photograph taken in front of the smoking debris. I stood for a second too, as though entranced, until I remembered why I had to keep moving. I told myself Elsa must still be at home. But surely there was no home now. I had a flashback to the moment in the garden, the young boy David in my arms, and the dead certainty of something hurtling towards us through the inky darkness. The blast, the immense pressure – how had I even survived? I knew I would be returning to nothing but rubble. Oh God, Elsa. The thought of her set me running.

When I reached Lansdown, there were chilling sights along every street. Great piles of fallen masonry where shops and houses used to be, trees blasted bare of leaves and branches, roads burst open. Everywhere, there were groups of workmen, desperately attempting to shore up the roofs and walls of damaged properties. Memories of the first night of the bombing flooded my brain – the rescue squad I had joined at the beginning of the war – a lot of retired builders and civil engineers and me, tunnelling into the maws of obliterated cellars, amid screams and smoke. Did someone tunnel in and save Elsa? I had a sudden thought of how strange it was, to be making this familiar journey home and to be fearful that everything I knew and loved had been destroyed.

On turning the slight corner before the terrace that led to my own home, it was clear there had been a direct hit on the street.

Several buildings were little more than jagged remains, ghostly amid the black dust clouds. Silent rows of men dug at the ruins like some nightmarish harvest. My eyes sore and teary with grit, I had to feel my way past two trucks parked in the road, my back aching, my head throbbing horribly. Two boys ran through the fog toward me, laughing, one carrying a painting in a grand wooden frame – it depicted a quiet country scene. A man shouted, 'Come back, you little bastards! You'll be hung for this!'

I reached the Barneses' house and knew I was almost home. A gap appeared in the smog and I stopped dead and looked up, breathing heavily.

'My God,' I said.

Avon Lodge was still there. The windows were all blown out, some roof tiles were broken, and a length of guttering had fallen down – that was the extent of the visible damage. The same could not be said of the house which used to adjoin my own, and the next two further up the street – all obliterated. A man I recognised from one of the local civil defence meetings wandered over to me through the smoke, wearing dusty overalls and carrying a pickaxe. He was obviously attached to one of the work parties trying to shore up the street.

'Is that your place, lad?' he asked, taking a battered cigarette from his pocket and nodding toward Avon Lodge.

'Yes,' I replied in a dazed far-off voice.

'You're bloody lucky,' he continued after lighting the cigarette. 'Three bombs hit further up the road. Blast took out a whole row. The house next to yours got dragged down with 'em,' he nodded at Avon Lodge again, 'but this'n stood its ground. Then another bomb hit further down the street. Four bangs in a row. Usually it's five. The Luftwaffe missed you out, lad.'

'My garden was hit,' I said.

This time he shook his head, smiling. 'You might have caught some shrapnel from the blasts up the road.'

'But I was standing out there. I saw it coming down.'

'Lad,' he said. 'If you were in that garden when a bomb hit, we wouldn't be here talking. I'd be collecting bits of you in a wheelbarrow.'

But I was certain. Perhaps the apparently uninjured façade of the house was a gruesome trick hiding an apocalypse behind it. I fumbled in my trouser pocket for my key, opened the door and burst into the hallway.

'Elsa?' I shouted.

There were books all over the floor in the study and a few of my mother's ornaments had been displaced from the shelves in the parlour and smashed on the floor, but nothing else. I rushed through to the kitchen. Here there was more damage – the windows had been blown out and the frames splintered to smithereens leaving gaping holes in the wall. Dust and rubble covered the floor and work surfaces like muddy snow. I ripped open the cellar door and ran down, taking three of the narrow steps at a time. No sign of her, our Morrison shelter empty and unused.

'Elsa?'

I ran upstairs banging open the doors as I went. The bathroom, the guest bedroom, and then our own bedroom, all virtually undamaged, all desperately quiet. By some miracle, the house was safe. But Elsa?

And then I had the strangest thought. Mother's ornaments, her horse brasses, her china figurines of Victorian children – we had packed them away last year. Elsa had never liked them, but she had politely suffered them with great patience for as long as she could. Then one morning, we were reading in the parlour and she turned to me and said, 'I'm sorry, Will, either they go or I do.'

And we wrapped them in newspaper, placed them gently in an old wooden crate and took them down to the cellar where we tended to store everything we didn't need or like. Why were they back in the parlour?

A chill ran down my spine. I have no idea why I did this, but I found myself walking slowly toward the wardrobe in our bedroom. I opened the door.

Elsa's dresses were gone.

In a frenzy, I checked every drawer in our dresser – everything of hers was missing. I looked around the room. All the little prints and photographs she had pinned to the picture rails, mostly torn out of art magazines, were gone, as were her books. I walked backwards and stumbled into the bed, sitting down heavily. I put my hands up to my head and rubbed at my eyes. The room was swirling in and out of focus.

'Elsa?' I shouted again. 'Elsa!'

I told myself I had to stop, calm down and think. I had to be logical.

Her aunt, I thought. She's gone to her aunt's – that's where she had been living before she moved in with me. But that made no sense – she would have left a note. My thoughts coddled like sour milk, the gash in my head was bleeding again. I pictured Elsa, the last time I had seen her, standing in the doorway to the back garden. She had been calling something, but I couldn't hear her above my own desperate thoughts. Now, in the quiet of the bedroom, I realised with a start what it was. 'Go back.' She had been screaming at me to go back.

Where are you? I thought. Oh Elsa, where are you? I staggered away down the stairs and had to stop and vomit. Then somehow, I was standing in my kitchen doorway, as Elsa had that night, looking out over the garden. The lawn was strewn with debris – great

15

chunks of blackened brick and mortar, the back of a wooden chair, a doll's head, a lot of glass – and there was a wide, shallow crater in the vegetable patch I had dug in the centre of the garden. But this all seemed to be debris from the houses hit further up the road, as the workmen had told me. I stepped out into the cool air and looked back at the house – apart from the windows and frames, and a few gouges in the brickwork, there was little damage. But surely the bomb I saw would have brought down at least the lean-to? I staggered over the garden, preparing myself to find her body. I knew from the first night of the bombing that death was capricious and random – we would be digging beneath destroyed houses and finding people alive with only scratches. But then we'd discover someone who had been killed by a single piece of shrapnel as though targeted by a sniper.

I found nothing of Elsa – and part of me knew I wouldn't. Because it wasn't just Elsa who was gone, it was everything she'd ever brought into our home. Had someone taken it? Had someone taken *her*? My head was thudding, my guts swilled. And then I fell to my knees and looked around. There's that phrase *jamais vu*? It means 'never seen' – it's when you look at something that should be familiar but it suddenly seems alien. That's how I felt – about the garden, the house, everything. I had a recollection of that night, of holding David in my arms, looking upwards, and the swirl of light around me like a vortex, and it had felt, at the very end, like I was falling. I thought to myself, where have I landed?

I started shouting again, 'Elsa! Elsa, where are you?' whirling about like a madman. And then everything was black, and it would be black for a long time.

Part Two

A FUTURE

Chapter One

October 2007

Standing outside the decrepit house in the lashing autumn rain, I am struck with the certain knowledge that I'm in completely the wrong place – and also, if I am being honest, the wrong life. I am tired. I am wearing an anorak. I have no direction, no drive, no friends.

I check my watch. It is 9.47 a.m. I am having my first existential crisis of the day. This seems about right.

Leaning my old Raleigh bike against the garden wall, I push my glasses back up, then drag my personal organiser out of the saddle bag, flipping to the page where I'd scrawled down the address. No, this is it: Avon Lodge. I shove the organiser under my anorak so its pages don't turn to papier-mâché in the rain, then look up again at the large, dark Victorian house in front of me.

It probably would have been beautiful once. Bath stone, bay windows, two ornamental turrets above the attic rooms, to give it a sort of fairy tale grandeur. But now the façade is blackened and pockmarked, and there are huge cracks in the stonework around the windows – which are themselves spotted with mould. Rain streams down the wall from a vast crack in the iron guttering; the front door is missing a glass pane and the porch roof seems to sag with age and damp. There are black sacks filled with rubbish piled next to the wall. The way that it is set back from the road, separate from both a smart row of houses on one side and a vast construction site on the other, Avon Lodge looks as though it has been quarantined with some horrible contagion.

Surely no one could actually live here? Especially not an eighty-seven-year-old man?

I check the address again, taking the organiser out, looking down at the paper then up at the house. It still feels like something is wrong. Actually, it feels like *everything* is wrong. Here, now, yesterday, the day before. Stop. Calm down. I just have to breathe deeply. In through the nose, out through the mouth. I'm in the right place. It might not be the place I want to be, but that's okay. I need to block out the voice in my head that tells me I will mess everything up. Unfortunately, it always comes up with such interesting new ways to torment me.

I decide I should walk up to the house and try to peep in through one of the windows, but when I push the garden gate it collapses from its rusty hinges and falls to the path with an almighty clang. Once I've recovered from the shock, I try to lift it back up, but it is too heavy and wet, and it falls from my grip, landing only millimetres from my feet. Deep breaths. I nudge my glasses up again and then check my hands for injuries because I don't want to get tetanus and die in convulsions. I examine them at some length, turning them over, letting the rainwater wash off the mud and rust. When I eventually look up again I realise with a start that the porch door is now open and a man is standing there staring at me.

'Can I help you?' he says.

Three months ago, I moved back in with my mum. She came to collect me from a hospital in South London and drove me home. For a few weeks I barely left my bedroom, and then one morning she opened my curtains and told me it was time to get a job. 'I have a friend who runs a home care agency,' she said. 'They're desperate for staff. Two weeks' training, then all you have to do is travel around Bath talking to old people. You can manage that.' I didn't get a say, but that was probably fair. Her twenty-nine-year-old daughter was living at home again, doing nothing but slouching about looking sad and untidy and watching crap television.

So I started work at the Regency Home Care agency. It sounds posh but is in fact housed on the second floor of the ugliest 1960s office block in Bath town centre. I did my training, learned first aid, learned how to dress and wash other people, how to manage medications (particularly ironic in my case). Then they unleashed me on a few clients – a stressful month of burnt meals, buying the wrong shopping, eking out awkward conversations with confused pensioners who wanted to know where the other carer was – the one they liked. I figured I'd be let go as soon as my probation was over. But I wasn't.

Then on Monday, Jane, the managing director, called me into her office. I like Jane, but I also fear her. She is smart and steely and together. Eight years ago, she was working part-time as a TA at the secondary school where my mum is deputy head – she was divorced with two kids, busy as hell, but also caring for her elderly mother. It all got too much so she put her mum into a care home, thinking it was the kind thing to do, but her mum was neglected

and bullied by the staff and she died a few months later. Instead of being racked with guilt, Jane studied management at college, then quit her job and opened her own home care agency – a whirlwind of guts and resolve. I know that my mum supported her; she helped her financially, she babysat for Jane's children when the going got tough. Now Jane is returning the favour.

'We have a situation,' she said. A familiar sinking feeling started dragging at my insides. Clearly, this was it, my notice of termination – Mum's influence clearly had its limits. Another crisis for her to cope with.

'Last week I got a call from a colleague in social services,' she explained. 'They are very concerned about an old gentleman named Will Emerson who lives next to the big property development on Lansdown Road. There was some sort of accident at the site a couple of weeks ago – a gas cannister exploded, huge bang, and the neighbours found Mr Emerson lying in his back garden in a hysterical state. They called an ambulance and the police arrived too. Mr Emerson told the attending officer that his wife Elsa was missing and they had to help him find her. But the officer checked with a few of the neighbours and they said he lived on his own and had done for as long as anyone remembered, and there were no records of anyone else occupying the property. Thing is, he's been reported to social services several times in the past – people have seen him wandering the garden in his pyjamas late at night, calling out for someone. Social workers visited a couple of times, and he repeated the same things – that his wife had gone missing, but when they asked for more details, he became evasive and aggressive. They're worried he's going to go off looking for this Elsa person and end up dying of hypothermia or getting run over.'

I didn't know where this was going, but the image of the old man wandering the neighbourhood at night – confused, barely dressed – it brought back memories of my own. I felt a tinge of recognition. Of sympathy.

'Social services need to carry out an intervention and a full review, but they're snowed under,' continued Jane. 'So they called me. They'll pay for three months of care – they want us to see how he's doing, if he has friends or relatives, if he is mentally sound, and if it comes to it, they'll consult with us on potentially re-housing him. I asked Rob to pop over on Friday, but the chap told him to bugger off. Sandra went over on Monday. Same thing.' She shuffled a few papers on her desk like a newsreader at the end of a bulletin. 'I thought you should have a try.'

'Why?' I managed. 'Why me?'

Jane looked at me conspiratorially.

'You wanted to be a researcher, didn't you? Well, here is something for you to research. Plus, you're an attractive young woman in your own way: that might make a difference. It's worth a shot. Also, I've got no one else available.'

I stared at her, shocked and uncomprehending. Jane saw the look on my face and burst out laughing, before recovering into a look of cloying sympathy. She leaned across her desk and gently touched my arm.

'You'll be *fine*,' she said. 'He's a very old man. He's only a little bit scary.'

She stopped smiling, realising what she'd said.

'Older men can be dangerous too,' I told her in a small voice.

'Yes. Yes, I'm sorry. Look, I'm not expecting anything. At this point, all I need you to do is go and see him – perhaps find out if there ever was a wife. He probably won't let you in and if he does, just talk to him about the care package. If he accepts, we can always send someone else to take over.' Her fingers gripped my arm a little harder. 'I know things have been tough. All of that stuff in London.'

23

Flashback. Walking slowly along a road I don't recognise, night-time, cars speeding past. I look down – my feet bare and bloody.

Of course Mum had told Jane everything. I could imagine the conversation: 'Please help my useless daughter, her life's a gigantic mess, but she's a good listener.'

Jane was still holding me. 'Maybe this will be good for you – a nice little challenge.'

When I left Jane's office I was shaking. I wasn't being fired, I was being handed a hopeless case instead. I went through to the toilets, shut myself in a cubicle and sat with my head in my hands for several minutes.

Laura James, care assistant. This was not my great ambition. I tell myself this is just temporary, something quiet and non-stressful while I am getting myself back together, but I know how quickly time can slip by. I keep having these moments when I think, hang on, what am I doing? How did I get here? And then I remember how and I always really wish I hadn't. So yes, things are working out for me on every conceivable level.

And right now, I am standing on an old man's path in the pouring rain, staring at him.

'I said, can I help you?'

It strikes me immediately that he doesn't look eighty-seven. He is tall and thin, and not at all stooped. His face is craggy but alert, his eyes a glinting steely grey within their deep sockets. His white hair is almost trendily styled into a messy crop. He reminds me of a Samuel Beckett photo our English teacher put on the classroom wall – his face similarly hewn out of angles and deep lines like canyons. He is wearing thick corduroy trousers, a striped shirt and a dark green cardigan with patches on the elbows. It is an eccentric, old-fashioned look, but it is definitely a 'look' rather than something wrangled onto him by a carer. He seems fitter and sharper

24

than the men I have cared for in their seventies, but at the same time, there is something off, something not quite 'there' about him. It's not that dour, droopy absence that dementia usually brings; it's something else, like there is some aspect of inner life that has been taken from him. His eyes lead nowhere.

'Mr Davidson?' I shout through the downpour. I look at my notes again, but the ink is running away and this makes me panic a little. 'Mr Will Davidson?'

He glares at me. 'Emerson,' he snaps. 'Who are *you*?'

'I'm from the Regency Home Care Agency.' I pull my hood back from my head to show my face so that he can see that I am not a psychopath. The driving rain trickles into my mouth. 'I think you have met some of my colleagues?'

He looks at me blankly.

'I have no idea what you're talking about.'

'We've been asked to visit you by social services. To see if you need any assistance?'

'I don't,' he says. 'Good day to you.'

He starts to close the door, and for some reason I find myself trying to stop him. Jane told me during my training that the most important thing is to make people feel safe, which is ironic because I never feel safe.

'Mr Emerson,' I say, stepping forward. 'I won't take up much of your time . . .'

'You are quite correct,' he says.

'But it's very wet out here, it would be lovely to—'

'To get home? Don't let me stop you.'

'If you would just let me in for a few minutes, I could take my clothes off and—' What the fuck. 'I mean my coat, my wet coat . . .'

He stops closing the door and stands looking at me for a second.

I can feel my face reddening. God knows what I look like, bedraggled on his doorstep like a lost child. And now I have also offered to strip in his lounge.

'I'm sorry,' I clarify. 'I didn't actually mean I was going to take my clothes off.'

'I see,' he says.

There is a pause, the only sound coming from the rain battering at the roof of the porch. The tension of the moment brings a familiar swooping feeling to my stomach, accompanied by a sense of distance and dizziness, like when you start getting a cold and you don't feel quite with-it.

'Well, I'll go,' I say. 'I'm sorry to have bothered you. Also I have sort of wrenched your gate off its hinges.'

'Yes, I watched that happen.'

'I could try and move it off the path?'

'I think you've done enough . . .'

'I'm sorry. I'll go.'

I pull the hood back onto my head, but without me noticing, it has been filling with the water cascading off the roof of the porch. A tidal wave pours over my face and down the back of my neck. I look up at the old man pathetically.

'That was really cold,' I say. There is no expression on his face, not even a pitying smile. I turn away and start back up the path, desperate to escape this new lesson in discomfort and rejection. At least I can tell Jane I tried. At least . . .

'I'm just making some tea,' he says. He shouts it loudly so I can hear through the rain. 'Why don't you join me . . . um?' I realise he is waiting for my name.

'Laura. I'm Laura.' I look up at him. 'Tea would be nice,' I say. He grunts.

'We could hang up your coat next to the fire to dry,' he says.

'Although, what sort of man-made material is that? It will prob-ably ignite.'

With that, he walks back inside, leaving the door open, clearly expecting me to follow. Standing on the threshold, a wave of dis-orientation and disconnection hits me. Grasping the door frame, I look around again in order to ground myself. I am at Avon Lodge, which is just past the really posh part of Lansdown Road, the long, steep thoroughfare winding out of the city toward Bath's northern suburbs. I am here to do my job. I can leave when I want. I glance up at the house again – it is so different to the ones around it. Out of place and ghostly, crumbling into its own untended grave. This thought does not make me feel better.

I step into the hallway and the theme of decayed grandeur is very much continued inside. The ancient floor titles are faded and broken, and some are completely missing; the thick patterned wallpaper is peeling away, exposing large sections of blackish plas-ter. Ahead, there is a narrow staircase, its painted handrail now chipped and rotten, and beside it, the hall narrows into a shadowy passage leading toward the rear of the house. It reminds me of the shitty flatshares I used to rent in London, minus the stench of dope and takeaway curry. Mr Emerson comes back toward me.

'Give me your coat,' he says. 'I'll hang it by the oven, it'll dry faster out there.' I take it off and hand it to him. From somewhere, I can hear the sound of classical music playing. 'Please, go into the parlour,' he says, pointing at a door. 'I'll make some tea.'

During my training, I dreaded going into their houses for the first time – I have already seen my fair share of scary stuff. Massive collections of creepy china dolls; giant moth-eaten moose heads mounted above fireplaces. There is always the chance of cat shit. Cat shit on the rug, on the sofa, and once, on a dining table, like a decorative centrepiece. But the hardest things are the photos of

27

lost husbands and wives – their young faces black and white and hopeful, their whole lives ahead of them. They make me really sad. So before I walk into the front room, I steel myself for the worst – and when I see inside this one, I almost gasp out loud.

It looks like some kind of neglected 1940s museum, like a National Trust property that has been intricately dressed to give an authentic sense of the past, but then abandoned. The wallpaper, a garish maze of now faded pink and blue blooms, clashes violently with a burgundy rug that takes up most of the floor space; it too is decorated with flowers that are now almost lost to age and ruin. A floor lamp with a badly torn shade stands next to a sofa heavily upholstered in a sickly olive green material, which is dotted with dark stains. There is an armchair next to the small fireplace in which coal is half-heartedly smouldering. A carriage clock sits on the mantelpiece ticking loudly. Most noticeable, however, are the vast dusty cobwebs hanging from the ceiling like veils, blowing slightly in the breeze, speckled with the skeletons of long dead insects. I can almost imagine Miss Haversham sitting in the empty armchair amid the wreckage of her bridal gown. The idea makes me shiver.

On one side of the chimney breast there is a set of warped shelves where I spot the source of the music: a vintage wireless set that looks far too aged to still be working. On the shelf above it, there is a row of old leather ring binders, stuffed with A4 sheets of paper turned sepia with age. I check the door to make sure Mr Emerson isn't watching, and then I gently take one and open it. Inside are dozens of typed pages, the ink faded, sections crossed through, like a novel manuscript. I catch the words Avon Lodge and something about Bath, then I hear a noise from the kitchen and I quickly slide it back and walk away. Is it some sort of memoir?

In the middle of the room a walnut coffee table has a vast

newspaper spread across it – the old man was clearly reading before I wrenched his gate off the wall. I don't really keep up to date with current affairs, but this is clearly not today's edition: the pages are yellowing, the black-and-white photos are blurred, and the lead story is about German U-boats attacking British convoys in the Atlantic. Then I notice the date at the top of the page – October, 1940. Okay, that's fine, he's reading a paper that is exactly sixty-seven years old. That's not strange at all. Maybe he's a history buff.

I catch a scent in the air, sweet and floral like vintage perfume. I'm trying to work out what it is when a very unsettling feeling hits me. It is a sudden, strange sense that something once happened here, something immense – like a furious, horrible row – and that the electricity of it still hangs in the air. The music from the radio is replaced with loud static, like the feedback from a broken microphone and I look around, fingers in ears, desperately searching for the source of the interference. Then, a realisation hits me in a cold ripple.

Something is in the room with me.

I don't know how I know it, I just do.

I whirl around, thinking Mr Emerson must have crept in without me seeing, but he's not there. No one is there.

And then it all stops and there is music and emptiness again.

I stand breathing heavily for a few seconds, then sit down on the sofa, trying to collect my thoughts. I realise I am biting my nails. I have to pull myself together. It was a breeze from somewhere, and the noise was water in my ears or in the pipes – I bet the plumbing in here is even more ancient than Mr Emerson. He is taking a long time. I hear a drawer being pulled open in the kitchen and a lot of clattering, and I try to joke about it in my head: what would I do if he suddenly came at me brandishing a knife? Was it possible to be attacked by someone in their late eighties? It is the sort of thing that would happen to me. But no, he comes in holding a tray loaded with chipped china cups, a teapot and a small jar filled with sugar cubes.

As he pours the tea, his hand shakes horribly.

But I'm okay. I'm fine.

'So you live here alone?' I ask as he busies himself. I open my organiser and slide the pen from its little holder. He looks at me quizzically.

'Are you taking notes?' he asks.

'Yes,' I say. 'I'm sorry, it's just so I have a record of what we've chatted about.' But that's not quite it. For weeks, my memory has been scrambled. I can't hold on to my thoughts. I keep forgetting little things like what I had for lunch, or my debit card PIN, or the last eight years of my life.

'Yes,' he says. 'I live here alone. I have for a long time. Which does make me rather curious as to why I am suddenly receiving all this attention.'

He passes a cup to me, his hands still trembling. I take it, and immediately see that it's filthy. I put it down on the table wondering how I should explain what I'm here for.

'We were asked by social services to come and see you,' I say. 'They are worried. Apparently you had a fall in the garden last week?' Silence. He looks at me in bewilderment. Does he remember? 'Do you have neighbours who you talk to?'

'I do not get on with my neighbours,' he said. 'They are busy-bodies. They're always telling lies about me. You can't trust them.'

'How about friends or relatives?'

He shakes his head then sits down slowly and heavily in the armchair.

'It is just me,' he says. 'By the time you get to my age, everybody you ever knew or loved is a memory. And memories fade.'

I don't want to ask, but I have to.

'Were you ever married?'

Just then, the carriage clock strikes ten and the sound echoes around the room. He goes silent again and out of the corner of my eye, I can see him staring at me. Just staring. His face is quizzical and angry.

'You are very familiar,' he says. 'Do you live around here?'

'No, I live in Bear Flat.'

'You lived here in the past? Many years ago? I've seen you, I'm sure.'

I shake my head. Many years ago? How old does he think I am? Maybe he *is* losing it. I can't think of anything to say so, despite the state of the cup, I take big gulps of the scorching tea and look around the room for inspiration.

It is only then that I notice it – on the wall near the window. A large print of a modernist painting. It depicts a naked woman curled up on herself, her eyes closed, her red hair splayed out around her shoulders. Amid the staid, old-fashioned clutter of the room the image stands out sharply, like something from another universe. I feel myself blushing and quickly look back to the book-shelf, but the old guy has obviously been watching me.

'Do you recognise it?' he says. 'The painting?'

This feels like a test. I stare at it again, trying to access the mem-ories of my Art History A-level; I recognise the style – the rich, almost golden colours, the wan expression on the model's face, the soft tones of her skin. I just have to remember the name . . . I catch a glimpse of myself at seventeen, sitting on the hill beside the school field, reading Gombrich, the sun on my face, killing time, not wanting to go home. Putting off the inevitable.

'It's Klimt, isn't it?' I look back at Will with a hopeful expression.

He nods joylessly, walking slowly over to the painting and

studying it. 'It is *Danaë, the mother of Perseus*. She made love to Zeus who is represented as a river of gold between her legs. At the time, people thought Klimt's work was pornographic.'

I am very unsure about the conversational route this could lead us down – it may take me somewhere incredibly uncomfortable. Time to change direction.

'So, social services think you may benefit from a little assistance. Is that something you'd be interested in?'

No reply. He is now just staring languidly at the painting. Lost in it.

'We could help with medication or shopping. There may be funds available to help pay, if you can't afford it?'

'Do *you* think this picture is pornographic?' he asks.

Here we go. I do not need this. I do not need to be made to feel weird and uncomfortable. Not right now. The anxiety bubbles inside me, like volatile chemicals being mixed together. It doesn't take me long to go from nought to completely stressed out. It's always been like this. I know why.

I stand up quickly – quickly enough to make the old man jump a little.

'I'd better go,' I say, putting my teacup back on the tray. 'I've got another meeting soon, I can't be late. If you don't want us to visit, it's fine, I can tell my boss you're okay. You look okay to me. Are you okay?'

Finally he is drawn away from the painting and he stares at me again.

'*You're* the professional,' he says. 'Shouldn't you know?'

I don't say anything and he tuts loudly. 'I'll fetch your coat,' he sneers.

He walks slowly out of the room and I take one last look around. Even though the fire is crackling away, there is an iciness in the room. I pull my hands up into the sleeves of my jumper, bunching the thick fabric into my fists. Keen, now, just to be out of there, I turn to walk through into the hallway. But to my shock, Mr Emerson is standing right there, watching me. I gasp involuntarily before realising that he's holding my anorak up, clearly expecting to put it on for me. Begrudgingly I walk over, turn my back and let him.

Outside, it has stopped raining but there is an odd dullness to the light, as though night is coming in.

'Goodbye,' I offer. He doesn't say anything until I have stepped over the gate and out of his garden.

'You didn't answer my question,' he shouts after me.

I stop and turn back, confused.

'The painting,' he says. 'Do you think it is indecent?'

I look at him, slowly raising my hood over my head once again.

'No,' I say. 'I think it's beautiful.'

For a second, he stands in the doorway scowling, but there is something else in his expression, a hint of recognition. It passes across him like a wave. And then he slams the door shut. Clearly, he detests me.

That is the last time I'll see *him*, I think. And I open my organiser, turn to my 'to do' list for the day and put a line through the visit. Then I pop it back in the saddlebag. I think about my last words to him – 'No, I think it's beautiful.' Why did I say that?

Just as I am removing the bike lock (as if anyone would steal this thing anyway), a young woman approaches on the pavement, pushing a buggy.

'Have you just come out of that house?' she asks, jabbing her cigarette toward Avon Lodge.

I nod. 'I'm a carer. Do you know him?'

'Stay clear of him, love,' she says. 'He's a fucking old weirdo.'

With that, she yanks the buggy forward and strolls casually past.

I sit on my bike watching the woman veer off toward a low block of flats further down the road. What the hell was that about? I take a last look at the house and I am already wrong about never seeing Will Emerson again. Because there he is in his front room, just visible through the musty window. He is standing very still, and he is staring at the painting.

Chapter Two

It is late afternoon by the time I get home. This is the house I grew up in – a pretty little Edwardian place, right at the top of a steep street leading to Alexandra Park. I should have felt secure here as a kid, surrounded by perfectly nice, perfectly identical terraces. But I didn't. I try not to think about my childhood, but it is tough when you find yourself back there every day.

As ever, the living room is scrupulously tidy and sterile – my mum is very particular about this. There are lacy net curtains and they're perfectly white, the carpet is freshly vacuumed and conditioned, the cushions plumped, the mantelpiece dusted. But if you were to open any of the cupboards, or the sideboard, or the little chest of drawers next to the sofa, the years of crap Mum has crammed into them would spew out and crush you to death. Nothing is ever discarded in this house, but everything is tightly repressed. I once asked Mum if she'd got all her interior design tips from Sigmund Freud – 'No,' she replied, 'I don't watch those fancy home decoration programmes.' I'm pretty sure she knew what I meant, but she keeps all the real stuff hidden under a relentlessly sunny persona – it's always been the same. If she is angry, she has this expression like she's stubbed her toe really hard but she is trying to smile through the pain while serving light snacks at a funeral. As well as being the deputy head at her school, she also doubles as a counsellor for the more troubled pupils. I desperately want to know what the poor kids make of her, this buttoned-up, efficiently caring sixty-year-old. She was a bit of a rebel once, then she married the intense older man all her friends warned her about. Her friends were right.

I traipse upstairs, still tired from cycling and my legs ache when I reach the landing. I have barely an hour before Mum gets back from work and I want to use that time constructively by having a nap. My room is the same one I had as a child and then a teenager. One whole wall is covered in corkboard tiles that I put up when I started at UWE, thinking I could pin all my notices and research to it – it's empty now. After I moved back in, I spent a frenzied few days tearing down posters, chucking away cuddly toys and clothes and crap. I was desperate to make the room look like a chic, self-contained studio flat in East London, all Farrow & Ball paint and Bo Concept furniture. I wanted something that didn't remind me of the crappy places I'd been renting with strangers and fleeting work colleagues. But my budget hadn't stretched, and the whole thing exhausted me, so the walls are painted in Homebase own-brand white emulsion. You can still see the Blu-Tack stains underneath. My pathetic 'lounge area' is an uncomfortable sofa with wonky arms, and an offensive plywood television cabinet which holds a cheap TV from Argos and a second-hand PlayStation 2. The floor is a disaster zone of crumpled clothes, damp towels and old copies of *Grazia*. It is less 'studio flat in East London' and more 'communal lounge in dangerous Earls Court youth hostel'. There is even a microwave oven in the corner for the times I *really* can't face going anywhere.

I collapse on my bed, determined to relax and let the day flow out. But now I am here, I can't switch off. Instead, I roll over and stare at the contents of my bedside table: a clock radio, a cheap cordless telephone covered in dust, a copy of *Meditation For Beginners*, which I have started about eighteen times and never got past chapter three. Next to the bed, there is a wastepaper basket because I keep waking up feeling sick, sometimes being sick. This is what it's been like for weeks.

I close my eyes and try to clear my mind, but it buzzes like a coffee rush.

I must have fallen asleep because when I drowsily look up, Mum is standing at the end of my bed. For a second it reminds me of that moment in the horror movie *Misery* when Kathy Bates looms over James Caan wielding a sledgehammer – the only difference being that Mum is wielding two boxes of ready-made meals.

'Lasagne or fish pie?' she asks.

She is wearing one of her standard-issue work outfits – Marks and Spencer dress and blazer – and her hair is in her official work bun, but there are strands frizzing out in all directions as though she's just staggered away from a wild romantic clinch with a Van de Graaff generator.

'What time is it?' I groan.

'Dinner time,' says Mum. 'I'm thinking lasagne, glass of pinot, there's a new crime drama starting tonight with whatshisface from *Doctor Who*. How was work?'

'Lasagne is fine. Work was okay. Had to visit a weird old guy. It didn't go well. He was ...'

'Lasagne it is. I bought some baby leaf salad to go with it, and they had vine tomatoes on offer, which I don't usually buy because they are just like regular tomatoes except on twigs and they're a

37

pound more expensive. You look very dishevelled, have you been drinking? I'll give you a call when dinner is ready.'

She is about to leave, but stops and looks at me, then comes back and sits on the bed.

'You're still feeling tired all the time?'

'Yeah. It's like it takes all my strength to stay awake. I still feel sick, I feel shaky, I can't remember things . . .'

She gives me a sympathetic nod. I don't tell her that I'm also gaining weight, because she can probably see that, and it feels shallow to bring it up. Like, what does it matter anyway? Who else will notice?

'Just remember that the GP said it would pass. When you start on these antidepressants, it can be tough.'

'But I've been taking them for three months,' I say.

I remember when Mum came to collect me from hospital, she took me straight to her GP. He listened quietly and kindly to me and said he would put me on the waiting list for therapy, but that it may take six months to get an appointment. Mum squeezed my hand while he wrote out a prescription for something called paroxetine.

'You've not had any panic attacks though? Nothing like what happened in London?'

Bare feet bloody on the pavement.

I shake my head.

'Good. That's good. I know it's hard, but you're seeing the doctor again in a few days – he'll know what to do. Just keep taking them for now, okay? Promise me?'

I nod at her, but look away.

And then she is gone, trotting down the staircase to the kitchen. I sit up and bury my face in my hands, thinking about how I'm going to tell Jane that my mission failed, that Will Emerson turfed me out into the rain.

I can't get anything right.

I look down into the bin. Among the tissues and grubby cotton wool balls is an empty strip of antidepressants. I ran out four days ago.

The next morning I get a phone call. It's Jane, asking me to come into the office, even though it's my day off. I have to drag myself out of bed, my legs feel like they're filled with wet sand. It takes me almost an hour to walk in and when I arrive, she is waiting for me in her office, her face as unreadable as ever. She gestures to the chair opposite her desk and I slump into it, balling the sleeves of my cardigan into my fists.

'Laura, what on earth did you say to Will Emerson?'

Immediately, I feel the emergency sprinkler system of fear and tension flooding my chest. He obviously complained about me; he probably told them I threatened to take my clothes off if he didn't let me in, and also damaged his property; he is reporting me to social services. I'll be sacked and humiliated.

'I don't know,' I gulp. 'I don't remember. I'm sorry, it was clear he didn't like me.'

'Well, he phoned the office just after you left him, and—'

'Oh, Jane, I'm sorry. I'm really sorry.'

'What are you sorry about? He's agreed to a home care assessment. Three visits a week starting on Thursday. But he said it has to be you, Laura. He doesn't want to see or speak to anyone else. Just you.'

'Oh.'

'So this is it. This is the real deal. If you do this, you'll have three months to look after him and assess his mental and physical state. Social services will want you to file a report – then a decision will be made on whether or not Mr Emerson is able to stay in his home or if he needs to be put into care.'

'You want me to assess him?'

39

'Yes. It looks like there's a lot of pressure to re-house him – the neighbours are making a fuss, the property developer next door wants something to be done about the house. They say it's unstable. I think they have an eye on the land.'

The 1940s room with the musty smell. The old man with the vacant eyes. The feeling of something weird in the air.

I gulp and try to swallow but my mouth is dry.

'You think I can do this?'

She pauses for a second. 'I do, yes. Look, I know things have been hard – all the problems you've had because of your father. But you've got to let all that go. It was a long time ago, and it's not like he ever ...'

She stops suddenly, but I almost want her to go on. I want to hear her say it. What so many people have said to me before. The memories flash in like a crazed movie montage.

'What? It's not like he ever what?'

'Nothing. Sorry. Let's just get back to the matter at hand – Will Emerson, because he told me he knew he needed help, but that no one understood. He said he thought *you* would. I have to admit, it was quite a strange phone call. He had a sort of mania about him and he was repeating things ...'

'You think he has early stage dementia?' I say, trying to be professional.

'It's likely, given his age and his isolation. Look, if he's difficult, if he scares you, let me know and we'll hand him straight over to social services and he can be moved. But if you think he can stay at home, they'll probably fund his care, which is good for us. Ultimately, it will be up to you. Social services are stretched to breaking point – they'll just rubber stamp whatever you report. You've got three months to prove that he can live alone. What do you think? Will you do this?'

And while I am still scrambling to come up with an excuse not to do it, because clearly I am not ready for this sort of responsibility, I hear a voice saying 'Yes.' It's only after Jane thanks me and says goodbye that I realise the voice had been my own.

Chapter Three

I am a child and my father is in the house, but I don't know where. Mum is in the room with me and she is saying, 'Stay away, not today, stay away, not today.' She repeats the phrase, her voice getting louder and louder until it is a horrifying yell, and then she is not there and I can hear my father approaching, his footsteps stomping up the stairs. I know he is coming for me. Then I see the door handle rattling and I am filled with utter paralysing terror.

I wake suddenly, my whole body jerking like a fish on a boat deck. I look at my own door handle and it seems to move, the door creaks open, just a little. I think I can see someone there.

A nightmare. I've been having them a lot recently. As soon as I can, I sit up in the bed, breathing deeply, waiting for it to pass. When I was in London, I started suffering from sleep paralysis. You wake up and you can't move because your brain hasn't told your body that it's not sleeping anymore, and then you see things – shadowy figures above you on the bed. A doctor told me it's common in people with anxiety disorders. It hasn't happened for a while, and this time it felt different – like the divide between sleep and life was blurring.

The first thing I do when I return to Avon Lodge is try to pick the gate up. It is still lying on the cracked stone path – a symbol of my uselessness and an obvious safety risk to callers. After several deep breaths, I grip it firmly and with all my might manage to lift it slowly into an upright position before manoeuvring it over to the garden wall, the base of it scraping noisily along the ground. I then lean it gently against the crumbling brickwork, wiping my hands together in a gesture of self-congratulation. If only I'd put 'Pick the gate up' on my 'To Do' list for the day. Perhaps I can add it, then cross it off immediately. That would not be not cheating.

'I don't think the wall will support that weight,' says a voice from behind me.

I spin around to find Will Emerson standing in the open doorway of his house.

'Jesus!' I yell. 'You've got to stop doing that!'

He stares at me, his usual impassive, unshifting expression. Does he recognise me?

'I'm Laura. From the care agency. We met on Tuesday?'

Nothing.

'Why do you have such a massive gate anyway?' I continue. 'It's like a bloody portcullis.'

'Perhaps you'd better come in,' says Mr Emerson. 'When you have finished blaspheming in my garden.'

He shakes his head, tuts and disappears into the house. I pull my hands into my sleeves and follow him.

The hallway is as sullen, dark and cold as I remember, and as we pass I glimpse into the front room again, and see the olive sofa, the flowery rug, the cobwebs and the vintage radio, which is once again playing a classical piece.

'You like music?' I say.

'It takes me back,' he replies, and for a few moments, there is a spark of enthusiasm in him. 'I was obsessed with it when I was young. Classical, jazz, swing, blues . . . When it's not playing, the silence reminds me that everything is gone.' He pauses and looks at me. 'Music is life,' he says.

Through the opposite doorway there is another room, lighter than the parlour and much tidier. There is a green leather armchair in the centre with a matching footstool, and along the far wall, a large rather, beautiful radiogram and an old upright piano. A wooden bookcase is utterly crammed with old newspapers, books and records. I wonder if this is where he spends his evenings, alone, listening to music, reading. That actually sounds nice. Most of *my* books have been lost along the way: lent to flatmates I barely knew, left behind in rooms I rented for a few months before running away – usually with little time to pack properly. I'd managed to keep a few battered paperbacks: the *Twilight* series, some Austens, a copy of *Tom's Midnight Garden* that my dad bought me. He had written inside, *This world is all wrong. Keep hold of something.* It makes me tearful and angry to think of it. But I can't seem to throw the damn book away.

'That's the study,' says Mr Emerson.

'You have a lot of books,' I say, trying to encourage him.

'Mostly on radio and telecommunications. Nothing to interest you, young lady.' With that, he wanders off toward the kitchen.

'Sexist old bastard,' I mutter under my breath.

He stops by the staircase and turns back.

'For an old bastard, I still have very good hearing,' he says, his voice terse and cold. I can feel my face blushing what must surely

44

be an irradiated crimson colour. You are definitely not supposed to insult the clients – rule number one. If he phoned Jane now, that would be that. One hundred per cent sackable offence. What else am I going to get wrong? How else am I going to annoy him? I fiddle with the strands of hair that have loosened from my ponytail, trying to draw them over my face like a guilty schoolkid.

'Go in and have a look,' he says. The tone of his voice is almost placatory. He shuffles on toward the kitchen, shaking his head once again.

The books are mostly as he described. Dull, musty old tomes on radio technology; a few classic works of literature dotted about. It's the newspapers that catch my eye. They are haphazardly piled on the bottom shelves and many have slopped out onto the floor into an unruly pile. When I look at them, I discover they are very old, from the 1930s onwards. Most are copies of *The Times*, its gigantic front pages a mass of tiny classified advertisements, and of the *Bath Chronicle and Herald*. I pick up the delicate artefacts gently, releasing a musty fragrance into the air. Will wanders in and hands me a mug of tea.

'Why did you keep all these?' I ask.

'I don't know. They were important to me once. I think I started collecting them after I was injured during the bombing. I seem to recall I was looking for something, but I can't remember what. Perhaps I just needed them to remind me about life before the air raids.'

Bombing. Air raids. I wonder if he was living in London during the Blitz. This could be the root of the problem. People who have suffered serious concussions can be more prone to dementia in later life.

'Did you have amnesia?' I ask him.

He shakes his head. 'Not quite. There are a few years after the

45

war that are . . . cloudy. I was in such a mess.' He looks glumly at the
piles of yellowing pages. 'Perhaps if they were in order, and neatly
stacked, I would be able to look through properly and remember
something.'

'Are you asking me to sort them out?'

He shrugs his shoulders. 'It'll give you something to do instead
of following me around looking miserable,' he says and walks out
again. It *would* be nice not to have to make any more awkward
conversation. And I do like sorting.

After an hour I have found that all the papers date from 1937 to
1942. While organising them, I thumb through the pages, vaguely
taking in the headlines about victorious battles and heavy losses,
about bombing raids and the advance of German troops toward
the Soviet Union. More importantly, I see that intermittently,
through the papers, especially in the *Bath Chronicles*, there are
stories that have been outlined in pen. These are often accompanied by scrawled question marks, often three or four in angry rows.
Sometimes the stories have been crossed through multiple times,
and a few have small handwritten notes, which I can't decipher
because they're so faded. I read a few of stories – something about
Bath's MP and the Fascist party, a piece on a company producing
radar equipment, something about a German woman cautioned
by the police. There seems to be nothing to connect them.

Just as I'm finishing, I find another issue of the *Bath Chronicle*
lodged right under the lowest shelf, which looks newer than the
rest. As I get closer I can see it is from 1977. I pick it up and leaf
through the pages – there are articles about the Silver Jubilee, new
road layouts and drugs raids, but nothing has been marked in the
same way as the others. I flick past a photo, a group of serious-
looking people standing around some archaic piece of technology,
under the headline ALL CHANGE AT WASHFORD, and I'm three

pages on before I realise something with a start, and swipe impatiently back again. One of the group, standing somewhat behind the others, looking sullen and indifferent, is a man with dark hair and a handsome rugged face, whose piercing eyes look startlingly familiar. I put it on the shelf with the others.

When I've finished, I walk through to the kitchen and see that, here too, everything is ancient, dirty and broken. There's a scratched-up Butler sink near the back door, cut into a scarred wooden work surface, and it is filled with washing up. I see mould clinging to the plates. A 1950s kitchen cabinet with fading sky blue doors stands next to an old oven, a blackened relic with a multitude of little doors and massive rusty iron hobs, splattered with who knows what. He should rent his home out for BBC period dramas. Or horror movies.

'It looks much better in the study now,' I say.

'Sit there,' he replies, pointing toward an old pine table in the centre. I walk over obediently and put my organiser down, opening it in case I need to make notes.

While he is busy making more tea, I try to think of polite conversational material in order to redeem myself for the 'sexist bastard' debacle. There are a few reliable opening gambits when talking to old people Jane told me: the weather, gardening, family, any personal trinkets you spot lying around the house – if you can steer them onto nostalgia, things tend to run pretty smoothly. As with first dates, current affairs and religion are to be avoided – as are my own problems. I definitely do not think Mr Emerson wants to hear about how I wake up every morning with a nameless dread that hangs about me all the time. He doesn't want to know that I cry in the shower so Mum doesn't hear me. *Nobody* wants to know about that. I decide to go with nostalgia.

'One of the papers was from 1977,' I say. 'You were in it.'

He looks up from the kettle, but there's nothing in his eyes.

'It was when they were removing all the old equipment from Washford transmitting station,' he says.

'You worked there?'

'Your powers of deduction really are extraordinary.'

'All your life?'

'No. I went to Washford later, in the fifties. I helped to maintain and update the broadcasting equipment. But by the end of the 1970s, those things were ancient fossils, like myself.'

'It must have been fascinating.'

'It was miserable,' he says. 'Everything after her has been miserable.'

Her? Does he mean his wife? I wonder if I should push him further, but decide not to. I get the feeling that if it's going to come, it will be on *his* terms. Instead, I get up from the table and wander over to the kitchen window. It's another overcast day, with bovine black clouds plodding across the sky in ceaseless herds – but the view is beautiful. Will's garden dips steeply toward some sort of large shed, but beyond that you can see the whole of Bath, quaint and tiny like a model village. In the centre, the spires and clustered Georgian buildings, then the suburbs, crawling out from the edges and up the hills, the snaking roads cutting through dense blocks of houses like cracks in paving stones.

'Wow,' I say, mostly to myself. 'That's quite a view.'

He shuffles over and stands next to me, handing over a steaming mug of tea (a mug this time, not a china cup – perhaps we are out of the formal stage). He winces out of the window for several seconds.

'I suppose you must get used to it after a while?' I say.

He turns and gives me a look of utter incredulity.

'I think you would have to be a bloody terrible cynic to ever take a view like that for granted,' he snipes.

And there we go, scolded again. Will this be the routine? Morning after morning, meeting this man, watching everything I say? The scenario wrenches up all too familiar feelings and memories. I do not want to get upset here; I do not want to end up tearful. I cup my hands around the mug, trying to enjoy the safe familiarity of its warmth. The seconds feel like hours, like torturous hours. He says nothing. Why am I even here? What does he want?

Turning away from the window, dreading the next exchange, I spot a narrow door on the wall opposite, a short way along from where we came in. I wonder if it leads to a pantry or something. I don't know why this catches my eye, but somehow I can't look away.

'What's that?' I say.

'The cellar,' he replies – somehow he knows what I'm looking at, despite the fact he is still staring out of the window. 'It used to be for coal, when my parents bought the house.'

Out of sheer desperation, I say, 'Can I have a look?'

'No.' He says it instantly, in a sharp loud tone. 'I haven't been down for years, the steps are steep and rotten. It's not safe. There's nothing down there now apart from an old Morrison shelter.'

'A what?'

'A Morrison shelter. Do they not teach history at school anymore?'

Exasperated, I go to put my mug down on the work surface, but I am too quick and it becomes a slam. The tea sloshes and spills onto my hand.

'Look, you don't *have* to be rude to me,' I say, trying not to sound upset but feeling the liquidy glug of emotion in my throat. 'You rang my boss and told her you wanted to see me, but if you've changed your mind, that's absolutely fine, I can go.'

He stares at me with a combination of surprise, horror and anger – and although this is a fairly common resting expression for an old man, I get the sense I've really done it this time. This is clearly where he tells me to bugger off. Through the silence that follows, I hear traffic passing on the road outside, and then the clock chimes loudly from the other room. He clears his throat to speak.

'A Morrison shelter is a reinforced metal cage about the size of a dining table,' he says. 'They were used during air raids in the Second World War.'

Partly I am thinking, what is going on with this man? But I am also remembering that Bath itself was bombed. Mum once took me to a war exhibition at the Victoria Art Gallery. They had all these old photos of the damage, there were gas masks and ration books on display, and they showed a video of survivors reliving their memories.

'So you lived here then, when Bath was bombed? Did you fight in the war?'

Will continues to look out of the window, his eyes slightly watery. I do not want to say anything crass or dumb now, so I just stand there too. But the longer the silence stretches out, the more I wonder if he is having memory problems. Is he struggling to recall anything at all?

'I didn't fight,' he says at last. 'I was here in the city. I had what they called a reserved occupation. It meant I couldn't be conscripted.'

'What did you do?'

'I worked for a company called Anderson Wireless as a research engineer. I helped to design radio components. When the war started, we were sequestered into military work.'

'Is that one of your radios in the living room?'

'No. That is quite clearly a Pye 25 set. Pye was one of the most important radio manufacturers in the world and they were based in Cambridge. You can tell it's a Pye by the giant Pye logo on the front.'

50

'Right,' I say. 'Obviously I should have recognised it. Did you work at Anderson all through the war?'

'No, only until 1942.'

'Why 1942? Did you leave or …' A thought occurs to me. 'Oh wait, wasn't that the year Bath was bombed? Was the office destroyed?'

'No,' he replies, his voice quiet and controlled. 'I was.'

I look at him, a little confused.

'What do you mean?'

He turns away and shuffles over to the dining table, leaning on it heavily and then slumping down into a chair.

'I lost my wife. On the second night of the bombing raid.'

Silence. His whole body seems to slump in on itself. Suddenly, he looks extremely frail and miserable. For the first time, I can see in his face all of his eighty-seven years.

'I'm so sorry,' I say, and I walk up and reach out for him. 'Do you want to tell me about her?'

'Actually, I think it would be better if you left,' he says. His voice is soft yet firm.

'But we have another hour?'

In my training, Jane told me it is really common for people with dementia to switch mood in an instant from happiness to the depths of misery, sometimes even to anger. You have to be ready. The correct response is 'comfort and distract' – make them feel safe, change the topic. But in this moment, I've got nothing.

I hover near him, considering whether I should put a hand on his shoulder. When I finally do so, his whole body seems to jerk and then freeze, as though he has never been touched before.

'Please,' he says. 'Please just go.'

'Are you sure you're okay? I can—'

'Get out, I said!'

It is so very loud. The burst of it takes me right back to my childhood. My dad. Quiet, quiet, then rage and volume. All those emotions punch me in the stomach. I feel now what I did then: head down, guilty. Tears prick at my eyes. I collect my coat from the back of the chair. I know what it is like to be hijacked by your own emotions, but in this moment, I despise him. The air is so thick and leaden in here; the outside world feels miles away. I back out of the room and walk quickly along the hall to the front door, breathing deeply. Pulling my shitty anorak on makes me feel even more sorry for myself. I've got to try and keep it together, at least until I'm outside. I yearn to be free from everything. But when I reach for the door latch, I stop abruptly.

My organiser is still on the kitchen table.

There is no way I can leave it – it has all my 'To Do' lists, all my contacts, addresses, notes, bank cards . . . I have to get it. I back up against the wall in frustration and disbelief and wipe my eyes with my fingers. I've just got to do this.

I take a moment, then I am creeping slowly back up the hallway. I can't hear anything from him and I start praying that he's gone out to the garden or something, but when I reach the kitchen, he is still at the table, his face buried in his hands. He is sobbing. His bony shoulders, his bent back, all shaking. I freeze. Should I try and comfort him? I know I ought to, but I am desperate to escape.

I edge toward the table and pick up the organiser, expecting him to hear me, to sit up with a start, to shout at me again. But he is lost in misery. I turn back toward the door and step away. Halfway along the hall, I hear him saying something, very quietly at first, but then louder. Repeating the same word over and over.

'Elsa,' he moans. 'Elsa, Elsa, Elsa.'

It is the sound of terrible, wretched sadness. I know it well. I head quickly to the front door and open it, but when I go to walk out I feel a weird kind of resistance, a change in air pressure. It feels as though something is only grudgingly letting me go – pulling me back, even. I have the feeling again, of someone suddenly being very close to me. I turn around, ready to greet Mr Emerson, but he's not there, just a faint sweet scent in the air. A shadow moves across the wall in the hallway. The door to the study wavers.

I walk quickly out of the house and toward my bike. As I'm riding away, I glance up at the row of Georgian houses just along from Avon Lodge. In one of the bedroom windows, there is an old woman staring right at me. When she sees me look back, she moves away and the curtain closes.

Chapter Four

There is a reason for the organiser. I've always been very into lists and schedules, but when I started on antidepressants, I began to have this weird feeling that I was only partially present in the world. Sometimes, it's as though I'm on a raft and everything is floating by, far away. I've become even more obsessed with trying to record and retain information, to anchor onto reality. My organiser is my ship's log, and my distress beacon. When I reach the end of every day, I cross it through on the year planner at the front – my life represented as neat diagonal lines on a page. Every Friday evening I check my 'To Do' lists, always adding uncompleted tasks onto the Monday of the following week. In this way I keep in touch with reality as the days drift. And I really *must* keep it together now because I have a job to do.

Mr Emerson didn't call Jane to cancel my visits. Neither did I. Even though he clearly hates me, even though there is something just so unsettling about him, I am drawn to that house. I see it when I close my eyes. I just have to keep going – not because of the job, but because there is something there I need to find out. There is something wrong. It seems no one has ever taken Mr Emerson's grief and trauma seriously. I know what that's like. I know how it feels not to be believed.

On the next visit, I decide not to mention that I saw him crying at his kitchen table. My plan is to keep things airy and casual, yet also caring – like a daytime TV presenter talking to the victim of a recent tragedy. I am walking up the pathway when I hear music coming from inside as usual, but this time it has a different quality. It is being played on a piano, surely the one in Mr Emerson's study, but the sound echoes and fades in and out as though moving through a cavernous space. When I knock on the door, it stops. Then Will is there, glaring at me.

'How are you doing today?' I ask.

'I am an eighty-seven-year-old man, living alone in a house that might well collapse on me at any moment.'

I breathe deeply. I'm not sure I can face much more of this.

'We have four hours a week together,' I say. 'So it might be useful for us to think about what we can get out of that time.'

He harrumphs.

'What can I do for you, Will? May I call you Will?'

For a second, a strange look overcomes him, like he has just recalled a powerful memory. His eyes are almost watery.

'I think,' he says quietly, 'I think Mr Emerson is more appropriate.'

'What can I do for you, Mr Emerson?' I continue, unperturbed. 'For example, can I help you with medication?'

'I take half an aspirin a day, I'm certain I can manage that.'

'I can do your food shopping?'

'There is a Co-op up the road and the exercise is good for me.'

'Or we could just go for walks. You're very close to Hedgemead Park.'

'I know where I live, Miss James! As it happens, my father was there when the park was opened.'

This is how things go. Every polite conversation I try to start, he bats it away. He has the air of someone who is waiting for something to happen and becoming increasingly frustrated that it is *not* happening and might never happen. Perhaps there is a question I am meant to ask that will unlock everything. Somehow, I need to move past this awkward stage of him detesting everything I say or do.

He goes off to make tea, so I sit in the front room, looking at the antique radio, the print on the wall, wondering if the large damp patch on the ceiling above the window has always been there. I get a horrible memory of the last flat I rented in London. One day I pulled the wardrobe back and found the whole wall swarming with cockroaches. Then a thought strikes me about the room, and about all the rooms I've seen so far. No photos. Old people always have photos on display. Always. Photos are memories; they are proof, when everything else is fading, that a life has been lived and shared. If he really loved Elsa, if he misses her desperately, where is she? Where is the evidence of her in this broken house?

When Will comes in he is holding two mugs, which are sploshing wetly together as he shuffles. I leap up off the sofa and take one from him, eliciting his standard 'tut and grimace' response to any human contact. I sheepishly return to the sofa. He lowers himself into the armchair and sighs loudly. It is going to be a long hour. The clock ticks. The sound echoes around the room. Out of desperation, I take my organiser out and open to the diary pages, pretending to check on where I am going next. Perhaps he'll fall asleep, or just leave the room. Instead he clears his throat and points.

'What *is* that thing you carry around everywhere?'

'It's a personal organiser. It has all my lists of things to do and my contacts. I write down things that have happened, too. Actually, I couldn't help but notice . . . ' I'm looking up and pointing to the folders I saw on the shelf, filled with typed pages. 'Did you use to—'

'Did you read those?' He is angry again.

'No, I just saw them and thought they might be—'

'They are private! I would very much appreciate it if you refrained from snooping around!'

'I wasn't snooping, Mr Emerson. I'm sorry.'

I look down at my organiser, gripping hold of it, wishing my way out of here.

'I thought everyone had a mobile phone now,' he says, his tone quiet and measured again.

'I don't.'

'All young people have phones. I see them walking about constantly prodding at the buttons.'

'I used to have one. Not anymore.'

'Why?'

I shift on the sofa and realise I am playing with a thread from the sleeve of my jumper. This is what I do when I am trying to be invisible. When I look up Mr Emerson is still waiting for an answer. That's the problem with old people – they have time.

'I . . . I don't like them,' I say and my voice is almost a whisper because I don't want to get into this.

'Why?'

'I don't know.'

'Yes, you do.'

'I don't want people to be able to contact me whenever they like. Why are you interrogating me?'

He looks suddenly crestfallen; mortified. 'You are the only person in thirty years who has asked me about my life, and really *listened*,' he says. 'I am trying to remember how I ought to respond to that.'

In this moment, and not for the first time, I feel a painful similarity between us. No one has ever really listened to or believed me, either. I want to think of something placatory to say.

'I liked that music you were playing on the piano before I came in,' I say. 'Was it an old tune?'

He fixes me with a bewildered stare. The look in his eyes is almost chilling.

'I wasn't playing music,' he says.

'But I heard it when I arrived.'

'I have never played the piano. It was my mother's and then it was Elsa's.'

He's forgotten, I think to myself. He's forgotten what he was doing barely minutes ago.

When our time is up, I grab my bike, clamber on, and, lost in thought, jam my foot on the pedal without looking up at the pavement in front of me, almost crashing straight into a man walking towards me. Luckily, I spot him at the last moment, skidding to a halt in front of him.

'Oh shit,' I say. 'I'm so sorry.'

I'm dreading another telling off, but he smiles warmly.

'Oh no, my fault, I wasn't looking either,' he says. He's eccentrically dressed in a mustard-coloured woollen coat and a very long purple scarf, and he has a friendly, ruddy face. 'You've just come out of Avon Lodge?'

'Yeah.'

'Poor old Will Emerson,' he says. 'A very misunderstood man.'

With that he carries on up the road. I'd been thinking of talking to Will's neighbours, seeing if there was anything I could learn from them – I recalled my encounter with the young woman pushing the buggy past his house, warning me to stay away from him. I wanted to find out if this was the consensus. The idea of knocking on doors and interrogating complete strangers filled me with anxiety, but here was a chance to talk to someone who looked pretty harmless.

'Excuse me?' I call after him. I say it before I've thought about what I want to ask, and now the man has stopped and is looking back at me. 'Do you live around here?'

'I don't, but my mother lives there.' He points at a house further down the road. It's the one where I saw the old lady watching me from the upstairs window.

'I'm a carer, I'm looking after Mr Emerson. I was just wondering . . . do you know him at all?'

'Not personally,' he says in a quiet, thoughtful voice. 'I've been visiting my mother here for ten years and the most I've got out of him is "good morning".'

I'm about to thank him for his time, but he's not finished.

' . . . A few of the residents on this part of the road have their own online forum – his name comes up quite a bit.'

'What do they say about him?'

'Just that he's a bit of an oddball. A couple of years ago, someone held a firework party in their garden. After a few bangs and flashes, he was out in his garden yelling and screaming. Scared the life out of the kids apparently. I know social services have been called. These houses are worth a million each now. The people moving in here, they're well off, they have power, they want things to be a certain way. They think Avon Lodge brings down the tone of the area – they don't want it affecting the property prices. I mean, I'm a property developer myself, so I have some sympathy for them, but I feel sorry for the lonely old bugger. And he is good to my mother – he takes round vegetables from his garden. She's housebound, so it's comforting. I'm glad he has someone visiting him. I've never seen anyone else go in or out of that house. What *is* he like?'

'He's still a bit of a mystery. I want to find out more, but he doesn't seem to have any family. The house is a mess.'

'It's a beautiful place, though. My mother is obsessed with it. She was here as a child, she remembers all these houses as they were. I'm sure she'd be happy to chat to you. I have to admit, I'd love to get my hands on the place, it would be a wonderful project. Anyway, I'd better get on. Nice to meet you.'

With that, he walks away in the opposite direction. I glance up to his mother's house, just in time to see the curtain swishing back into place.

Chapter Five

The consulting room is small and bare, but the window looks out onto a wide leafy street and a row of beautiful townhouses. I am visiting my GP, Dr Bedford. He is in his late thirties, friendly and awkwardly handsome in the nerdy English way familiar to fans of Richard Curtis movies. He is wearing a smart plaid shirt and brown knitted jumper. I'm wearing the long baggy sweatshirt I slept in. My skinny jeans are too tight so the top button isn't done up. I would have made more effort but I spent the morning hyperventilating over this appointment. He looks up at me from his computer and his face betrays no obvious repulsion at my appearance. I feel guilty because I am lying to him. Through the fog that has taken up permanent residence in my head, I know that I need his help, but I've let him down.

'So, Laura, the last time you came in, you were not getting on well with the medication. Are things any better?'

He looks hopeful and I don't want to disappoint him. But I have to.

'Not really,' I say quietly, looking down at my hands, my fingers knotted together.

'Can you tell me how you're feeling?'

'Tired all the time. Constantly anxious. I keep forgetting things. I feel . . . shit. Just totally shit . . . You did ask.'

I promised myself I would hold it together.

'Oh dear,' he says, turning to his keyboard and rapidly typing something in with two fingers. 'That's not ideal.'

'It really isn't.'

'This kind of antidepressant, it can take a little time to bed in, sometimes it . . .'

'It's been three months. I've been taking them for three months.'

I still can't make eye contact and I feel like a petulant child. I can sense him studying me. Waiting for me to fill the growing silence. Outside, huge 4×4 cars pass by, no doubt wealthy parents dropping their children off at the school next door. The sun is warm through the window and the world outside looks pretty and carefree. By his keyboard Dr Bedford has a mug with the Bath rugby logo on it. I stare at it for a few seconds as an unwanted memory drifts in. He notices where I'm looking.

'Are you a fan?' he asks.

'My dad took me once.'

I was seven, the stadium was noisy and I didn't understand the rules. After a few minutes, I got fidgety, so when the game reached half time, Dad wrenched me off the seat and dragged me home. He told Mum 'this little brat ruined the afternoon for both of us' and didn't talk to me for two days. Why is it I can recall things like this, and not what I had for lunch yesterday? It stings so hard. I can taste blood in my mouth. Dr Bedford is waiting.

'I just feel like I want to come off them. I don't think they're right for me. It's not helping. I can't . . .'

The sentence gets lost and I can feel tears in my eyes. Then they're rolling down my cheeks, and I'm trying to wipe them away with the backs of my hands and my fingers.

'Sorry,' I say. 'Sorry.'

'Don't be.'

He turns back toward his desk, pulls a couple of tissues from a box then leans in and hands them to me – this is probably the extent of the physical sympathy he's allowed to show. I blow my nose extremely loudly.

'I want to stop right now,' I say.

He nods slowly, like a chess grandmaster considering a move.

'Not a good idea,' he says. 'You really mustn't do that.'

I feel a spasm of worry.

'Why?'

'Because these are quite powerful psychotropic drugs; they make changes to the brain chemistry and when you come off them suddenly there can be withdrawal effects.'

Shit. 'What like?'

'Insomnia, dizziness, headaches, mood swings . . .'

'I have those already!'

'There can be slightly more serious things too. Sensory disturbances, for example.'

'Sensory disturbances?'

'Sometimes people hear, see or even smell things that aren't there.'

I get an image in my head of Avon Lodge, the sense of something in the room with me.

Dr Bedford sees my expression and his face softens into a reassuring smile.

'Look, that's very rare, don't worry. And you're still taking them . . . aren't you?'

'Yes. I mean, of course.'

'Good. I think the best thing is to reduce the daily dose and see how it goes for a month or two – then we can try something

63

different. The important thing is, we get you to a place where you're managing your anxiety. We need to make sure that what happened in London never happens again.'

The splintered memory of that night hits me once more. The wet pavement; bare, bloody feet; and then Lambeth Bridge. Just past midnight, the wind buffeting over the dark Thames. A police officer holding out her hand. 'Come down, love. Come down.' Car horns bellowing. Did this happen? Did I dream it?

'I see you're still on the waiting list for therapy,' Dr Bedford continues. 'I'll see what I can do about speeding things up. I think that will really help. Because you do need a bit of help, Laura.'

I nod, but my throat feels as though there's a bowling ball lodged in it and I can't reply. When you spend a lot of time trying to pretend nothing is wrong, it is weird to be confronted with the fact that actually, everything is wrong and has been for a long time. All the scaffolding collapses. He sits back in his chair.

'How is everything else?' he says in a brighter tone. 'How is work?'

He is giving me the chance to get myself together.

'It's okay,' I say. 'I'm caring for this guy who is almost ninety years old. I have to decide whether he can stay in his home, or if he should be taken into care.'

'That's a lot of responsibility. Are you okay with that?'

'I have to be. He refused to speak to anyone else. I need to be capable for once.'

'I think you'll look after him really well.'

'I don't know. Everyone else thinks he's senile.'

'But you don't?'

'There's something about him – it feels important to understand. I don't know why. Do you have any tips on dealing with challenging clients?'

He smiles at me again, and then turns to his computer and taps away.

'I've ordered your repeat prescription, you can collect it on your way out,' he says.

'Thank you.'

He watches me get up and grab my bag from the chair next to me.

'There's always a story,' he says.

I turn back to him.

'I'm sorry?'

'Difficult clients. There's always a story behind who they are. The trick is in helping the person to tell it. People give themselves away in the stories they tell. When you understand the story, you know what to do.'

'Okay,' I say, pulling my arms into the sleeves of my anorak.

'One last question,' he says. 'Why do you think the old man spoke to you and no one else?'

'I don't know,' I shrug. 'Probably because it was really pissing it down when I first visited him and he felt sorry for me.'

Dr Bedford crosses his arms and smiles a warm, indulgent smile.

'No,' he says. 'No, I don't think that's it at all.'

Cycling away, I think about Will and how to get to his story. I need to find something to talk to him about. There are two things I *know* he is interested in: vintage radios and erotic modernist art. I decide to concentrate on the former. Instead of going straight home, I take a detour to Bath Central Library, and to my surprise find *two* books on the early days of the wireless industry, including one about the history of Pye. I don't think they have been borrowed for many years.

I spend the afternoon at home in my room, lying across the

sofa reading up on the history of radio – the early crystal sets, the arrival of moving coil speakers and superheterodyne technology in the 1930s, the spread of transmitting stations across the country – making notes as I go. I wonder if this is a bit pathetic – learning about radios so an eighty-seven-year-old man will be nice to me. But it is more than that. I want to help him. It's up to me now to show he can live in that house. I have to give him the chance to prove it.

And then I'm falling asleep and I need to find a bookmark. I dig around in my bag for a piece of paper and find the prescription that Dr Bedford gave me. I forgot to pick up the pills at the pharmacy. I should go into town tomorrow and collect them. I should do that. I really should.

Chapter Six

It is not long before I get to test my new-found expertise in pre-war radio sets. I am sitting in the parlour at Mr Emerson's, on the olive sofa. We are drinking tea with absolutely nothing to say to each other, the awkward silence mercifully undercut by the sound of classical music from the wireless set. I get up and casually walk over to the bookshelf. Deep breath.

'I see you have the model B version of the Pye 25,' I say, trying not to sound too rehearsed. 'I don't think the rising sun motif was used in the model A version, was it?'

Mr Emerson looks at me blankly. I don't know if it's boredom or shock. I decide to carry on anyway.

'And then after the war, they phased out that logo completely, didn't they? Because of its connotations with Japan?'

Nothing. I feel ridiculously crestfallen. My gambit has crashed and burned and I have another hour to fill. I'm just about to sit down again, when he clears his throat.

'It's a model C,' he says tonelessly. 'Not a model B.'

A response! And it doesn't matter that I'm wrong. After all, the best way to engage with a man is to make a minor factual error about something he's interested in.

'. . . But,' he continues, 'they look identical. There's no way you could know without looking at the components. How did you find this out?'

'I went to the library and they had a couple of books on the subject. I made notes.'

He looks at me. I feel like he's sizing me up.

'Why?' he says.

'Because I'm interested. I like how these old wirelesses look like pieces of furniture, not just gadgets. They were designed to fit in with the décor of a room, to be looked at. Also, I thought it would give us something to talk about, Mr Emerson.'

There is a slight movement in his expression.

'Call me Will,' he says. And he almost, *almost* smiles.

Bingo.

'There's a lot I still don't know, Will. I guess I should go on the internet.'

He shakes his head. 'If you really want to learn,' he says, 'there is something I ought to show you.'

Our walk through the garden is silent, but there is a sense of trepidation in the cool fresh air. It's mostly laid to lawn, but there's a large vegetable patch with rows of carrots and what look like beetroots. The door to the workshop is slightly warped but Will heaves it open with practised efficiency. When I peer inside I understand that I have been transported into the vintage equivalent of a man cave (an old man cave?). In the centre of the room is a large, solid, wooden work table, the surface of the chunky edifice littered with tools, wires and ancient components that I cannot identify. Along three of the walls are shelving units, placed closely together, all of them cluttered with rows and rows of old radios. Some are in wooden cabinets, dulled with dust and cobwebs yet still grand and beautiful, some are in faded Bakelite, others have their covers removed, the innards exposed. In the gloom, they resemble ornate tombstones. Opposite the door there is a smeared window offering a slightly lower view of the Bath skyline than the kitchen, and beneath it a desk piled high with arcane communications equipment – black boxes covered in switches and dials, and in front of them an old microphone. It looks like some ancient BBC studio and I know from the books I've been reading that it's a radio transmitting station. Nearby, there is a large metal chest of drawers, and a whole wall where various screwdrivers, spanners and unidentifiable little tools are hung up like implements of torture.

'Wow,' I say. 'Is this where all old radios go to die?'

Will smiles. An actual, genuine smile this time.

'Go on, have a look,' he says.

I walk in and stroll slowly along the shelves, running my fingers through the dust on the cases, beginning to feel like a child at some eccentric local museum. It strikes me how different, how unique, each of the wireless cabinets is. Some have huge dial displays and swooping art deco mouldings, others are squat little boxes. One looks like a bizarre science fiction space helmet.

'Where did you get them all?' I ask.

'Some I bought, some were given to me because they were broken, some were from the office.'

'Do any still work?'

'A few. A lot of them used an early type of battery called an accumulator – you had to take it to a bicycle shop or motor garage to get it recharged. Some did use mains power, though. A couple are plugged in if you want to listen one day.'

I nod, hoping to encourage him to keep talking.

'I started fixing these things when I was nine or ten,' he said. 'I just ... understood them. I was something of a prodigy I suppose. Neighbours would bring their sets over to me for repairs. Then I started to send off for components so I could build them myself – it was much cheaper than buying ready-made sets from the shops.'

'Is that how you got your job?'

'Indirectly, yes. My father knew Harold Anderson – they were in the same regiment during the First World War. I'd just finished at technical college and he asked Anderson if I could go for an interview. I think Father rather despaired at ever finding a role for me.'

'That sounds familiar,' I tell him.

'I went to meet Mr Anderson and he showed me their latest wireless model. I examined it carefully and then I told him how it could be improved. He called me a rude, precocious little brat ... '

'Oh, so you've always had good people skills?' I say. I immediately worry I've gone too far, but he merely pauses and retains his wry smile.

'What happened next?' I say. 'Did he throw you out?'

'No. He offered me a job in his research division. At eighteen, I was by far the youngest person there – the rest were university graduates, engineers, scientists ... It took them a while to warm to me.'

We're silent for a few minutes.

'Why do you keep them all?' I ask.

He looks up.

'They remind me of the person I was,' he says. 'Elsa used to get very frustrated with how long I spent in here, tinkering about. But then she decided to come in too. She'd sit reading while I worked. And all the while she was quietly learning about radio communications.' He looks toward the transmitter station under the window.

70

'Elsa? That's your wife?'

He nods distractedly. 'Elsa Klein,' he says, then again to himself in a whispered chant, 'Elsa Klein, Elsa Klein.'

'That's a beautiful name. It sounds Dutch?'

'She was Austrian.'

'And you met her before the war?'

'Yes, at a dance.'

He shuffles over to the far wall and picks up one of the smaller wireless sets from the shelf; its darker wood case appears almost black in the gloomy lighting. 'This is one of ours, the Maestro. I helped design the tuning set-up.'

I walk around the desk to take a closer look, and I'm on the verge of asking about it when an incredibly loud bell noise suddenly erupts from somewhere in the room.

'Jesusfuckingshit!' I yell.

'That's someone at the front door,' says Will. 'I had the bell wired up here years ago. It's probably the postman.'

'I'll go,' I say, trying to calm my thudding heart.

'No, you stay. Look around. I'm not an invalid. Yet. But please – don't touch anything.'

With that, he walks around the work table and out, leaving me alone in his shrine to ancient communications.

The atmosphere is immediately different in his absence. Heavier somehow, as though the silence has its own weight. I notice now the huge cobwebs hanging along the walls and the rotten wooden rafters. Feeling slightly spooked and claustrophobic, I walk over to the window and peer out through the cold, hazy glass, but I can't see much of the city below through the dirty pane. Instead I look down at the microphone and for a few odd moments it looks familiar. I get a snapshot, a memory of it, that feels distant but res-onant. I tell myself I must have seen something similar in one of

71

the old black-and-white movies I end up watching with Mum on rainy Sunday afternoons. But then it's not just the microphone that looks familiar, it's all this equipment, this window. It's like déjà vu, but more powerful. A vision of the room in another time. Feeling faint, I put out a hand to lean on the transmitter and feel a jolt of something, like an electric shock. Suddenly, there's a blast of static from the speakers. It's so loud the dust seems to reverberate in the air around me, and I have to jam my fingers in my ears, a wave of fear crashing over me like icy cold water. Something clatters outside, and as it does, the noise immediately stops. The door begins to open and then Will is standing there. I double back in shock, almost falling over.

'What on earth is it?' he says.

'That radio just turned on,' I say, pointing backwards into the room. 'Didn't you hear it?'

'I told you not to touch anything!'

'I didn't mean to!'

'I should have known I couldn't trust you! This is valuable equipment. It's all I have! Which set did you switch on?'

'I didn't switch on anything.'

'Which one was the noise coming from?'

I turn and point to the equipment under the window. His face drops into an expression of disbelief, then he pushes past me, over to the transmitter and starts pushing at the buttons, peering inside the case at the blackened valves and snaking wires.

'I'm sorry,' I say again. 'I just leaned on it and it started.'

'Whatever you think you heard it couldn't have come from this transmitter.'

'Why not?'

'Because the damn thing hasn't worked since the war.'

*

The shock of the noise stays with me all afternoon, as do Will's dismissive words. When I leave the house, I cycle away slowly, still feeling unsettled, and as has become almost habit now, look up at the old lady's window a few doors down. Sure enough, she is there, staring out at me, her thin face impassive and inscrutable. I feel a cold breeze across me that makes me shiver. What *is* her deal?

I jam on the brakes.

I am acting on instinct as I lead my bike to her front door, laying it down gently on her path. I breathe deeply, eyes closed, heart thudding. My finger pauses over the door buzzer for several seconds, then I press it.

And just like when I met her son, I have no idea what to say until it's too late. I hear the sound of a latch turning on the other side of the door. It opens enough for me to see her.

'How can I help you?' she says. Her voice is spookily high and mannered, like a child's. She is wearing a long patchwork cardigan matched with a necklace of large colourless stones. Her long, almost white hair is in two thin plaits down her back. She looks at me expectantly, as though my visit had been prearranged.

'I'm sorry to bother you,' I stutter. 'I'm a carer for Will Emerson who lives at Avon Lodge. My name's Laura James.'

'Hello, I'm Florence Barnes,' she says.

'I'm trying to find out a bit more about Will. I met your son. He told me you have lived here a long time?'

She looks me up and down. 'Come in.'

I am shown into a dark little living room with ancient blackened floorboards and sooty whitewashed walls. There is an open fire, and a large sideboard cluttered with thick church candles which have oozed wax all over the surface. 'Please, sit down,' she says, gesturing to a sofa, buried beneath knitted throws. She sits in a wooden rocking chair, and watches me silently for a few moments.

73

'Now, what do you want to know? I cannot tell you much about Will, I'm afraid. I see him occasionally, but he's not a big talker as you have probably found.'

My heart sinks. Another dead end. For a second, I'm not quite sure if there is much point in carrying on. But at least she may be able to tell me about Elsa. I just have to think of the best way to get there.

'So you grew up here?' I ask.

She smiles indulgently.

'Yes. I was born in this house in 1935, although I started at a boarding school when I was ten and was hardly at home after that. I moved away when I was married. But my parents left the house to me when they died and I came back when my husband passed. I have glimpses of Will from my childhood – he was rather hand- some back then, although very quiet, as I said.'

I pause before asking the next question. I feel like so much is riding on the answer.

'When you lived here as a child, was he dating anyone, do you know?'

She looks at me with a sense of confused, questioning surprise.

'Not while I was here, no,' she says.

'Are you sure?'

'When I was seven I contracted scarlet fever and then pneu- monia. I was virtually bed-bound for a year. I was so fragile, the doctors doubted I would ever recover. I spent a lot of time looking out of my bedroom window watching the world go by. Apart from his mother, I never saw a woman near that house.'

'Oh,' I say. This appeared to contradict all of Will's memories. The love he felt, the stories about Elsa, their relationship. Was it all the product of dementia? This is perhaps what loneliness does if given enough time.

'He is a strange fellow, but he has always been good to me,' she says. 'I think people see someone who is a bit different and feel threatened. And now we're both old, we're getting rather left behind. Lots of younger families are moving in – we're seen as relics, if we're seen at all. Avon Lodge is a mess now, but it was beautiful once. When I was a child, we used to run along the alley at the back of the houses, all the neighbourhood kids did. Will didn't mind us messing about in his garden, and he was always playing music from one of his wireless sets. But there was a lot of chatter about him in the street. Especially when he disappeared.'

'He disappeared?'

'Yes, after the bombing. He was gone for a number of years. No one knows where. There were rumours about it.'

'What sort of rumours?'

'That he'd been arrested for something, some terrible crime, and that he was in prison. There was even talk of a murder. But I was very young, I was only told so much.'

Prison? It didn't seem credible. Surely there would be records? But then, when I talked to Will about the newspapers he'd collected, what had he said? The years after the war had been 'cloudy'? Was he blocking something out?

'Do you think it's true?' I ask her.

She shakes her head. 'He's a troubled man, I think, but no. Not that.'

'Do you remember the bombing?'

'Oh yes. After the first night, my mother took my brothers to stay with her sister in Batheaston, but I was too ill to move so my father stayed with me in the house. When the bombers returned, I heard the sirens and lifted the blackout blinds to watch. Two bombs dropped along our road, but quite a way from us. Then my father rushed in and carried me down to the cellar.'

'Did a bomb hit Will's house?'

'No. No, it couldn't have. It would have damaged our house too, and the others along this terrace. The bombs dropped further up the road, past Avon Lodge. Where they're building now.'

But Will had said he was injured in the bombing. Another false memory? For a second I don't know what to say, and she seems to pick up on it.

'You met my son Matthew the other day,' she says. 'Did he tell you to come and see his eccentric old mother?'

'He said you wouldn't mind chatting about the war.'

She smiles at me.

'The street was ours then. It feels like we're outcasts now, us old folk. All that property development, expanding out, swallowing up houses. The past is just an inconvenience to them. They don't understand. Bath is an ancient place. The past is very much alive here. Anyway, I'm afraid I'll have to get on. I have a friend coming over in a bit.'

'That's fine. Thank you for inviting me in.'

We get up and walk through to the front door; she opens it halfway before stopping and turning back to me. Her expression is one of puzzlement.

'Can I ask – did you have close relatives living in Bath during the war?'

I shake my head. 'No. Not that I know of.'

She studies me closely. I hear a low noise in my ears, like traffic, but none is passing.

'You look so familiar,' she says. The intensity in her voice is unsettling and she is wincing at me, as though dredging up some distant memory.

'I've been visiting every other day, you've seen me riding past.' I say it with a nervous little laugh, to try and break the weird tension. But she is not smiling.

'No, I recognise you from before; from long before this.'

I have a sudden dizzy spell and my legs feel so shaky I have to lean against her wall. 'I should get going,' I say, but my voice is slurred and I have no idea if she hears or not.

A few yards down the street, I have to stop pedalling, get off the bike and throw up into a bush. I retch until there's nothing left. When I get home, I go straight up to my room; I open the bottom drawer of my desk and pull out my battered old university laptop, the case covered in stickers, the screen smeared and dusty. I stop for a while and take some deep breaths because this thing has baggage attached. I remind myself that the email app was deleted years ago, so I won't see any notifications popping up. No unwanted intrusions. I plug in the cable and power it up, then spend forty minutes updating the operating system and the web browser. When it is finally ready, I pause, gathering myself, thinking about what I am doing and why, and what it will mean. I say to myself: to make progress, I have to interact with the world and I have to be able to deal with what it tells me. And then I google 'Elsa Klein'.

Chapter Seven

I'm in Jane's office for our regular catch-up. Between us on the desk is a plate filled with bourbon biscuits. This means the meeting is serious.

'So,' she says. 'Here are the questions we need to answer. Is Will coping in his house? Does his memory of his own life make sense? If not, does he have dementia and is he really safe alone?'

She takes a biscuit, which is my cue.

'I searched for his wife on the internet,' I tell her. She leans forward. We both know if there's anything I can get right, it's this.

When I was nineteen, I started a degree in Media and Communications at UWE. I lasted two terms before some things happened, my anxiety exploded, and I left. But one subject I loved was Research Methodology. Sitting alone in a silent library, tapping away at a computer, making notes, methodically working through evidence. I could do that. It was calming. I aced it.

'And what did you find?' asks Jane.

'Obviously there are thousands of Elsa Kleins, but I couldn't find any who lived in Bath in the 1930s. Then I checked the marriage register – there's nothing for anyone called Will Emerson or Elsa Klein in Bath during that period. I'm worried he made her up, or imagined her.'

'And you understand about confabulation?'

'Yes. Confabulation is false memories – they are a symptom of dementia.'

'It could also be PTSD – some trauma from the war,' Jane says. 'It could even be schizophrenia or bipolar disorder, in which case he needs professional psychiatric care. Or he could just be lying to you.'

'Lying?'

'He's a lonely old man. He might be looking for companionship, or an ally, someone to fight his corner. I've heard some whoppers in my time. Lonely people do desperate things.'

The thought had occurred to me, too, and it brought a memory. I used to ask my dad about his childhood, and he'd tell me elaborate tales about his fascinating, loving parents and a beautiful house, and travels all over the world. But much later, I found out he'd told mum his parents abandoned him and he'd grown up in a children's home. The details kept changing. I should have been angry, but despite everything, his need to make up stories about his past made me pity him. There was always a sadness there, deep down, eating him from the inside. It ruined him and it ruined us. And then one day, he just packed a bag and disappeared.

'So what are you going to do?' asks Jane.

'Talk to him some more. If I find out anything new, I'll look into it, but I doubt I will.'

'Are you still happy to be doing this?'

'What do you mean?'

'You just look ... exhausted. You look frazzled. Social services will act on whatever you tell them – considering what's going on in your life, that's a lot of responsibility. Perhaps we should just pass this back to them now, tell them he is ill and be done with it?'

The idea that Jane is ready to give up on me really stings. I know she ought to, I know the rest of the staff resent me. They're all out seeing seven or eight clients a day, while here I am, barely holding on to one. Teacher's pet.

'I need to do this,' I reply. 'His wife is the key to it. If she is real – *was* real – maybe he doesn't have dementia, maybe he's still grieving and he just needs support. If I can find out the truth, there's a chance he can stay. I have to try.'

When I get up to leave, she just says, 'Be careful.'

At home, lying on my bed, I run through the experiences I've had recently. Feeling exhausted and sick, getting really anxious all of a sudden, the weird sensations at Avon Lodge. Are these the symptoms Dr Bedford warned me about? Is this about me failing to take my medication, like I fail at *everything*?

Deep breaths. It will all be fine. Deep breaths. I'm not useless.

I awake in an all-too-familiar situation: late evening, fully-clothed, damp patch on the pillow beneath my mouth. Mum is sitting down on the bed looking at me. Perhaps she will say something comforting, something real. Mum leans closer.

'We're having shepherd's pie and broccoli,' she says. 'Shall I steam or boil the broccoli?'

'Steam,' I mutter.

'How are you doing?'

I want to tell her that I'm not taking the drugs and that I might be hallucinating.

'I'm okay. Just tired.'

Mum puts a hand out as though to hug me, but seems to falter and then pats me on the leg. She gets up to go back downstairs, stopping in the doorway.

'We'll eat dinner and then find something terrible to watch on TV,' she says. 'There's a new reality show where they make over the inmates in a women's prison.'

'That sounds educational.'

'We have salted caramel ice cream in the freezer.'

With that, she begins to retreat through the door. I sit up.

'Mum?'

She pops her head back in. 'Yes?'

'When I close my eyes,' I say, 'it feels like I'm falling – like I'm really falling and there's nothing to hold on to.'

Three months ago, she went out to fetch her daughter and came back with a sad and broken houseguest, a ghost, disconnected from her own time, her own place, wherever that was. Where was it? I can't remember. Somewhere along the line, many miles back, I derailed.

She looks concerned for a second but quickly hides it. 'I'll catch you,' she says.

Chapter Eight

Outside, the low November sky is blotted with dense black clouds. I know I'm tense because I am attempting to pedal really fast up the steep slope of Lansdown Road, rather than just getting off and walking it like usual. I have to confront Will about the past – about Elsa. Because if she doesn't exist, if he's imagined her or lied about her, I can't help him.

When I arrive, breathless and sweaty, it takes him several minutes to answer the door. To my surprise, he is dressed in old blue work overalls, stained with oil and singed in places.

'I am tidying the workshop,' he says. 'Follow me. You can help lift some of the wireless sets.'

And with that he is off down the hall, and all I can do is follow him and worry: this was not part of the plan. How can I broach things now?

Inside the workshop, several of the old wireless sets have been moved off the shelves onto the table in the centre. The light from the window illuminates the vast galaxies of disturbed dust in the air. He hands me a cloth.

'You just need to give the cases a wipe, then check for wood-worm and mould. These wooden models can be eaten away entirely if you're not careful.'

Then he moves around the table and begins to silently inspect a large Bakelite model. I go to one of the other sets and we work in silence for a while. At first, I'm frustrated that my plans have been waylaid, but then I realise this activity is a distraction that may let me in. I see the battered old armchair in the shadows at the far end of the workshop.

'Is that where she used to sit?' I say.

'Who?'

'Elsa. You said she sat there while you worked.'

He nods absently. 'She liked to listen to broadcasts, and she was very interested in *that.*' He gestures to the transmitting station under the window. 'She liked the idea of being able to communicate with people all over Europe. She thought she might be able to use it to get news about her parents or her sister.'

I don't answer for a moment, working the cloth between the dials of the radio.

'You told me before that you lost her in the bombing raid,' I say. 'What happened?'

'I don't know,' he says.

'Was she killed in a blast, or . . .'

'She wasn't killed . . . she disappeared.'

'What do you mean?'

He turns back to his wireless.

'Will, I'm trying to understand.'

'You won't. I don't understand it and I've thought about little else my whole life.'

I look away from him, wondering whether or not I should mention what I found online. If this is a confabulation or a lie, is it really worth challenging him?

83

'What is it?' he says, and now he is looking at me with that cold, hard stare.

'Nothing.'

'Come on. Spit it out.'

'It's just that there are no photos of your wife anywhere. I searched the marriage register. There's no record of you and Elsa.'

His hangdog expression shifts upward, from indignation to something approaching anger.

'You've been checking up on me?'

'I'm worried about you. I wonder if we should make an appointment with your GP, just to get you checked out – make sure everything is okay?'

He is silent for a few seconds and I wonder if the fantasy is beginning to break apart. But when he looks at me again it is defiance I see.

'You think I'm mad?'

'I think that perhaps you've got a bit confused or you—'

He raises a finger to stop me, and I stop.

'You don't believe she existed?'

'I want to. I know that *you* believe it.'

Will lets out a short, bitter laugh.

'Spare me the psychiatric clichés.'

'I'm sorry,' I say. 'I didn't mean to upset you.'

'This is what I've always had to deal with!' he roars. 'Decades of mistrust and suspicion! No wonder I began to doubt it all myself!' He drums his fist on the table with surprising force, his face red with rage. In this instant, I remember what Florence had said, about how Will had disappeared for years after the war. The rumours about prison. Is this whole story an attempt to avoid his own guilt?

It takes him a few seconds to catch his breath.

'We weren't married,' he says quietly. 'Not officially. We were engaged, but we decided to wait until after the war. We thought that by then, we'd know about Elsa's family. She wanted them to be there – even if it was just a registry office. But this was Britain in the 1940s – judgemental, prejudiced. People didn't live in sin, especially not with immigrants, not with Jews. It was easier to tell people we were husband and wife. Are you satisfied now?'

'But do you have any photos of her? Any letters?'

'They're all gone.'

'Did you throw them away?'

'They disappeared with her.'

'What does that mean? Will, I want to help you, but I need to know what happened the night of the raid.'

I look at him and he stares right back, and I am shocked to see that there are tears in his eyes.

'I don't know,' he says. His voice is guttural. 'I don't know. Don't you think I ask these questions as well? As the years go on, things start to fade. God help me, what if it's not real?'

'Okay, let's take our time,' I say. 'Let's go back inside and sit down in your study. And then when you're ready, perhaps you can tell me what you remember?'

'I'm not going to sit down and tell you my life story!'

'I'm just trying to help you! Maybe there's a chance I can figure it out, even if you can't.'

He doesn't answer for a long time. Instead, he looks upwards as though wrestling with some great moral dilemma.

'I can't tell you the story,' he says. 'But I can show you. The folders in the parlour – you found them on the first day you visited. Many years ago, I cannot recall when, I wrote down what I remembered of Elsa; how we met, our life together. It's all there, for what it's worth. You can take them and read them all.'

Then he walks out of the workshop toward the house, with its black windows and weird energy and the shadows slipping across the walls. He stops and turns toward me. 'I'm going back,' he says.

And I know that if I want to keep him in this house, I have to go with him.

Part Three

A PRESENT

Chapter Nine

October 1938

It was Smithy who spotted her first. We were at the Bath Pavilion, on a rainy Saturday night. She was with another woman, amid the crowds lurking at the edges of the dance floor. The band was playing through a repertoire of popular tunes, trying to drum up some interest, but it was still early, and most people were busy ordering drinks, chatting, their cigarette smoke swirling into a thick fog above our heads. This suited me as it meant I could stand and enjoy the band without feeling I ought to ask some poor girl onto the floor. I did not really go in for dancing; none of us did at Anderson – we were an awkward bunch of chaps: bony, brainy and bespectacled, all elbows and left feet. We were also rather tired from another busy week at work, but it was Smithy's birthday and we felt we ought to make an effort, especially with how things were in the world. Chamberlain had just flown off to Munich to make his useless peace with Hitler; everything was paused on the precipice, waiting to tip.

There were four of us from the Research and Development department. At thirty-two, Smithy was the oldest and most technically brilliant. A bird-like fellow with quick black eyes and a beaky nose, he surveyed the room as though scanning for predators. Giles Cooperton was small, chubby and red-faced – he had the nervous air of a bullied schoolboy, but dressed in fine suits from Bond Street tailors, which rather flattered him. Paul McDonald fancied himself as the matinee idol of our bunch with his sports jacket and cravat and his dark hair slicked back like Errol Flynn – hard to believe he was an absolute genius in long-range radio communications. Smithy should have been married ages ago and his parents were beginning to worry so attending these events had taken on an air of desperation. We'd spent an hour chatting awkwardly, scanning the place for young girls who looked single and not too terrifying. McDonald joked about me being more interested in the music than the girls, which was true – I had heard Teddy Joyce and his Orchestra on the BBC and was keen to see them play. It was the sole focus of my evening. Then Smithy saw her.

'I say, look over there,' he said, angling his thin neck toward our left.

Our eyes scanned past a group of young men in army uniforms tapping their feet in unison to the music and some giggling young girls in bright floral dresses who seemed altogether too silly to attract Smithy's attention. And there she was, refusing a cigarette from some smarmy young chap, smiling politely, looking out at the band. She was wearing a jade-coloured dress, sleek and shimmering in the half light, the swooping neckline daringly low. Her face was perhaps more handsome than conventionally beautiful: her eyes were stern, her nose broad and somewhat crooked, her jaw strong and wide. It was her hair that really set her apart – a mass of fire-red curls that seemed untamed and untameable.

McDonald said, 'Good lord! She looks like some sort of mythological warrior queen. She is very obviously out of reach for you, Smithy, old pal. I shall see you boys later. Will, my lad, watch and learn.'

He handed his empty glass to Smithy and sloped off toward the girl, adjusting his cravat en route in a way he clearly felt was rakish. I watched him go, sipping from my glass of tepid beer. 'Why does he always do this?' I said to Smithy. 'He usually gets knocked back.'

'You have clearly not studied John von Neumann's work on strategy games,' Smithy replied. Cooperton and I inwardly groaned. Smithy had a scientific reference for every occasion. 'According to his minimax theorem, it is worth taking any risk where the reward for winning is greater than the remorse of losing. For McDonald, this is a sporting event.'

Cooperton let out an anxious giggle, which was more or less his response to everything, and as McDonald sidled in toward the girl, he began commentating as though presenting a test match on the wireless. 'The bowler approaches the crease, his head held aloft, ready to pitch the trickiest of spin balls . . .'

At that point, the band brought on a vocalist, a young woman, and worked its way into a ballad. I immediately recognised it as 'Someday I'll Find You', a Noël Coward confection that I rather adored. Clearly their hope now was to send a few soppy couples swishing out onto the dance floor, but their playing was so good I was rather overcome by it. Right there, in the darkened dance hall, having glimpsed a quite singular woman, I felt this song of passion and longing with my whole being. And as I listened to the lyrics about searching for a lover and finding them, as though in a dream, in the blueish light of the moon, I had this odd feeling, like déjà vu. I thought to myself, I have been here before with this girl and I will be again. It made no sense.

91

It took me a minute to snap out of it, and when I did, I saw McDonald leaning in close to the girl and saying something over the swoop of the strings. To my shock, she was staring right at me. I jerked my eyes away, embarrassed, but curiosity forced me to turn back. McDonald was still talking, but once he'd finished, she said a few words to her friend, then slipped away. He stood blinking for a few seconds, then started back to us.

'That was quick,' said Smithy, a wry smile creeping across his face. He always enjoyed witnessing McDonald's failures.

'She's a bloody kraut,' said McDonald. 'No sense of humour obviously.'

'What's a beautiful young German woman doing in Bath?' giggled Cooperton.

'Whatever it is, she's doing it alone with that attitude.'

Then he turned to me.

'She asked about you, though.' He said it in a begrudging tone.

'Me?' I said.

He nodded, looking out at the band. 'Can't imagine why.'

'Oh, there is something about a handsome man who doesn't know it,' said Cooperton, putting a hand on my shoulder. 'Beauty and humility. A very potent combination.'

We all turned to stare at him, and he laughed self-consciously, letting his hand fall away from me. 'Sorry, I have been reading Elinor Glyn. Mother keeps forcing her on me.'

'What did she say?' I continued to McDonald.

'She said, "Who is the gentleman so enjoying the music?"'

Feeling bashful and noticing McDonald's growing resentment, I thought it best to change the subject.

'Anyone for another drink?' I asked. I looked back to where the woman had been standing, but she was nowhere to be seen.

Outside the main room, at the long bar opposite the entrance, I squeezed in amidst the crowds of young people still arriving through the sharp autumn rain. It was a relief to be away from McDonald for a few minutes. A scowling barman in a stained white dress shirt took my drinks order and as I waited, I was aware of someone weaving in and standing next to me, bringing with them a beautiful flowery perfume. It was somewhat unusual for a woman to be buying her own drinks at the bar, and I didn't need to look up to know it was *her*. I just felt it. I glanced sideways, as subtly as I could, only to find that, for the second time that night, she was doing the same toward me. When our eyes met, she smiled, and I found myself gripping the bar, my legs having become completely insensible. I thought the beer must have been stronger than we were used to. In close up, her strong face was even more impressive; her eyes were a radiant dark green and seemed to have their own light, like the sun shining through some beautiful stained-glass window. She was quite obviously astonishing. I smiled back at her stupidly, hoping to think of something witty to say. Nothing was immediately forthcoming.

'I saw you caught up in the music,' she said. 'Are you a fan of Noël Coward?'

McDonald had been right – her accent was Germanic, but not overly harsh; her English was excellent, with a hint of Somerset about it.

'I like his love songs,' I stammered. 'They have a . . . a wistfulness about them.' She looked at me encouragingly, and it gave me some confidence. 'There is something about his use of melody, the way the tune swoops around the vocalist as though they're dancing together. I'm sorry, I am rather a bore about music.'

'I like it,' she said. 'It is so nice to meet a man who has come here to appreciate the band rather than make moves on young girls.'

'There you go, sir,' said the barman, and then I had four glasses of beer in front of me. I turned back to her.

'May I ask where you are from?' I said. 'Germany?'

'Austria,' she replied. 'Though it is all the same now, I suppose.'

I understood this to be a reference to the Anschluss, the annexation of Austria into Hitler's Germany. While I was trying to think of a way to approach this subject, she asked for her drink and was quickly served some sort of orange cocktail.

'It's very English, though, isn't it?' she said, taking a sip. I looked at her, perplexed. 'Noël Coward's music, I mean. Very cut off from what everyone else is making now.'

Without thinking, I fired back, 'I simply don't agree.' And I was startled to discover that I had begun an argument with this enchanting woman. 'I mean to say that, well, you could easily compare him to the German composer Kurt Weill in his mix of romance and cynicism.'

She gave me a sly little smirk then looked away. 'I have been approached by several men this evening. Most of them told me how wonderful I look in this dress and then tried to get me tipsy. You argue with me about Noël Coward.'

I thought I had ruined everything by contradicting her, but when she looked back to me, her smile was so warm and radiant, I felt the whole place spin. 'You enjoy Kurt Weill?' she asked.

'Yes. I heard a broadcast of *The Threepenny Opera* on the wireless, with Lotte Lenya singing. She is astonishing.'

'She was born in Vienna – like me.'

I could have stayed and talked to her about music all night, but I was aware I had been away a while and the chaps would want their drinks.

'I'd better get back,' I said. I was hoping to lift all the glasses in an impressive show of balance and gumption, but the task was beyond me.

'Here,' the woman said. 'I'll take yours. Can you handle the other three?'

'Aren't you buying a drink for your friend?' I asked, immediately realising this would make it clear we had been watching them both.

She said, 'I hardly know her. I brought her because my aunt said I shouldn't come alone. It is not the done thing, apparently.'

'I suppose not,' I replied.

I didn't know what to say about that, but she smiled again and started to cut through the crowds, men parting in her path, staring at her. I picked up the drinks and followed, trying to keep up.

The music was a little faster now – a popular new tune with an energetic beat. As we approached the boys, I drew up alongside her to make it clear we had been chatting and were now acquainted. Cooperton saw me first and dug his podgy elbow into McDonald's ribs; they all turned to look at the girl and then at me, their jaws dropping in unison like in some daft cartoon. I handed out their drinks and she passed mine to me as the music played on and the couples danced.

'Thank you,' I stammered.

'You're welcome,' she replied. She walked away as the song ended and in the moment of silence that followed, she turned and winked at me.

Thoughts of what I should have said to her bombarded my brain, but then the bandleader cried, 'Now for some fun,' and the opening strains to 'The Chestnut Tree' drifted out across the room. Usually novelty songs were kept until the end but it did rather feel like there was a desperate air to the evening. A cheer went up and at last, the dance floor swarmed with people.

McDonald turned to me and said, 'What on earth was that about?'

'I don't know,' I replied.

'Did you get her name at least?' asked Smithy.

I shook my head, looking out at her as she disappeared between groups of drinkers, the cigarette smoke enveloping her.

Cooperton giggled into his drink.

The following Tuesday I took my packed lunch to the Victoria Art Gallery. I often went there during the week, enjoying the silence of the exhibition room; the modest collection of local artists, enlivened by the odd Gainsborough. It was rarely busy, just a few old dears patrolling the room unsteadily. I thought I would do a lap, then sit on one of the two long benches at either end of the room and eat my sandwiches.

I had barely begun appreciating Sebastian Pether's 'Moonlight Scene' when I spotted her. I couldn't believe it: the Austrian girl from the dance. She was dressed in a smart wool skirt and jacket, browsing a glass display case in the centre of the gallery. I suddenly regretted wearing the patterned sleeveless jumper Mother had knitted for me. I watched her moving around, looking at the porcelain collection with cool detachment. Then she glanced up and saw me through the glass. I turned quickly toward the wall and paced away, pretending to be lost in the art.

As I passed an old couple arm in arm and admiring the portrait of an old Bath mayor, I glanced back, and she too was walking, circumnavigating the central displays in the opposite direction. She was still looking at me. I moved on to the next wall pretending to examine the paintings, and I was aware that she was moving too, always keeping the glass display between us. I could barely breathe. The next time I turned around to see her, there was a small group of schoolchildren skipping across the room in matching caps and duffle coats, holding hands and laughing. We both watched them but we were still moving in time, as though involved in some extraordinary dance. The children passed and our eyes were back on each other as we silently promenaded.

Eventually I halted, pretending to look at a large painting in front of me but actually trying to clear my head and think of what to do next. I was something of an innocent; I'd just come out of two years at technical college studying Electrical Engineering – it may as well have been a boys' school. Or a monastery. My only contact with women was at Anderson's – there were the diligent, aloof secretaries and then the women who assembled the prototype wireless sets in the factory below our office, but they were rough and intimidating and I had learned to avoid them. All I knew about romance I'd picked up from visiting the pictures and reading the garish novels I surreptitiously borrowed from the library. I tried to remember some of the advice McDonald had given me, but I remembered he had failed rather spectacularly with this girl at the Pavilion. I stood and thought and panicked.

'Is this painting a favourite of yours?'

Her voice was directly behind me. I spun around to find her right there, smiling mischievously.

'Um, well, yes. As a matter of fact, I rather like paintings of . . .' I turned again, realising I had no idea which painting I had been gawping at for the last few minutes – my mind had been directed elsewhere the whole time. It was a work entitled 'Canterbury Meadows', a rather austere Victorian painting of some livestock sitting in a field.

'I rather like paintings of . . . of cows,' I announced. Before adding, 'It seems.'

'I see,' she said.

'They're very relaxing creatures.'

'Yes, they are.'

'Are you an art lover?'

97

She stepped in beside me so that we were both looking up at the picture, side by side, like scholarly friends. I had, once again, lost radio contact with my legs.

'I am,' she said, 'but perhaps not this sort of art.'

'Ah,' I said with a wry grin. 'Is it perhaps too British – like our poor Noël Coward?'

She glared at me with mock reproach. 'It's not *that*,' she said. 'Everything is so old-fashioned.' And she made a sweeping gesture that accommodated the entire gallery and perhaps the whole city beyond. 'All these portraits of people who have been dead for hundreds of years and these nice country scenes and these cows. It's not telling us much about the world we live in now, is it?'

'No, I expect it isn't. What art do you like, may I ask?'

She moved behind me and stood now at my other side, still looking at the painting, still seemingly toying with me a little, but – I felt – not in a cruel way.

'Last year, the architectural institute in Munich held an exhibition they called *Die Ausstellung "Entartete Kunst"* – the exhibition of degenerate art. The Nazis put it on. There were works by Ernst, Kirchner, Kokoschka, Klee – all considered enemies of pure Germany. Hitler meant to show everyone how rotten and depraved these paintings were; they hung them badly and wrote graffiti on the walls. But everyone went, thousands of people every day. My father took me and I'll never forget it.'

She leaned in closer to me and said, almost in a whisper, '"*Entartete Kunst*". Degenerate art. That's what I like.'

We stood in silence for a number of seconds.

'Were there any cows?' I asked.

She burst into loud laughter, visibly shocking an elderly gentleman next to us, and eventually gripped my arm as though to regain her balance and decorum.

'Not many,' she replied. 'You would perhaps not have enjoyed it.'

We were quiet again for a little while. I thought I ought to admit something. 'I'm afraid I don't know any of the artists you mentioned,' I said.

'Do you know about modern art? About Surrealism and Expressionism? They're the future.'

I shook my head, feeling very stupid and uncultured. I remembered seeing a newsreel about an art exhibition in Paris filled with what I thought at the time to be strange, monstrous images. The delusions of mad men.

'I don't,' I said. 'I ought to. I am certainly interested in the future.'

'Well, let me tell you: there is a book in the lending library downstairs, called *Art Now* by Herbert Read. It is a little dry but I read it while I was learning English and it is very good on the basics. I suggest you borrow it. If you really do want to find out more?'

'I do,' I said.

'Good. I'm glad. Things are so awful, you have to look ahead. Everything is changing – art, music, movies – it's very exciting. But here in Bath . . . not much is moving.'

Just as she said this a guided tour of the gallery came to a halt around us, and a curator with a sombre expression and drooping moustache began to explain the works of Gainsborough to a group of dispassionate visitors. Unsure of how to continue the conversation and now feeling rather self-conscious, I looked back at the sad old painting before me, with its harmless bucolic scene, and I thought to myself, should I ask her out? Could I? I considered suggesting the Holburne Museum at the end of Great Pulteney Street, but I wasn't certain we would find much degeneracy there either. Perhaps tea one afternoon? Was tea too boring?

At last, I gathered the courage to ask if she would at least entertain the notion of meeting again . . . but she was gone. I looked around, and then elbowed my way through the small tour crowd, but she was nowhere to be seen in the gallery. Filled with something like panic, I made a couple more desperate circuits, then vaulted down the wide stone steps to the entrance vestibule. Outside, traffic hummed along Bridge Street and pedestrians scuttled by under the dark clouds. I could not see her. She had escaped once again – and it seemed very unlikely I would encounter her by accident a third time.

Disconsolate, I sloped back into the building and stood for a second, trying to make sense of everything. I decided I should go through to the lending library, which was on the ground floor, beneath the gallery. I thought perhaps I would look for this art book and perhaps take *something* from this wasted encounter. Beyond the broad issuing desk, the room was lined with tall dark wood shelves, spaced very closely so that each narrow passage felt crowded with people reading and browsing. As a child my parents had brought me here every week. My father tried to encourage me to read adventure stories, but even then I was only interested in books on electricity and telecommunications.

I walked along the cramped rows, thinking of her, the way we had stalked each other around the gallery, watching and smiling. Her wild red hair and stylish clothes, her eyes on me as we moved in time; two bodies separate but orbiting, suddenly pulled together by some quirk of gravity. To her it was probably just a game; to me ... it was the most exciting thing I had known. It was as though I'd received a glimpse of something, some completely different life, exciting and unusual, only to have it snatched from me.

I found the art section (which was an unfamiliar area to me) and ran my fingers along the worn spines of the books. Sure enough, there was one copy of *Art Now*. I picked it up to flick through and inside were many photographs of strange artworks – collages of

100

shapes and tones. As I reached the back pages, a piece of paper fell from inside. I bent down to pick it up, thinking it was perhaps a library ticket. But it wasn't. It was a note in rather large, scrawled handwriting. My heart thudded in my chest as I read it:

So here you are! Please let me know
what you think of the book.
  1 Bloomfield Crescent, Bath 2950.
                                Elsa.

And in the bottom corner of the note was a small yet easily identifiable sketch of a cow.

Chapter Ten

2007

I have information now. The memories are a jumbled mess, but from the sections I've read, I have a date, a setting, a cast of characters – all things I can use. This afternoon I went to the art shop in town and bought a roll of A2 graph paper. I cut off a long section and pin it to the corkboard on my bedroom wall, drawing a line along the middle with a black Sharpie. At one end I write 'October 1938', at the other 'April 1942'. This is the timeline I'm working with. This is where the truth of Will's life is hiding. I pin on index cards with the names of all the people he has mentioned so far – they are almost certainly all dead, but do they have family? It's easy to find people if you have an internet connection and know the right websites. I learned the theory at university, then discovered the practice when my dad started trying to get in touch with me after he left us. If you have a phone number, an email address, a social media presence of any kind, if you vote or buy a house, someone can find you – even if you don't want them to, even if they made your childhood a misery.

Sitting alone in my bedroom, I open the laptop then click on Internet Explorer, pausing for a few seconds to gather myself. Before I can change my mind, I register a new email address, then sign-up-for-free trials on an ancestry website and an address directory. I make anonymous accounts on Facebook and LinkedIn so I can search those too. My plan is to tap in the names I have, tracking their lives through birth and marriage certificates, property purchases, electoral rolls and census records – hoping to find living relatives, anyone who can corroborate Will's memories. It makes me shudder to think: this is what my dad did to get at me. A panicky wave of heat and nausea rushes over me so fast I barely have time to make it across the room before I'm retching bright yellow bile into my waste-paper basket. For a while, I lie on the floor clutching my stomach, waiting for the cramps to pass. Tears feel sticky on my cheeks. I want to shout downstairs, I want someone to hold my hand, but I can't let on how bad this is getting. I have to get through it. Just focus. Focus on the research.

There is almost nothing on Smithy. His whole life seems to have been lived away from official record. Paul McDonald died in the 1960s, but had a son who was once arrested at a National Front march so I decide not to make contact with him. Josephine Klein, Elsa's aunt, with whom she was living at Bloomfield Crescent, had a sister and a brother, both with families, including a nephew named Miles Frankland, living in Bristol. I emailed as many as I could, asking if they could phone me, rather than emailing me back. I felt I could send messages, but receiving them, seeing the notification icon blinking away on the screen – it was too triggering. I couldn't face it.

There's a knock at my door and Mum comes in with a cup of tea, placing it on my desk. She looks at the corkboard and then at me.

'Are you solving a murder?'

'No, I'm trying to work out what happened to Will up until the bombing; whether or not he had a wife, and if so, what happened to her.'

'I once watched a documentary about murderers during the war,' she says. 'They used to creep around in the blackout, kill people and then hide their bodies on bomb sites.'

'Thanks, Mum.'

'Do you think that could be it? Perhaps he murdered his wife.' She laughs to herself but then sees my serious expression and stops. 'Are you sure you should be doing this – going on that computer, looking things up – after everything?'

'I have to.'

'Do you, though?'

I ignore her and go back to it. Mum sighs and slips away. It turns out Giles Cooperton had a younger sister, Valerie, who is still alive. There's a story about her on a local news site; she'd once been a fashion designer, but more recently worked as a clothing consultant on period dramas. Her phone number's not listed anywhere official, but I eventually find it on a not-entirely-legal directory website. After many minutes of trepidation, I call. She's not there so I leave a garbled message about Will and Giles and Anderson's. By the time I'm finished, my tea is stone cold.

The next morning, Jane wants me to check in with her, so we arrange to meet in a small coffee shop opposite the Guildhall.

'So, is it official? Has he lost it?' she asks as I arrive.

It is crowded, so we have to perch on two of the high stools in the window, next to a young guy who is tapping away on an Apple laptop.

104

Do cafés hire these men in? They are a part of the interior design nowadays. Jane is jabbing at her mobile phone, apologising while she's doing it, like someone guiltily eating a steak in front of a vegetarian. She is wearing a Hermès pullover and a grey woollen skirt. I am in yet another Gap hoodie and yet another pair of jeans that I had to fight to get into because I've gone up a size and a half since I bought them.

'I don't know,' I say, staring into a giant cup of peppermint tea, the steam creating its own halo on the window beside me. Outside it's cold and bright and the sun glints off the tour buses as they thunder past on their way to the abbey.

'On Tuesday, I asked about his wife, Elsa, and he got so angry and muddled. But then he let me read some of a memoir he'd written years ago – starting with the night of the bombing.' I share as much of the story as I can with Jane, using the hasty notes I'd jotted down in my organiser for reference. I tell her about how he woke up in the hospital and then walked home through the wrecked streets. I tell her about how he arrived to find Avon Lodge intact, but no Elsa. I tell her about their meeting at the Pavilion and then at the gallery. 'It could be a confabulation,' I say at the end. 'But the detail of it, the emotion – it was so convincing.'

Jane gives me an indulgent smile. 'Before you worked with us, we cared for an old gentleman named Sidney Grange. He convinced one of our most experienced carers that he'd been a bodyguard to Harold Macmillan. He told astonishing stories and even provided intimate details of Number 10 Downing Street.'

'Let me guess: not a bodyguard for Harold Macmillan.'

She shakes her head. 'Pipe welder for an engineering firm in Bristol. Carers are a captive audience and men do love to tell stories about themselves.'

'It's just the *way* Will wrote it. There was a texture to it. I felt like I was there.'

105

Another faintly patronising sigh from Jane. I look out of the window at the crowds strolling past. A group of French teenagers in matching anoraks and backpacks; young mothers pushing prams, cooing at their babies. Then my stomach lurches. Over the road, outside the market hall I glimpse a familiar figure, a haggard man, staring right at me, his face locked into a hateful grimace. I feel utter dread fall on me like a rusted cage. Everything else fades out.

'Are you okay? Laura?'

Jane has her hand on my shoulder and she's gently shaking me.

I snap awake as the noises of the café flood back in. I look out at the market entrance again. No one there.

'I'm fine,' I say. 'Just tired. What were you saying?' I try to pick up my cup but my hand is shaking so much it clatters against the saucer.

'We've got another slight problem,' she says. 'Someone has reported Avon Lodge to environmental health. They're complaining about the smell and the rubbish bags outside the house.'

'I'll deal with it.'

'We could get a contract cleaning team in, but budget-wise . . .'

'I'll do it, it's fine.'

Jane looks up for a second.

'I think this sort of thing is going to keep happening,' she says. 'I don't think Will has made many friends up there.'

I know this is another warning, another subtle suggestion that I should think about giving up and handing Will to social services. Maybe this is her way of solving the problem I have become, getting me to the point where I quit and she doesn't have to make her mentor's daughter redundant.

'You have to assess,' Jane repeats while studying her phone screen, 'whether you think he is safe in that house by himself. If not, social services will ensure somewhere else is found for him.

From what you've told me, he's struggling – he's regressing to some imagined past. My guess is he needs to be in sheltered accommodation where there is specialised care.'

I look at her and, not for the first time, I am sure I would not have this job if it weren't for my mum. Seemingly reading my train of thought, she leans forward.

'It's okay for you to let this one go,' she says.

For a moment I feel a surge of relief at the thought of it. I would be free. But then what? Where has freedom got me in the past? I know the thoughts that come when my mind wanders.

'I should keep going,' I say. My voice cracks with uncertainty and I know it sounds like I'm trying to convince myself, not Jane. 'I need to find out more about his life, about Elsa. If there's *any* truth in it, it means he's an old man who has suffered a trauma and just needs to talk it through. I owe him that.'

'You don't owe him anything.'

'Myself then,' I snap. 'I owe it to myself.'

Jane's phone vibrates and she looks down at it again. 'I've got to go,' she says, already standing up and lifting her coat from the chair next to her. 'Have you had a good look around his house for photos, letters, clothes . . . There must be something?'

'He said everything of hers has gone.'

At this, Jane stops pulling on her coat and adopts an exasperated expression.

'Is there any chance she just packed her bags and left him? The old bugger is probably in denial.'

'No,' I say, feeling myself becoming frustrated and upset. 'Why would she do that to him and never call again? People can't just disappear out of your life like that. Christ, I know well enough.'

Outside, it has begun to rain, a sudden cold wind lifts the umbrellas of the passing crowds – I search their faces, looking for

107

the figure I saw before. Was he really there, just over the road? I shake my head and allow myself to be swallowed up in the rush toward the abbey.

When I get to Will's I notice that one of the rubbish bags in his front yard has been gouged open by foxes, leaking empty tin cans and some sort of carcass onto the pathway. It takes an age for him to answer the door and when he does, he gives me that familiar look of confusion followed by slowly dawning recognition. Last night I felt like I was making progress, with my chart and my index cards and my laptop. But here I am again, the smell of rot pervading this damaged house, the threat of an environmental health visit lurking, dread in the pit of my stomach like an undigested meal. Every step forward, a knock backwards. I guess, this is how progress will be – cyclical.

'I need to read some more of your journal,' I tell him. He looks down, then wanders into the parlour, resigned to this intrusion. I follow him, guiltily. In order to figure out the future, we'll have to delve about in the past, even though neither of us can really face going there.

'Where now?' he asks, standing beside the shelves.

'Somewhere positive,' I reply.

He takes out a folder and hands it to me.

'Our first date,' he says.

Chapter Eleven

November 1938

A few days after my chance encounter with Elsa, I was sitting at my work desk, her note in my tremoring hand, considering whether or not I had the courage to contact her. There was no doubt I wanted more than anything to see her again, but I was scared and inexperienced, and it was obvious she had seen so much more of the world than I. On top of this, things were busy at Anderson's. We were working on a new prototype, a very small portable wireless, with a less cumbersome battery than other contemporary models. Our workshop was a hive of activity, the oak desks laden with technical drawings and prototype components, our laboratory machines whirring and buzzing like Dr Frankenstein's laboratory. Mr Anderson had been taking meetings with a succession of serious-looking men in dark suits. Some wore military uniforms. We were told not to disturb them.

'Have they come to conscript us?' said Cooperton.

'Hardly,' said Smithy. 'We're more valuable to them here. They'll have us designing death rays.'

'And besides, the army doesn't take your sort,' said McDonald to Cooperton, aiming a grotesque wink at him.

I supposed he meant because Cooperton was so fat. The poor chap looked rather startled and hurt, and no one else in the office would meet his eye – when he turned to me, I smiled at him and nodded, but I feared my gesture of brotherhood was too subtle to give him much comfort.

After another few minutes of staring at the note and running my finger across the little drawing of the cow, I heard Smithy groan loudly and get up out of his chair.

'Are you going to telephone her or not?' he said.

'I don't know,' I replied. 'Aren't there conventions to follow? Shouldn't I see her at another social occasion before I contact her directly?'

'Dear boy, *she* contacted *you*,' said Smithy. 'And hardly in a conventional manner. I do not feel she is a stickler for romantic rules.'

'She is probably a con artist,' said McDonald. 'After your inheritance. I'd be wary of her. For a kraut she had suspiciously good English. Perhaps she's a spy.'

I turned back to the note.

'For pity's sake,' said Smithy, leaping from his chair and approaching me. He dug into his trouser pocket and produced a shiny new two-shilling coin. 'If you can't decide, let's allow the universe to do it. Heads or tails?'

The others looked over, their interest piqued. I stared at Smithy dumbly.

'Come on,' he said. 'It's not a difficult question.'

I thought I might as well go through with it, if only to satisfy him.

'Heads,' I said. 'No, tails.'

'Oh for God's sake, man!'

'Tails,' I repeated, with more resolution this time.

110

Smithy flipped the coin high into the air. As it spun, it caught a glint of sunlight from the high window, and looked almost like a falling star. It landed in Smithy's outstretched palm, and he slapped the coin onto the back of his other hand, covering it from my sight.

'Now,' he said. 'Isn't it fascinating – at this point you both are and are *not* asking this lady on a date.'

'Oh, heaven help us, not this again,' groaned McDonald, plunging his head into his hands.

Smithy had been boring us all with a thought experiment he had discovered in one of his science journals. It had been proposed by some obscure Austrian scientist and was something about a cat trapped in a box with a radioactive substance, and the cat was both alive *and* dead until observed – or some piffle like that.

'Just tell me,' I said, beginning to feel irate. Smithy lifted his hand with a theatrical flourish and stared at the coin for an unreasonable amount of time.

'Sorry, dear boy,' he said. Heads then, I supposed. I felt a curious swell of relief – this would give me an excuse not to pursue the matter any longer. The girl was strange anyhow, very forward and perhaps even pretentious. But Smithy wasn't finished – this was a performance. 'You will have to gather your courage. The universe has decided in favour of the lady.' He showed me the coin. It was tails.

I decided to wait until the rest had gone home before calling her. I spent the afternoon summoning what little courage I had, working through what I should say and how. When the office clock struck five, people started to drift away until only Cooperton was left. With his coat over his arm, he shuffled to my desk. Lost in my romantic plans, it took me a few seconds to look at him, and when I did I was astonished to see that his eyes were almost teary.

'I just wanted to say thank you,' he said.

'For what?'

'Your support this afternoon. It was very much appreciated.'

He saw Elsa's note in my hand.

'Be yourself,' he said. 'Don't worry about custom or convention – that is not how you will win this maiden.'

And then he put on his hat and left. Though I considered him a close friend, that little man was such an enigma to me.

A few moments later, I picked up the office telephone and dialled the operator. I gave Elsa's number in a stammering voice. There was a long delay before I heard a voice at the other end.

'The Klein residence.' It was a woman, but not Elsa. This voice was British, sharp and refined.

'May I speak to Elsa?' I asked.

'Who should I say is calling?'

I realised that Elsa did not know my name. How should I introduce myself? This was already an utter disaster. I struggled to think of what to say next.

'Hello?' said the voice again. 'Are you still there?'

'Yes, sorry. My name is Will Emerson. I met Elsa at the Victoria Gallery on Tuesday and I was wondering . . . '

'Oh, that was jolly quick!' she yelled in a tone that seemed both amused and incredulous.

'I beg your pardon?'

'Elsa told me all about the young chap in the gallery and the note she left. Isn't she a devil?'

I had no idea of the etiquette I was to follow from this point. Who was this woman? Was it Elsa's mother? The dalliance seemed very amusing to her. It was most unorthodox. Before I could summon a response, I heard a muffled voice calling, 'Elsa? Elsa darling, there is a telephone call for you.' This was it, I thought. My throat became parched, I could almost feel it closing like an airtight valve. Then a familiar voice on the line.

'Hello?'

It was her. My whole body felt light and distant. Blood swooshed in my ears.

'Hello, it's . . . it's Will Emerson.'

'Good day, Mr Emerson.'

'We met at the gallery.'

'I remember.'

'I discovered your note.'

'Yes, I suspected as much. You liked the cow?'

'You are a talented artist.'

'What can I do for you, Will? May I call you Will?'

There was something in the way she asked me, in the very phrase itself, that seemed oddly familiar.

'Yes, of course. I wondered if . . . I thought perhaps . . .' My voice was a pathetic squeak. 'I wanted to ask if you would like to meet me. Perhaps for tea? I understand, of course, if this is not appropriate . . . I'm afraid I . . .'

'Yes.'

'Pardon?'

'Yes, I would like to meet you for tea. What about this Saturday?'

There was only the ghostly rustle of static interference between us.

'Saturday would be perfect,' I managed.

'Midday?'

'Yes.' I decided I ought to try and seize the initiative back. 'Shall I call for you?'

'That would be very kind. You have my address.'

I did. Bloomfield Crescent – the terrace of tall, thin Georgian townhouses just out from Bear Flat, on the other side of the city.

'I will see you on Saturday.' My voice was regaining some of its timbre. 'I very much look forward to it.'

113

'I do too,' she said. 'Goodbye for now, Will Emerson.'

The line crackled and went dead. I walked back to my desk and sat down. Smithy had left the coin there. Just think, if it had fallen differently, I would not have made the call. It all would have ended there. I took the coin in my hand and turned it over in my fingers before putting it in my drawer beside the library copy of *Art Now*. I became aware that I was smiling very broadly. The laboratory had been in semi-darkness since the late afternoon, lit only by desk lamps, but now everything around me seemed very bright, like my own private summer.

Saturday took an age to arrive. Thursday and Friday were like glacial epochs. When the day finally came, I woke early and dressed, deciding to walk all the way to Bear Flat rather than take a tram. The exercise would help clear my head and calm me, I thought. The day was crisp and cold, the streets unusually quiet. As I strode up the steep incline of the Wellsway, taking in the view of the vast brick warehouses along the Broad Quay, I wondered about what this day would bring, and what would be required of me. My parents, bashful and old-fashioned, had not prepared me. My brother, who was older and more dashing than I, had said we would 'have a chat' about girls when he returned from Spain. We never got the chance.

It wasn't the time to dwell on that.

A housekeeper answered the door at Bloomfield Crescent and invited me into the large entrance hall. She went off to inform someone of my arrival and I stood marvelling at the décor. The interior was extraordinarily modern, the walls and tiles all white, the only furniture a deco sideboard and an almost industrial-looking anglepoise lamp. As I was inspecting it, a tall figure in a dark tweed suit emerged from a doorway on my right. Elsa's father, I guessed. But then to my astonishment, I realised it was a woman.

She was perhaps in her mid-forties, with short, neat hair, and an angled, almost handsome face. I was dumbfounded.

'Mr Emerson,' she said. 'I am Josephine, Elsa's aunt.' She held out a hand for me to shake. Incredible. 'I expect she is still getting ready, do come through.'

Still rather shaken by her masculine appearance, I followed Josephine into a small drawing room, which was as modern and minimal as the hallway. It was so unlike my own home – crammed, by my parents, with honest, unremarkable furniture. I also noticed a very good wireless on the sideboard: the beautiful Ekco Model AD65 in onyx green, its distinctive circular casing designed by the architect Wells Coates. An instant design classic. She sat down lightly in an armchair, took a cigarette case from her pocket and offered it to me. I declined. She took a cigarette for herself, lit it and sat back, observing me.

'So,' she began, before coolly exhaling and watching the white smoke curl in the sunlight. 'What exactly are your intentions?'

'I beg your pardon?'

'Your *intentions*. With my niece.'

Silence. I gulped somewhat audibly. There had been nothing in my life to prepare me for this moment. I stared at her and she stared back. Was I expected to commit myself to a relationship with a young woman I had met only once?

'Well, I . . . I'm not sure that . . . '

Time seemed to stop – as did my capacity for rational thought.

'Aunt Jo, are you torturing our guest?'

The voice came from the doorway, and I spun around in utter relief to find Elsa standing there in a dove grey woollen coat with a luxurious fur collar, her hair, once again, loose and unstyled. She was smiling broadly.

'I was merely trying to ascertain what the young gentleman

has planned for your outing today. It seems he wishes to keep it a secret.'

'I'm sorry,' I said at last. 'I did not mean to appear rude, it's just that ...'

'Perhaps you are not used to being interrogated by strangers?' said Elsa.

'I am not.'

Elsa leaned against the door frame, turning from me back to her aunt.

'Mr Emerson is taking me to the Grand Pump Room,' she said. 'Something you have unkindly refused to do.'

'I am?' I asked. Elsa nodded at me, and I turned to her aunt. 'I am,' I said.

'My aunt thinks Bath society is stuffy and elitist.'

'Full of ancient crones and colonels,' said Josephine from her smoky corner of the room. 'The whole town is falling apart around them as they roll about in their invalid chairs. But if you two want to spend your time amid that rabble, do go ahead. Oh but please, don't get on one of those death traps into the city.'

'She means the trams,' said Elsa. 'There was apparently an accident a few years ago on the Wellsway. Do you recall? The brakes failed on one tram and it rolled all the way down the hill straight into another. There were some terrible casualties. Auntie Jo has not forgiven them.'

Josephine stubbed her cigarette into a chunky glass ashtray at her side and looked at me seriously.

'We shall call you a taxi,' she said. 'Today, young man, you are escorting precious cargo.'

We did not really speak as the car wove into the city. Although I tried to think of things to say, Elsa stared out of the window, transfixed, it seemed, by the view. We pulled up outside the Odeon on Southgate Street and I got out, running around to the other side, but finding the driver already opening Elsa's door. She refused his hand and stepped out unaided. The street was bustling with traffic and shoppers, the cars weaving impatiently between buffering trams.

'Why the Pump Room?' I asked as we walked up toward the building.

'I want to see what the tourists see,' said Elsa. 'I have been in Bath for months and I've barely seen anything. Aunt Josephine is such a snob. I had to sneak out to the gallery last week because she says its collection is "musty and obsolete". She is correct, but I am glad I went anyway. Come on!'

She headed off into the crowds of shoppers dawdling their way along in heavy coats and scarves, and just like at the dance, I did my best to keep up. We passed the entrance to the King's Bath, its grand stone walls the colour of burnt honeycomb, scarred and weathered. I remembered that my father used to come here for hydrotherapy – he was badly wounded at Ypres and our doctor thought it would be helpful, even though the worst of what the war did to him would never be helped or healed by warm water.

We wandered on, under the colonnade and toward the Pump Room entrance in the Abbey Square. At the kiosk inside, I bought tickets to taste the waters, which also got us what I really wanted: access to the afternoon concert. After dropping our coats at the cloakroom, we went through to the Grand Pump Room, which I had only previously seen on picture postcards and illustrations of its Georgian heyday. It was an odd experience. Architecturally, it was still impressive, the high walls punctuated with doric columns, shafts of light streaming in from the giant windows, bringing life to the stuffy air, thick with pipe smoke. Hanging from the ceiling

117

above us was the monstrous bronze electrolier, which must have seemed modern thirty years ago, but now looked burnished and ugly. Indeed, everything seemed tired. The painted walls had turned yellowish, like curdled cream, the floorboards were battered, the dozens of wooden chairs scattered around the room looked spindly and uncomfortable, their cloth seat covers worn and moth-eaten. Only a few were occupied, mostly by old folk, their heads dipped as though in church. There was a more ordered group of chairs near the ornamental fountain where staff handed out glasses of the spring water to taste. This space was reserved for Pump Room subscribers, a group of ancient chaps in three-piece suits, ensconced behind newspapers.

'Where is the dancing?' said Elsa. 'Where are the courting couples?' She looked crestfallen. 'This isn't what Jane Austen promised.'

'Come on,' I said. 'You have to try the water. It has miraculous healing properties.'

We walked over to the fountain together, our footsteps echoing. A young girl in a starched white dress and apron handed us each a glass of cloudy liquid.

I sipped at mine, knowing a little of what to expect, but Elsa lifted hers in an extravagant gesture and said, 'Bottoms up.' I went to stop her but was not quick enough – she glugged it all down in one.

'*Mein Gott!*' she yelled. The loud exclamation in German caused a symphony of rustling newspapers behind us. 'It's horrible!' Her face had collapsed into a grimace of revulsion.

'I tried to warn you,' I said.

'It's like seawater!'

'That's the high mineral content.'

'And it's boiling hot!'

'Which is why there is steam rising from the—'

'Why do people do this?'

I had no answer for that.

'Ahem,' the girl at the fountain said. 'Taking the waters cured King Bladud of his leprosy.'

'But was it worth it?' gasped Elsa.

The girl smiled, despite herself. In the sallow half light of this once stately room, amid the empty chairs and the sad tokens of Georgian Bath – the tired statues, the faded portraits – Elsa seemed to be the only thing truly bright and alive. I knew even from this early point that I was gone. I was lost to her.

It was too early for afternoon tea so we took lunch on the terrace, its arched windows overlooking the historic Roman Baths, the glass hazy from the steam. Couples perched at the small round tables as staff buzzed about. The chequerboard marble floors and rows of exotic plants lent a vaguely Parisian feel.

'Tell me about yourself, Will Emerson,' said Elsa as she scrutinised her cod steak and potatoes. 'What do you do?'

'I am a research engineer at a wireless manufacturer. I help design smaller and more precise components. We're working on a very compact portable model. It's quite exciting.'

'My father is fascinated by the wireless,' she said. 'He listened to classical music broadcasts in his study while he worked. I would sit on the armchair beside his desk, reading. Sometimes we would listen to the BBC and he would get me to translate.'

She looked very wistful, almost melancholic.

'Was this in Vienna?' I asked.

'Yes. We lived in an apartment in Alsergrund, close to Sigmund Freud's office. My father is a lawyer. He is quite successful and well known – at least he *was*. My mother is a musician, she played

119

violin in an orchestra. They were very cosmopolitan. There were always interesting people around – singers, artists, scientists. We'd go to concerts and galleries all the time. On Sundays, my father took us to his favourite patisserie. He drank Turkish coffee, which they served in copper flasks. My sister and I ate cream cakes. It was wonderful. We didn't know how lucky we were until it all ran out.'

'And now you are here.'

She nodded silently.

'When Hitler took power in Germany, things changed very quickly for Jews in Austria. People who had always agreed with the Nazis began to feel bold. There were groups of men in the streets making salutes, fighting. And then the Anschluss happened ... Jewish businesses were stolen or destroyed. My father lost almost all his clients overnight – people he had worked with for years, people he thought of as family. They turned on him.'

I was naïve about the world, but I had read the papers and watched newsreels. I had seen footage of the German army marching into Austria, the crowds waving and cheering, Hitler waving from his open-top car.

'So you all left?' I asked.

This time she shook her head, her eyes would not meet mine.

'My father has people to help, he and my mother are still in Austria, I don't know where. But he sent my sister and me away. It all happened very quickly. He managed to get a French visa for her because she had attended university in Paris. But I was studying Art at the State Academy in Vienna – I was not ready to leave home, you see. The baby of the family. My father contacted his brother Levi in England – that's Aunt Josephine's husband – and he pulled the strings. I was granted a British visa. That was just the beginning. Father had to bribe the officials in Vienna for the correct travel papers so that I could get on a train to Holland.

120

German soldiers came aboard at every stop and asked everyone questions. Sometimes they grabbed people and dragged them away. I have never been so terrified. One day I was the little girl reading in her father's study and the next I was travelling alone across Europe with nothing but a suitcase and twenty marks in my purse. The last time I saw my parents, they were waving me away at the station. I'll never forget my mother's face when I got on that train, not for as long as I live. I saw it happen, do you understand? I saw her heart break.'

Elsa ate in silence for a few moments. I watched her, imagining the bravery that had brought her here, trying to think of something to say, some perfect sentiment to encapsulate what I felt. I had never admired anyone so much, not even Guglielmo Marconi. But once again, language failed me. She looked up at last, sweeping a stray curl from her face. Her eyes glistened but she was smiling.

'Anyway,' she said. 'Before I left, my father told me it is my duty – my *duty* – to live, to laugh and to have exciting times. That is why I am going to order the peach Melba for dessert.'

After lunch, we walked down to the concert room and took our seats for the afternoon performance. It was the soprano Vera Maconochie, singing a selection of ballads accompanied only by piano, and her voice filled that grand chamber. The metal chairs were tightly bunched so that Elsa and I had our arms pressed together. Our hands touched and then our fingers. I felt the music through her; it resonated along our limbs, as though our bodies were part of the orchestration.

It took a few songs for me to concentrate on the music, but then Maconochie sang a piece I recognised, 'Young Love Lies Sleeping', and as I listened, as the voice soared, I thought about Elsa and all she had been through. She had lost everything, her life was in turmoil, but she had chosen to spend this afternoon with me. It was the music, I think, that unlocked the depth of my feeling, because, as the song reached its beautiful crescendo – the individual strains meeting and parting in the thick air – I'm afraid to say I felt tears gather. I wiped them away quickly so that no one could see.

Afterwards, we decided to walk back to her aunt's. It was already getting dark as we left the Pump Room, the air had a steely edge that threatened frost. Elsa wrapped her coat tightly around her.

'Are you sure you wouldn't rather take a cab?' I asked. 'It is rather chilly.'

'You think this is cold?' she laughed. 'When I was young, I joined a Jewish girls' group and we'd go hiking in the Wiener Alpen. *That* was cold.'

We chose to head up the Holloway, passing the steep woods leading to Beecham Cliff and the ancient Magdalen Chapel, hidden behind the splaying, knuckled branches of a Judas tree.

We talked a little, moving seamlessly between local and international matters, tapping gently into each other's lives. Elsa's Uncle Levi, it turned out, was something of a theatrical impresario, who had produced shows in Vienna and London, but was now in New York, making moves into Broadway and even motion pictures. Josephine was apparently a writer of some repute, her identity hidden behind a male pen name. 'If I told you, you would recognise it at once,' Elsa smiled. Elsa's uncle had met Josephine in Vienna, while she conducted a grand tour of Europe. Two days later they were engaged. 'That's what my family does,' said Elsa. 'We collect people. My great-grandmother was Scottish, which perhaps explains *this*.' She pointed to her hair.

All the way, she probed at my own family history. I was not intentionally evasive, but there was nothing to match her story.

122

'My father managed an engineering company, but he was injured in the war and was never the same again,' I told her. 'My brother went to fight the fascists in Spain.' It took me a few seconds before I could continue. 'He was killed there.'

'I'm so sorry.'

I shook my head. 'This is an age of sad stories,' I managed. 'My mother found it hard to be in our house after that – too many memories, too many ghosts. And we didn't get on. She wanted to talk about my father and brother, to grieve, but I didn't know how to help her. I wasn't very sensitive to what she needed. She said it was like trying to talk to a clod of earth. So she moved to Bournemouth to live with her sister and I stayed in the family home.'

'You live alone there?'

'Yes. I am the caretaker, really.'

I don't know why I couldn't say more after all she had shared, but she did not press me. Instead, she slid her arm through mine until we reached Bloomfield Crescent.

'You must come in for a drink,' she said.

'I should get home,' I replied. The truth is, I wanted nothing more than to be with her, but there was part of me that felt exhausted by the weight of what was happening.

'At least let us get you a car?'

'I like to walk. It will give me time to think about today.' I smiled at her. 'I will have a case of Bath spring water delivered to your home.'

'Was I that awful?' she said.

Our breath caught in the air and rose around us. The sky was a sheet of deep blue velvet, pinpricked with stars.

'Goodnight,' I said.

'Goodnight, Will Emerson.'

She leaned against me and kissed my cheek. Her lips were warm and the feeling expanded outwards like ripples on a pond.

She started back toward the house, and in a sort of trance, I walked away.

'Can I ask you one thing before you go?' she said.

I spun round to face her again.

'Of course.'

'Why did you hide it?'

'What do you mean? Hide what?'

'In the concert, why did you hide how much the music moved you?'

I looked away, feeling caught out, like a guilty schoolboy.

'I'm afraid I rather let myself down, didn't I? Music can sometimes have that effect on me. Throughout my life, I've often felt as though I could see sound. As a child listening to my grandfather's old gramophone, I would picture the separate waves produced by the different instruments, each with its unique pitch and timbre, carried through the horn and out into the room, the strands formulating into something whole and beguiling and magical. This afternoon, with you by my side, I felt that again. How very silly it must seem.'

She walked back to me until she was very close, then put a hand on my arm.

'No,' she said. 'I think it's beautiful.'

I knew I would never forget those words. When I listen to music and when I think of her, I can still hear them.

Chapter Twelve

2007

The detail of his story, the emotion – I lay awake that night thinking it over. Can a man who seems to have barely left Bath imagine for himself the life of a Viennese refugee? Can he conjure a love affair from nothing? Once I had finished reading, the air seemed thick with her. I could almost smell her perfume. I'd ridden home from Avon Lodge through the busy streets, taking a detour to pass the Pump Room, the bare wooden space of his memory now lavishly furnished and busy with tourists taking afternoon teas. I wanted to see the building as they had, I wanted to get off my bike and go in, to walk where she had walked. I wished I could meet her. I wished I could ask how she had coped. I needed to know more, to know everything.

But when I arrive at Avon Lodge for this morning's session, he is not at home. There is a note pinned to the door inside the porch, addressed to me.

Gone for shopping, spare key under doormat. Let yourself in.

This doesn't seem like a sensible thing for an eighty-seven-year-old man to do. I look at the note again. The handwriting is neat and slanted, and something about it troubles me. I stand in the doorway for a second, the note in my hand, trying to figure it out. And then it hits me.

Heading into the study, I go straight to the piles of newspapers and flick through until I find one of the little notes I'd discovered while tidying up – then I compare it to the message Will left for me. The handwriting is completely different. Was someone else trying to help Will regain his memories? Who? Why?

I decide to wait for him in the parlour, and as I walk through, there is the familiar smell of mould and damp, which reminds me of environmental health and how we need to think about cleaning the place up. Each time I come, the blackened wallpaper seems to be peeling away ever further like diseased skin, exposing the grimy bone of the plaster. The sunlight pouring in through the tattered curtains draws my eyes to the Klimt picture, the woman's hair lit golden red by the dusty rays.

That's when I hear it.

A sort of thudding coming from somewhere above me. I stop still and listen, holding my breath. Surely it was outside? I can feel my heart beginning to pound. There it is again. Knock, knock, knock. It is definitely in the house. My instinct is to walk right out, to get away, but I tell myself it must be the wind or something. It is nothing weird. There isn't someone up there waiting for me. There is no such thing as ghosts.

Instead of leaving, I creep to the base of the staircase and glance up. From here, I can only see a couple of closed doors. And somewhere up there, a clock is ticking.

'Will?' I call.

Nothing.

I put a foot on the stairs, and then another. The wood groans under the pressure. I think of all those dumb horror movies when you find yourself yelling at the person on the screen, 'No! Don't go and investigate!' But I am ignoring that obvious life lesson. There is something driving me, a gruesome curiosity. At the top of the stairs there are four wooden doors around the large landing area, all firmly shut, and another narrower staircase leading up to another storey. A worn Persian rug runs the length of the floorspace, pockmarked with holes, and there is a grandfather clock against the wall between two of the doors, its baritone tick-tock, tick-tock, echoing off the walls.

I've almost convinced myself the whole thing was in my head when I hear the thudding noise again. Louder, more insistent. I know now where it is.

It is coming from the attic.

'Will?' I try again. If it is not him, what will I do? I should just get out of here. I hear cars pass outside. Would anyone hear me if I screamed? Should I have a weapon? I am being ridiculous. My breathing is fast and shallow. My heart is beating so hard I can see my anorak tremoring across my chest. And then somehow, I am on the second staircase and it is leading up toward a narrow, shadowy corridor. The window at the top has an old piece of black cloth pinned across it, the sickly light barely seeping in at the edges. As I climb, it feels like there is growing pressure in my ears, there is a ringing noise like tinnitus. The wooden stairs are horribly soft and I have to step over one that's caved in entirely. At the top, there are two doors and as I look at the nearest I hear movement again, a thud and a muffled crash. What am I doing? What am I doing? I am edging toward the door. The handle is missing, so if I'm going to go in, I will need to push it open. I have a flash forward to ambulances in the street, a body being carried out on a stretcher. And that image seems familiar somehow. This house. A body carried out.

I push the door. The hinges make a high-pitched moan. If there is someone there, they know I'm coming. Slowly, as the door opens, I see, through half-closed eyes, the space inside; an attic room, utterly neglected and derelict. The plaster has collapsed from the sloped ceiling, exposing festering wooden beams and above them roof tiles, all snaggled and broken, letting daylight through. The sunken floorboards are mottled with bluish mould, and the small window has two panes of glass missing. I step in, and as I do the door closes slightly behind me; almost in slow motion, I turn to it and my breath stops in shock.

Something is upon me in a blur of motion. It whirls around and I feel it at the back of my head, like hands grabbing. I scream and put my arms up shielding my head and staggering backwards, panic exploding as the room swirls. The thing is clutching at my hair in vicious jabbing movements and then wrenching away. The noise is close up and on me, filling my ears – a horrible loud flapping.

Flapping.

It's wings.

I open my eyes, just in time to see a pigeon, skinny and half bald, reeling high up toward the ceiling then battering along the walls like a giant moth at a lampshade. For the first time I notice that there is bird shit everywhere – all over the window sill and down the walls. There are dirty feathers in the air like flakes of ash. I am almost sick. The trapped pigeon whirls around and flies at me again, straight at my face. In a single spasmodic jerk of movement,

I lunge for the door, prise it open and launch myself out, yanking it shut behind me.

'Fuck!' I yell at myself. I'm bent over in the corridor, cowering, stupidly shocked.

After a few seconds, I manage to stand up. I've seen enough. I creep dizzily back down the stairs to the first-floor landing, breathing hard, picking gross feathers from my hair. I stand by the grandfather clock for a while, breathing, breathing, just trying to get my heart rate down. The house seems to be closing in on me, the bulging walls, the sagging ceiling. I can smell a hundred years of grime and dust in the air, like stale breath. It is just then that I realise something. There is complete silence. Something is missing? I look around and then I see it.

The clock has stopped.

The time is a minute off a quarter to four. It stopped while I was up there.

'Laura?' It is Will's voice from downstairs. I hear his shuffling steps in the hallway.

'I'm up here,' I say, still reeling, but also feeling ashamed at being caught snooping around. 'I, um, I'm just using the bathroom.'

'Do you want tea?'

I shout yes, and then push open the bathroom door. It is not quite as wretched as the attic room, but still an awful mess, the ancient linoleum torn and stained, the walls exposed down to bare brick in places, the frosted window at the far end covered in some sort of green slime – it's like the washroom in a shitty student night club. The ancient toilet has a wall-mounted cistern and a rusted chain flush, and on the opposite side there is a sink and a freestanding ceramic bath that was perhaps once white but is now a yellowish brown, its surface a labyrinth of cracks. I don't really want to touch *anything*, but I go over to the sink, wrench on the cold tap and splash my face. This is no good, I think to myself. He can't live like this.

When I get downstairs I find him in the kitchen, taking a shop-bought Victoria sponge cake out of a cardboard container, sliding it onto a plate on his kitchen table, and I notice again how much his hands shake.

'I thought I'd get us a treat,' he says. And perhaps it is my imagination but his expression seems to soften when he sees me, as though he is glad I am here. 'Are you all right? You look rather flustered.'

'I'm fine,' I say, standing awkwardly in the doorway, catching my breath. 'There was a pigeon. A pigeon in your attic, I heard it . . .'

'Not again,' he says. 'I should fix that window. Would you like some?'

The contrast between my panic just minutes ago and Will's strange calm is disorientating. He is standing looking at me, his knife poised above the cake.

'Thanks, but I shouldn't have any.'

'Why not?'

'I'm sort of watching my weight.'

He looks dumbfounded.

'What on earth do you mean? You look perfectly healthy. You look nice.'

I take a sad moment to reflect on the fact that this is the first compliment I have received from a man since I moved back to Bath. But we have to talk about the attic room. The roof is caving in. Something has to be done.

'Look, Will . . .'

The doorbell rings and it startles me – I'm still jumpy from the pigeon attack. We look at each other, puzzled by this unexpected intrusion.

'I'll get it,' I tell him, and the thought hits me that it might be the environmental health officer making an early appearance. I see a figure through the mottled glass of the porch door. If it's them, it's over – I haven't even shifted the bin bags piling up in the front yard. Slowly, I open the door, dreading the confrontation, only to see an elderly woman in shop overalls, a concerned expression on her face.

'Hello?' I say.

'Is Mr Emerson there?' she asks in a thick Somerset accent.

'Can I help you?'

She checks around, up and down the street, and lowers her voice.

'I'm Edith, I work in the little supermarket down the road. The thing is, he just walked out without paying.'

'Oh, I'm so sorry. How much does he owe you? I'll sort it out.'

'It's £2.50, love.'

I delve into my jeans pocket hoping that by some miracle I have enough money. When I hand it over, she gives me a pained look of gratitude and sympathy.

'It's just that it's happened a couple of times before. Usually, I manage to stop him and get him over to the till.'

'Thank you. Thank you for looking out for him.'

'Are you his granddaughter?'

'No, his carer.'

'Maybe you should do the shopping for him in the future, look? He's lucky I was there. If the manager had caught him, he'd be in trouble.'

'I understand. Thank you again.'

'It's no trouble, love. I don't take no notice of what they say about him round here.'

'What do they say?'

She looks sheepish, checking up and down the pavement again

like a spy about to disclose state secrets. 'There's always been rumours that he's no good. They go back ... oh, to when I were a girl. He went missing for a while – just after the war, this were. Some say it was several years, and the house was all shuttered up. Thing is, a few folk used to say he'd been put away. For treason or some such, I don't know. People make up stuff, don't they? I'd better get back. Just remind him to pay in future, look?'

With that she turns around and marches back down the path and away. It was the same rumours Florence had talked about when I visited her – something happening to Will after the bombing, disappearing for years. I'm on edge anyway after the incident in the attic, but the return of this little snippet of gossip has riled me.

By the time I get back inside, Will has shuffled through to the parlour where I find him in his chair by the fire, eating a huge slice of cake amid the cobwebs and stains and dust. I sit down on the sofa.

'Will, when you went shopping, do you remember paying for the cake?'

'What? Of course I paid.'

'Did you? You remember going to the till?'

He looks at me aghast, his old eyes searching my face as he thinks.

'I think I do. I ... I went in. I chose and ... I had a ten-pound note in my wallet. I paid with that!'

He reaches into his jacket pocket and takes out a worn leather wallet, which he opens quickly. He stares into it for a few seconds, then pulls out the ten-pound note. He looks at it with incomprehension. And then at me.

'I forgot. I forgot to pay.'

'It's okay,' I tell him. 'We've all done it. I once came out of Sainsbury's with ...'

Then I notice.

The carriage clock on the mantelpiece has stopped. The time is the same as the clock upstairs. Three forty-four p.m. 'That's weird,' I say. I rush through to the kitchen beginning to feel nauseous. The clock on the wall. Stopped. Three forty-four p.m. I edge away, out into the centre of the room and as I move, it seems the shadows on the walls are following me. There is tension in the air like a tightening rope.

I stride back into the parlour, feeling anxiety prickling at me.

'Have you stopped all the clocks?' I say, my tone is accusatory, like I'm telling off a child.

He looks up, bewildered.

'No, I ... I didn't realise they had stopped.'

'They all stopped at the same time, Will. Did you do it?'

'No! I don't think so ... I got ... No, I didn't. Why? Why would I?'

'How have they all stopped at once, then? What is going on?'

'I don't know. I don't understand.'

'Jesus!'

My head is in my hands and I'm breathing so hard my shoulders are bunching. The pigeon, the shop assistant, now this. Now this. I can feel panic coming on, like a car engine revving. I've got to calm down. It's nothing. A weird coincidence. I feel my way to the sofa and collapse into it. My breathing is laboured and asthmatic.

Calm down.

'Would you like some water?' asks Will and I'd almost forgotten he was there.

'I'm fine,' I say. Stay grounded. Why are you here and what is the plan? I'm here to help. I need to hear his story and work out if it's true.

'Just give me the next journal,' I say to him, catching my breath. 'Just ... something, *anything* more about Elsa.'

And I need her – I need her story to distract me, because …

(Shit this is so stupid, so stupid.)

… because part of me is sure that, as I ran through the house checking clocks, I was being watched; something was there. I felt the crackle of a presence just out of sight. Am I being tested? Or warned?

Chapter Thirteen

December 1938

I only saw Elsa once more before the Christmas of 1938. I took the day off work and we met on Milsom Street, perusing the festive shops together, marvelling at the lavish decorations in the windows of Jolly's and Colmer's department stores. I took her briefly to see my office – we weren't allowed to bring people in, due to concerns about industrial espionage. Instead, we stood outside and I tried to explain to her the research and manufacturing processes behind modern wireless sets.

'This is fascinating,' she said. 'Do you think we could go for cake now?'

As we were about to leave, Mr Anderson walked out, dressed in a smart beige raincoat over his pinstripe suit.

'Emerson,' he said. 'What in God's name are you doing lurking about outside the office? You have a day off.'

'Yes, sir.'

'Who is this?' he said, gesturing toward Elsa.

'My name is Elsa Klein,' she said, extending her hand in greeting. 'I am a friend of Will's.'

Anderson took her hand and made a sort of puzzled expression. 'You're from Germany?'

'Austria.'

'Ah,' he said. We all stood for a second, looking about. I couldn't help but feel there was something guarded in his manner, although perhaps it was merely the awkwardness of the situation. 'Well, I'd better get on,' he said. 'Lovely to meet you, Elsa. Will, take this young lady somewhere more interesting than our workshop.'

We met again in early January. She telephoned me and asked if I had ever walked to the castle on the hill, the one visible from the Grand Parade. I knew she meant Sham Castle, the folly built by Ralph Allen in the 1750s, but I wasn't sure if she knew it was just a façade.

'Apparently, there is a nice walk up there,' she said. 'Would you like to come? Auntie keeps giggling whenever I mention it.'

'I would be happy to,' I said.

It was a beautiful wintry day, so cold that our breath caught in the air around us, but utterly clear and bright. We had arranged to meet on the South Parade, and when I spotted her in her beautiful long coat, I was still unsure of how to greet her, so I slowed my pace as I approached, straightening my jacket, removing my hat. She saw me and for a second her mouth froze in a surprised 'Oh' as though she hadn't recognised me – then she walked quickly to me, kissing me on the cheek, her hands on my shoulders. The motion was unabashed but there was a slight tremble in her hands that I put down to the cold weather.

'Your face is lovely and warm,' she said. It was a few moments before she drew away, and the fragrance she always wore, sweet and flowery, lingered between us.

'What is your perfume?' I asked, my lips still close to her ear.

'Violets,' she replied, drawing away at last. 'There was a confectioner on the Kohlmarkt in Vienna. The empress of Austria used to go there. I'd visit every week with my friends to buy violet sweets. The smell reminds me of home.'

'It's beautiful,' I said.

We walked together through Sydney Gardens, over the river, and on to the steep path winding up between the terraced houses off Sydney Road. The castle stood in a muddy meadow, its central gatehouse flanked by two small towers at either end of the wall. My brother and I used to come here as children, picking wild flowers for Mother, climbing over the stones, looking for grass snakes. We enjoyed the fact that when you got close, you could see that it was just like a theatrical set – a wall rather than a castle. A discovery Elsa was apparently yet to make.

We were a hundred metres away when she stopped and looked at the building, then at me, then back again. She walked up to the nearest tower and glanced behind and around it.

'I don't understand,' she said. 'Is it a ruin?'

I smiled and shook my head. My suspicions were correct – she didn't know about this place. Her aunt hadn't told her.

'It's not real,' I said. 'It's a folly.'

'A what?'

'A folly, an architectural decoration. The entrepreneur Ralph Allen had it built so that he could see a castle from his townhouse.'

'You made me walk all the way up here to see a false castle?'

'I didn't make you,' I said. 'You asked to see it.'

'I thought it was real! Why didn't you tell me?'

I couldn't stop myself from smiling. 'I was interested to see how you'd react.'

She was standing red-faced in the shadow of the tower, her hands on her hips. And then she came at me.

'You swine!' she yelled, and she slapped my arm hard. For a second I was worried she was serious, but then I could see she was smiling too. She slapped me again and I feigned cowering away. 'I can't believe you didn't tell me!'

'It is a perfectly valid historical monument,' I said, stepping back from her.

'It is a wall!'

'But look at the view,' I said, pointing out toward the city.

She looked down at the buildings, so densely packed between the hills. It was a clear afternoon, the Abbey tower and the spires of St James's and St Andrews' piercing the soft plumes of chimney smoke. We were quiet for a while, viewing the city as though it were a work of art.

'It looks like a model village,' she said. 'It is so beautiful. Every building looks to have been carefully placed to be pleasing to the eye. You would never know, when you look at it, that terrible things are happening in the world.'

And even though I had viewed the city many times before, I don't think it had ever looked so small and sweetly ordered, so separate from cold reality, as it did that afternoon. Along with it, my life had never seemed so minuscule.

I stood as close to her as I dared.

'You must miss home terribly,' I said.

'More than I can put into words.'

We could just hear the metallic roll of the trams and the hum of motor cars.

'But it is not all bad,' she said, and our arms were touching now. 'There have been some good things.'

'Like standing here beside Bath's fine castle?'

'It is *not* a castle.'

'You don't like our art and you don't like our castles. What is it, then? What *has* been good?'

I knew what I was angling for. I had never been so forward. I felt light-headed with the fear and thrill of it.

'I have met some nice people,' she said, brushing her hair from her face with the back of her hand 'But only a few.' And then she wandered away as though that was obviously the end of the conversation and no further clarification was required.

During our walk back into town, I went through my usual paroxysms of anxiety, thinking about how best to ask her out once again. I still wasn't sure what I had to offer, or why she bothered spending time with me, so I was not confident in my ability to extend our friendship indefinitely. But I had to try.

'There is another concert coming up at the Pump Room that I thought might interest you.' I phrased it as a casual observation. 'A performance of works by Schubert. I believe he was Austrian?'

'He was,' she replied with no visible emotion.

'I wondered if I could take you?'

'I . . . I don't think so.'

My heart plummeted.

'I see. Of course. I am sorry, that was presumptuous of me.'

'No, it's not that.'

'Then what?'

She didn't reply for a few seconds and we trudged silently up the track.

'Schubert was a favourite of my mother's. She was an amazing musician. She taught me to play the piano before I could even read. We used to play together on Sunday evenings. A lot of Schubert. I remember . . . ' But whatever she wanted to say, she couldn't go on.

'Oh goodness, I'm so sorry.'

'It is quite all right. You did not know.'

'I would love to hear you play.'

'I can't,' she said. Her voice was so quiet I had to lean in towards her. 'I can't play again until I know my family are safe. It hurts me to play now. The feeling is too much. Just to listen to music, any music, sometimes it is hard for me.'

'I am so very sorry. If I'd known I wouldn't have taken you to the concert that day.'

'No, I'm glad you did it. Seeing your reaction, it was wonderful. It is something I lost when I left Vienna and I want it back. Music is life. But I will not play until I know what has happened to Mother and Father, and my sister, that's just how it is.'

'I wish you had told me.'

'I didn't know you then,' she said. 'But I do now.' She grabbed my arm. 'I have been waiting to find someone in Bath who I could talk to about art and books and music, and now here you are. Come on, let's pick up the pace, you are a very slow walker, Will Emerson!'

She raced ahead and I tried to keep up with her – a situation I would need to get used to. We stopped at McIlroy's, the grand furniture store on the Arcade, and lunched in its Georgian restaurant beside the elaborate Adams-style fireplaces. As we were looking at our menus, I could see Elsa intermittently glance up at me, a slight smile on her face.

'What is it?' I asked.

She was radiant in the sunlight streaming through the glass.

'I'm just looking at you.'

'Why?'

'You really don't know, do you?' she said.

'Have I got something on my face?'

I thought perhaps I was splattered with mud from the walk,

and that Elsa hadn't told me as revenge for Sham Castle. But she shook her head.

'It is so funny,' she said. 'You build these wonderful contraptions that can pick up signals from all over the world – but you are so bad at it yourself. Your aerial is of very poor quality.'

It was an inexplicable exchange, but I was glad to see her laughing again – even if it was at my expense.

Chapter Fourteen

2007

I wake up at 6.30 on Saturday morning with an incredible amount of energy. I feel it exploding along my veins. There's so much, it can't really be mine, like I'm borrowing it and somehow I will have to pay it back with extortionate interest. For now, I should make use of it. I need to tackle Avon Lodge just in case an environmental health officer arrives on Monday.

I am at the kitchen table eating toast when Mum walks in.

'What are you doing up?' she asks, her face moves quickly through a spectrum of emotions from shock to concern. She is wearing the Marks and Spencer dressing gown I bought her for her birthday last year because it reminded me of the one she used to wear when I was little. When things were bad and I couldn't sleep, I would snuggle into her as close as I could get; I would breathe in the scent of talcum powder and lily of the valley perfume, my heart rate calming.

'I'm going over to Will's. I want to try and clean up his house a bit.'

She fills the kettle and gets two mugs out of the cupboard. 'I'll come,' she says, while she drops a teabag in each one. 'I'll help.'

'Oh no, you don't have to. It'll be gross.'

'I have to regularly inspect the boys' toilets at school, Laura. Nothing can shock me now.'

'Honestly, it's okay, I'll manage.'

'I want to,' she says, now more firmly. 'It'll give me a chance to see where you're spending your time. And I can meet him.'

There is something protective in the way she says it, and I understand that she is not really offering to help. She is worried. She is monitoring me.

'Fine,' I say.

'Besides, it'll give us some time together,' she adds, making a pained smile as she pours the boiling water.

Mum drives us. On our way we stop at Homebase and buy a bucket, wipes, scouring cloths, multi-surface cleaners and bin bags; we even buy a mop, which only just fits in the Corsa.

'We don't have to go mad,' I say. 'We just have to give the impression he can still look after himself.'

'Can he?' she says.

I don't answer. Everything feels sharp and brittle.

Will is standing at the front door, ready to greet us with his typical expression of bewildered disgust.

'This is my mum, Carol. She's come to help me clean up today.'

'Clean up?' he says.

'Yes, you remember. We need to make the place a bit more presentable.'

He wanders into the house. I glance at Mum and then follow him, carrying the buckets and bags of cleaning products. Mum walks through behind me, looking at the walls and floors with undisguised horror. She is holding the mop like a weapon.

We quickly divide the work. While Will decides there is urgent business to attend to in his workshop, Mum starts attacking the cobwebs in the parlour with a duster and I begin in the kitchen. It is backbreaking work. I wash the floor, scrub the blackened work surfaces, scrape rotten gunk out of the corners, dry-heaving quietly to myself. I throw away food that is so far past its sell-by date it is a biological hazard – at the back of a cupboard, I find a tin of Ovaltine from 1979 and something that used to be a packet of Oxo cubes. I fill two bin bags with unidentifiable waste. In the living room, Mum pulls whole blankets of cobwebs down and wipes the shelves, filling the air with a glittering fog of dust; she lifts the rugs and screams when she discovers a squirming colony of unidentifiable insects, which she then hoovers up using Will's ancient vacuum cleaner. I head up the stairs and do the same in the bedrooms and bathroom, filling more rubbish sacks, getting through three pairs of rubber gloves, my eyes stinging with detergent fumes, my arms aching. I leave the attic, because I can't face any more unexpected pigeon interactions, but on Monday I can arrange for the office handyman to come round and fix the window. We are getting things done. I am useful.

While I clean, I look for clues, I look for *anything*, that suggests Elsa was ever here. I look beneath the sofas and behind bookcases; I look in the wardrobes, in shoeboxes and ancient suitcases beneath the bed. But I don't find anything that tells me *she* lived in this house. If she was here, where did she go? Why did she take everything – like, literally *everything*? Or did someone else?

In the early afternoon, I make mugs of tea and take one to Will. I find him standing in the garden, in the same spot I have seen him standing in before, staring up at the sky, muttering to himself. I hand him the mug and without looking he says, 'Thank you, Elsa.' He then turns and smiles at me but doesn't acknowledge his mistake. It's as though he has drifted away to the past – or some fantasy of it. Heading back to the house, I glance over at the row of houses next door and catch the old woman again, this time watching from a rear window. She makes a small almost motionless wave.

And there is something I have been avoiding, but if I am to be thorough, and while I have the energy and strength of mind, I know I have to do it. The cellar. The only place I haven't been. What if all of Elsa's stuff is down there?

The little door is stiff and takes a good shove to open. When it gives, the smell of damp earth coming up from below is almost overpowering. There is an old-fashioned light switch on the wall and I flick it, not expecting anything, but a weak, orange glow emits from the depths and I see the narrow, steep wooden staircase leading down. I hear a buzzing from somewhere, and I don't know if it's the fridge or something else. It sounds simultaneously close and far away.

I take each step slowly, feeling the spongy give in the wood, and as I descend, I see the shelter that Will told me about – a low metal cage the size of a double bed, placed against the rear wall. What must it have been like, to crawl into these things and wait and pray? Another couple of steps, then I am standing on the muddy, wet floor, beneath the bare light bulb. Will had said that the shelter was the only thing down here, but it's not true. When I turn, I see that behind the staircase there is some sort of metal bunker, maybe for coal, and two shelving units crammed with wooden and metal boxes. Is this it? Is this all her stuff? The buzzing is louder down here. It is not the fridge. It is something else. There are currents in the air, like eddies in a fast stream.

I start opening the boxes. What I find are old family relics: framed photographs of two little boys – Will and his brother, I suppose – at beaches, at a park; the whole family maybe around a table at Christmas, a cricket match. The images are sepia and stained with brownish splodges. There is one of the family, all posing together in the garden, the boys on their parents' laps, smiling; Will's father in a smart old suit, his mother, her hair neatly styled, looking slightly away from the camera, as though not quite ready, caught in a motion that ended long ago, but was happening then. I look closer and see that the father has his arm across the smaller son, who I guess is Will, hand open, protective but loving and comfortable. There are no photos of me and my mum and dad like this. We always felt broken.

I find an old food mixer, a TV set from the early 1970s. In a dark corner there is something that looks like an old cash register but then I realise it's an electric typewriter, bulky and black with IBM written across the front, a blank sheet of paper loaded, ready. Is this what he used to write his memoirs? There are objects wrapped in old cloth and they turn out to be china figurines and brass ornaments; a painting of a small boy crying; a presentation box containing silver cutlery, a jack-in-the-box, but the handle is broken. When I dig deeper I find an old 78 record and a small portable gramophone player. Bits and pieces collected by Will's family that were perhaps precious once, now sent down here to rot. The air becomes chilly for a second and I get that sense again, of some distant tragedy that still exists here, somehow frozen. The buzz has become a throbbing noise, like an idling engine.

And then the bulb flickers and goes off.

146

For a second, I am plunged into blackness and I almost scream, but the light comes on again, much dimmer than before. There is that sweet smell in the air again, like flowers. I need to get out of here. I feel my way back toward the stairs, trying to fill my brain with thoughts so I don't have to hear anything, closing my eyes against the darkness in case something appears. I put my foot on one of the steps and hear a crunching sound; the same on the next one. With every movement it comes. Crunch, crunch, crunch. I stop, worried I'll bring the whole staircase down.

But then I hear the sound again. And again. And then, with horrible certainty, I realise what it is. It is the sound of typewriter keys striking paper. I turn and slowly, so slowly – my body seemingly shutting down through fear – turn back, toward the shelves. The noise is louder and I try to calm myself with the idea that maybe Mum has put the washing machine on, and that that is what I'm hearing. But I know, I know, I know.

I know something is down here with me.

Tap . . . tap . . . tap.

I turn round the corner, to the shelves, close my eyes for a second, then slowly open them and look towards the typewriter. I shuffle closer and lean down to it, swallowing heavily. Woozy now with tension. There is a line of text on the paper. In extremely faint letters, the ink running to almost nothing, are three words.

Who are you?

Panic, instant and flooding. In two lunging strides I'm at the stairs, and upon them, too terrified to care about whether or not they'll hold up. The air isn't coming when I breathe, and anything I manage to heave into my lungs is staying there like thick suffocating smoke. The throbbing in my ears is so loud it is like aircraft

147

overhead. There is someone right behind me, I feel them with every pore of my skin. Just as a step literally crumbles under my feet, I reach out and grope for the door, grabbing it as the whole staircase groans and shatters. I explode through, falling into the kitchen and dropping to my knees, fighting for breath, almost convulsing with panic. Mum is in first, running from the parlour at the noise I'm making; she sees me on the floor and there's a look of horror in her eyes as she kneels down to me and tries to scoop me up.

'What is it? Oh Laura, what is it? What happened?'

I'm hyperventilating and shaking on the floor.

'She was there,' I say, my voice hoarse and strained.

'Who?' says Mum, looking around, looking out toward the garden. I follow her gaze and Will is standing in the doorway.

I shake my head.

'No one,' I say. 'Nothing. I was in the cellar, the light went out, I got freaked out. I'm sorry.'

Mum brushes my hair back from my face. The smell of dirt and old cloth is still on me. 'You silly girl,' she says quietly. 'My silly girl.'

Will comes in and looks down into the dark void of the cellar. 'I told you those stairs weren't safe,' he says.

In my mum's arms, my breathing starts coming back. She pulls me to my feet and helps me to the table, where I sit down on one of the rickety wooden chairs, leaning heavily against the wall. 'I'll make tea,' she says, and while she goes off to fill the kettle, Will sits down opposite me. We are quiet for a while, then he leans in.

'What did you see?' he asks. 'What did she say to you in the cellar?'

When I look at him, his eyes seem distant, as though he is not quite there and he is not quite looking at me. He tries to put one of his hands on mine and I jerk away.

I don't want to go. I don't want to go where he is going.

I tell Mum I'll walk home, and as I'm heading down Milsom Street, past Jolly's department store, I remember the part in Will's journal where he mentioned Elsa's perfume. I divert into the shop and speak to a man at the cosmetics counter; he beckons me over to a display of traditional scents. 'This is called Spiced Violet,' he takes my wrist and sprays some on. Slowly, I lift my arm to my nose, pause, and breathe in.

Later, when I get home, I trudge upstairs physically exhausted and certain that Avon Lodge is testing me, toying with me, draining me, mentally and emotionally. But as I sit at my own desk in my own bedroom, in front of my old uni laptop, I get a moment of clarity. The typing was so faint, I could have imagined it; maybe the text was always there. I see it all for what it is – my fear and imagination going into overdrive, with that creepy house bringing it all out. What if it is doing the same to Will? What if the last thing he needs is to be alone in that place with his broken memories? What if it's all in his imagination too? I look up at the chart on the cork board and feel sort of silly for thinking there was anything real in all of this. I need to go back to the doctor and tell him what's happening. I need to tell him that I messed up with the drugs and that I might be falling apart a tiny bit.

Frustrated and tired, I get up to go to bed, and it's only when I'm lying there I see that there is a message on the answerphone. I hit play and a forthright woman's voice thunders from the speaker. 'This is Ms Valerie Cooperton leaving a message for

Miss Laura James. I am not sure how you found my number, but I suppose we can meet . . .' And here we go, I think. Here we go into the unknown.

I drift off, near to sleep, my hand close to my face. I can still smell the perfume I tried at Jolly's, and my sleepy brain tells me it's just a coincidence. It's just a coincidence that this sweet powdery violet scent is the one that follows me around Will's home.

Chapter Fifteen

1939

I remember the first time I brought Elsa to Avon Lodge. It was a Sunday afternoon and we had been for a long walk through the city. She had devised a literary tour for us, taking in the houses of Henry Fielding, Jane Austen and Oliver Goldsmith, and the Saracens Head pub where Dickens had boarded.

'Now I would rather like some tea,' she said. 'And cake.'

'You seem to be settling into British habits very well.'

'Aunt Josephine is a strong influence. Afternoon tea is a holy ceremony for her.'

'My mother bakes excellent fruit cakes,' I said. 'One arrived in the post from her yesterday morning.'

'Are you inviting me to your home or merely boasting?'

'I think perhaps the former.'

'Come on, then,' she said, taking my arm. 'You can give me the tour.'

*

It was a very modest tour. A quick peep in the study, which I still saw as Father's room, though I was beginning to import my own books and records; a look in the parlour, still cluttered with Mother's ceramic statuettes; and upstairs, a fleeting visit to the spare room where Mother sat sewing in the evenings. Then on to the kitchen. While I boiled the kettle on our smart new stove, Elsa looked out of the window.

'It is a very different view of the city,' she said. 'You see it edging up the hill into the distance, and . . . What is the little house at the end of the garden?'

'It's my workshop.'

'What do you have in there?'

'A few top-secret projects.'

'Very intriguing.'

'Would you like to see?'

'That depends. Can I bring my cake?'

The row of ceiling lights hanging from the rafters flickered into life above us revealing the work bench in the centre of the room and the shelving units lining the walls, dotted with wireless sets, boxes of valves and piles of batteries. I walked in, shadowed by Elsa, and it was surreal to bring her into this personal place, this little shrine to radio communications. Her perfume mixed with the familiar smell of wood and dust. It was intoxicating, this unlikely meeting of worlds.

She walked slowly around the table, slice of cake in hand, inspecting the wireless sets with the same detached amusement with which she had studied the art in the gallery.

'They're rather beautiful,' she said. 'I have never seen so many.'

I followed her, as close as I dared.

'Which is your secret project?' she asked.

152

I pointed to the half-assembled wireless on the work bench. Without its Bakelite cover it was just a mess of wires and valves, like a model of some futuristic city from a science fiction magazine.

'This is the latest Anderson. It is very compact, but the speaker and antenna are excellent. I think it will be one of the best on the market.'

'Does it work? Can I hear it?'

'It's not quite ready and without the cover the acoustics won't be perfect, but I can play it. It plugs into the mains here.'

I plugged it in and slowly turned the dial, the sound of static quietly building in the room. Guiding the pointer to the local BBC frequency the air was full of music – the lilting strain of Haydn's violin concerto No. 4 in G major, the notes rich and vibrant against the quiet magnetic hum of electricity.

'I'm so sorry,' I said, remembering what she had told me about music, and how it reminded her of her family. I went to turn the dial, but she took my hand.

'Please don't,' she whispered. 'I am trying to enjoy it again – even if I can't play. It's important. My God, it's like the musician is in the room with us.'

Her eyes were very slightly moist as she walked away toward the rack of equipment in the corner beneath the window.

'What is this?' she asked, keen to change the subject.

'It is a radio transmitter and receiver station,' I said. 'With that Morse code contact key, I can communicate with other radio users from all over Europe. We are also trialling a microphone for voice communication.'

'Could you reach my sister in France?'

'If she had access to a transmitter and a receiver I could. I'd show you, but really I am not supposed to be using this equipment. It should have been confiscated.'

She noticed the dozens of small printed cards I had displayed on the walls around the transmitter, each with a different illustration, and lines of handwritten text.

'What are these?'

'They are QSL cards. When you speak to another amateur radio operator, you exchange these cards through the post – it's a way of confirming that you established meaningful contact.'

She studied them closely. 'You have communicated with all these people? From Norway and Belgium and Morocco?'

'Yes,' I replied, feeling a small sense of pride.

In the background the concerto was reaching its climax, the violin accompanied by a gentle piano refrain.

'Here,' I said and I clumsily opened the drawer on the desk, pulling out one of my own blank QSL cards. I'd had them printed on stiff card, light blue in colour, and in the corner was an illustration of the Royal Crescent, which I'd chosen to represent my location. I took a pen from the desk and filled out the details of my equipment and usual transmission frequency, then handed it to Elsa.

'For you,' I said. 'This was my whole world, really. Until I met you.' And then I blushed at the silliness of my gift and my declaration.

She smiled warmly, putting the card into her deep coat pocket. And with the sounds of the violin ebbing away behind us, she drew very close to me and brought her hand up to my face; her palm cool on my cheek, her fingers tangled in my hair. Closer still, as the music slowed, and the lights seemed to blur around us. Then, her breath on my face. I wanted to say, 'I'm not very experienced,' but the words wouldn't come, and they were not needed. As the concerto ended and the audience began to applaud, her lips touched mine, and the sound melted away.

'Meaningful contact,' she whispered.

Chapter Sixteen

2008

We meet in the café at the Assembly Rooms. Giles's sister told me she would be far too busy to see me before the new year (in contrast, Mum and I had very little to occupy us over the festive season) so it's not until the first week in January that she fits me in. I'm not sure who I'm looking for when I arrive in a fluster, several minutes late, but it's a drab Thursday afternoon and most of the tables in the tall, grand room are empty. Behind a group of young mums surrounded by their buggies, I see a woman in her eighties wearing a salmon pink 1960s skirt suit and a very brightly coloured silk scarf, sitting alone in front of a pot of tea. She looks like an elderly Jackie Kennedy. I approach cautiously, feeling a tightness in my breathing. When she spots me she gives me a cautious smile and beckons me over.

'Um, hi,' I say. 'I'm Laura, and I hope you are ...'

'Valerie Cooperton,' she says in her clipped, confident tone. 'Please sit down.'

Valerie had told me that she lived on North Road, the snaking lane leading along the fringe of Bathampton Down, but would be 'happy' to meet me (although she didn't exactly sound happy) in town. Now we are here in the Assembly Rooms: me, and an actual fragment of Will's life.

'Giles was thirteen years older than me,' she explains while pouring the tea. She pushes a china cup and saucer toward me. 'He was very technically minded, very precise – whenever a new gadget came out, he knew exactly how it worked within minutes of taking it apart, which is what he invariably did, much to our father's frustration. It was inevitable he would work in technology. But he also adored fashion. He used to take me to tea in Selfridges and explain to me what all the women around us were wearing. He taught me that clothes are engineered just like motor vehicles or wireless sets; he said style is a science. It's because of him I became a dressmaker.'

'You got on well?'

'Not until we were older because of the age gap, but he was my brother and I loved him. Most of all, I found him interesting. He had so many ideas, he saw connections between things. How many people in your life can you say are genuinely interesting? When you think about it, there aren't many.'

I don't have to think about it for long, to be honest.

'He sounds lovely,' I say.

She nods and smiles briefly, but a shadow moves over her expression.

'He never really fitted in here – far too flamboyant and unusual. He left Anderson's soon after the bombing and moved to London. He used some inheritance money, bought a little house in Kensal Rise and opened his own shop on Denmark Street, selling wireless sets. He was obsessed with that place. It is still there as a matter

156

of fact; his business partner took it over. It's all modern hi-fi equipment now.'

'Did Giles talk about Will Emerson?'

She shifts in her chair.

'They got on well. Giles thought that Will understood him better than most.'

Will as an empathetic friend? It's a little difficult for me to square with the cantankerous old man I know. Perhaps there *was* once something about him that may have appealed to a well-travelled woman like Elsa. It adds a sliver of plausibility to the tale.

'Did Giles ever say that he'd seen Will with a woman?' I ask, trying to make it sound casual, as though this isn't the whole reason for the meeting. I lift the teacup to my mouth, but my hand is shaking.

'Not as such,' she says at last. I feel myself deflating. 'Giles tried to help him in that regard, but not with much success. Will was always a lot of work.'

'Did they see each other after Giles moved to London?'

Eventually she shakes her head while staring into her cup.

'He didn't keep in touch with anyone from Bath after that.' She seems unable to look at me, and I wonder if she is embarrassed that her brother had given up on his friend. 'It was the war – there was rather a lot going on. Sometimes the past is best left in the past; I don't particularly want to go rooting through my family history – there are painful things buried there. You're a young woman, I don't expect you to understand.'

For a second I want to say 'I do, though, I do'. But this woman doesn't want to hear about my past, my issues. When we finish our tea, we sit awkwardly for a while, and I'm desperately thinking of more questions, fiddling with my sleeves.

'Will is . . . he's very old,' I say. 'Social services think he might

157

have dementia – they want to move him into a care home, but he doesn't want to go. I'm trying to help him.'

'Do *you* think he has dementia?'

'Maybe. He remembers a lot about the past, about the war. I'm trying to find out if those memories are reliable. But sometimes, the intensity of his feeling – it scares me. That must seem stupid.'

She gives me a narrow smile.

'You know this building was hit in the bombing?' she says. 'It had only just been renovated. It took several years and many thousands of pounds – and then in one night it was gone. My whole family went to take a look at the damage. What we saw was ghastly. The roof gone, the interiors blackened. My father burst into tears. I'd never seen him cry before. Nothing else that happened during the war frightened me as much as that. I tried to comfort him but do you know what he did? He pushed me away and called me a silly little girl.'

Those words trigger such vivid memories for me I flinch.

'Oh,' she says. 'You've had experience of this?'

Her perceptiveness catches me off guard.

'My dad had . . . *issues*,' I say in a mocking tone, but I can see in her eyes that she won't let me make light of this. 'He didn't fit in either. He always wanted to be a cinematographer. He was obsessed with cameras and movie making. But it never panned out. So he drank and he got angry. I wanted to help, but he took every chance he could to tell me I was useless.'

She looks at me for a while as though assessing the truth and depth of my statement.

'It is astonishing, isn't it – the lasting damage a little cruelty can do?'

It is time to go, and we walk together out of the main entrance, into the brash sunshine. I thank her for her time, and we're almost going our separate ways. But something occurs to me.

158

'Can I ask you a question?' I say. She stops too. 'If you don't want to talk about the past, why did you agree to meet me?'

Her face is unreadable as she thinks.

'I wanted to find out what you knew about Giles. There's a lot about his life in London that he kept very private – even from me. I think we are both leaving this meeting a little disappointed. May I ask *you* a question now?'

'Yes.'

'Why does it matter so much to you that Will's story is true? It's not just about his care, is it?'

As I'm thinking of how to answer, a coach party of Japanese tourists arrives, and we watch them file quietly past us toward the building, staring upwards with undisguised delight at its majesty.

'I want to believe it's possible,' I say. 'A love affair so brilliant and beautiful that nothing dims it, not even after sixty years. I'd like to know such a thing exists.'

She gives another tight smile.

'It was nice to meet you, Laura,' she says. 'I'm sorry I couldn't help more.'

She doesn't say anything else, but with a sort of guilty look she makes a little wave and disappears beyond the crowd. If she's holding any secrets about Will's past, it's clear she will never share them with me.

159

Chapter Seventeen

Monday morning is cold and damp. When I try to get out of bed, I have a dizzy spell and need to wait for a really long time before standing up again. It's a withdrawal symptom, I tell myself, recalling Dr Bedford's words once again. *You can't just stop taking antidepressants.* I never did pick up that repeat prescription. It will pass. I decide to use the time by flipping open my laptop and doing a Google search on Cooperton's store in Soho, but when the screen comes on, I see something that sends a bolt of alarm through me. An email notification. Blinking away, waiting. It can't be *him*. He can't know I'm back online. But the weird thing is – over the past few days, I've felt him edging closer again. I close the laptop immediately and the dizziness returns. I'd better walk rather than cycle to Avon Lodge.

Today, we are meant to be heading into town because Will wants to take me on some kind of nostalgic tour. I have no idea where we are going, or how much ground we will be able to cover considering his age, but the idea seems to have given him some impetus and enthusiasm. Is it a good idea to encourage Will's unreliable reminiscences? The fact that he's motivated is positive, but what happens when reality catches up with him? If only I'd managed to find something from Cooperton's sister to corroborate his history. For now, I choose not to mention I met her.

When I get to Avon Lodge I find Will waiting for me in the small porch area, wearing a grey raincoat and a trilby hat like a very old Agatha Christie detective.

'You look a little pale,' he says.

'I'm fine, let's go.'

It is a slow walk down Lansdown Road, Will shuffling uncertainly and then stopping every few yards and looking around like some intrepid explorer getting their bearings. When we reach the Paragon, Will surveys the long row of beautiful townhouses.

'This street was hit,' he says. 'Further up there. High explosive bombs, second raid, first night,' he says. 'A whole household killed in an instant. We dug at the wreckage for the rest of the day, but no one was left alive.'

He shakes his head, and I feel guilty because really I'm looking the other way along George Street with its vodka bars and nightclubs. I'm remembering being eighteen, clinging on to the outskirts of various social circles, desperate not to be cast away.

'Does it look the same as it did back then?'

'Yes, I suppose. Although most of the buildings were filthy black. The local coal gave off a lot of dust when it was burned, and because the city is in a valley it hung in the air and got into the stone.'

'Didn't people clean the walls?'

He smirks. 'We had more important things to worry about back then.'

We cut down the narrow alley to Walcott Street and I have to

161

help Will as he descends the steps tentatively, the high walls either side seemingly closing in around us. I get a brief moment of nausea and have to steady myself – we're like two invalids, split off from a day trip, lost and unwell. At the bottom, we head left toward an antique store housed in an old Victorian warehouse, the pavement outside crowded with little stone statues and tin baths leaned up against the wall. Will walks toward the building and puts his hand against the brick.

'This is where I worked,' he says gently. 'This was Anderson Wireless. Downstairs they assembled the prototypes, upstairs was the laboratory. There was also a large factory in Somerton where the finished sets were built, but this was the heart of it. I'd walk here every morning, past the market stalls and the tramworks, the smell of grease and oil in the air. Come on.'

We walk toward Pulteney Bridge, the abbey visible above the shops and cafés, stark and tall in the grey light. He looks around for a second, his face a mask of confusion, as though somehow he had been transported here from another country. It seems as though he is very far from me, fading into some distant past, like a figure on an old sepia photograph.

'Bath is a kind of palimpsest,' he says as he walks. 'Do you know what that is? It is a document that's been written over several times, so that beneath each layer there is another, older text. Somewhere near here was the druid settlement, Bladud and all that, then there was the Roman city with its baths and villas, and then the mediaeval city with its narrow streets and its wall. After this, the Georgian city . . .'

'Jane Austen.'

'Yes, and Beau Nash and Ralph Allen, and the architects John Wood the senior and John Wood the younger. There is an industrial city too, and then the modern city of high-rise blocks and shopping arcades. They don't replace each other, they exist side by side. The mediaeval city is still here, the city I grew up in is still here. Sometimes when I walk through Bath, I catch a glimpse of someone who looks familiar and I realise it is someone I knew back then – a friend, a workmate – just walking along among the other pedestrians, looking young, as I remember them.'

'Like ghosts?' I say.

'No,' he says quietly. 'Just ... there.'

He wanders off again, and I have no choice but to follow. We're heading toward Pulteney Bridge. 'There is one more place to show you today,' he says.

I haven't been inside Victoria Gallery for years. There was the time Mum and I came for the Second World War exhibition and before that I came with my art class and we had to sit along the plush velvety benches in the centre of the room and choose a painting to sketch. Now, in the upstairs gallery again, I feel that little has changed though I recognise almost none of the paintings, only the familiar pale, pinched faces of Gainsborough portraits. The climb up the stairs was an effort for both of us, and for a while we stand silently, watching visitors idly strolling from one work to the next, occasionally stopping and pointing their phones at a picture.

'I think I remember where I was when she came and stood behind me,' says Will. 'We often wondered what had brought us both here, on the same day, at the same time. It seemed almost too perfect. Too ... Ah, there it is!'

He walks off, but when I try to follow, a group of schoolchildren wander between us, all huddled together in their coats and hats. Holding hands. The dizziness comes again, and I reach for a display case in the centre of the room to get my balance. I look around for Will but I can't see him, and when I finally do spot him, he is looking up at a large painting on the far wall, in an elaborate gold-painted frame. It's a country scene, a rugged hillside, dotted with cows. *They are very relaxing creatures.* In this moment of recognition I have a horrible feeling, as though I'm somehow in the centre of an orbit through which the room and its inhabitants are spinning. I want to call for Will, but I'm embarrassed at the state of myself. Instead, I stagger forwards a little, and grope my way onto one of the large central benches, hearing the rush of blood in my ears and the thud of my own heart – a cacophony that seems to drown everything else. The swirling is faster, and there is heat and light at the centre of it. Sparks ignite at the edges of my vision.

Then there is blackness.

'Are you okay?' a voice fades in. It is kindly and female. 'Someone has gone to fetch you a glass of water.' I open my eyes and I see one of the art gallery staff standing over me. I realise with a flood of embarrassment that I'm lying on the bench and there are a lot of people around. I hear myself say 'Thank you', and when I sit up someone is handing me my glasses so I put them on. My organiser slips out of my hand onto the floor. Will is standing there too, looking concerned.

'You fainted,' he says. 'One minute you were there, the next . . .'

I close my eyes and rub my head. My hair is all knotted and it must look crazy.

'Should we call an ambulance?' a voice says. 'Are you okay?'

'She's fine. She needs air.'

'Can everyone stand back now?'

I let my eyes close – I feel drugged and tired – and when I open them again, the tourists have moved on, bored of the show. The schoolchildren have disappeared. Someone returns with a glass of water and I sit up to take it. The staff member sits next to me.

'Take your time,' she says. 'Small sips.'

'I'm sorry about this,' I reply softly.

'It can get very stuffy in here, especially when it's crowded. Have you been to the gallery before?'

'A few times,' I say, aware that she is keeping me talking so she can make sure I'm okay. It reminds me of that night in London; the bridge, the ambulance ride, the nurse asking patient questions as they decided whether or not to section me. 'I came with my mum to see the war exhibition a few years ago.'

'Oh yes, the Bath Blitz exhibition,' she says brightly. 'That was my first as a curator. It was all right, wasn't it?'

I feel like I'm slowly coming to my senses, but I totally appreciate this woman's quiet easy conversation. And don't want it to end just yet.

'You had those interviews, with the survivors . , .'

'Yes, that was tricky to organise, but fascinating. Lots of amazing stories. A few rather too amazing to feature in the exhibition. A couple of our interviewees came up with some pretty weird and wild tales. I suppose the whole experience must have been surreal.' She looks up at Will. 'Are you a local? You look like you could possibly have been around then?'

'Let's get you some fresh air,' Will says to me, and I nod, too weary to challenge him. We take it slowly. Down the steps, through the vestibule and onto the street, then toward the bridge where we stop. Gently, in a way he never has before, he takes my hands.

'I'm worried about you,' he says. It is a shock to hear it from him.

'It's fine. It was just hot in there.'

'No, there's something else. I see it in you. I know what it's like — to have something you can't talk about. Something locked away.'

I feel a lump in my throat that I have to swallow down hard.

'It's fine,' I say again. He is still holding my hands.

165

'You're a good person, Laura James. Do you understand?'

And he's staring at me with those deep-set eyes, waiting. But I'm looking away. Finally, he lets my hands fall.

'Perhaps we should have a little wander around the block,' he says.

We walk down past the Empire Hotel and around the Orange Grove. I'm starting to feel better when Will stops and stares at the restaurant next to the hotel.

'That was once the police station,' he says. 'It is where they took Elsa when she was arrested. Come on, we should probably get back. We can take a taxi.'

'Elsa was arrested?' I say. I feel like there is bait dangling from the line, and I have taken it.

'One night in 1940,' he says. 'The decision was made to round up all the German and Austrian immigrants in the city – there were fears about Fifth Columnists, especially with the Admiralty based here. Elsa told me there had been postcards and leaflets left in parks and posted through letterboxes, encouraging people to listen to the Lord Haw-Haw broadcasts. The government was setting up internment camps all over the country. I . . . I didn't realise how serious it all was. The police just took her away.'

'Oh my God, what happened next?'

He grimaces at me. 'Does it matter? Perhaps I imagined the whole thing.'

I can't figure out if it was always his intention to bring me here. Was there cunning intent behind this story? Whatever the case, it takes me a while to realise what it means. If she had been arrested, there would be a record of it somewhere. There would be proof.

Chapter Eighteen

1939

I have a confession. The year Britain slipped into the nightmare of the Second World War was the most wonderful of my life. While the rest of the city took on a dour mood of purposeful dread with endless Civil Defence meetings and air raid drills, Elsa and I began our courtship in earnest. Determined to wring all we could out of the remaining peacetime, we danced at the Pavilion every Saturday evening, we ate at expensive restaurants and drank cocktails at the Grand Pump Room hotel. Giles took us on several jaunts to London revealing an astonishing knowledge of the city's salacious nightlife, from private Soho bars to the glorious Florida Club with its revolving dance floor and lively house band.

But there were quieter times too. On Saturday afternoons, Elsa and I would lounge around in the study at Avon Lodge listening to the wireless or gramophone records, foisting our favourites upon each other. I would play Elgar and Vaughan Williams, she would bring Schoenberg, Debussy and sometimes even Schubert. We discovered American jazz together, buying 78s by Cab Calloway and Bessie Smith, revelling in the exciting new sound, stomping about the room, annoying my neighbours in the process. One sultry day, I dug out my 78 recording of the song we had heard at the Pavilion, 'Someday I'll Find You'. As soon as Elsa arrived, I opened the door and said to her, 'Come, listen.' We walked through to the garden, and there was a smoky light and the heady scent of flowers in the air. I had brought a portable gramophone out and when I put the needle down onto the disc, Elsa recognised it immediately. 'This time, let's dance,' she said. And we did. We danced together beside the low orange sun, our arms about one another, barely moving, lost in each other's eyes. We could feel the music on our skin; it was between us and inside us. A perfect resonance. I never played that record again.

On Sundays, I cycled to Bloomfield Crescent for the day; if it was sunny we would walk up into the hills, following the skyline around the city, and up to Little Salisbury Hill. But if it was rainy, we would sit on the small settee leafing through Uncle Levi's collection of books on art and theatre. My world was broadening, as though the curtains were being opened on a vast, incredible new landscape. It was here, on these lazy afternoons, that Elsa introduced me to Schiele, Kokoschka and Klimt, the artists of her home country. Klimt was her favourite. For my birthday, she bought me a large monograph covering his entire career – it had photographs of fifty paintings, including ten beautiful colour plates. I had never seen anything like these images. The women sultry, lithe, their skin blushing, their clothes all harlequin colours bathed in dazzling gold light. I recall the afternoon we first studied that book together, turning each glossy page, sitting very close, her head almost resting on my shoulder ... The feeling of it, I couldn't describe it, I just knew we had passed some kind of threshold. I became very aware of her body, her breathing. New emotions swelled in me. It seemed as though I had suddenly come alive.

But it wasn't always easy, this opening up of a new life. In many ways I was still the shy lad brought up in a rather old-fashioned city by quiet, conservative parents. Some evenings, we joined Aunt Josephine at sherry parties, meeting her crowd of faintly bohemian writers and thinkers. On the night before my nineteenth birthday, there had been one such occasion at the home of the artists Clifford and Rosemary Ellis, who lived in a large townhouse further along Lansdown Road. It was a rather sultry evening as Elsa and I strolled down, me in my one good lounge suit, she in a beautiful dress with a print of frolicking cupids. She took my hand and said, 'You're shaking. It's just a little party.'

'I don't know anyone. This is very much not my crowd. My God, the Ellises are famous.'

'You'll be fine, I promise. Talk about what you know; talk about radio. These people love an enthusiast. Trust me.'

I wanted to believe her, but I already felt so damn insecure, and when Rosemary herself opened the door to us, drink in hand, mid-conversation, I almost ran for it.

'Elsa,' she said, pushing away a strand of dark curly hair from her eyes. 'How lovely to see you. Jo is already here. And you are Will? Jo was telling the truth – you really are very tall and dashing. Come in.' She guided us through the hall, which was crowded with guests, the noise of chatter almost deafening in the narrow space. In the living room, many more people, almost all older than me, were grouped into discussions. The walls were covered with beaut-iful paintings; ancient leather-bound books were crammed into a row of wooden shelves. A gramophone was playing a fast-paced jazz song, almost drowned out by the babbling conversations.

Elsa spotted her aunt and rushed off to greet her, leaving me blinking into the imposing crowd. Rosemary swam past again, pushing a glass of scotch into my hand. I took too large a sip and it burned my throat. I was desperate not to embarrass Elsa, not to show myself up as a philistine. I joined one group gathered around an architect named Frederick Bond, a small excitable man in a musty three-piece suit, who was explaining a complicated-sounding theory on psychic energy and alternative dimensions, and who was in the area hoping to carry out archaeological excavations in Glastonbury.

'You are all aware, I assume, that the whole of Bath is riddled with lay lines; they criss-cross the seven hills, they come down this very street, in fact. You know, there are modern druids still holding ceremonies in the city.'

'Oh Frederick,' someone said. 'You are my absolute favourite crackpot.'

'You may mock,' Bond continued, 'but there is an energy in the air here. In psychic terms, Bath is a sort of vast wireless receiver.'

'Speaking of which,' said another member of the little group before turning to me, 'I believe this is our neighbourhood expert on such matters. Will?'

'Yes, hello,' I said, trying not to sound either self-conscious or oafish.

'Arthur Ellis,' he said, putting a hand out for me to shake. 'You're a wireless man, aren't you?'

'Yes, I work in research at Anderson's. We're developing a new model, very compact, but with excellent tuning capabilities. Cutting-edge stuff.'

While I spoke I was desperately looking around for Elsa, worried that I was being a bore and hoping for her to rescue me, but she was deep in conversation with Rosemary and her aunt. When I turned back, I realised the small group was waiting for me to continue. They were listening.

'Well, we're innovating with superhet technology to better isolate incoming short- and medium-wave radio signals, and—'

'Superhet?' someone asked.

'Superheterodyne. It's a modern sort of radio receiver that generates a local oscillator signal that combines with the incoming signal that you want to listen to, allowing you to block out all the other radio noise. It means you get exceptionally clear reception, even if you are listening to a broadcast from the other side of the world.'

'You can do that now?' said an older gentleman.

'Yes,' I said. 'Just the other night, I picked up a broadcast from Tokyo.'

'Good grief,' said the man. 'I don't quite believe it.'

I looked at the faces around me, interested, but somewhat sceptical of this young lad, throwing around technical phrases. Then I did something I can't account for. I downed my whisky, handed the empty glass to Arthur and said, 'I'll show you.'

In a flash, I was out of the house, sprinting up the road, buoyed I expect by the heady mix of nerves and scotch. I rocketed into my workshop, gathering up my finest Anderson set, together with its long wire antenna. I lifted the set, testing its weight, realising I could probably make it back without any sort of calamity, and then I hobbled out.

The group, still together, still chatting in the living room, were somewhat dumbfounded to see me, standing in the doorway, a large wireless set grasped in my arms. A few other heads turned to us now.

'Can I put it on the table by the window?' I asked, my voice calm, but showing the strain of the weight I was carrying.

171

'Absolutely,' replied Arthur, clearing a couple of sketch books and a candle holder from the surface. I put it down carefully, and looked about, trying to work out where to put the antenna. Usually, in a home situation, I'd run it along the picture rail, but the paintings here looked extremely valuable and I didn't want to cause any damage. Besides, I figured I'd need more height.

'Can we help at all?' asked Bond. 'Is there some ceremony we need to enact?'

'I just need to run the antenna somewhere high up.'

'You can tie it to the chandelier,' suggested Arthur. 'Actually perhaps not, Rosemary will be upset if we bring it down.'

Then, looking around, I had an idea.

'The window,' I said. 'Can someone go upstairs?'

And that is how, on the night before my nineteenth birthday, I found myself standing on the window sill outside the house of Bath's foremost artists, stretching upwards, holding the end of an antenna wire, while Arthur Ellis, leaning out of the first-floor window above, held fast around the waist by a notable architect, flailed about to reach it. After a minute or so of ridiculous effort, we finally made contact and Arthur took the wire into the upstairs room.

When this was done, we all thundered back into the living room, squirming through the others, like schoolboys at some silly game, converging in front of the set.

'Now,' I said, switching it on, watching the dial display glow into life, 'it will take a few minutes to warm up.'

I put my fingers to the bandset and bandspread controls. 'This knob will get me in the vicinity of the correct frequency, and this'll allow me to get closer still ...'

I knelt at the radio like a safecracker, listening in as the speaker warmed, hearing the growing fuzz of static. I was no longer nervous, no longer performing at competency – I knew what I was doing. There were whines and tics as I tweaked the signal; a few false starts as sounds ebbed in and then away. I felt the little crowd grow restless around me. And then, very quiet at first, but louder as I turned the volume dial (even allowing myself a little flourish, like a magician pulling a rabbit from a hat), there it was. A voice. The words incomprehensible, but very clearly – even amid the tide of gravelly interference – Japanese.

'Good lord, the boy has done it,' said Arthur. 'Rosemary, come and listen to this. It's bloody Tokyo calling.'

She approached, taking her husband's arm, and we stood enraptured, listening to this voice from thousands of miles away.

'Isn't it astonishing?' said Rosemary. 'The voice is in Tokyo but it is also here. Such distant places at the same time. It's like time travel.'

'Considering what we are beginning to understand about the universe,' says Bond, 'space and time have a lot of surprises in store.'

'Well, we're all neighbours now,' said Rosemary. 'The whole world is the size of a room.'

'Pity we're on the verge of destroying it,' said her husband. 'What do you think the gentleman is saying?'

'He is probably declaring war on us,' someone else said to a ripple of cynical laughter. I looked around, flushed with pride as a barrage of questions erupted from the group. And over the other side of the room, standing by a single lamp with an extravagantly jewelled shade, was Elsa, lit in reddish-orange, and dotted with sparkling reflections. She was watching, smiling, and when she caught my eye, she held her glass of scotch aloft to me as a sort of salute. She was so beautiful, so ... present, everything else faded – the voices, the wireless broadcast from the other side of the globe – all drowned out by the signal of her. Of us. Together. Glowing.

173

Just before midnight, Josephine had someone call a taxi and we walked out with her when it arrived. I expected Elsa to say goodnight to me and accompany her aunt, but this time, the two of them kissed then looked at each other for a few moments before Josephine got into the car alone.

'Are you staying at the party?' I said to Elsa as the car pulled away.

'No,' she said, finally drawing her eyes away from the car and toward me. 'You're taking me home. To Avon Lodge.'

'I am?'

'Yes.'

I was torn between desperately wanting to be sure of what was happening while at the same time desperately not wanting to ask exactly what was happening in case it broke the spell or betrayed my lack of experience.

'I see,' I stuttered. 'And if I could just clarify . . . '

'I'd like to stay the night,' she said. 'With you. As long as you have no objection.'

'I assuredly do not.'

We walked back in silence, not because we had nothing to say, but because it seemed as though the time for speaking was over. We were somewhere else now. I fumbled a couple of times with the key in the lock, but then, remembering my return here earlier in the evening and feeling steadied by that, I got the door open. Elsa shut it behind us and pushed me against the wall, looking into my eyes the whole time. She took my hands and put them on her, moving her body against me. I could feel the whole contour of her. Instinctively, I brought her in even closer, and her lips were warm filaments on my neck, her fingers in my mouth. There was something in the air and it crackled between us.

Later, in bed together, the sheets discarded, we lay for a long time, lost in contemplation.

'It was a nice party,' she said at last. 'I told you it would be fine.'

'You did.'

'You should trust me.'

'I know.'

Then we were silent again. We didn't know that soon Elsa would be required to show bravery and strength that belittled my own.

Chapter Nineteen

2008

The Bath Record Office is a little warren of rooms in the basement of the Guildhall. It is not somewhere I ever thought I'd find myself. A Google search for 'Bath police records' suggested a few artefacts, including historic charge sheets and arrest reports, remained in the city's collection, so here I am. Walking down the worn stone steps to the archive, clutching my organiser to my chest as a defence mechanism, I feel like an impostor. I'm not a researcher. I'm not a student. I will probably be asked to leave. Beyond a corridor lined with old wooden filling cabinets, there is the small reference library, its dozens of shelves filled with ancient books and battered folders. A middle-aged woman sits quietly at a reception desk, tapping at a computer. When she notices me, she smiles warmly.

'Can I help you?' she asks.

'I don't know. I'm looking for someone, well, not someone now, someone who lived in Bath during the war, except I don't know if she existed, but if she *did* exist, I think she was arrested.'

It all comes out in a single garbled sentence. The woman seems unperturbed.

'I'm afraid we only have limited records from the Bath Central Police Station during the Second World War. Do you know when she was arrested?'

'It was in 1940. She was a Jewish refugee from Austria. I think there was some sort of mass arrest in Bath one night, and she was taken.'

'"Collar the lot",' the woman says.

'Pardon?'

'"Collar the lot." It's what Winston Churchill said in 1939 about the refugees who were arriving in Britain from Germany. The government decreed that they should all be put in prison camps until the war ended, just in case they were spies. Anyway, I'll have a look through our collection, but a more accurate date might help. Perhaps while I'm looking, you could check the *Bath Chronicle* newspaper? We have every issue on microfilm. If she was arrested, there may have been a news report. Have you ever used a microfilm reader?'

'Uh, yes. A few times. At university.' I lift my fingers to my mouth and start biting at a nail. Looking around the room, I notice the table in the centre – there is one old man sitting there, looking at a large map rolled out in front of him, his face inches above the yellowing paper. He seems totally comfortable here. Why can't I be like that?

'Come this way,' she says.

She leads me to another room where there are rows of filing cabinets, and at the far end, two giant microfilm readers, with large blank screens like old computer monitors. She goes to a cupboard, searches through then pulls out a reel of film. 'Sit down,' she says, gesturing to a chair in front of one of the readers.

'This reel has all the *Bath Chronicle* newspapers from 1940,' she says, placing it onto a spool beneath the screen, then winding the film under a plate of glass and through the other end. It's a different reader than the ones at the university library but I recognise the controller for spinning the film back and forward and the bank of buttons for zooming in and out, and refocusing. The woman switches the screen on and the quiet hum takes me back to some of the nicest memories I have of uni.

'It's quite straightforward,' she says. 'But come and get me if you're stuck. I'll see what I can find in the Bath police station archive.'

Then she disappears. I open my organiser, laying it on the desk with my pencil. Now I have a few hundred newspapers to search – and for an hour, I fruitlessly slog through, rolling past stories about wartime preparations and local controversies, past adverts for concerts and whist drives and savings bonds. The mechanical clicks and whirs of the film spooling and the pages whizzing by on the softly lit screen are almost hypnotic. It's lunchtime when I spot a photograph that makes me stop. It's next to a story about the completion of a building called Kilowatt House, 'an ambitious modernist masterpiece' on North Road. At first, the photo appears to show a man and a woman standing in front of a large white building; they are smiling and holding champagne flutes. The woman is wearing a pale dress, the man is in a tweed suit – he is handsome, but also rather boyish. And it takes me a couple of seconds to realise, the man isn't a man at all. The caption says, 'Architect Molly Taylor (left) and friend Josephine Klein'. It is Elsa's aunt. I feel a rush of excitement – a fragment of Will's recollection is real. But as I trawl on, through dozens more issues, with no further leads, I get a growing sense of frustration. It's possible Will had also seen Josephine's name in one of his old newspapers.

Maybe he'd plucked it out randomly to become part of his tale.

But then my eye is drawn to a small article with an intriguing headline: ENEMY ALIEN AT BATH. It sounds like some sort of extraterrestrial invasion, but it is about a young German refugee named Hilda Knapp who had moved from Bath to Frome without informing the police of her change of address, which was apparently illegal. It's from May 1940. The authorities have started to crack down on immigrants. I scroll through the next few issues slowly. There are more stories about German people getting into trouble for not registering their arrival in Bath, and reports on Bath council meetings about the problem. And then, halfway down the list, I spot a search result that sends a shiver through me. Dated 1 June 1940, the headline reads simply, ALIEN REFUGEES ROUNDED UP. I pause for a second, my heartbeat loud in the small quiet room, then I click on the link.

A number of alien refugees resident in Bath – mostly women – have recently been rounded up and removed to a place of detention.

They were escorted from their homes by police officers and taken to the Central Police Station in the early hours, later being conveyed in a charabanc to their destination.

Was this it? Was this when Elsa was arrested? I go back to the help desk, barely able to stop myself running. When the staff member sees me, she lifts up a folder.

'I think I've found the date of her arrest,' I say. 'June 1940.'

'Okay. This lists everything we have in the archive relating to Bath Police Station,' she says, opening the folder to reveal pages of text and reference numbers. There are lists of items under headings such as POLICE OPERATION RECORDS and CIVIL

179

DEFENCE PROCEDURES, together with dates and details about what's been archived.

'This might be something,' the woman says. 'It's a small collection of police photographs and there are several from the summer of 1940. I could fetch them for you to look at?'

'Yes, please,' I say eagerly, like an attentive student.

She heads off into another room but it seems so unlikely there will be anything to do with Elsa. This woman from another country, this ghost, this figment . . . how could she really be contained in a photograph in a basement in Bath? The research assistant returns with another folder, sits down, and carefully slides out a small collection of photos then begins to flip through them for me. There are faded shots of policemen at work – patrolling the streets, controlling crowds of people at some sort of sporting event – and a couple of the police station itself, one with a group of young women standing outside. She flips past a couple more of crowded street scenes, and then the show is over. It's over. I can go home, I can break it to Will that there's nothing, no sign, no proof, no . . .

The women outside the station.

'Can we go back a few?' I ask. The assistant rearranges the photos on the desk, until I see the one I want. There are maybe fifteen women and a couple of men, most with tired and bewildered expressions; I look along the row from person to person, like a crime victim at a police line-up. And then I get to a young woman who looks different to the others – she is staring at the camera with a look of defiance and contempt, her wild curly hair billowing about her face, her hands clenched into fists. I let out a gasp of surprise, because somehow I know.

'It's her,' I say. 'It's her.'

*

Late one night, in May 1940, a woman named Elsa Klein was taken from her home and brought in to Bath Central Police Station with at least twenty other German and Austrian aliens. At some point during this process, perhaps while the wretched group was waiting to board a bus to the detention centre, someone took a photograph.

The research assistant makes a photocopy for me and I look at the image again. The more I stare, the more certain I am: the woman is not looking at the camera, she is looking at me. She is challenging me.

And I wish I could ask her – what happened next? Because if she was taken away to a detention centre in 1940, surely she would have been interned for the entire war. And if that were the case, how the hell was she living with Will in Bath in 1942?

Chapter Twenty

I am standing at the door to Avon Lodge holding a manila envelope containing the photo of Elsa Klein. I don't know how this is going to play out. Part of me is terrified about showing the image to Will. What if he doesn't recognise her? What if he *does* recognise her and has a breakdown? How involved should I really be in all this? But I *am* involved. I really am.

I hear the dull click of the latch and then the door opens, the hinges groaning loudly. There is Will, in high-waisted baggy trousers, a shirt and knitted tank top, his dour glare a strangely comforting constant.

'Hello, Will,' I say brightly, but I know there's an edge of trepidation. 'I've found something.'

Despite all our cleaning efforts, the kitchen has slipped back into the awful mess it was before; the clutter, the filthy sink and oven, the underlying smell of backed-up drains. I sit down at the table and when he brings tea over, he shuffles onto the chair beside me with almost maddening sluggishness. When he is finally ready,

I put the envelope on the table as though I'm presenting a vital exhibit in a courtroom drama.

'I went to the Bath Record Office,' I tell him. 'I searched for Elsa's arrest in the *Chronicle* archive.'

He nods vacantly, and at first I'm not sure he's even understood what I'm telling him.

'I didn't ask you to,' he says. His voice is firm but cracked. He puts down his tea and rests both hands on the table, palms down, as though preparing to hoist himself back up again.

'I wanted to.'

He's looking away from me, staring down at the floor; there is a tremor to him, like his whole body is shaking. 'I'm sure she would never have been in the news.'

I clear my throat. 'But she was.' Finally he turns to me, his deep eyes wide and shocked. 'I mean, there was a story about the night all the refugees were arrested.'

'How did you know about that?'

'You told me.'

'I didn't.'

'Yes, you did, when we walked past the Orange Grove the other day.'

He shakes his head. 'There was no record of her ... I'm certain I went back to the police station to check. I'm sure I did. What is in that envelope?'

'I'll show you. It was in amongst the—'

'No, wait,' he says, and he grabs my hand. 'Please wait!'

'What is it?'

He looks as though he is trying to say something, but the words, the emotions, are far beyond reach in some distant corner of his brain.

'Please,' he says again. 'I can't. All I have, you see, all I have are memories. The time I was with Elsa, it's the only real thing in my life. Every day, I relive it. Everything that happened afterwards, the years that went on and on, they were empty. There's nothing else. So what you have in that envelope . . . it's terrifying. The past is all I have and it's terrifying to me. Do you understand?'

There is something in the words he uses, the raw fear in his voice, that triggers a similar sense in me. The terror of the past. The tyranny of it. Out of nowhere, familiar memories and emotions engulf me, as sudden as a flash flood.

'I do,' I say. I try to control my voice but it's already mostly tears.

I expect him to scoff at me. How could a twenty-nine-year-old woman know how he feels? I've barely lived.

Instead, he nods.

'I saw it,' he says quietly. 'I saw it in you the first time you stood at my door.'

I hear the gentle hum of passing cars, and the sound of heavy things being moved on the property development.

'What happened to you?' he asks.

'I can't.'

'Because people haven't believed you? They haven't taken you seriously?'

Years of that. Years of it. Friends and flatmates, always sympathetic at first. Then after a few rough days, a few panic attacks, I try to tell them, I try to explain, and almost imperceptibly they move away. Because what happened really? How bad was it really?

'Tell me,' he says. 'Because I will believe you. I know how to do that at least. And it will help me too, Laura. Before I see whatever you have in that envelope, I want you to tell me what happened.'

'It was my dad,' I say. I have to stop to compose myself. Will lets me. 'He'd always wanted to be this great cinematographer – he grew up in Slough and he told me it felt like a sign because he was so close to the Pinewood and Shepperton studios. He was obsessed with cameras, he loved making films – he said that nothing was real unless there was footage. But he couldn't break into the industry; people just ... didn't like him. He ended up taking a job as a cameraman on the Bath local news. He hated it. He hated it here. He took it all out on us. On me.'

The memories don't sound that terrible in isolation. I could pick from dozens of them. Hundreds. I am ten years old, sitting at the coffee table at home, a sketchbook in front of me and felt-tip pens all around. I've eaten one of the microwave meals Mum bought for me, she won't be home until late, she's left me a note that says, *Tidy up before Dad gets home*. But I'm excited because I've been to see *The Little Mermaid* with my friend Jessie and we talked about it all day and now I want to draw Ariel and Ursula. But then I hear Dad's car in the driveway and a cold panic is on me. I pick up as many of the pens as I can, shove them in my pencil case and run upstairs. It's better not to be around when he gets home. He needs some time. From my bedroom, I hear the front door open and slam shut, and I crawl to the furthest corner of the bed, right against the wall, the colouring book in my hand. I hear him shout something, and then his feet on the stairs. Thud, thud, thud. I brace myself. Because there's always something I've got wrong. My door swings open.

'I've told you a thousand times!' he says. His greying brown hair is all messy, his face is contorted and he has a fistful of my pens. 'When I come home, I want the living room to be tidy! I need to be able to relax and I can't relax if your shit is everywhere!'

He throws the pens at the bed. They hit the wall and scatter. I see that a couple have lost their lids.

'I'm sorry,' I say.

185

'You're always bloody sorry!'

There is silence for a few seconds and he breathes loudly, then runs his hand through his hair. There are sweat patches under the arms of his shirt even when it's cold.

'Is that what you've been colouring?' he says, pointing at the book.

I nod. He bundles into the room, and this is the part where he tries to be interested and kind. He really tries. 'Let's have a look.' He takes the book from me and I get as far into the corner as I can.

'You need to stay in the lines,' he says, flicking through the images. 'You'll never be an artist.'

He throws the book back to me, then clutches at his forehead with both hands, as though he has an agonising headache. There is something he wants to say, there is always something he wants to say, but he can't. I just want him to go. I want to find the lids, so my best pens don't dry up.

Hundreds of days like this. I have left a mess in the kitchen, I tread mud into the house, I'm watching a TV programme he thinks is silly or noisy. Weekends of him slumped in a chair, reading, drinking until he can't speak. I know not to ask him if he wants to play. Most evenings, Mum will come home late and downstairs there will be shouting, shouting, shouting. She'll creep to my room, sit on the bed and say, 'What meal did you get from the fridge?' and then she'll nod when I tell her but not really listen. 'Good choice,' she will say, but not much else.

But here is the hardest thing. Sometimes, Dad is lovely. He'll show me how to use one of his camcorders and we'll make a film together. He is fascinated by space and science and the universe, and he'll read me his favourite books and discuss them with me. He takes me on day trips. One day, we go to the London Planetarium. We sit in the darkness watching the stars. I have this wonderful feeling that there are limitless possibilities out there for me, that I have a brilliant future to explore. I have never experienced such excitement – the thrill of a whole life to come. I turn to my dad and say, 'It's so beautiful, I don't want it to be over.' He smiles and whispers, 'Nothing really ends. Everything is always happening.'

But then, on the train home he shouts because I spill my Coke on the table. All the rare bright moments end like this, broken and ruined.

On like this for weeks, for years, the deadening normality of it. Nothing better, nothing worse. Whenever I try to tell people about him, they are always waiting for the punchline; they want bruises and busted teeth. But there are no great horrors, no fists. Just tension, taut as a drum skin, over every moment I am at home. Each time something happens, my heart breaks because I know he is good; deep down he is good, but that good man is falling further and further away, and the monster is winning. The sound of the footsteps toward my bedroom, the door opening, and all my things around me, all my hopes and ambitions, all useless, all targets for him and his rage.

Now I am in Bath, in this house, with its strange buzz, its electricity of longing. I'm a grown-up, I have a job. But wherever I am, whatever I do, I am in that room.

Will is looking at me.

'The place I was in before the bomb, I'm still there, with Elsa,' he says. 'Nothing that's happened since feels real.'

We sit together for a while, not really knowing where to go from here. Two people viewing their lives from a distance, trying to work out how to get home.

'Is this why you never looked for her? You've had sixty years – to search newspaper archives, or police records, or track down her relatives. But you didn't. Is it because you were scared of what you'd find?'

He stands up and steps away from the table. 'When I came out of hospital after the bombing, I got home and all her things were gone, the house seemed utterly unfamiliar. I just broke down; it was as though everything went dark. I ended up back in hospital for several weeks. The doctors told me it was trauma or brain damage. I had all these memories that were bright and vibrant and alive, but they didn't fit with what the world was telling me – they were like pieces of the wrong jigsaw. The rest of the war, the years afterwards, I can barely remember them. It was like sleepwalking. I began to fear that everything I had experienced before the bomb was a dream. When I started to pull myself together, I couldn't face searching for answers and then finding out the woman I loved was some figment of my imagination. So I clung to the journals I didn't even recall writing and I hoped they were memories and not stories.'

As Will mentions the empty years after the war, I recall the rumours Florence and the shop assistant brought up; those whispers of prison. What *really* happened when he was discharged from hospital? Did he just sit alone in his study, endlessly reliving the past? Or was there something else?

'And you never ... you never thought of letting go,' I say. 'You never thought of finding someone else?'

He looks at me with a terrible sorrow, but I realise it is not for himself, it is for me. It is pity.

'We're told that love is everywhere, that there's someone out there for all of us. But this is what I've learned in my eighty-seven years. It's not true. Most people never have love – what they experience is desire and then routine. Real love, lasting love – it is rare. There isn't enough to go around. So no, there was no one else for me.'

He sits beside me again. 'Everything was very dark for years. And then you came to the door. You seemed to feel something in the house. It gave me hope again. The past is terrifying, but so is hope. Whatever you have in that envelope, I am frightened of it.'

Now I'm frightened too. Because what if I'm wrong? What if this is a different Elsa Klein – or she doesn't match the broken memories he has? But then, we've both got to stop running eventually.

'It's a photograph,' I say. 'It was taken in May 1940 and it shows a group of refugees at Bath Police Station, waiting to be taken away. I'm sure that one of them is Elsa.'

He sits down again.

'Show me,' he says.

Slowly, I open the envelope and pull out the photocopy. I slide it across the table to him. He picks it up and holds it close to his face, his hands tremoring.

If it is her, I know I have to do this properly. I have to find out what happened and link her to him. If it isn't, then there's something wrong with both of us. He is old and his mind is going; I am a wreck, coming down from the drugs that were meant to keep me sane and functioning, and their tendrils are pulling at me. It's probably for the best if it is not her. If it's not, we can part and no one will rely on me. I am not reliable. All I've ever done is get by.

I look across. His face is rigid and he's shaking his head.

'It's not her?' I say.

He turns to me slowly – it is a great effort to remove his eyes from the image.

'It's her,' he says. 'It's Elsa. I haven't seen her face since I was twenty-three. She is everything I remembered.'

He leans across and embraces me, saying 'thank you' over and over again. His clothes are musty and need a wash, but I hold him for a really long time. I look over his shoulder at the photo on the table. I say to the woman with the determined expression, *I am going to find out what happened to you.* But a question remains in my head. I gently separate from him.

'Will, I need to know something. If she was arrested that night – if she was taken away to be interned for the rest of the war – how was she with you the night of the bombing?'

He stares at the photo and I don't know if he's even heard me.

'Did they let her out?'

Eventually he shakes his head. 'It didn't happen like that,' he says.

'Then what did happen?'

'I need to rest. I'm sorry. I need to be alone for a while.'

He wrenches himself up from the chair and goes through to his library, shutting the door behind him. I take the mugs over to the kitchen sink, trying to put my thoughts into order. What I do know is that I had an instinct about something and it was right. I feel something like confidence. I start filling the washing up bowl and look up at the clock on the wall.

It has stopped again. Three forty-four p.m.

Then I see something else, something outside. I feel fear move through me, from my throat to the pit of my stomach.

Inside the workshop there is a shadow moving.

I put down the mugs. I close my eyes for a second and I sense the weird underlying tone of the house again, like a speaker humming. Almost in a trance, my hand is on the back door, pushing it open. Then down the garden path, and halfway the sound seems to be accompanied by some weird glint in the air, the light shafts visible and complex like fractals.

Through the doorway to the workshop, into the cool, dark interior. Everything in the room seems incredibly solid and hyper-real, every object pushing itself into my consciousness. I don't know why I say it, but I do anyway.

190

'Elsa?'

There is utter stillness. It's almost like I can hear the particles of dust colliding in the air. I am going mad, I think. This is it. This is what it feels like.

'Elsa, are you there?'

I see movement at the far end of the work table, and I jump, searching the gloom for its origin – but then I hear a bird flapping outside. It reminds me of the incident in the attic room and I almost laugh with relief. 'I'm losing it,' I say quietly, and I'm already moving toward the door.

At that moment, there is a blast of noise so loud and shocking, I put my hands to my ears and scream. For several seconds my mind is in utter turmoil as the horrible hissing cacophony continues. The first coherent thought to strike me is that there's been another explosion on the building site next door. But no, the sound is not coming from outside, it is in here with me. Every functioning wireless has been switched on, the volume turned to maximum; the glow from a dozen radio dials emerging from the darkness like the eyes of wolves in a forest. Then it stops.

I cower, afraid to move. After a few seconds, I take my hands away from my ears. My eyes fall on the transmitter station.

This was a warning. It feels like a warning.

I look down and am surprised to find that I have the photo of Elsa gripped in my hand.

Chapter Twenty-One

1940

Harold Anderson came from a long line of inventors. His great-grandfather designed and built industrial equipment for the glove-making trade, his father was a firearms innovator. As an officer in the Great War, Harold had become fascinated by radio communications, bringing home a decrepit field radio transmitter to disassemble and experiment with. He set up Anderson Wireless a year later, and by the end of the 1920s it was one of the major manufacturers of consumer sets in the country. I gave this potted biography to Elsa, as the taxi took us up Bathwick Hill and then along the meandering driveway to his home.

None of us had ever been invited before. It was a shock when, the previous Friday, Cooperton and I had been ushered into his office and asked if we would like to attend a little party he was throwing. 'It's a business do, really,' he explained from behind his desk, as cluttered with blueprints and components as our own work stations. 'This is a very different war to the last. It is an information war – communications and surveillance will be paramount. Which is obviously an opportunity for us.'

It was the spring of 1940. The Admiralty had been moved to Bath, with thousands of staff arriving from London. They took over the city's grand old hotels and constructed a village of hutments on Foxhill. The RAF was completing its airfield at Colerne and would soon begin Charmy Down. We were being drawn into the centre of things – and Anderson saw growing potential.

'There will be important people present,' he explained. 'I need you two around to answer questions, explain our technology, impress them. You may also have a pleasant time, although that is secondary. Please feel free to invite partners.'

Cooperton and I had looked at each other with a combination of surprise and foreboding. Just as we were leaving the room, I turned back to Anderson.

'May I bring Elsa?' I said.

'The pretty Austrian girl?'

'Yes.'

'There's no chance she's a Nazi spy?'

'I don't think so, sir, she's Jewish.'

He mulled this over, pulling at his moustache.

'Very well.'

And so there we were, Elsa and I. In the taxi, enjoying the warmth of the spring sun through the thin glass. I'd picked her up from her aunt's and when I saw her, all the breath left my body. She was wearing a long dress with a modern print of jagged lines, her hair, for once, artfully pinned back and controlled into a sculptured style. She was wearing long lace gloves.

'You are astonishing,' I said. 'I mean, you *look* astonishing.'

But I had indeed meant the former.

Anderson had told us the dress code was 'relaxed formal' so I was wearing a grey lounge suit, and I'd put pomade in my hair, which was already turning liquidy in the warm air. I could feel it running down my temples like fragrant sweat.

'Your carriage awaits,' I said to Elsa, holding out my arm for her to take. 'I must say I am rather nervous. Apart from Cooperton, I don't really know anybody and these are important chaps. I'm very significantly out of my depth.'

'I'm here,' she said. 'I'm with you.'

'Have a lovely time with the military moguls,' shouted Aunt Josephine from the sitting room. 'Don't come home until you have stopped the war.'

Anderson's house was a beautiful Georgian villa set amid acres of pristine gardens with views down toward the city. As we rolled up at the grand portico front entrance, two doormen rushed out to greet us, helping Elsa from the car. Someone offered us glasses of champagne from a silver tray, and we stopped to take in the entrance hall, bright and large, and crammed with people. Most of the men were dressed more formally than I, befitting their obvious military standing, the women in slightly old-fashioned party wear. Elsa and I nudged together, holding our glasses, unsure of what to do.

'Perhaps I shouldn't be here,' she whispered to me, and I noticed her face was suddenly ashen white.

'Why on earth not?' I replied, a little louder than she appeared to want.

'I should be keeping a low profile considering everything that's happening.'

'What do you mean?'

'German immigrants are being arrested. Haven't you seen the

194

news? And there is not much love for Jews in your country either. I shouldn't be drawing attention to myself.'

'Oh Elsa, you have nothing to worry about here in Bath.'

'Really? There are leaflets being put up around town, surely you've seen them? "Jews out," they say. And the other day I read that a German woman was taken to the police station because she'd made a mistake when she registered. What if they decide to just round us all up?'

'That won't happen. We're civilised people here.'

Anderson spotted us and raced over. I was glad I hadn't mentioned his question about her being a spy.

'Good to see you, Will,' he said with a genuinely welcoming smile. 'And lovely to see you again, Miss Klein. Will tells me you are of a musical bent. You must meet my wife.' He craned his neck beyond a group of older men, huddled in a conspiratorial scrum. 'There she is.'

He led us through the throng, until we reached a woman engaged in conversation with a short African man in a beautiful suit, surrounded by his own staff. As the eccentric-looking group departed, the woman was left alone looking somewhat flustered.

'Daphne,' said Harold. She turned to us when he spoke and gave us a broad but vacant smile, clearly trying to place who we were and if she should know us.

'Darling,' she said. 'The next time you invite royalty to our home, could you please at least give me *some* warning?'

'This is Will from the office,' he said. 'And this is his friend Elsa.'

'Ah, Will,' she said, holding my shoulders and placing a kiss in the air beside my right cheek. 'And Elsa, I hear you are from Vienna, home of the waltz. Thank you both for coming. There are people bringing around drinks and canapés, and later we have a chamber orchestra arriving from London. I know the cellist. Frightfully talented. Suzanne!'

With that, she was away, swimming gracefully through the crowd.

'She's got the jitters,' said Harold, as he watched her go. 'We don't usually entertain. It's been weeks of hard work for her.'

'What did she mean by royalty?' said Elsa.

'Oh, the gentleman she was speaking to is Haile Selassie. The emperor of Ethiopia. He is in exile here in Bath. Pleasant chap, very quiet. I did not expect him to accept the invitation.

'Anyway,' he continued, looking around until his eyes stopped on a tall man in Navy dress uniform. 'Ah, there is Captain Robertson. He's with the Naval technology team. I've been telling him about our latest developments.' Anderson took us over and introduced us. Robertson cut a dashing figure, and was somewhat imposing. He looked amused by everything.

'So you're the whizz at miniaturisation,' he said.

'I am. Are you enjoying Bath?'

'It's been bloody chaos,' he said, taking a cigarette from a silver case. 'We're getting there, slowly.'

He lit the cigarette and blew smoke away from us.

'You have some nice offices, though? Bath's finest hotels must make up for the inconvenience?'

He made a sound like a snort.

'My God, they're falling apart,' he said. 'No one is staying in them anymore, apart from old spinsters. The interiors and plumbing haven't been upgraded for thirty years. When we took the Empire Hotel we had to fit wooden braces from floor to ceiling to stop the bloody place falling down. At the Pulteney, the staff told us that if we have meetings of more than ten people in a room we will have to sit around the outside or the floor will cave in. Jerry won't have to bomb this damn city – they can just wait for it to fall down of its own accord.'

I felt rather indignant at this and was about to set him straight, when Elsa nudged me almost imperceptibly in the ribs.

'Look at that beautifully dressed man who has just arrived,' she said. 'Isn't that one of your friends, Will?'

I turned to where she was gesturing. It was Cooperton in a striped sports jacket and white slacks, looking terribly at ease; he swooped past a waiter taking a drink as he approached.

'Good afternoon,' he said. 'I say, isn't this perfect?'

We chatted for a while and, very subtly, Elsa took a deep breath, visibly readied herself and parted from us. At first she wandered along the walls, looking at the paintings, and then people started to draw her into conversations. Cooperton and I talked a little about work and what would be expected of us here, but really I was watching her. She had that air, I realised, that indecipherable quality of charisma, of social magnetism. People wanted to talk to her and were interested in what she said. But at every moment she could, I noticed that she was looking back toward me. At first her expression was concerned, but as she became more comfortable, her glances were brighter and then slightly mischievous. Eventually, she got to Anderson again, and the two of them spoke for several minutes.

'Elsa is a marvel,' said Cooperton, noticing my distraction. 'No wonder McDonald still has the hump.'

We'd noticed he had become distant at work, not joining us in the pub on Friday evenings, disappearing at the weekends. With a start, I remembered that one of the secretaries said she'd seen him going to a meeting of something called The Link, some organisation that supported better relations with Germany. There were rumours they were affiliated with the British Fascist party. Might *he* cause problems for Elsa and me? Oh bother, I thought, it was all rumours and nonsense. Cooperton was heading off to find more drink when Elsa came back to me.

'Come on,' she said quietly. 'Mr Anderson says we must see his library.'

'Should we be creeping off? I feel like I'm at work really.'

She drew up to me very close. I could feel the heat of her face. Her body pressed against me.

'The library is very well stocked apparently, and very quiet. I think we will find something to interest us.'

I did not understand why she was suddenly so keen to see a lot of books, but I followed her anyway. She moved through the crowds to a closed door on the opposite side of the hall. She opened it just a little and slid in, beckoning me to follow. Inside, the curtains were half closed, so there was a sort of darkness, but immediately it was clear this was a substantial collection, the shelves lining each wall from floor to ceiling. Once inside, Elsa turned toward me, and in one graceful pirouette, took my collars in her hands and backed me up against a set of encyclopaedias.

'You look very handsome in your suit,' she said. I realised we were not here to read.

We were just about to kiss when we heard the sound of crying, coming from the far end of the room. Slowly, Elsa and I moved apart from each other, trying to look as inconspicuous as possible, then turned toward the sound. It was Harold's wife, sitting at the writing desk, her chair turned toward the window. Its high back had hidden her from us when we crept in. My first thought was to try and tiptoe out again – if she was upset, it was none of our business. But Elsa was already walking toward her.

'Madam?' she said. 'Are you all right?'

'Oh, good gracious,' Daphne exclaimed, immediately attempting to compose herself. 'I'm very sorry, I didn't see you come in. Forgive me.'

'What is the matter? Can we help?'

'The orchestra can't make it,' she said. 'They just telephoned from Newbury. The trains are backed up, some fault somewhere. Oh, dash it all.'

She was tearful now and shaking slightly. I had no idea what to do.

'Everyone will understand,' I said.

'This was my job, my responsibility,' she said loudly. 'Harold wanted the Pump Room Orchestra but I insisted on my friends. Oh damn, damn, damn.'

Elsa stepped forward now, and put her arm on Daphne's back.

'It's not your fault,' she said softly.

Daphne tried to smile but could not.

'I wanted to get everything right. This party is so important to Harold. I am not one for social functions, I have not been a regular host – it has been noted by some of the others. I'm a bit of an outsider here. I tried so bloody hard this time. Now I've got to go out there and tell everyone that there will be no entertainment after making such a big fuss.'

Elsa handed a delicate handkerchief to Daphne and she dabbed her eyes with it.

'You must think me an awful bloody fool,' she said. 'My husband told me you've been ripped from your family – and here I am wailing away because I don't have music.'

'I don't think you're a fool,' said Elsa. 'You're upset because you care.'

Daphne managed the faintest of smiles.

'Well,' she said. 'I'd better go out there and tell them. I just have to face the music – or rather not, as the case may be.'

She handed the handkerchief back to Elsa who I could see was deep in thought about something – there was a sense of internal struggle about her that was obvious even to me.

'Don't tell them that. You have a piano, don't you? Tell them there has been a change of plan. There will be a solo recital.'

'But I have promised concert-class musicians,' said Daphne. 'I can't just go up and bash out a Beethoven sonata. Thank you, dear girl, but—'

'You won't be playing,' said Elsa quietly. 'I will.'

A pause. Daphne regarded Elsa silently. Surprised and concerned, I watched her too.

'Tell them to expect a recital of modern and classical piano works.'

'But Elsa . . .' I started. She directed a very forceful glance at me.

'I don't have the sheet music,' said Daphne.

'I don't need it.'

Daphne shook her head, but more out of confusion than refusal. 'But . . . I . . .'

Elsa took both her hands.

'Trust me,' she said.

Daphne nodded, got up and opened the large wooden door onto the grand hall where most of the guests had assembled themselves. Before I could ask Elsa if she was okay, if this wouldn't cause her immense pain, Daphne cleared her throat loudly and the room was silenced.

'Thank you everyone for attending,' she said. 'I'm sure my husband has dealt with the formalities, I just wanted to give you some news. I'm afraid the chamber orchestra we had invited to perform has been held up in Newbury.' A few sympathetic noises from the crowd. 'However, we are lucky to have with us an excellent pianist, Miss Elsa Klein, who will entertain us with a recital. If you'd all like to follow me down to the conservatory?'

Daphne headed off and the crowd began to chat and follow her down the wide stairs to the lower floor. I took Elsa aside.

'My goodness, Elsa, are you sure about this?'

'I was sure until she said "excellent".'

'But you said it would be too painful to play again.'

'You saw her,' she said. 'I couldn't let her suffer.'

She was shivering.

'I think this is a bad idea, it's just a silly party. I'll go and tell Anderson you've had second thoughts.'

But she grabbed me by the arm and there was fury in her eyes I'd never seen before.

'No!' she hissed. 'You're not listening to me! This is important.'

'I don't understand.'

'Try,' she said. And she looked at her hands as they shook.

The one thing I did know was that her strength, her courage came with a cost.

'Come on,' I said, smiling, trying to bring things round again. 'Let's get this over with. There is a lot of champagne to drink. No matter how awful you are, it will all soon be forgotten.'

'That is not very reassuring.'

I took her hand and we walked down the stairs together. Inside the conservatory, chairs had been laid out for the guests and everyone was sitting, a murmur of anticipation passing between them. I took the last empty seat at the rear of the room and smiled at her, mouthing 'good luck'. But she was gone from me now, walking silently toward the piano, her footsteps tapping on the wooden floor. When she reached the front, a gentle applause started, and she bowed slightly. Then, in silence, she pulled out the piano stool and sat down.

Elsa closed her eyes and breathed. She removed her gloves.

There are rare moments in your life so vivid that you know they will be unforgettable from the very outset. They have about them an ethereal quality separate from other events in our lives. The few

201

silent seconds before her fingers touched the ivory keys had about them a shimmer, like heat on a road surface. Outside I could hear the birds singing in the ornate gardens, a gentle breeze rattled at the doors, but all else was still, as though we were waiting for some fresh, better world to be born.

And then she played.

And my God, she was wonderful.

Perhaps there were people in the room who had never heard Debussy or Ravel or Prokofiev – they certainly hadn't heard them performed like this. The notes could have been too sharp in the brittle acoustics of the room, with its solid floors and vast windows, but her playing was so sensitive and controlled that the sound elevated to her touch as though undergoing some miracle of auditory massage. It was joyous. At the close she played Schubert's 'Sonata in B flat Major' – her mother's favourite composer, a piece no doubt filled with meaning and resonance for her – and the phrasing was so delicate, so alive with emotion, it was as though she was telling the room about her life in Vienna, about being thrust from her parents and sister, about the nightmarish train journey through Holland. It was all there, clear and sad and beautiful, and I saw people in the audience overcome with it.

She played for forty-five minutes and they passed in a second. When she finished, the last moments stayed in the air, drifting about us like incense. There was no applause at first – I think people were afraid of breaking the spell. Then a couple of the older men in Admiralty dress uniforms got to their feet and began to clap, then others too, and in the end, a roomful of people were standing, applauding, and it was so loud, almost too loud to bear. Elsa stood and bowed. She looked around the room, and I broke away from the seats to the aisle down the side, where she saw me at last. She smiled and pretended to sigh with relief. I mouthed 'well done'. People formed a circle around her and congratulated her and asked about the pieces, and when I got to her finally, she took me aside and said, still smiling, 'Please take me away.' She put her hand in mine and it was still shaking.

I guided her through the crowds, determined and resolute, parting the waves of admirers, allowing her to follow and not seem rude. When I got her back to the library, I closed the door behind us and turned, wanting to express my admiration, but she had already fallen to her knees, sobbing hopelessly.

'Mama,' she whimpered. 'Oh Mama, please. Oh please, be safe.'

I sank down too and I held her.

Yes, she had played wonderfully. But she had also performed an act of beauty, strength and extraordinary kindness that perfectly symbolised who she was. What she saw in Daphne was not a rich woman hosting a silly party, but a fellow human being, upset and afraid, and she knew how to help. We sat for some time on that floor, the smell of old books in the dusty air, the bustle of the party outside, all of eternity ahead and around us.

In that room, on that spring afternoon, what I desperately wanted to tell her was 'I love you and you are not alone'. But I couldn't communicate, I couldn't traverse the distance between us.

Later as we were leaving the party, while Elsa was fetching her coat, I explained to Anderson and his wife about Elsa's pledge not to play the piano, about how painful it was – I couldn't help myself, I was so proud of her.

'Oh goodness, that poor girl,' said Mrs Anderson with tears in her eyes. 'She put herself through that for me? I shall never be able to repay her.'

'I'm sorry, I didn't mean to upset you,' I said.

'No. I'm glad you told me. It is good to know how far people will go to be kind.'

I didn't realise at the time how important my moment of indiscretion would turn out to be.

Chapter Twenty-Two

2008

The next day, Jane insists I accompany her on one of her own visits, just so we can 'catch up'. She collects me in her silver BMW at eight in the morning, and when I squeeze into the passenger seat beside her, she heaps her laptop bag and several files and folders on top of me. 'Sorry,' she says, pulling away from the kerb without really looking. As the managing director, she doesn't have to take on clients of her own anymore, but she maintains a light rota to 'keep her hand in' as she puts it. I think she enjoys meeting people whose lives are in disarray. It is like therapy. Or tourism.

'So,' she says, the car weaving along the narrow street, avoiding the wing mirrors of numerous parked vehicles by fractions of a centimetre. 'How is it going with Mr Emerson?'

I tell her about the most recent visits, and about my trip to the Bath Record Office, and while I'm talking the thought strikes me that the nervous energy I've been carrying around lately might be a sense of achievement. I did research and I found what I was looking for. And it was just me. That is something, isn't it?

'So I have confirmed at least part of his life story,' I say.

I want her to be impressed – I almost need it. But she shakes her head.

'You don't really need to be doing that,' she says. 'You're just there to look after and assess him.'

'I know,' I say. 'But with Will, I think understanding what has happened to him is part of caring for him. I don't mind doing it. I'm interested. Anyway, isn't that why you sent me there? Because you thought he'd like me?'

She shoots me a condescending look. 'I didn't think he'd get you playing at Miss Marple, looking up all sorts of things that might not have happened, that he's imagined or constructed for himself.' Then she turns her head away from me and out toward the road ahead. 'I do wonder if this was a mistake. I worry that he's taking advantage of you . . . in your suggestible state.'

'My what?'

'I just think maybe he knows that you're a bit vulnerable and he's playing with you. Feeding you an interesting story so you'll get involved, so you'll feel you have to do what *he* wants when the time comes to make your decision and file your report – which is next Wednesday. Do you think you are ready?'

Do I? Am I ever?

We're driving up Bloomfield Road now, past the park, the line of ornate houses built high up onto the side of the hill, the mansions, now turned into hotels and luxury flats. I'm gripping my fists and I can feel my broken jagged fingernails gouging into my palms.

I look out of the window, and further up ahead I see the entrance to Bloomfield Crescent, an arched row of tall, slender houses towering over the steep pastureland leading back toward the city. It's probably Jane's erratic driving, but I feel a sudden wave of nausea.

'What if he hasn't imagined it?' I say, trying to breathe deeply and ignore it. 'What if it's not a confabulation?'

'It doesn't matter,' says Jane. 'He's an old man who needs care. Don't get too sucked into it, that's all I'm saying. Chances are, social services will take one look at your report and have him transferred to sheltered accommodation. Did I tell you Will's solicitor has been in touch? Will has apparently given them lasting power of attorney if necessary. When you ... Are you all right?'

'Can you stop the car for a second?'

I start trying to offload all of Jane's stuff from my lap to the back seat, and she has to help, because I am struggling to get out, certain I'm about to throw up. I yank the door open and clamber away. There are shadows at the edges of my vision. I take a huge lungful of breath, and another, and then glance at the nearest house on the crescent. I have in my head a moment from Will's journal – a moment at this house. Elsa in her winter coat. A shock of red hair. I can almost see her, waving him away at the entrance to the mews. She is not there, but I want her to be. I want her to be close to me. I slump back against the car.

'Laura!'

It is Jane. I am half sitting, half lying on the pavement, my back against the car door, vision blurred, mind scrambled, as though I'm drunk and unable to focus on where I am or what I'm doing.

'I'm okay,' I drawl. 'Can a person ... Can people be in two different times at the same place?'

Jane gives me an odd glance. 'I thought you looked peaky as soon as you got in the car. You're almost see-through.'

'I'm fine. I just keep getting dizzy spells.'

'Have you been to the doctor again?'

'Honestly, I'm okay.'

I look up at the house. Through the window, the rooms are empty.

When I turn back, Jane is staring at me.

'We are getting you an appointment right now,' she says. 'Get back in the car.'

'What about your clients?' I ask, climbing back into the passenger seat.

Jane checks the road and pulls away from the kerb.

'They're not going anywhere.'

I am sitting in the small consulting room, opposite Dr Bedford who is wearing a Bath rugby shirt.

'It's dress down Friday,' he explains. 'For charity.'

I fiddle with the sleeve of my cardigan.

'So, your friend told the receptionist that you've had a panic attack?'

'It wasn't a panic attack!' I almost shout it, hoping my shock and indignation are obvious. 'I just felt a bit dizzy! Believe me, I know what a panic attack feels like.'

Flashback to me lying on my bedroom floor in a shitty flat in Ealing or Acton or Hammersmith, hyperventilating wildly, lungs burning, back spasming, someone banging on the door. Sometimes it was about paying the rent, or not paying it, sometimes the fear of losing someone, sometimes the fear of seeing them.

'Okay, so you felt dizzy and a little sick?'

I don't want to give him too much. I don't want to be told I'm not coping. He taps something at his computer.

'And you've not noticed any other symptoms with the anti-depressants?'

I can't help but look down, pulling at threads.

His voice is calm. 'You *are* taking the antidepressants?'

Long pause. Traffic passing. Maybe it's time to come clean for once.

I shake my head. 'I stopped.'

'When?'

'Before I last saw you.'

He moves away from his computer and rolls his chair towards me. 'Why?'

'They were making me feel ill and strange and spaced out. I was putting on weight, I was fucking exhausted all the time but I couldn't sleep and when I slept I had terrible nightmares.'

'But, Laura, it is very risky to simply stop taking them. When we last met, I told you there can be serious withdrawal effects. I think that is what you are experiencing. Have you had any other symptoms?'

'I don't know. Maybe. Everything is really weird at the moment – with work.'

'What is your work?'

'I'm a home carer. I'm looking after this old man and his house is ... Something happened to him a long time ago and it doesn't make sense. I'm trying to help him, but I don't know if any of it is real. When I'm in his house, I feel ... I feel like there is someone watching me. It feels like there is static in the air.'

He nods slowly; then he is back at his computer, his fingers poised over the keyboard as though he isn't quite sure what to write.

'These sound very much like withdrawal symptoms. People who come off SSRI antidepressants, they talk about experiencing feelings like electric shocks in their brains.'

I don't say anything, but he sees recognition in my eyes.

'Laura, I really think we need to get you back on the medication – just a very small dose, if only for a few weeks. Perhaps then we can try something else.'

'No!' I almost shout it at him and I can feel my jaw trembling with the effort not to cry or yell some more. 'I'm done with it!' I wipe at my eyes with my sleeves, trying to ride out the adrenaline. He looks at me for a while, and I realise how young he is in his rugby top and his hair all scruffy.

'I can't go back.' My voice is a whisper from a long way away.

I get up to leave.

'Laura,' he says. 'Please think about what you're doing. The symptoms may get worse before they get better. I'm here to help you. I'm not the enemy.'

My hand is on the door knob, but I stop and turn back to him.

'I won't go back,' I say.

Then I'm gone.

I wake in the night and I am scared and disorientated. I've been sleeping naked because my body feels like a furnace, and now I have the duvet wrapped around my legs, damp with sweat. I get the feeling someone else is in the room, but when I switch on the lamp, knocking everything else off my bedside cabinet, I am alone. It is 3.44 in the morning. My head is pounding, like I have banged it really hard. This is how I wake up now.

A week skulks by. I go to Will's almost every day, sometimes, I leave the house and I'm not aiming for Avon Lodge, but then half an hour later I'm standing outside. We have developed a routine around the clocks. I tell Will they have stopped and he tells me he has wound them again. We don't talk about what is happening. Sometimes I wonder if he's winding them at all. I feel like I'm losing my grip and that possibly Will is loosening it. Yesterday, walking back to the house from the back garden, I saw a figure in the kitchen that wasn't Will, but when I got in, there was nothing.

I booked another appointment with my GP then immediately

rang back and cancelled it. What can I tell him? That I think I'm seeing the ghost of a woman who died during the war? That I think she's trying to contact me? When I'm feeling lucid, I know I'm imagining things, I know it. But when I'm in that house, it's like I fall under some kind of spell. I feel like the past still exists in there and it wants to tell me something. There is something I am supposed to do, but I don't know what it is.

Lying here in bed I can't get Will's story out of my head – the people, the places, the things that don't add up. It's all spinning around and I can't grasp any of it, but I can't sleep either. At the core of it is her.

I need more information. I go to the timeline on the cork board, and I add the new events and people I've learned about from reading further into the journals, cross-referencing from all the scribbled notes I have taken; I add more places that seem important – the houses, restaurants and galleries that have figured in his tales – together with all the rough dates I have. It all tumbles out of my fervid, insomniac brain in a rush of lines and words and numbers and boxes. By the time I've finished it's 4.30 a.m. and the board looks like a cross between a complex flow chart and a con-spiracy nut's pet theory. I sit on my sofa, legs curled up beneath me, and I stare at the diagram, imagining – in my weird sleep-deprived mania – that I am a detective attempting to unpick a tricky case. What I have to concede straightaway is that I still have nothing directly and incontrovertibly linking Will with Elsa. This is still a tale told by a nearly-ninety-year-old man with signs of dementia to a woman who dropped off an antidepressant cliff edge and is hitting every withdrawal symptom on the way down. We are not credible witnesses to our own lives.

I hear Mum wake up, get ready and go to work; I hear the street, empty of cars; then the mid-morning sounds of whistling postmen and crying babies being pushed past the window. When Mum gets home from work I'm still here, still in the same grotty T-shirt and jogging bottoms, staring at the screen. I hear her coming up the stairs then there is a knock on the door.

'Come in.'

She's in one of her more executive-style suits so there must have been important meetings at the school. She brings with her the fresh smells of outdoors.

'Darling, it's very stuffy in here,' she says, walking briskly to the window and thrusting it open. 'Have you even left your room today?'

I shake my head, while staring intently at the screen.

'I wish you'd go out. I wish you'd make contact with people.'

'I *do* make contact with people.'

'People outside of work. People your own age.'

She stands there in the doorway, a hand on her hip, watching me.

'I know, Mum.'

'What about your old school friends? What about Gemma or Mary or Katie? Why don't you get back in touch with them?'

I could tell her that Gemma went to Edinburgh University to study PPE and now works at the Scottish Parliament; Mary is married with two children and lives on a boat in Cornwall; Katie went off travelling in South East Asia and never quite came back. But really, we lost touch in the months after our A-levels, when it was clear they had trajectories, they had momentum, and I didn't. All I had were crippling insecurities I couldn't articulate. I was exhausting to them. I exhaust everyone. It would be bizarre to make contact now.

'They've moved on,' I say.

When she leaves with an exasperated sigh, I open my laptop. I've got to prove to myself, to her, to Jane, that I can make progress.

And there it is: the unread email I have been putting off. Blinking at me. Before I can change my mind I click on it.

It is not from my father, as I had dreaded.

It's from Miles Frankland. Josephine's nephew. He was one of the relatives I contacted when I first took out my laptop and began my search for anyone connected to Will's past. He wants me to visit him at his home so he can show me some family artefacts that might be helpful. But this will mean going to Bristol. The place where everything really started going wrong. The place Dad turned up again.

Chapter Twenty-Three

2008

I know the train journey from Bath to Bristol by heart. The slow trawl through Oldfield Park and Keynsham, then out into the sliver of countryside between the two cities, the floodplains along the Avon, the old Cadbury factory. Then you see the great expanse of tower blocks and terraces that make up Bristol's messy sprawl. I can't quite believe I am doing this. The journey is barely fifteen minutes, but it feels like travelling across the cosmos. I'm going backwards in time. Shivering and bunched up on a seat, the old feelings start simmering away in me.

I should have known, really, that university would be too much. The course was hard work, so many essays and projects and deadlines. And I was alone. I lived at home instead of the halls of residence because I was too anxious to leave Mum, but it meant I couldn't connect with people. I felt like an outsider.

It wasn't just the stress and loneliness of uni life that got me. One afternoon, I was leaving the lecture building in a rush, late for a seminar, and there he was waiting outside. My father. I hadn't seen him for many months. He looked terribly old and haggard, like some vengeful wraith. I almost screamed. 'I just want to talk,' he said. 'I want to explain everything.' I was shaking so much, I could barely stand up. I managed to shout at him, 'Go away. Leave me alone!' Some other students noticed and came over. I heard one of them say, 'I think you'd better go,' and he did. But a few days later, the mobile phone calls and emails started. He just wanted to explain why he ruined my childhood.

As the train pulls into Temple Meads station there is the derelict postal building, surrounded by scrubland, like a miniature apocalypse. As we grind to a halt, I'm already at the door, jabbing the button, desperate to get away.

Josephine's nephew, Miles Frankland, lives in Stoke Bishop, one of Bristol's wealthiest suburbs. I take a bus, then it's a five-minute stroll through leafy streets to his address and the quiet of the place calms me down a little. His house is what estate agents call 'an executive family home' – a vast modern edifice with a mock Tudor upper floor, a triple garage and a lawn the size of three tennis courts. I stand beside the wooden gates at the entrance and briefly wonder to myself, what am I doing here? How has this happened? It is as though I have started doing things without my own permission.

When I buzz the bell, the door opens straightaway, and a man in his fifties is standing looking at me. He is wearing a blue-and-white tracksuit and his face is sheened with sweat. His skin has a weird artificial tan, the colour of builder's tea.

'Laura James?' he says in a sort of plummy drawl, his smile straying close to a leer. 'Come on in.'

He holds the door open in such a way that I have to pass close to him to get inside. The large entrance hall has a magnolia carpet

215

that's so utterly spotless I instinctively yank off my trainers and throw them outside. There is a set of golf clubs leaning against the wall. 'I'm afraid you've caught me after my workout,' he says. 'I was expecting you at 11.30. I would have showered.' He gives me a weird, suggestive look again, and I smile back, but alarm bells are already ringing.

The living room is as tidy, ordered and soulless as the hall. In the centre, two rich red Chesterfield sofas face each other over a chunky coffee table on which someone has displayed a selection of classic car magazines. Behind them, a giant fireplace houses a wood-burning stove that doesn't look like it's been used, the logs piled carefully on either side. The walls are painted a creamy white and lined with watercolour paintings of forlorn seascapes. There is an odd feel to the place, like a showroom, like no one actually lives here.

'Would you like tea?' he says, wandering through the room to a doorway at the rear. 'Sit down, I'll bring it through.'

I perch on one of the sofas, feeling awkward and unsettled. I've got to try to make this normal. He's not *that* strange. Everything is fine.

'Your house is beautiful,' I say.

He pops his head back around the doorway.

'Thank you. It's just my wife and I now the boys have left. She is in France at the moment, otherwise I might not have invited an attractive young woman home.'

He winks. Everything might not be fine.

Unexpectedly, the tea comes not in bone china cups but in giant Sports Direct mugs, so full and heavy I can barely lift mine. He sits on the sofa opposite, his arm along the back of it, his legs wide apart.

'I'm afraid I only met Aunt Josephine a couple of times,' he says. 'She and my uncle moved to the United States before I was born.

216

Once, when I was fourteen, my family travelled out to see them in New York. That was an extremely memorable holiday.'

'What was she like?'

He makes a show of thinking, putting his mug down and cupping his chin in his fingers, as though he is trying hard to find the right words. He pushes his legs out and his foot touches mine under the table.

'She was very eccentric,' he says finally. 'She wasn't quite the black sheep of the family, but definitely an exceedingly dark grey.' He laughs at his own joke. 'We are a very traditional, very conservative bunch – the men are all boring old bankers and accountants, the women are . . . what do we call housewives now? Home-makers? But Josephine was different. She was wild – almost uncontrollable, apparently. My mother said she was expelled from two very expensive private schools, and then when she was eighteen, she fled alone to France. She ran around Europe for two years, refusing to come home, and when she did, she was married to a Jew. You can probably imagine how that went down.'

'Not well?' I guess.

He shakes his head. 'She was kept very much at arm's length from that point on. Anyway, when she came back to Britain with her new husband, Levi, they bought that weird house in Bath – this was all in the late Thirties, I think. But they didn't stay for long. He had been a big deal in the theatre in Germany, a very respected producer and director, and he left for the States. He ended up producing Broadway shows. She went out to join him.'

He lifts his mug and for a few seconds his face is eclipsed by the giant ceramic monstrosity. After he has taken a sip, he lowers the cup and is looking at me.

'My wife doesn't like me to use these mugs in company,' he says. 'But while she's not here, we can be naughty.'

My awkwardness is beginning to melt into panic. There is a prickly feeling down my spine. Bizarre thoughts pop into my head – that this is a trap, that he's going to drug me and lock me in a room somewhere. I put the mug down on the coffee table, trying to control my breathing. Perhaps sensing my discomfort, he leans back in the sofa again and folds his arms, creating a little more distance.

'Do you know anything about Levi's niece, Elsa?' I say. 'You said on the phone that you might have some photographs?'

'Straight down to business!' he says brightly. 'I like that.' He gets up, wanders over to a sideboard and picks up an ancient-looking photo album. Instead of going back to the other sofa, he sits next to me, very close, opening the book and leafing through the pages. I can smell a mixture of sweat and a very pungent aftershave.

'I don't know much about her,' he says as black-and-white photos of family gatherings and holidays flick by. 'I know she fled from Austria alone, a very brave girl. But she was arrested in Bath sometime later. And something happened, some sort of tragedy. But I'm afraid, my mother didn't say much and I didn't listen. Oh, here is Auntie Jo.'

He stops on a photo of someone in a leather jacket and goggles standing beside an ancient-looking motorbike, sliding the book onto my lap. I recognise Josephine immediately from the picture in the newspaper.

'Quite a character,' he says. His hand is still on the edge of the album and I feel his fingers on my leg. 'There is another one with a young girl, it might be your Elsa.'

He flicks forward a couple of pages, edging nearer to me, the sofa squeaking as he moves. And then we're looking at a large image of Josephine, this time in what looks like Parade Gardens, sitting in a deckchair, reading a newspaper and holding a ciga-rette. But right there, sitting in a chair next to her, beautiful and unmistakable, is Elsa. Her hair is blowing across her forehead and she is scowling at the camera. She is wearing a beautiful dress with a flowery print and holding a hardback book. I have to lean forward to read the title. It says *Art Now* by Herbert Read. I have a sudden urge to rip the photo from the album and run.

'Is it her?' he says. I just nod. 'She's very attractive, isn't she?'

I feel his hand rub my leg beneath the book and instantly lurch upwards, banging my legs on the coffee table as I stand.

'I should go,' I say and my voice is ridiculously shaky.

'So soon?' he replies incredulously. 'You're welcome to stay for lunch. You may be able to tease some more memories from me.'

But I'm already pacing toward the hallway, determined to keep ahead of him so he can't get between me and the front door. 'No thank you,' I say. I'm out of the room into the hall, and now he's following. Whatever I could have learned here, it's not worth it.

'I do have one titbit for you,' he says with increased urgency. I stop close to the front door and turn to him.

'There was a book about Broadway theatre, Aunt Josephine gave a copy to my mother when we visited that time. I think the author was Gerald Dutton or something like that. There is a little section about Levi and I'm certain Elsa was mentioned. If you want to know what happened to her it's all in there. Are you sure you won't stay? I have it inside . . . '

He moves forward again, and for a few seconds I consider it, but then I get this feeling, like, actually *I've* been uncovering stuff myself. I don't need this man.

'Thank you,' I say, 'but I can manage. Goodbye.'

I open the door, tug on my trainers and walk away through his neat garden.

'It's been out of print for years, you silly girl,' he shouts. 'You'll never find it.'

It's only when I clear his long driveway and turn onto the pavement that I realise how much my heart is thumping. A few hundred yards down the road, I stop and try to ground myself. Deep breaths, look round, remember the day, the time. It's all right. It was just some creepy middle-aged guy. It's fine.

On the train home, I think to myself that here I am again, shaky and alone, just as I was when I used to make this journey every day from university. But then I think of the photo of Elsa and the fact that I have a lead. There is a book with her story in it. And as the train pulls back into Bath Spa station, I remember something from my degree: in the first term, we did a whole module on how to use legal deposit libraries. Later tonight, I can visit the British Library website and do a catalogue search for 'Gerald Dutton' and 'Broadway'. I've got this.

But when I get home, Mum is waiting for me in the living room, standing not sitting, wearing a troubled look.

'It's Will Emerson,' she says. 'You need to go to the office right now. The police have been called.'

Chapter Twenty-Four

May 1940

The phone rang just before midnight. I was in bed reading, half asleep. At first I ignored it, but when it refused to stop, and I realised the late hour, I had a growing sense of apprehension. Out of bed and dragging on my robe, I thought perhaps it was my mother, phoning with some imagined emergency, but when I got downstairs and picked up the phone, the operator told me the call was from a Mrs Josephine Klein, and suddenly I was wide awake.

'Will? Is that you?'

'Yes. Has something happened?'

'Elsa has been taken to the police station.'

The words made no sense.

'What? What on earth for?'

'Two policemen came to the door. They said they had been ordered to collect her – something about bringing in aliens from Germany. I told them she's Austrian but they said it didn't matter – she had to be taken.'

'I don't understand. She is registered with the police,' I said. 'She has the correct papers.'

'We told them that,' said Josephine breathlessly. 'But they said Bath was now in the Severn protected area, because of the Admiralty coming here. They said they had to take anyone who could pose a threat to national security.'

'This is absurd,' I said. 'They can't just turn up in the night and take people away!'

'They gave her five minutes to pack a bag. They said if I got in the way I would be arrested too.'

With a horrible sinking feeling I remembered Elsa's concerns at the Andersons' party – the newspaper story she had seen about a German woman being arrested ... I had assured her there was nothing to worry about; that this couldn't happen in Bath. She came to me with legitimate fears and I barely listened. Had Elsa been reported somehow? I thought of the rumours going around about Fifth Columnists. About McDonald and the group he'd joined. Surely no one had accused her?

'I told her not to worry,' said Josephine. 'I told her to do what they asked and that it would all be sorted out at the station. But I don't know, Will, I don't know!'

She told me about how the policemen looked at her with a steely sort of intransigence. It was as though they were not hearing her.

'I felt as though I was dreaming,' she said. 'It was the shock. When Elsa came down in a dress and coat, clutching an overnight bag, I almost didn't recognise her. It made no sense.'

'Have you called anyone else? Can any of your friends help?'

'I'm too much of an outsider to beg favours from powerful people. Oh, Will, she was frightened at the end. She told me not to worry, but her eyes gave her away. They took her arm and almost dragged her to their damn car. I shouted, "You don't need to manhandle her! We're civilised people!'"

And yet still, they took her. I imagined Elsa stretching out her hand to her aunt, to me, but I saw the grip loosening and falling away. I felt a horrible finality.

'I'll go to the station!' I shouted. 'I'll get her out!'

But even as I said it, I knew it wouldn't be so easy. I was no one, I had no clout, and amid the growing tension of the war, the gentle traditions of life in Bath were breaking down – we were all becoming cogs in a much greater machine. For an hour I paced up and down the hall, trying to think of what to do, of who to call on, my brain a whirlpool of possibility and panic. My mother, who had never even met Elsa, would be next to useless; I had no friends in the legal profession. It is testament to how bewildered and terrified I was that it took me so long to come to the only possible candidate.

The walk was long and difficult. The unlit night streets were treacherously dark and populated only by ARP wardens, who glared suspiciously at this fraught-looking lone traveller as I passed. Walking down the grand parade of Great Pulteney Street, I was struck by how dead the stately houses looked, as though there had been some grand desertion. Behind a few of the blackout blinds you could just make out a weak orangey glow – the dying embers of untended fires. And then, once out of the city, the suburban lanes were in absolute blackness. I had to navigate at a snail's pace along Bathwick Hill, my arms outstretched like a sleepwalker.

It took me an hour to reach Anderson's house and I had no idea what I would say or if anyone would even answer the door. This was an unthinkable intrusion: almost 2 a.m., turning up unannounced at my employer's private residence. I believed there was a possibility it might even cost me my job. But I was operating on instinct, on desperation – I had to get Elsa out of that place. I had to try.

The house looked stark and monolithic beneath the weak moonlight – a huge contrast to the welcoming sunshine of the party. When I reached the entrance, I paused for a moment to collect myself, then pulled the handle beside the door and heard a bell sounding inside. There was no going back now.

For what seemed like several minutes there were no other sounds from inside, and a cursed thought struck me that perhaps the whole household was away. Or maybe the police had already been called. But then there were faint noises from somewhere within – a bump, some footsteps, then the clatter of a lock mechanism. The door opened a few scant inches, and I could just make out an elderly housekeeper. She was in nightwear and holding a lamp, which gave her face an unholy glow.

'What on earth is it?' she asked.

'I'm sorry to call at such a late hour. My name is Will Emerson, I am an employee of Mr Anderson. I'm afraid I have something of an emergency. I desperately need his help.'

'Will, is that you?'

The voice came from the vast curving staircase, leading to the mezzanine floor above. It was Anderson in a luxurious house coat, also holding a lamp, also looking dishevelled and somewhat demonic.

'Yes, sir. I'm so sorry, sir, something has happened. I need your help.'

'Can't it wait? My God, man, it's two o'clock in the morning.'

'It's Elsa. She has been arrested as an enemy alien. They have taken her to Bath Central Police Station.'

Anderson made the last few stairs and approached the door. His initial look of bewilderment gave way to something else.

'This was always a possibility, I'm afraid.' He said it as though placating a small child. 'Bath has become an important town – the Admiralty are here, there is top secret work going on. She's a lovely girl, but how much do you know about her really?'

'Are you saying she could be a spy for the Nazis?'

Anderson said nothing.

'Sir, she's Jewish. Her father's law firm was shut by the Germans, their home was taken. For all she knows her parents have been arrested. Her sister is in hiding in France. For pity's sake, she hates them more than us!'

'That's as well as may be, but what do you want me to do?'

'You have connections, sir. I just thought . . .'

'Dammit, boy, I can't just march into the police station and make demands.'

Then another voice from the stairway.

'Harold, who's at the door? What's going on?'

'Now you have woken Daphne,' said Anderson.

I turned to her as she approached the door. I must have looked half mad.

'It's Elsa,' I said. 'Remember, from the party?'

'Of course I remember her, what's happened?'

'Darling,' said Anderson, 'you don't need to get involved. Go back to bed.'

'She's been taken by the police,' I said to her. Anderson threw me an angry glare, but I was desperate. 'They're rounding up German and Austrian aliens. She's going to end up in a prison camp, God knows where . . .'

Harold looked at his wife with a sort of benign exasperation. 'I'm trying to explain to the lad, that this is wartime – whatever contacts I have, I can't just—'

'Oh yes you can,' said Daphne, her voice filled with resolve. Harold looked momentarily winded. 'You can and you will.'

'But, darling, I . . .'

'Harold, have I ever once asked you for favours regarding your connections in this city?'

'You have not.'

'I am asking now. Get her out. Get her out of there at once.'

With that, she walked back up the stairs and into the shadows, utterly confident that her demands would be met. Harold looked back at me.

'Well,' he said, 'I had better get dressed, it looks like I am going to the police station.'

'I'll come,' I said.

'No, you will not – you have done quite enough already. Go home and get some rest, you look like a bloody maniac.'

'I can't go home, I have to—'

He put a single finger up to silence me – a gesture of such polite, measured fury that perhaps only an Englishman of a certain status could manage it.

'I'll contact you if you are needed,' he said. 'And I will drive over to your house as soon as I'm finished so that I can explain the situation. But I have to tell you, I do not expect to be successful. This war is bigger than the lot of us. We'll all experience loss before it's over, believe me. Just go home and get some rest.'

But there would be no rest. For hours, I paced the house, obsessing over every imagined outcome. Would she be held for months? Years? There were rumours of refugees being sent to other countries, sent home even. In the bleakest moments of that long night, I imagined losing her for ever. My stomach lurched at the thought. I rushed to the bathroom and retched at the horror of it. When I allowed myself to sit and rest, I slipped into mournful reverie, recalling glimpses of our year together, a year in which life had blossomed into something more vibrant and colourful than I'd ever imagined. It couldn't really be over like this, could it?

Gradually, the first light began to seep in from behind the black-out blinds, but halfway mad with fear and worry, I couldn't bring myself to lift them and welcome the day. What could it ever bring without her? Every time I heard the distant sound of a car, I stood alert, my heart pummelling at my ribs, but one by one they passed by. Had Anderson given up and gone home? Perhaps he was unable or unwilling to face me with terrible news?

I was picking up the telephone receiver to call his house when yet another vehicle glided slowly past. This time, however, I heard it stop and reverse. I put the receiver down and walked through to the parlour. From just outside, came the sound of a car door opening.

Chapter Twenty-Five

2008

Jane is in her office, and from the expression on her face I assume Will has had an accident; he has been found by a neighbour lying somewhere, gravely injured. It must have been serious if the police were called. A fear hits me and I am shocked by the force of it. It's a fear for him, for his safety, but also for me. If he is injured, he will be in hospital then a care home and the decision about his life will be taken away. A little part of me is crushed that I won't get to solve the mystery that's been haunting us for three months, that was starting to make me feel competent and assured. I get an image of Will in his baggy old cardigan, shuffling through his empty life, and I understand in that instance that I liked and cared about him, but also, while the uncertainty over his past remained, he was an opportunity for me to prove myself. What if I've lost that? Guiltily, selfishly, I feel robbed.

Jane waves me in and I can't hold back. 'What's happened?' I ask. 'Has he fallen in the garden again?'

For a few seconds she seems unsure of how to progress.

'No, nothing like that,' she says. 'Will has been involved in ... an incident. He was questioned by community police officers this afternoon.'

My first thought is that I just completely misheard what she said, because it makes no sense whatsoever.

'I don't understand. What happened?'

'Apparently, a boy from down the road climbed into Will's garden this afternoon. Instead of taking him home, Will invited him to his workshop to look at the radios, and when the parents found him there they went bloody mad. They accused Will of abducting him. So there's a big shouting match, some other neighbours got involved, then the police were called. They phoned us and as I couldn't contact you, I went up there to sort it out.'

'Is he okay?'

'He was very shaken,' says Jane. She stops for a second. 'The little boy's name is Josh, but Will kept calling him David. He said he'd promised to show David how radio transmitters worked. And when Josh's dad turned up at the door, Will refused to hand the boy over. He was going on about how the man at the door couldn't be David's father because David's father was shot down and killed in an air battle in 1942.'

'Oh,' I say.

'Do you know what he was going on about?'

'David was a little boy who lived up the road from Will during the war.'

I think about what Will told me, how he was holding David when the bomb fell. But Jane doesn't need to hear about that – it won't make the situation sound any less troubling.

'Are they going to press charges?' I say.

'It doesn't look like it. The police gave him a talking to, that's all.

But, Laura, this is extremely worrying. He is clearly disorientated. I think your report needs to reflect—'

'He's fine!' I say, surprising myself with my tone. 'I'll talk to him about what happened. He's not a danger to anyone.'

'Laura, the police were called! Will was babbling about a boy he knew over sixty years ago!'

'He just gets confused.'

'Your report is due on Wednesday. You've got until then to finish your assessment of him, and I want to see some bloody compelling evidence that he wouldn't be better off in full-time care.'

'I understand.'

But under everything, I know what's motivating me. It is not Will's well-being, it's the house, the growing certainty that there is something I need to do, to solve.

'I'm going to see him,' I announce, and I'm already marching toward the door.

The wind is strong against me, blowing my hair in my eyes as I stride through the evening streets. I'm tired from Bristol, but that trip seems like days ago and the whole world is shifting on its axis, sending everything sliding away. I cut along Milsom Street, past swarms of students in their best clubbing gear, yelling at each other.

My legs tiring, I slow to a striding walk up Lansdown Road, wondering which house Josh's family live in. Is it one of the nice ones in the row next to Avon Lodge? Or the ugly flats beyond? If the police do nothing, will this family look for their own vengeance? Villagers with pitchforks and torches.

The house is in darkness, just one light showing in the first-floor windows, the wind rustling through the branches of the trees outside. Shivering to myself, I look along the road both ways, just in case.

There is no answer when I knock. I leave it a few seconds and try again. I can hear a noise inside – a whining, like the wind under a doorway.

I take the key he gave me out of my jacket pocket and slide it into the lock, turning it slowly and quietly, as though I'm sneaking in, scared of what I'll find. The door opens with a long, loud creak, the street light edging into the bare hallway, lighting it fraction by fraction. I'm nervous. I'm so nervous and I don't know why.

Hitting the light switch by the door, everything is illuminated for a few seconds, the peeling wallpaper and broken floor tiles looking garish and sickly. But as I walk in and close the door behind me, the bulb immediately pops, plunging me into a darkness so sudden and complete, I gasp with shock.

There is a bump upstairs. The bird in the attic.

'Will?' I call.

I grope my way forward and try the switch near the stairs, feeling immense relief when the landing lights go on. But as soon as they do, there is a groaning noise from somewhere above.

'Will?' I call again as I start up the stairs. At the top, I hear the unmistakable sound of radio static. It is coming from his bedroom.

When I open the door, he is sitting on the edge of the bed, hunched over, face in shadows, wearing striped pyjamas and a threadbare dressing gown. I smell it at once, the bitter sting of cheap whisky, sloshing about in the stale air. There is a large almost empty bottle of Bell's on the dresser under the window, and he has a tumbler clutched in his hand. The scene sends a shudder of recognition through me like the shock of diving into a freezing lake, and I feel bile rising in my throat.

Dad.

Dad on a bad day. A bad week. His thin brown hair a knotted

231

mess, face unshaven. *Stay out of his way, Laura.* My mum would sound irritated at me more than upset with him. *Just stay out of his way, can't you?*

'What do *you* want?' growls Will between halting, crackling breaths.

I back out into the doorway.

'I heard what happened today. I came to see how you are.'

He shoots me an angry look, but he can hardly focus, his eyes rolling in his bony face.

'You've seen me. Now bugger off!'

I look around the room trying to find the source of the radio noise. But there is nothing up here.

'Will . . .'

Dad would come home drunk and disappear upstairs. Sometimes I wanted to help him, and so I'd creep up and find him in the bathroom, slumped next to the toilet. I'd stand there, trying to work out what to do. 'Why are you staring at me? You're always sulking. No wonder this bloody house is so miserable.' I'd tell him I was sorry. I was always so sorry. I was sure some part of him was sorry too.

'But you asked me to help,' I say to Will. 'You asked me.'

'I wish I hadn't. I wish you'd never come here.'

Memories flowing now, awoken by the stench of whisky. The Sunday evening when I was twelve, and I desperately needed help with my maths homework. He was sitting in his armchair, hunched over a newspaper. That horrible sweet-sour smell was all around him.

'Dad, please, can you help . . .'

'I'm busy,' his voice liquid and raspy.

'But I can't . . .'

'Oh, for God's sake, there's always something with you! I get no bloody peace, no peace at all. Sometimes, I wish we'd never bloody had you!'

Mum told me later he hadn't meant it, but I knew it was the truest thing he'd ever said to me – even if he hated himself for it. It provided a weird sort of clarity. It explained everything.

Stop. Blank it out. I have to keep everything together.

'Come on,' I say quietly to Will, sitting down on the bed next to him. 'Why don't you tell me about David?'

He sinks into himself, breathing heavily, his face questioning, uncertain of this change in tone.

'He was a lad from up the road. Six years old, a funny little thing. His father had been in the RAF, but during the war he was shot down over the English Channel and never found. I don't think David ever understood what had happened. His mother had three other children and couldn't really cope, so David found his way to us – he loved Elsa. After she moved in with me in 1941, he'd run along the alley behind the houses, and let himself into the garden. She would let him sit with her while she worked.'

'She got a job? What did she do?'

'She became a musical adviser to local operatic societies – she would translate and arrange German scores. She also taught piano and violin – after the Andersons' party, she felt able to play again. She gave David lessons. When I got home, he'd come out with me to the workshop. We were like a family in a way. It suited all of us.'

'Will, what happened to him – the night of the bombing?'

'No one would ever tell me. I am certain he died. He was in my arms, I was trying to protect him. If only I'd ...'

He buries his face in his hands, sobbing to himself, his grief utterly insular and unknowable.

'Will, it's okay,' I say, moving closer.

He turns to me sharply.

'It is not okay! This is a mistake. It's all a mistake! Rummaging about in the past, dredging this bloody nonsense up.'

'I don't think it's nonsense. I was in Bristol today. I was checking on something about Elsa's uncle. I found out about a book that—'

'For heaven's sake, are you not listening to me? You won't find anything! There's nothing there!' I try to speak but I can't. 'What if I never did meet her, what if none of it happened? Jesus Christ, after the bomb, I woke up in the hospital, half mad, my head split open. I barely even knew myself let alone anyone else. It took me years to ... Oh, what does it matter?'

'Will ...'

'The boy – I didn't hurt him, did I?'

'No, of course not.'

'I don't know what I was thinking. I don't even remember how we came to be in the workshop. What is happening to me?'

'It's fine. You're tired and a bit confused. It happens.'

I try to put my hand on his shoulder but he pushes it away, his deep eyes like glowing coals. At that moment he wrenches himself to his feet, his mouth a horrible grimace.

'Leave me alone! I don't need you meddling in my life, my past, like it's some sort of stupid game. I don't need you at all!'

He stands by his bed, ancient and wretched, swaying slightly, the whisky tumbler clutched in his skeletal hands. I stand too, a swell of fear and self-sorrow driving me backwards toward the door, my stomach cramping like it's being squeezed in a vice. I feel like I'm being pulverised. He won't look at me, and the rejection of it is so familiar it is unbearable. The detail drags me back to my dad and me throughout the whole of my childhood. The grinding tension in every moment. And Will is not finished.

'You barely know your own past, let alone mine! What are you doing with your life? You're wasting it here, you're wasting it. If you can't look after yourself, what good are you to anyone else?'

All those years, then running to London, and even there I couldn't get away. 'Please,' I say to him, trying to catch a breath, trying to force a clear thought through the convulsions. Stepping slowly backwards. I can't see for tears.

'Stop snivelling, you stupid useless girl.'

'Oh please, oh please, don't.'

My hands are gripping the door frame and I realise this was always me – bracing myself against the onslaught, terrified of being swept away.

'I said, go!' he yells. And with unfeasible speed and strength, he throws the glass, not at me, but near enough that when it hits the wall and shatters, the whisky sprays across my face. I stumble out of the room, sobbing now, grasping at the bannister and dragging myself down the stairs, the emotions from twenty years ago as sharp and bright as daggers. In the midst of it, part of me recalls the first time I left this house, feeling insulted and belittled, and how things had changed since then, how I'd pulled out of a nosedive, how I'd begun to feel there was a purpose here. But now this and I'm useless again. On the last step my legs give way and I crumple to the floor, fighting for breath, snot running down my face. I might have to crawl out of here. And where then?

'My God.' A voice from the top of the stairs. I look up and he's there on the landing, his face wracked with confusion and horror. He's staring down. 'I'm so sorry. I didn't mean it. I didn't mean any of it.'

Despite everything, I feel a wave of relief, because maybe he is snapping out of it. Maybe he was just drunk and scared, but now he's back in control. The Will I knew – dignified and true and sane.

And yet, although his eyes are on me, it's like he's looking through me to something else.

'I'm sorry,' he says again. 'It's been so long.' He shuffles forward. 'I almost didn't recognise you, Elsa.'

Chapter Twenty-Six

I am home. Last night, Mum had to catch me at the door and half
drag, half carry me to the living room. She deposited me on the
sofa, wrapped me in my duvet and tucked in a hot water bottle.
The official anxiety disorder recovery position.

I told her everything that happened at Will's – how he turned
on me, how it triggered memories of Dad; how I ended up at the
foot of the stairs, bawling like a baby. She listened carefully and I
expected her to deliver advice or judgement. Instead, she stroked
my hair until I fell asleep.

Now it is morning and we're sitting in the kitchen together and
I feel better and stronger after four rounds of toast.

'I think the best thing would be for you to write your report and
advise that he goes into a care home,' she says. 'Then forget all
about him and his past. Walk away.'

I nod silently, sipping at the milky, cloyingly sweet tea she has
made for me. In the background, BBC *Breakfast* is on TV, the
sound down so all I hear is occasional laughter.

'I was going to check one last thing,' I say. 'There's a book that might have information about his wife in it. I was going to look on the British Library website to see if they have it there, and then I was going to find it and read it.'

'Go to London? After everything that happened there? Oh, Laura, you've done everything you could for Will, but look what he did to you. He's a bully and surely we've both had enough of them.'

It is the closest she has come to mentioning Dad since I've been home. It's something I really need to hear right now. I need her to talk about it.

'Can I ask you something?' I say. 'About Dad?'

'Of course.' But her voice is guarded.

'How did you meet him?'

She looks away from me and I feel the thread of connection fraying.

'You need to get outside. You look so pale. Have a walk – breathe some fresh air. It's a lovely day.'

'I want to know. I need to know.'

At first I don't think she'll answer. It's always been like this, whenever I've asked about the past. She'll change the subject, claiming to be protecting me, and I've accepted that, secretly relieved. I don't want protection anymore. I want information. When she looks at me again, I think she sees that.

'I tell you what,' she says. 'Let's walk into town together. If you want to know about how it started, come with me and I'll show you.'

It is early Saturday morning and the shops are not quite open, so the streets are calm and quiet, the only noise coming from the seagulls fighting over rubbish bins. We walk through the cobbled Abbey green and the warren of little streets beyond the churchyard, all tea shops and cosy pubs, and I wonder if Will and Elsa trod these same pavements. It makes me feel better about him. The raw shock of his anger has faded to become a kind of dull background sadness, like a throbbing headache. Mum takes my arm and we walk up Walcott Street, past the horrible 1970s Hilton hotel and the old cattle market, past the comic store I used to come to with my pocket money and the vintage clothing shop where I bought my first pair of cherry red DMs. There too is the place Will worked. He took Elsa there once, and the thought of her brings a sort of warmth. Our memories are becoming entwined. Toward the top I start to feel breathless. 'Not far,' says Mum.

Turning the corner onto London Road, she stops in front of a steak house built into the corner house of a battered terrace.

'This was a pub,' she says. 'The Hat and Feather. It was my local. It's where I met your dad. It was a cool place, a bit rough, full of crusties and drug dealers. Perhaps that should have been a warning sign.'

She steps forward, but reaches back for my hand.

'I'd just broken up with someone, I was having an awful time at work. We got talking at the bar. I was twenty-nine, your age, he was already in his forties, but looked younger. He was moody and interesting – he told me he was a cameraman working in news and documentaries, but he dreamed of making movies. We just drifted into seeing each other. My friends were worried about the age gap – and they thought there was something dangerous about him. That just made me want him more. Yes, I was that idiotic, but there were moments he could be wonderfully kind and loving. And then a year later, the best thing that ever happened in our relationship came along. Which was you, by the way.

'He was a good dad for a while, but when things started going wrong with his career, he became more impatient and aggressive – with both of us. And the drinking got worse. I blocked it out, or put it down to his artistic temperament. But he was drunk every weekend, and that became drunk every night. I tried to protect you. I tried. I thought the answer was to keep you two apart as much as possible. To compartmentalise everything. I knew there was something in his past that had damaged him; I thought if we could deal with it, things would be better. But it was too late, and I should have known. I should have thrown him out long, long before he left.'

'Mum, it's not your fault.'

'Let's walk along,' she says. 'I'll show you where we lived.'

London Road, the artery leading out of the city, is congested already. The high old tenements, built far back from the road, are grubby with dirt and neglect, all divided into tiny flats, the skeletons of long-dead bikes locked to their railings. We get to one blackened building and Mum stops and points to the first-floor window.

'That was mine,' she says. 'I bought the flat myself, the mortgage was brutal until your dad moved in.' She looks around vaguely. 'I was here for five years. I used to stand at that window, looking out at the road. I'd stand there for hours, thinking about my life, the future ... When I drive past, I'm always scared to look into the flat ... I half expect to see myself as I was then, still standing there, still watching. That must sound mad.'

'It doesn't. Will says the past is not buried away, it is here now. It lives with us. It's like a thing Dad once said to me: everything is always happening.'

'He was always like that, always trying to work out the meaning of things. You got that from him, I think. You were such a good girl, Laura. You were so thoughtful and clever. Sometimes, I think, if things had been different ...'

'I wouldn't be such a fuck-up?'

She looks shocked and guilty.

240

'No! That's not what I meant.'

But it was and we both know it. I should have stayed at university, got my degree, gone to London with a good career and stayed there. Instead I dropped out, and every time I thought I'd hit the bottom, I'd find more space to fall.

'I feel scared all the time, Mum. It's like a weight on me. I wake up with it, I go to bed with it. There is always something. But I was the one Will let in – not the others. I am the one who found the photo of Elsa. And maybe I'm not completely broken. There are things I can do. There are things I understand. I can't explain it.'

'You don't have to. I know.'

'Do you, though? Most of the time, I'm just a problem you have to manage.'

'That's not true. That's not how I feel about you at all. I've always seen those things in you. I've just been waiting for you to see them too.'

At home, I go to the kitchen to put the kettle on. When I come out with two cups of tea, Mum has fetched my laptop and put it down on the dining table. The screen is open, the British Library website ready on the browser.

'If you need to prove his story is real, go to London and prove it,' she says. 'But not for Will, for you.'

Chapter Twenty-Seven

Two days later, I am going to London for the first time since I fled the city. The book is at the British Library. I filled out an application to reserve it.

I shower and dress and pick up the backpack I prepared last night, which contains a bottle of water, my organiser and a battered old A-Z. There is a drizzle coming in as I walk down Holloway towards the station, and unlike Saturday, the city looks tired and weather-beaten in the grey light. I arrive early, and I'm shivering, so I get a coffee from the little sushi place on the platform and cup it in my hands to stay warm. I keep looking up at the train times on the electronic display, hoping that everything is cancelled and we all have to go home. Then I see the train as a dot in the distance, trundling unstoppably toward me.

I lived in London for six years – although 'lived' is not really the right word. I existed in London. After I quit university, a friend from school was looking for a flatmate in Hackney, so I headed there instead of going home and facing my mum's bright-faced disappointment. I mean, who drops out of a Media degree? I maxed out my student loan just before I left uni and that paid for a few months' rent. I had no plan, no ambition. I just wanted to be somewhere I could get lost. And I did.

My friend and I fell out after a month. I moved and then moved again, chasing shitty jobs across the city. Coffee shops, pizza restaurants, temping agencies. I lived with strangers I don't remember and got into relationships I don't *want* to remember. I was having panic attacks on the Tube, in workplace toilets, on my bedroom floor. I was on beta blockers, but I kept needing to sign up with different GPs so my meds got messed up. There was worse to come.

I had three dissociative episodes. I'd find myself walking miles from my flat, sometimes in the middle of the night, and I wouldn't know how I'd got there. The last time, the police picked me up wandering along Lambeth Bridge at four in the morning. Jogging bottoms, T-shirt, no shoes. They were certain I was going to jump; I couldn't convince them they were wrong. An ambulance took me to hospital and someone bandaged my feet. The staff talked about having me sectioned. Mum rescued me. The end.

When I get off the train at Paddington, I am buffeted along the platform by swarms of urgent people and have to find a seat in the vast concourse area to rest for a while, my legs weak, my chest hurting. I'm paranoid I'll bump into someone I knew back then and I have to keep reminding myself that London is six hundred square miles. All I have to do is get the Tube to King's Cross.

But then the oddest thing happens. Without really thinking about it, I get off the train at Baker Street and take the Bakerloo line down to Piccadilly Circus. Something has been on my mind. When Valerie told me about Giles she said he had a shop in Soho – she said it's still there. I think to myself, why not just go and look?

*

243

I find the shop on a terrace of dark-bricked Edwardian buildings, down a narrow lane just off Greek Street. As I turn into the road, the bustling crowds of Soho recede behind me, making it feel like I'm somehow stepping into an entirely different place or time. Walking along, completely alone, all the doors are painted glossy black, the windows empty, the blinds closed. An old man emerges from one of the houses wearing a long grey raincoat and an old-fashioned hat, and the noise and motion of his presence is shocking against the growing silence. He watches suspiciously as I walk by. I have this growing feeling of tension, but it is not anxiety. It's adrenaline.

When I get to the store, I approach cautiously as though a dangerous and unpredictable acquaintance lives there. The windows are larger and brighter than all the others along the street, and inside there are brushed steel spotlights illuminating columns of expensive audio equipment. A sign along the front says COOPERTON HI-FI. I breathe deeply, then push open the heavy door. There is no going back now.

Inside, it's warm and bright, the walls lined with thick black shelves, loaded with turntables and amplifiers. Jazz music is playing quietly, but the sound is all-encompassing, as though the band were performing live just behind a curtain somewhere. A young man in a skinny-fit light blue suit and a cool, highly sculpted haircut is fiddling with the buttons on the front of one particularly expensive-looking box. He turns toward the door smiling automatically, but then when he sees me he seems to hesitate. I guess he thinks I've wandered in by mistake on my way to Primark.

'Can I help you?' he asks.

'I . . . I don't know. I have a question.'

'What are you interested in – a turntable? An amp?'

'No, I mean a question about the shop itself.' He looks confused. 'Do you own it?'

'No,' he laughs. 'I'm just a sales assistant. The manager isn't here at the moment. Do you need him for something?'

'I'm not sure. Did he actually know Giles Cooperton?'

The assistant looks at me for an uncomfortably long time. This was clearly not on his agenda today.

'Can I ask what this is about?'

'It's a long story.'

'Well, as you can see,' he says gesturing around the empty store, 'I'm not exactly rushed off my feet here.'

He smiles again, but this time it seems genuine. Maybe he thinks I will end up buying a pair of £10,000 speakers if he's nice to me.

'Okay. So, I'm a carer and I'm looking after an eighty-seven-year-old man – I'm trying to find out a bit more about his history. I believe he once worked with Giles Cooperton, and I'm in London anyway so I thought I'd come and have a look at the shop and find out more about it. I kind of don't know why. I'm sorry.'

'It's fine!' he says. 'The manager will be in tomorrow. You can come back?'

'I don't live here. Don't worry. It's nothing.'

There is an awkward silence, so I start to wander about looking at the shelves, not sure how to extricate myself from this. I'm aware though that he is watching me. Is he worried that I'm going to steal something?

'Do . . . do you like music?' he asks, walking a little closer.

'Yeah, I suppose,' I reply.

'I get a staff discount if you need anything? It's not all really expensive stuff, some of the systems are pretty cheap. I mean, not that you're cheap. I didn't mean that.'

I give him a confused glance and his face is a deep crimson colour.

'Thanks,' I say. But this whole exercise has become weird and awkward now. What was I thinking? 'Right ... I guess I'll be going.'

I start to walk toward the door, keen to get out and make my way to the library.

'Giles didn't just own the shop,' the sales assistant says suddenly, and with a hint of desperation. I stop. 'He actually owned the flat upstairs too. I don't know if that helps?'

I have this odd tinge of excitement and for a second I feel like a detective.

'But he didn't live there, right?'

'No, his business partner, Jeremy Menzies, lived in it.'

'They ran the shop together?'

'From what I've been told, yes.'

'Did they get on? Were they friends?'

'Yeah, from what I gather. I think Giles spent a lot of time up in the flat. My manager is Donald Menzies, Jeremy's son. He basically grew up in here. He met Giles loads of times.'

'Does Donald live up there now?'

'No, we just use it for storage now. Don keeps saying we should sort it out, but he hasn't got round to it. It's been left pretty much as it was when Jeremy lived there.'

I nod, but don't answer – I just need to get out so I can quietly process all this. I came in here anxious and unsure and now I have gathered information. I'm almost lightheaded with pride.

'I have to go,' I say. 'But thank you, you've been very helpful.' Wow, I sound like Columbo. Oddly, the sales assistant looks almost crestfallen.

'Here,' he says. He takes a business card out of his jacket pocket, scrawls something on it and then offers it to me cautiously, like someone trying to hand-feed a squirrel in the park. 'It has my email and I wrote my own mobile on the back. Just in case you want to call me. My name is Josh. Josh Denton.'

'Oh, okay.'

Honestly, this is not the time for a sales pitch.

The Underground from Covent Garden is a nightmare. The trains are an ugly crush of tourists and late-running commuters, all jammed together in a fug of cold germs and coffee breath. I squeeze on amid a group of men in suits, my backpack clutched to my chest, eyes down. How did I do this every day – for months, for years? The warm glow of my assertiveness in the hi-fi shop sustains me.

Spewed out amid more crowds at King's Cross, then wrenched along the Euston Road, I feel like I'm lost in the undertow of a polluted river. It is only when I get inside the giant entrance hall of the library that I can breathe again. The whole sense of the place is different – it is hushed and austere, like some colossal modern cathedral. There are pockets of people in the café and around the entrance to the museum, but there is a sense of order.

After collecting my reader card at reception, I take the stairs up to the Humanities Reading Room and feel a pang of jealousy and failure seeing the rows of scholars, sitting at the long desks, their books and laptops spread out before them. It is the familiar impostor syndrome telling me I should go, tormenting me with humiliating possibilities: at the reader desk, the woman will tell me I've placed the online order wrong, or not placed it at all. She'll tell me to leave. But another part of me is thinking, today, I am one of them. I am doing research like them. I exist.

The librarian doesn't ask me to leave. She takes my details, walks away and returns with the book. I take it in both hands like a precious offering. I find an empty seat between a thin young man in a blazer and horn-rimmed glasses and an Asian woman typing neatly into an expensive Apple laptop. I smile nervously at the woman as I sit down, but she ignores me. I open my organiser on the desk beside the book, together with a pen for notes. I feel like I'm about to take an exam.

Almost too afraid to open the book and discover what – if anything – it can tell me about Elsa, I spend a little time just looking at it. It has a plain hardback cover in dull red, the words A BROADWAY STORY written in slightly faded gold leaf on the spine. I lift it to my face and inhale and it doesn't have that musty old book smell. As I'm doing this I glance to my right and realise the man next to me is watching. I've been here for less than a minute and I've already marked myself out as a book-sniffing weirdo. It is probably time to read.

I go straight for the index, hoping to find Levi and maybe even Elsa waiting right there for me. Tracing my finger along the lists of entries, my heart starts beating fast as I get to 'K' ... but there's nothing for Klein. My first reaction is that I've got the wrong book, or that Miles was lying, and I start to panic. Have I wasted a whole day and a £40 train ticket for this? I bury my face in my hands, the disappointment and frustration overcoming me. The silence of the room is suddenly sinister and oppressive.

It's okay, I tell myself. This isn't a disaster. Maybe it's just that he's not in the index. Surely the author hasn't listed *everyone* mentioned in the book? I try not to listen to the voice in my head telling me that if he didn't warrant an index entry, he can't figure that prominently in the text, and I start to flip the pages, not knowing what to look for, just hoping I see it. The first few chapters are about Broadway before the First World War and then into the 1920s – which I feel I can ignore because Levi didn't get to New York until 1936. I'm already halfway through the book before I get

248

to the mid-Thirties and that feeling of panic is rising again. I keep flicking pages, looking out for the name Klein or anything about immigrants or Austrians. I see mentions of Jewish stars – Max Reinhardt, Kurt Weill, George Gershwin – but nothing about Levi. The pages turn, the chapters pass, and with each sheet of paper, Elsa fades further into the lost past. Page after page after page after . . .

I glimpse a word that could have been Levi. Stop. Go back.

I gasp.

There it is, page 278 of 450. The name Levi Klein, buried in a long paragraph about a production of a musical called *Babes in Arms*. For a few seconds the words become a jumble of unfamiliar symbols and I have to shut my eyes and reopen them in order to focus. When I've composed myself, I read the rest of the page and the five pages after that – and when I've finished, I go through it all again because I can't quite process what I've seen. This time, I have to accept there is no mistake. I look up from the book. The words are unambiguous and they bring with them a shudder of nausea and grief.

Everything Will told me, everything I was beginning to believe, is a lie.

Chapter Twenty-Eight

1940

I approached the window slowly as though wading through deep water, lifted a flap at the edge of the blind and looked out.

It was Anderson's Daimler. I recognised it instantly, gleaming in the morning sun. He was out of the driver's side and walking around toward the house – my heart plummeted. He was surely alone. He had come to tell me that nothing could be done, that she was on her way to Liverpool or the Isle of Man or some other faraway place. None of us are bigger than this war, he had told me, and now he was here to prove it.

But he turned. He turned toward the passenger side. The sun on the car windows made it difficult to see as the door opened and a figure, masked in shadow, emerged. I squinted into the brightness, trying to make out any feature, any detail. Was it his wife? A policeman? The person stepped forward.

The sun on her hair, flame red in the brightness. Her face dazed and tired, but defiant.

I rushed through to the hallway and clawed at the door, dragging it open. Anderson supported her as she walked toward me and I covered the distance between us in a single stride, taking her into my arms. The scent of violets was still about her. 'Elsa,' I cried, 'Elsa, Elsa.' I almost choked on the word.

'She's exhausted,' said Anderson, standing slightly away, her suitcase in his hand. 'I offered to take her to her aunt's but she wanted to come here.'

'I'm so relieved,' I said. 'I'm so relieved to see you.'

'I need a glass of water,' she replied, her voice dulled by sheer fatigue.

With that, she slipped away, drifting into the house, almost like a spectre. I turned to Anderson.

'What did you do? What did you say?'

'It doesn't matter,' he said. 'She's here now.'

'I'll never be able to repay you. You saved her.'

He tipped his hat to me and began to walk back toward his car, but then stopped.

'The thing is,' he said, 'I didn't save her, and neither did you. She saved herself, the day she put aside her fears and played the piano to help my wife. Times like this make you think, don't they? About what bravery really is.'

When I walked into the house, Elsa was in the kitchen, a glass in her hand, staring out of the window towards Bath. Before I could say anything, she put the glass down on the worktop and turned toward me.

'I told you,' she said. Her voice was low and controlled but crackling with latent emotion. 'I told you this could happen.'

I was dumbstruck. I tried to formulate words but they would not come.

'I told you they would come for us, for me. But you wouldn't listen! Not here, you said, not in Bath.'

I recalled the conversations – about the harassment of German refugees and the undercurrent of fear in the city. It had all seemed so . . . far-fetched.

'I'm sorry, Elsa. I'm so sorry.'

'You have to listen to me!' she said. 'You have to really listen! This is the world we are in now. Things are going to happen that won't make sense, that aren't fair. I know, Will, because I have seen it! So please, listen to me! When I tell you to be afraid, be afraid!'

'I will, I will,' I said. But in my tiredness and fraught emotion, the words tumbled over me, and all I could take in was her anger. I had never seen her like this and I was afraid there was something terminal in it. 'Forgive me,' I begged, putting my hands out to her. She held on to them, but I could not tell whether it was an embrace or a means of restraint.

'I was scared,' she said. 'I was so bloody scared. I don't want to feel alone again.'

She released her grip on my arms and put her hands to my face. 'Listen to me,' she said again. And then with her pelvis she pushed me backwards against the table. There was a heat around her, a kind of energy I had never experienced. With her lips on my ear she whispered, 'We need to go upstairs, right now.'

Later, as she dozed in bed, I went back down and called Josephine to let her know that her niece was free and safe. Filled with adrenaline, I tidied the house, trying to make the place feel more welcoming. I took flowers from the garden and put them in a vase on the kitchen table. Once I'd finished, I crept up the stairs to the bedroom, understanding that she needed rest, but desperate to see her again. I stood outside for a few seconds, wondering if I should knock, still unsure of the rules with regards to privacy, despite everything that had happened between us. I pushed at the door and looked in.

She was asleep, naked, her legs pulled up to her chest, the sheets crumpled around her, entwined in her limbs, her hair spread out glossily on the pillow. The curtain was open and the light refracting through the thick glass spread jewels of colour across her skin.

In that breathless moment, the air was dense and still around her, as though the very atmosphere was enraptured by her presence. Her eyes opened and she caught me staring. I felt an instance of shame and guilt for spying on her, but she wasn't shocked or embarrassed and didn't try to cover up. I felt almost inebriated.

'What is it?' she smiled.

'You look like the painting,' I said. '*Danaë, the mother of Perseus.*'

She sat up a little, amused. 'You think I am a Klimt?' she said.

The resemblance was utterly striking. It was her. Timeless and boundless.

'Will you marry me?' a man's voice that sounded a little like mine enquired.

'Pardon?'

'I'm sorry. I'm very sorry. Tea. I meant will you want tea?'

She looked at me for a long time.

'The answer is yes,' she said. 'To both questions. Although I would like the tea first.'

There are some moments in life when your whole future suddenly seems to unfurl in front of you, like petals emerging from a bud. In an instant, everything that happened before is rendered obsolete and the future becomes something wondrous like a beautiful view, glittering and vast. I felt the universe could not contain my happiness.

Two years later, on a warm April evening, with the sound of aircraft in the fiery sky, I would discover I was right.

Chapter Twenty-Nine

2008

The 3.40 p.m. train back to Bath is waiting at Platform Ten when I emerge from the Underground into Paddington Station. The concourse is a little quieter now, and as I walk alongside the train, I'm relieved to see there are seats available and I won't have to deal with my thoughts while crammed into a vestibule with dozens of other travellers. As the train pulls away, I close my eyes. I have ninety minutes to sit and think about what I read.

Everything seems so dumb now.

I get a sudden burst of rage. I feel used by Will, let down by him; even as the vast cracks and contradictions started to appear in his story, I wanted to believe. Jane warned me about how dementia changes people; they create stories and lies, they can become manipulative. It's not his fault. It's mine. Classic me. I take a tissue out of my pocket and try to blow my nose as quietly as possible. I want the train to stop and I want my mum to collect me and carry me away somewhere. I want to tell her, I'm really sorry about everything. And this starts me sobbing, and I can't stop my shoulders shaking. My head thuds against the window as the world passes by unhearing and oblivious. When I get home, Mum is out and I am alone.

The following afternoon, I sit in Jane's office as she reads my report. I did consider emailing it, but then, it's not the only document I'm handing in this morning, and the other one requires me to be present. My conclusion: after three months of assessment, it is clear Will Emerson is showing significant signs of dementia, including a confabulated life story that resulted in him essentially abducting a child. His physical health is deteriorating and the house is unsuitable for an elderly occupant. According to the Mental Capacity Act, social services should intervene. Will's solicitor must take power of attorney and secure a care home place. I was able to write this in the required tone of dispassionate professionalism because, in truth, I feel disconnected from everything. Even though I have never written a report like this before, I know it represents my most competent moment in the job.

Jane turns the page, reads the final section then looks up at me.

'And you're sure he can't stay at home with, say, NHS supplementary care?'

'No,' I say. 'It's not just him, it's the house. It's badly maintained, the walls are riddled with cracks, the ceilings are bowing. I could get a survey but I don't think it's necessary.' I sound like a robot.

She nods, but she's still looking at me, seemingly waiting for something else. Regret? Sorrow? I have nothing to offer. 'Right,' she says. 'I'll share this with social services and see how they want to progress. Thank you, Laura. I know this hasn't been easy but you've done a thorough job.'

She puts the report in her in-tray and gives me a 'that will be all' glance. But no, that will not be all. I gulp silently.

'There's something else,' I say. And I slide the single folded sheet of paper across to her.

She picks it up, looks quizzically at me, then reads.

'Oh Laura, why?'

All last night I lay in bed, looking up at the ceiling, feeling blank, my monotone interior voice playing out its familiar recorded message. *You're done, it's over now.* At 4 a.m. I got up and walked over to the corkboard, then slowly started removing the index cards one by one. Down came the names of the people Will knew, the places he went, the dates, the connections between them. Last of all, I removed the drawing pins from the timeline so that it rolled up on itself and dropped to the floor. What did I ever think I would gain from unlocking this story? Afterwards, I took out my laptop and wrote the report and my resignation.

'I just ...' I didn't want to get emotional, but now I know it is inevitable. 'I can't do this anymore.'

'But you've done a good job with Will. You did everything you could for him.'

'I was stupid! I believed everything he told me. He needed someone to put him straight about his memories, not to indulge him. And it's not just that ...'

'What else?'

How do I put it? How do I explain what has led me here in terms that make sense? It's not possible. Because nothing about this makes sense. I take a deep breath, and look away from Jane. If I am telling her this story, I can't look at her.

'I started to have this feeling there was someone else living in the house. It was a sense, like static electricity, something in the air. I sensed her walking around the house. I felt that she knew I was there. That she was trying to tell me something.'

'She?'

'Elsa. Will's wife. I felt she was present in the house, but not as a ghost – that she was alive somehow, just not quite there in the same place as us. That's why I wanted to find out more about her. But she wasn't there. I was just ... getting sick. I need help. I need to just stop everything for a while. I have to protect myself.'

'You don't think Elsa existed?'

I look at her, surprised at how kind she is being.

'She existed,' I say. 'But she didn't have a relationship with Will. She never got the chance to have a relationship with anyone.'

The first thing I discovered at the British Library was that there's a reason Levi isn't in the index. Like a lot of Jewish émigrés, when he reached the US, he adopted a more American name. Throughout most of the book he's known as Larry Kaye. He was indeed a mover and shaker in the theatre business, working on a series of acclaimed productions with major stars. But then came the paragraph I copied down:

In January 1942, tragedy struck for Kaye. His beloved niece Elsa, recently released from an internment camp on the Isle of Man, boarded a merchant vessel bound for New York, planning to stay with her uncle and make a new life in the US. Elsa, who had fled from Vienna to Bath in 1938, was a talented musician, and Kaye was sure he could find her work in a theatre orchestra. Sadly, the ship was part of a merchant convoy attacked by German U-boats in the mid-Atlantic. It was torpedoed and sank with no survivors. Kaye's wife Josephine was devastated by the loss and he pulled out of two productions in order to care for her. The couple never fully recovered.

There it was, clear and unambiguous. Elsa couldn't have lived with Will because after her arrest in July 1940, she spent over a year in an internment camp before being freed and boarding a ship to New York. And she couldn't have been with Will during the bombing of Bath in April 1942 because by that point she was at the bottom of the Atlantic Ocean. Will has either imagined it all, or he is lying to me. There can be no other rational explanation.

Chapter Thirty

I'm standing outside Avon Lodge in the late evening, a bluey darkness coming in over the hills. I have to go in and face him, but what then for me – the woman who believed everything, who felt she was connecting with something in the house, privy to some secret knowledge? What a joke. There is nothing here beyond my own anxiety and the last vestiges of a drug misfiring in my system. I know I'm going to cry, so I put my hood up and pull the strings tight around my face. I can't get things right. I come at the world at the wrong angle and I miss. It was all there, all the evidence was really there – why did I keep ignoring it? I had in my head a possibility, as absurd as it sounds, that Elsa was still in the house, not as a ghost, as a resident. The two of them apart but co-existing. A double exposure. I want to toss my organiser and my stupid timeline chart on a bonfire and be rid of them. Then I want to hide away. I should have learned by now, there is no answer at the end of any journey – the questions merely follow you.

*

Jane has already been in to see Will; she told him about my report and my resignation. At least this way, I won't have to break it to him, and Jane will have dealt with the initial shock of it. I could have got away without coming here at all, but I owe him that. As I walk up to the door, I promise myself that if I smell alcohol on him, I'll go – I cannot cope with that again. But when I knock, there is no answer. I knock again and wait. No answer. I peep through the parlour window, but no lights are on and I can see through the gloom that the room is empty. I could use the key he left for me that time, but it already feels like an imposition. I'm not his carer anymore. One more knock. No sounds from inside at all. I'll go. I'll let Jane know. She'll be able to send someone to check on him.

I turn to leave, but just as I'm walking back up the path, I catch a subtle movement in the corner of my eye. A light has flickered on in the parlour. I walk back to the window and look through – the lamp is on, but no one is there. My breath forms a mist on the glass. Dodgy electrics, I tell myself. The wiring is shot. Then I notice the Klimt print is on the floor, the glass broken. The lamp goes off. And in the same instant, the porch light comes on.

I step away, a fearful possibility sparking inside me like embers glowing into life. The house wants me to investigate. No, it's over. There's nothing here. But I am taking the key out of my pocket anyway and my hand is shaking as I try to push it into the lock. Then as slowly as I can, I push the door open, the hinges groaning loudly. 'Will?' I say, almost as a whisper.

The hall is dark, and there is the smell of rotting plaster in the cool wet air. Loose scrolls of peeled wallpaper flutter in the breeze. 'Will?' Maybe Jane has moved him to a home already. Maybe he has fled, determined not to be re-housed. This is stupid. I should go. A shadow slants across the wall, I see it move like time-lapse footage. Something crackles in the air, but I know it's not real. As

I move further in, the putrid smell gives way to something else, the unmistakable undernote of sweet flowers. 'You're not there,' I say. 'There's nothing here.'

The porch light goes off behind me, and for a second I'm in utter darkness – just like that time in the cellar. I don't even have time to react, beyond making a solitary gasp, before there is another tremoring burst of light. The kitchen is now illuminated. I am being guided. The only thing that gives me the strength to walk through the hall is the belief that this is all nonsense, that nothing is happening here. And when I get to the kitchen and see that no one is there either, I am relieved. The lights are short-circuiting, a cruel trick. I'm such an idiot. I'm so highly strung. Wait until Jane hears . . .

A security light on the rear outside wall pings into sudden life, sending a beam of bright white light into the centre of the garden. At first, it's blinding and I can't see anything, but then as my pupils adjust, I do see. I do see it.

It takes several seconds for me to understand that this is real. It is an actual reality. Will is lying seemingly unconscious in the centre of the garden, utterly white. Blue white.

I run. I run to him.

Chapter Thirty-One

The Older People ward at Bath Hospital is bright and cool, with magnolia-coloured floors and patterned curtains around each bed. Some of the other men are sitting up chatting to wives and relatives, but at the end of the row, Will is asleep and alone. Several days after his fall, his face is still a map of reddish-yellow bruises; he looks so frail it seems a breeze from the window could pick him up and take him away like an autumn leaf.

I sit on the chair next to his bed, feeling cautious and guilty. I am certain it is my fault he is here. 'Will?' I say softly. I almost take his hand, but I'm worried the skin will tear in my fingers.

He had suffered a minor stroke. It probably happened only a few minutes before I found him. I called the ambulance and waited with him until it arrived, but I couldn't face going with him to hospital, so Jane went instead. For two days it seemed that he would not survive. He lay there staring into space, semi-conscious, silent apart from the pathetic wheeze of his breathing. Jane visited him every day, talking to the nurses and health visitors about the kindest options, discussing plans with his solicitor. Together they decided that, when Will was discharged from hospital, he would need full-time residential care as a matter of urgency. The house he had lived in for almost ninety years was quickly and quietly put up for sale. The construction company working on the land next door put in an immediate offer. Jane has even talked to a vintage wireless museum in Minehead about donating Will's radios. The Morrison shelter in the cellar will be disassembled and taken to a local museum. Everyone is being very efficient about tearing his life apart. Decades of possessions, picked through and dispersed. All over. All done.

'Are you Laura?' a voice from behind me asks.

I look up and see a middle-aged man with curly brown hair and steel-rimmed glasses smiling down at me, clutching a battered old folder in his arms.

'I'm Peter Robson, I'm the hospital social worker. Can we have a word?'

He leads me back down the ward and into a small treatment room with a bare desk, a metal gurney and several chairs. There is a watercolour of some flowers on the wall. He sits down and motions to another seat.

'You were caring for Will Emerson, weren't you?'

'Yes.'

'And how did you get on? I've heard he is quite a difficult character.'

'He was . . . it got easier.'

He nods and smiles, then opens his folder, pulling out some papers.

'We're working on a plan for his discharge, but I need to check we have all the details. He's recovering physically and they're desperately short of beds here, so he will have to go back to his home while his solicitor looks into residential care. I want to make sure there are no remaining relatives who should be consulted. I've managed to talk with Will, but he's very confused. As you worked so closely with him, I just wanted to check – did he mention anything to you about some long-lost niece or nephew? An old chum?'

'No. He was alone.'

'He was never married?'

'That's a complicated question.'

He gives me a quizzical look but then flicks through his papers.

'You see, I did a bit of digging around in the archives downstairs, and I found a few of his medical notes, going right back to the war. Did he tell you he was in psychiatric care?'

'He said that after the bombing, he ended up back in hospital for a few months.'

'A few months?' He shakes his head dismissively. 'According to these records, Will Emerson was committed to the Somerset and Bath Mental Asylum for eight years.'

I blink at him, trying to comprehend what he's saying.

'Eight years?'

'Yes, from 1942 to 1950. The diagnosis in his medical records is listed as acute war neurosis – what would have been known as shell shock.'

So that was it. The rumours that Florence Barnes and the woman from the shop had heard weren't quite accurate – he wasn't in prison, he was in psychiatric care. The terror of the bombings. The head injury he sustained. Perhaps the repressed grief of losing his brother ('I didn't know how to handle it.') The truth was there all along – no mystery, no lost love affair – he was ill, that's all. And so was I. The final brutal confirmation. Peter is still flicking through his papers, oblivious to my turmoil.

'I was looking through to see if he was visited by a spouse or partner at all,' he says. 'His mother made a couple of visits – it looks like she died shortly before the end of the war. That was it for his family.'

'Uh-huh.'

'But he had one other regular visitor.'

I'm barely listening as he studies the pages, brow furrowed. The room is silent except for a low humming from the strip lights.

'Giles Cooperton,' he says. 'Does that name ring a bell?'

'It was just someone Will worked with. He died years ago.'

The social worker lets out a disappointed sigh.

'Oh well,' he says. 'Another dead end.'

Before I leave the hospital, I feel I ought to say goodbye to Will. Still a little dazed, I sit down by his bed and watch him sleep, his skin waxy and white, his mouth agape. He looks as though he will never wake up.

'I'm sorry, Will,' I say.

I'm just about to get up when I see his eyelids flicker and then open. To my shock, he turns his head slowly toward me.

'You?' he whispers. 'I didn't think I would see you again. What are you sorry about?'

The tone in his voice is almost casual, as though I have woken him from an afternoon nap. I don't even know where to start.

'I'm sorry I wasn't a better carer,' I say, barely able to form the words. 'I should have done everything differently.'

He makes a barely perceptible shake of his head.

'It seems I have been living in a fantasy,' he says. 'They tell me I suffered from – what is it? – post-traumatic stress disorder? As real as Elsa was, I never knew her. Perhaps I saw her photo in the newspaper once. That's what the social worker thinks. Then the bombing . . . whatever happened to me that night, it knocked me for six.' He wheezes and coughs, his whole body wracked with the effort of it.

'Over time, as you get older, stories and memories ... they become inextricable, like the threads in a rope. I've spent my whole life convinced that I had a love affair so wonderful that I could never fall in love again. What a terrible trick, eh?'

'It's okay,' I say because I don't know what else I can do.

'You did the right thing,' he smiles. 'With your report. You did the right thing. I've been living on borrowed time. The worst of it is, I dragged you into it.'

'No, you didn't. I wanted to believe you. I wanted it to be true. I really thought . . . I thought that the house – that Elsa – was trying to tell us something.'

He tries to sit up but can't. Instead he reaches out for my hand and I let him take it. His skin is as dry and brittle as tissue paper.

'I think perhaps we were both mad for a while, weren't we?' he says. 'And now we must say goodbye to each other.'

I smile at him. 'I'll come and visit you again.'

He closes his eyes and sinks back into the mattress.

'Laura?'

His voice is almost nothing, like it's coming from another room, or the waking edge of a dream.

'Yes?'

'Please. Don't come back. There's nothing here.'

Part Four

RETURN

Chapter Thirty-Two

28 April 1942

I woke with a jolt and for several seconds I couldn't take in where I was or what had happened. The objects around me were unrecognisable. There had been a bright light, a wave of immense pressure, as though being flung back by a crashing wave, then blackness. Afterwards, there were fragments of memories – people gathered round, shouting. Then I was inside an ambulance. Then nothing for what felt like days.

A figure approached me through the blur.

'Where am I?' I groaned.

'You're in the Royal United Hospital in Bath. You've had quite a bump to your head.'

With this information, things swam into focus. I could recognise the chaotic activity of the ward: the rows of metal beds, nurses running, vast black blinds over the windows. My head felt like it had been split open, it was agony to breathe. In the bed next to mine, a woman I recognised from Lansdown Road was moaning weakly, her right arm and leg bandaged, her face ludicrously swollen and blackened with bruises. The bed on the other side was empty, but the ruffled sheets were smeared with dry blood.

The nurse hovered in my field of vision, her face gaunt and tired. 'What happened?' I said.

'You were brought in on Monday morning. You'd been hit by shrapnel and you were unconscious in your kitchen. Nasty gash on your forehead, nothing too bad, but you've had a shock – we'll need to check you over when a doctor is free. How do you feel?'

'Pain. A little bit of pain.'

'I can bring you some aspirin, but morphine is being rationed.'

She was about to race away to someone more deserving, but I grabbed her arm, thinking about the three of us in the garden when the bomb struck.

'Did ... did you ... was anyone else brought in with me?'

The nurse fixed me with a quizzical stare and my stomach lurched at the thought that she was trying to summon the courage to give me terrible news.

'According to the chaps who brought you in, you were alone. I'll check, but it's chaos here. We took some damage – there's no gas, we had no water for a day, the wards are all full to bursting.'

After that, I lay in a weird stupor for hours, floating between consciousness and dreaming. It was only when the nurse returned to me that I was able to reconstitute my thoughts.

'I've checked around,' she said. 'There were no records of anyone else being brought into the hospital with you.'

'I have to go.' I lifted myself up and the pain in my head was like a gunshot.

'You can't. We need a doctor to see you.'

I struggled to my feet. 'I have to find someone,' I said. 'Please, for God's sake, let me go.' The nurse looked around. They clearly needed beds – I could see exhausted ambulancemen bringing in casualties, everyone covered in grime; they were still digging people out from their wrecked homes. 'I'm fine,' I said. 'I will see a doctor at home. I've got to get out of here.'

It was another nurse who came by and handed back my clothes. They were blackened and torn, but I hardly noticed. Disorientated and weak, I half walked, half staggered from the hospital. A bus pulled up at the stop outside and I boarded with a rabble of similarly tattered and tired people. A smartly dressed elderly woman sat next to me. She turned and smiled.

'It's all right, my dear,' she said, 'we'll recover from this.'

There was little obvious damage as we drove down Coombe Hill in the afternoon sun, but then as we approached the city along Upper Bristol Road, the carnage became obvious – rows of houses with their windows blown out, roofs collapsed, whole buildings turned to mountains of rubble. Groups of workmen gathered at the sides of the road, shovelling rubble from one place to another. There were pieces of furniture lining the pavements, packed suitcases left abandoned, and over everything a grey haze drifted like some poisonous fog.

The road was closed before the turning up to Queen Square because of a ruptured gas main, so we all had to get out and walk. We formed a shuffling pack, padding slowly along the road, but then we stopped together when we reached the square and saw the Francis Hotel, its grand Georgian façade ripped in half, a fissure running through it like a valley. You could see what was left of the bedrooms on either side of the crater – the luxurious wallpaper, a nightgown hanging from the back of a door, a pristine bathroom sink with a washbag still perched by it. People stood around and gawped. A man was having his photograph taken in front of the smoking debris. I stayed for a second, entranced, until I remembered why I had to keep moving.

I had a flashback to the moment in the garden, the dead certainty of something hurtling towards us through the inky darkness. The blast, the immense pressure – surely nothing of the house remained? I would be returning to nothing but rubble. The thought of it, the despair of it, set me running.

When I reached Lansdown, there were chilling sights along every street. Great piles of fallen masonry where shops and houses used to be, trees blasted bare of leaves and branches, roads burst open. Everywhere, there were people stumbling over the wreckage, picking out belongings.

On turning the slight corner before the stretch of houses that led to my own, it was clear they had suffered a direct hit. Several buildings were little more than jagged remains, ghostly amid the black dust clouds. Silent rows of men dug at the ruins like some nightmarish harvest. My eyes sore and teary with grit, I had to feel my way past two trucks parked in the road, my back aching, my head throbbing horribly. Two boys ran past me carrying bags full of vegetables. A man shouted, 'Take those down to anyone who needs 'em.' As I passed them, a gap finally appeared in the smog. I stopped dead and looked up, breathing heavily. 'My God,' I said.

Avon Lodge was still there. The windows were all blown out, some roof tiles were broken, and a length of guttering had fallen down – that was the extent of the visible damage from the front. But the bomb hit the garden, I thought. Could this be a gruesome trick – the uninjured façade hiding an apocalypse behind it? I fumbled for the door key, and burst into the hallway.

There were books all over the floor in the library and a few paintings had been displaced from the walls in the parlour and smashed on the floor, but nothing else. I rushed through to the

274

kitchen. Here there was much more damage – the rear wall had almost completely caved in, dust and rubble everywhere. It was like some ghastly theatre set and I was drifting through it; the ghost of a long-dead actor.

And then I was standing where the kitchen doorway used to be, looking out over the garden. It was a scene of utter destruction. One side of the workshop had completely collapsed, the walls obliterated, the roof leaning into the void. The lawn was an immense smouldering crater, several feet deep and strewn with debris – great chunks of jagged bricks and mortar. I stepped out in the cool air and stumbled about, dreading that I would find some horrible evidence of ruined bodies. As I got closer to the workshop I looked in and was astonished to discover most of the shelves intact and many of the wireless sets dusty but safe. The transmitter was covered in rubble but not too badly damaged it seemed. Yet still, no casualties.

My head was thudding, I felt a swoop in my guts like seasickness. 'Where are you?' I cried, but I wasn't sure if it was aloud or in my head. I staggered back from the garden, stepping carelessly over the detritus and into the house. There was an official number we were supposed to phone to report casualties, I remembered. It had appeared in the *Bath Chronicle* just days before the bombings. I went to the phone in the hallway, picked up the receiver and asked the operator to connect me.

'Hello,' I said. 'I need to report a missing person. We were bombed in the last raid and they haven't been found.' The voice on the other end asked for a name.

I looked in the hallway mirror, but the room was swirling in and out of focus. I put my hands up and rubbed at my eyes. And there I was, the bloody bandage like a headband just visible beneath the curls of my hair, which was not red anymore, but black with soot and dirt.

'It's Will Emerson,' I said. 'He was with a young boy, a neighbour. His name is David . . . There's no sign of them here. Nothing at all.'

I turned my back to the wall and slid down it until I was crumpled on the floor, too bewildered and exhausted to cry.

In the afternoon, a rescue team stopped by and searched the garden and surrounding properties. They dug around, they moved great chunks of masonry. They discovered nothing. One man said to me, 'It's unusual, not to find shreds of clothing or bits of . . . well, of evidence that somebody was there.' They left after an hour – there were other houses on the street to search, other people's worst nightmares to render into truth. Eventually, I called Aunt Josephine and she sent a car to pick me up. The sound of her voice made me weep at last.

Afterwards, I climbed up the stairs, crept into the bedroom and began to pack some things, trying not to look at Will's clothes folded over the chair in the corner of the room, or the photos of us together on the mantelpiece. That's when I heard it. A voice, his voice, calling my name. It seemed to be coming from the spare room, and without thinking I rushed through and swung open the door, but he was not there; I felt something like a breeze, a weird tingling rush, and then his voice in our bedroom, and again on the stairs. I stood on the landing confused and frightened. 'Will,' I called. 'Will, are you there?' I knew it was madness, but I could sense him, I could almost smell his cologne in the air. Then he called again, and I followed him from room to room. Every time he shouted my name, I called back. I didn't know what it meant, but I felt it with every fibre of my being.

He was still here.

The car arrived in the evening, and as I left, I looked back, dumb with shock and confusion. And through the fog of it all I said to myself, my name is Elsa Klein. I fought my way out of Austria, I left everything I loved and knew – I got through that and now I will get through this. Will is not gone. He is somewhere. Whatever has happened, I will find him.

Chapter Thirty-Three

2008

The consulting room is extremely bright today. Outside the window, a low sun hangs in the cloudless sky beyond the treeline, bringing unseasonal warmth and colour. It is weirdly oppressive, as though the universe is trying to tell me to feel better – or feel *something*. I fiddle with the sleeves of my jumper, trying not to make eye contact with Dr Bedford. He is staring at me intently, his face a mask of pained concern. I am being softly interrogated while my mum waits outside. I've seen more of her over the past three weeks than I have since I was a child. I can't get rid of her these days.

For two weeks I didn't leave my room, curtains closed on the world, mind like a malfunctioning computer. I lay in bed, replaying Will's timeline – all the events in his life with Elsa – still with a part of me thinking, surely it can't all have been lies? Then one morning, I managed to get up and dressed, and I walked into town, with all the dates and events copied out into my organiser.

I spent three hours at the Bath Archive, researching as much as I could. It all fell apart, like ash in my hands. A pub he told me he'd visited with Elsa had been demolished a year before they went; the concert they attended on that first date didn't take place – Vera Maconochie had been involved in a minor traffic accident and didn't play at the Pump Room for another two weeks. If I'd found this out earlier, if I'd bothered to check, perhaps I could have helped him properly.

'Your mother said on the phone that you've had a couple of setbacks?'

I nod. The silence stretches out.

'When I saw you last, we talked about the possible withdrawal effects of coming off the medication so abruptly.'

'So you're saying, "I told you so"?'

'No,' he says in a more friendly tone. 'There's no blame here.'

He leans back in his chair, smiling, and it feels like a challenge. He's waiting for me to blink first. But I've got nothing to give him.

'One thing we have to do is get to the bottom of your anxiety – of where it comes from.'

'I know where it comes from,' I say quietly. 'My dad was an alcoholic and he hated me.'

I have this weird feeling of sudden clarity, as though my ears have popped. I'm not sure I've ever said it out loud before. We'd always been careful, Mum and I, about how we discussed it. He was a 'heavy drinker', he 'turned to the bottle', he 'sought solace in drink' – we used these phrases to edge around it. Because he couldn't be an alcoholic, could he? He had a job, he didn't drink as soon as he woke up, sometimes he was sober for several days at a time. And he wasn't abusive because he never hit us.

'I'm still trying to sort a therapy appointment,' he says. 'For now, we need to think about what I can do to help you. I want you to see me every week, okay? You need some stability. Can you take some time off work?'

'I handed in my resignation.'

'In that case, give yourself some time to rest. Avoid things that will trigger your anxiety. Are you able to cope financially?'

'I'm living with my mum.'

'And that's okay?'

'I'm almost thirty years old. It's the dream scenario.'

He laughs at this and it breaks the tension in the room. He goes back to his keyboard and types some more. I wonder if he's making a note of the fact that I still have a sense of humour. I feel like I need to break the silence, to keep the fragile rapport going.

'I thought I was getting somewhere, but I wasn't,' I say. 'I just want to wake up and not feel scared.'

'Is your father still in your life?'

'No. He tried. But no.'

Dr Bedford takes a sip from his mug and considers this.

'What are you most scared of?' he says.

I make an awkward smile.

'Whatever's coming next.'

He nods and goes back to his computer. As he bashes at the keyboard, he frowns to himself. 'Let's maybe try you on a course of diazepam, which is a mild tranquiliser, just for a while. We could also look at different sorts of antidepressants that will support you without the side effects you experienced last time. Does that sound okay?'

'Yes,' I say. And this time I mean it.

When I get up to go, he says without looking at me, 'And that man? Will? You don't have to see him again, do you?'

I don't answer, I just leave.

Chapter Thirty-Four

I have returned to say goodbye to Avon Lodge. This place has taken up my days and haunted my dreams; for a long while I thought it was trying to tell me something, something I half heard or half understood, but I was wrong. Now it's time for closure – it will soon be gone. Will is still being looked after here while a care home place is finalised, but I checked ahead and I know he's asleep in his room. I don't want to see him. He asked me not to, after all. Riding toward the house, I feel the first few raindrops of a coming shower. I remember the first time I arrived here, sodden from an October downpour, scared and withdrawn. I never did fix the gate.

As I prop my bike against the garden wall, I look up and I see what I instinctively knew I would – Florence watching from her upstairs window. I have to know something. I walk back toward her house remembering the time I visited before, the unease I felt. This time, when I reach the front door, she is already there, in her long cardigan, her tightly plaited hair.

'Do you have more questions?' she asks.

'Just one. Why are you always watching Will's house? What . . . what are you looking for?'

She gives me a kind of indulgent smile, as though this is something I should already understand.

'Do you really want to know?'

I just look at her, waiting.

'Something happened that night – the second night of the Blitz,' she says. 'I was in my bed as the first bombs came down. I heard the explosions getting closer. But then, there was an extraordinary light, so bright and pure I could see it through the blackout curtain. I sat up and looked out of the window. The light was all around Avon Lodge, like a halo. It was extraordinary; I felt I could see the individual particles glistening in the night. I watched for a while, I don't know how long, and then the light faded into itself and was gone, and my father rushed in and took me down to the cellar.'

I start walking backwards, away from her, away from this fantasy she has constructed.

I shake my head. 'It's not . . . none of this is real.'

'You must see it, though? In the garden, the way the light falls even now? There's still something there.'

I shouldn't be listening, I shouldn't be paying heed to this, but her tone is so honest, so direct, it disarms me. 'I need to go,' I whisper.

'Wait,' she says. 'Before the light faded, I saw something else. There were firemen and air wardens running about in the street, but there was also a young woman, lying motionless in the road. She had obviously been injured, she was bloody and unconscious. I wanted to bang on the window to alert someone. But then slowly and surely, and it looked to be taking an incredible effort, she got herself up, she got herself to her feet. And then she looked about with a sort of defiance, as though the chaos had come for her and she had beaten it. Then she looked up at me. And I waved. And I was so ill at the time, so pale and weak. But she gave me a bit of hope, this stranger. She allowed me to think that I could get better. Do you see? You never know where help will come from: a stranger, a friend, the past, the future.' With that, she gave me an odd sort of smile.

Unsure, really, of what to say or do, I thank her for her story, and walk back to Will's front yard, fumbling in my pocket for the spare key. I jam it into the lock for the last time, and then I'm in. The familiar smell of damp, lingering along the corridor and into every room, is almost comforting. I didn't need this nonsense today. Calm. Calm. There is a thick silence, like the house knows the end is coming. I hear no sounds, I feel no static in the air. My mind goes back to the night I found Will unconscious – the lights switching on and off – but I know that they were just flickering. I only *imagined* they were guiding me to him. I have to bury it.

When I walk through to the kitchen, the carer is there. She is calm and quiet, flitting about without urgency. I feel a moment of sadness and pain, but I push that away too. I'm here to let go.

'It's a mess, isn't it?' she says. I don't know if she means the kitchen or the whole situation. 'Will is upstairs in his bed if you do want to see him, but I wouldn't expect much. Has Jane kept you up to date?'

'She said he's deteriorated.'

'Physically, he's in incredible shape for someone pushing ninety. The physio has been getting him to walk around a little every day. But there's no communication, no awareness. It's like a power switch has been turned off. Sometimes, you see that, don't you? They just shut down. He's been through such a lot. I wonder if he'll even make it to the care home at this rate.'

With that, she heads off upstairs.

Alone again, I look out at the garden, overcome with the feeling that I have contributed to the demise of this house – it stood for a hundred and fifty years before I came along. Then I see through the rain shower that the workshop door has been left open. The radios, I think, should be looked after. Somehow, I'm furious about it. I rush out, through the back door, grimly determined, recalling the times the transmitter had burst into life. Did I imagine that too?

The wireless sets closest to the entrance are splattered with rain, and it will ruin them. I go to the work desk and take a cloth out of one of the drawers, and I am there for almost an hour, carefully wiping the wood and Bakelite cases; moving several further along the shelves so they are safer from the elements. It is calming, though I know, deep down, I am waiting for something to happen. Nothing does.

Walking back up the path, I think about the rest of the day and what I'll do. All of the days, all empty in front of me. The thought is terrifying. In the middle of the garden I feel a shift in the air pressure, and then a sudden gust of wind. My stomach lurches. The gale is so strong, it pushes me backwards and I have to brace myself against it, putting my arms up to my face, a swirl of dust and rain in my eyes. There is a movement near the house and I look up, blinking. Someone is standing in the doorway. It might be grit in my eyes, but the shape seems to be flickering and fuzzy like a poorly tuned TV image. The person is putting out their arms as though to stop me. I rub my eyes and look up again.

There's no one here.

Everything is quiet. Just one last illusion, one last trick. And such a horrible trick at that – because the face was pale and beautiful and framed with wild red hair.

Go back.

I have this instinct, this raw visceral instinct, to go back.

Almost robotically, I walk to the workshop again. I look around the room at these artefacts, these fossils of another era. There is still something I have to do here. I can't escape it. 'Tell me what you want,' I say. 'Just tell me.' Slowly at first, but gathering pace, I walk round the shelves, finding the power switches and turning the sets on. Finally, I get to the radio transmitter station, its intimidating bank of black boxes with their dials and buttons marked with unknowable abbreviations. I sit at the chair and study them, trying to work out how to power it all up, but I'm lost. I can't do it alone. I open the desk drawer hoping to find an instruction manual, but there are just dozens of QSL cards, musty and faded. I can't help wondering about the angles and connections I may have missed. A tiny part of me hoped until the end that there would be a fresh lead, that the mystery would live on. What else do I have? My brain is still buzzing, but there is nowhere to go. I know all I can about these dead people, the lives that momentarily converged then diverged, leaving no trace, leaving . . .

Wait.

I'm looking at the QSL cards when I spot a familiar name. Cooperton. His card is the most stylish, a beautiful font, an illustration of two men in smart suits sat together in front of a wireless. The contact date is February 1942, perhaps he and Will were testing some new radio equipment and exchanged cards as a nod to formality. On the back is a handwritten message.

To Will. Only connect. With love, your friend for all time. Giles.

That handwriting, I've seen it before. Think. I sit back and close my eyes, breathing in the smell of damp wood and varnish.

The newspapers. The weird notes on the newspapers. Giles wrote them.

Only connect. Your friend for all time.

What did the hospital social worker say? That Cooperton had visited Will for years in the asylum. Something doesn't fit. I reach into my pocket for the organiser and frantically search through until I find my transcription of the interview with his sister. She'd told me Cooperton had lost touch with Will right after he left Anderson's. 'They never met again,' she said.

But that isn't true. She lied to me.

Why?

Chapter Thirty-Five

It takes almost an hour to reach North Road. I freewheel Lansdown then swoop left past the grand curve of Camden Crescent, through Hedgemead Park and then Sydney Gardens. Valerie's home is a 1960s modernist edifice with a long sloping roof and huge windows sporting pristine white venetian blinds. Compared to the Georgian and Victorian terraces I have passed to get here, it looks like an alien spaceship. When I called her from Avon Lodge, she listened to what I had discovered about her brother and after a long silence told me, 'Come for tea. I'll try to explain.' I don't know why I am doing this, given what I found at the British Library, given that Will confessed he imagined the whole thing, given that he is fading fast. It would be easier for me to pull away from the whole damn drama. And sure enough, as I stand waiting at this stranger's door, I begin to feel tremors of fear through my body, my arms, my fingers – the old flight response. But there is something in me that isn't ready to quit, that has got used to being resourceful. So I stay.

She opens the door wearing another vintage dress and rainbow scarf, now matched with plastic bangles that rattle on her thin wrists. She makes an awkward smile.

'Come in,' she says.

Her living room is an explosion of Sixties kitsch. A lime green sofa and patterned orange armchair compete for attention in front of a lavishly decorated marble fireplace. Along the same wall is a giant display cabinet with mirrored interiors – the shelves a riot of strange ceramic vases. On the glass-topped coffee table in the centre of the room there is a giant yellow plate piled high with chocolate biscuits. Valerie ushers me to the sofa and then sits down beside me. She picks up an Orange Club and starts to slowly unwrap it while I try to acclimatise to the Technicolor fever dream I've just walked into.

'So you want to interrogate me a little more?' she asks. 'I told you, didn't I, that raking up the past is not always a good idea.'

'There's just something I need to check.'

She takes a bite of the biscuit and studies me.

'You look tired,' she says. 'Is Will keeping you on your toes? He was always very good at taking from people who cared about him.'

The remark is so pointed, it takes me aback.

'I'm not looking after him anymore. He had a stroke. They're looking to move him into a care home, but they don't think he's going to recover.'

For a few seconds, her wry smile drops away, but it quickly returns.

'Oh, he'll recover. He always does. He'll probably outlive us all.'

'Why don't you like him?' I watch as she finishes the biscuit then screws up the wrapper.

'He is good at getting vulnerable people to do what he wants, even if it's foolhardy, even if it's bad for them.'

She looks me right in the eye when she says this.

'I'm not here for him,' I say. 'I'm here for me, because I need to finish this.'

'Really? Isn't this all a bit sad? You're a young woman – you must have better things to do with your time than traipse around Bath chasing ghosts.'

She sits back in her chair, arching an eyebrow, clearly enjoying the provocation. But I'm done with it.

'Do you know how hard it is for me to be here – to even come to your house?' The words explode from me without my knowledge as though some internal authority has been bypassed. 'Every morning it's a challenge to get up, to put one foot in front of the other, to dress, to leave the house. I'm exhausted, I'm scared of everything. I dread every day. But I *have* left the house, I *have* pushed myself. Even if this whole thing leads nowhere, even if it's all in my head, I've found things out that no one else has found, and I've got through it. If you don't want to tell me anything, that's fine, I'll go.'

I leap up from the sofa ready to storm out, adrenaline scorching through me. Amid the muddle of emotions and thoughts, one realisation emerges: I'm not thinking of giving up and running home, I'm thinking of where I go next. When I get through the front door, I'll look somewhere else.

'Giles was in love with him.'

She states it simply, her tone of voice completely matter-of-fact. But I know in that second that it is something she has never said before. 'I think he was in love with him until the day he died.'

I sit back down again. She looks relieved.

'Why couldn't you tell me?' I ask.

'All my life I have protected my brother – it is a difficult habit to break. Ever since I was a very small child I knew he was … different, but it was always unspoken. He could never tell our parents – my God, Father would have killed him. All through school and college he was bullied and abused. It was fine at Anderson's – he, Smithy and Will were thick as thieves – but soon after the bombing, the company was bought out by a larger firm and Giles was the only one in the research division who wasn't offered a job. My brother questioned it and eventually they said the other men wouldn't work with a fairy. He came home and confessed and our father's reaction was to disown him. Thank heavens he moved to London. It was Soho in the Fifties; there were places to go, there was a scene. I visited him a few times, but he was very discreet about his love life, even with me. I wish he'd told me more; I just want to know that he was happy. I'm sure he never quite got over Will, though.'

Here goes. *This* is why I am here. I clear my throat.

'And that's why he visited Will at the asylum?'

She doesn't look at me.

'Giles would come back to Bath at least twice a month to see him. He couldn't stay at home, so he would take hotel rooms, or stay at Will's house. I would only see him briefly; he'd take me to tea rooms. It was painful for him to be here, but he came anyway. I resented Will for that; especially because of what he got Giles involved with.'

'What do you mean?' I say.

She reaches out to the yellow dish and takes another chocolate bar. 'The hospital records aren't quite correct – it wasn't just Giles who visited Will. Smithy would go too. Smithy left Anderson's at the same time as my brother and started working for Military Intelligence, listening in to German radio communications, that sort of thing. He was an odd man, an utter egghead. He convinced the others that something had happened to Will the night of the bombing, something ... unusual.'

'What was it?'

'Giles would try to explain, but it just sounded like ravings. I remember one time, this would have been the early 1950s, my brother and I met Smithy at a café – he'd just got back from a seminar in Dublin given by some famous scientist. Smithy was very excited because he said it confirmed his own theories.'

'What theories?'

She sighs a deep, frustrated sigh.

'He told me the universe we live in is not alone – there are others all around us where things happen differently. I didn't really understand, I still don't. But I do remember one thing he said to me: "Whenever a choice is made, all possibilities are explored by the cosmos. Everything is always happening."'

I am back in the planetarium with my dad, and he turns and whispers that phrase to me, a lifetime ago, staring up at the universe, the shifting stars. I feel a surge of electricity down my spine so strong I almost cry out.

'Smithy was convinced Will was in the wrong place, that the bomb had opened something up, it had dislodged him, but that the mistake could be corrected. How did he put it? "The machine can be fixed." All I know is, Giles believed it and put himself at risk coming back to Bath to discuss all this nonsense. He thought he could save Will.'

'Did they talk about Elsa?'

'I don't know. I was a young girl, I was just worried about my brother.'

It's too much. It's all too much to hear, to take in.

'I have to go,' I say. I am up again, almost as quickly as before. The blood rushes from my head and I feel faint, but I go for the door anyway.

'Are you okay?' she asks, following me. 'You mustn't take any notice. It consumed the three of them, they obsessed over it for years. It made Will worse not better. Then Smithy moved to Berlin for his job and they never saw him again. Whatever they had planned, it fell apart. You have to let it go.'

I'm outside now, but I stop and turn.

'Do you have any of Giles's things? Could there still be anything left? Anything of Will's? Anything important?'

My heart is thumping hard against my ribs like a fist at the bars of a cage.

'No,' she says, exasperated now. 'There's nothing here.'

Static in the air like a storm coming.

'Then somewhere else?'

'Just leave it alone.'

'Tell me!' I am shocked at my outburst and so is she.

There's the sound of throbbing engines a mile above us.

'I have to know if Will really met Elsa – that she saw him at the gallery, that something happened between them. If nothing else, I have to know that!'

'Why?'

'I don't know! I don't know!'

But I do. It's about that girl with the wild red hair who had the strength to cross a continent alone. If I can find one thing, one shred of proof that Will and Elsa met and fell in love, then maybe there is some truth in what Smithy believed. Maybe there is a way to bring her back.

A gale blows across the street. The noise fills my ears. My hair is in my eyes.

'Please,' I say.

'You are a very fragile young woman,' she says, looking me up and down – my baggy clothes, my knotted hair. 'You would do better to focus on yourself and your own life.'

'This *is* my life,' I say. 'I have nothing else.'

292

The two of us face each other.

'Giles kept a case,' she says at last. 'A large suitcase, with a few of Will's things from the office. That's all he had. When he died, I kept some personal items from his house in North London, but I didn't see the case – his business partner arranged for a clearance company to take the rest so it was probably sold at auction or it's rotting on a landfill somewhere. I'm certainly not going to help you anymore on this foolish errand.'

With that, she disappears into her home, sure that her part in this bothersome quest is over. Behind me, the whole city is there, a thousand years of it, pouring out down the hill into the hollow. When I cycle away towards town, I glimpse the old buildings from a distance and I understand that they are both the past and the future. Maybe every journey we make is in two directions at once.

And, Valerie, the quest isn't over. Because I know there is some-where else to look. I know where the case might be.

Chapter Thirty-Six

The train to London is busy and hot, but I find a seat and close my eyes, composing my thoughts. Here I go again. Back to the city I tore through for six years, the city that hid me and broke me. It is probably fitting that my last shot at this mystery should be here, down a dark anonymous street that might not lead anywhere at all.

I decide that I need to look professional, like someone you would divulge information to rather than pity. This morning, I apply make-up carefully, and I put on a dark green midi dress I bought in Jigsaw when I first moved back to Bath but never wore. For the first time in ages, I look at myself in the mirror and think, maybe I'm worth the effort.

When I step inside Cooperton's, the air is warm and dry, and as before, there is music playing, this time a slightly mournful piano piece. As soon as I enter, I see the sales assistant I met last time; the young man with his quirky haircut and cool suit. He's polishing an amplifier, and when he looks up to greet me, he does a sort of double take. It's as though there is some kind of recognition there, although that can't be it.

'Excuse me,' I say. 'You won't remember me, but ...'

'No, I do remember you,' he says, putting down the cloth and smiling. 'You came in a few weeks ago. You were asking about Mr Cooperton, right?'

'That's right.' Despite myself I smile too, and the revelation that he recalls my last visit makes me feel stupidly bashful.

'It's nice to see you again! How can I help?'

'This is going to sound weird,' I say.

'I like weird. Weird is good.'

'Right. Okay. So Giles ... Mr Cooperton ... once worked for a wireless manufacturer named Anderson's in Bath. While he was there, he had a friend named Will Emerson. I believe Mr Cooperton kept something from the office, something of Will's. In an old suitcase. I'm wondering if there's any chance it's upstairs – in the old flat he rented to Jeremy Menzies?'

Because this is what I'm thinking. Giles and Jeremy were more than just business partners. And if that's true, maybe Jeremy kept some things of Giles's. Maybe he kept the case.

The assistant stares at me, and I remember how he did that last time I was here.

'Just a sec,' he says. 'I'll fetch the manager.'

He disappears through a door at the rear of the shop and after a minute, I begin to wonder if he's just back there fretting over how to get rid of me. Then he returns followed by another man, this one in his late-fifties, with a ruddy aristocratic face. In his navy blue blazer, V-neck sweater and striped tie, he looks as though he's on his way to a country club.

'My name is Donald Menzies, I'm the manager. Can I help you?' His tone is noticeably more abrupt than the other staff member's.

I start to explain the whole thing again, but now my confidence is flagging and the adrenaline I brought in with me is beginning to curdle into something more familiar. Throughout my explanation

I see – out of the corner of my eye – the young sales assistant gawping at me, as though he can't quite believe this weird trashy person has once again invaded his sleek domain.

'So you've come here from Bath?' asks Donald.

My mouth feels sticky and my throat hurts.

'Yes . . .'

'Giles detested Bath,' he says. 'That place had very painful memories for him. And I certainly do not think he'd want a complete stranger going through the last of his personal effects.'

'So there *are* a few of his things upstairs?'

He looks momentarily rattled.

'It doesn't matter. Giles was a private man as was my father.'

Now he is truly flustered. I understand that he has given me something more than he wanted to. I recognise all the tics of anxiety. I am an expert in the subject. I need to be careful. Jane always told me that establishing trust with a client involves humility and reassurance – she said I was good at those things.

'I understand this is a lot to ask, and I'm sorry to bother you. And honestly, I'm not here about Giles. I don't want to pry into his life. The suitcase was full of things belonging to Will Emerson. That's who I'm interested in.'

There is the merest hint of recognition in his eyes.

'Giles mentioned him?' I ask.

'He may have done. It was all such a long time ago. I'm afraid it would be quite out of the question for a stranger to go rooting around up there.'

We stand at this awkward impasse for several seconds as the music plays, and the shop assistant pretends to polish some equipment while stealing the odd glance at this weird ongoing spectacle. The progress I thought I was making is slipping away from me. But still, I can't let it go.

'Look ... okay. Something happened to Will during the war, something terrible and tragic and inexplicable. And I think there may be answers up there. This is a bizarre request, I totally understand that, but I'll be so careful and quick, and I won't bother you again, it's just that Giles's sister Valerie was so sure this suitcase existed and—'

'You spoke to Valerie?' says Donald with surprise and genuine interest.

'Yes, we met at the Assembly Rooms and then again at her house.'

'I have been wanting to get in contact with Valerie for years. Giles often spoke about her, but he kept her a little separate from his life here in London. I have some things, some photographs and letters I think she might like. I've not been able to track down any contact details for her.'

'I found her online.'

'I'm not very good with the internet.'

This is it. This is my bargaining tool. I take out my organiser.

'I have her phone number,' I say. 'I'm sure she wouldn't mind me sharing it with you. She told me she wanted to find out more about his life here.' I copy it out onto a blank page and rip it out for him.

He stares at the note, his face still stern and determined, then he looks right past me to his sales assistant. He's going to have me thrown out.

'I won't be long, Josh,' he says. 'Buzz me if you need me.' Then he turns to me. 'Five minutes. But I doubt you'll find anything useful. Come with me.'

Dumbfounded, I follow him through the rear door into a small corridor crammed with empty cardboard boxes and packaging. Turning a corner, we start to climb a narrow, winding staircase past the first floor, then upwards, at which point the walls become bare brick and the floorboards are dark and ancient. Neither of us

297

speaks. We reach a door at the top, which Donald opens with a large old-fashioned iron key.

'This was their flat,' he says. 'We use it for storage now, but, well, I haven't been able to clear it out entirely. My father was rather tidy, but Giles was a hoarder, always collecting gadgets and taking them apart, even when he became ill.' He holds the door open for me and I step through.

'*Their* flat?' I say.

'Yes. Giles and my father lived here together. My father . . . let's say he came to terms with his true self a few years after I was born and he and my mother divorced. He met Giles a year later and that was it.'

'I thought Giles had a house in North London.'

'He did, but he was hardly there. He stayed in it when Valerie came to visit. He never told her about my father. He didn't want her to have to keep a secret from their parents.'

The flat is a gigantic bewildering mess. There are cardboard boxes piled to the ceilings bearing the names of high-end stereo manufacturers. There are shop display units and rolled-up posters stacked against the walls. But beneath it all, you can make out the remnants of a living room – a mildewed carpet; an old sofa crushed under broken fax machines and printers; striped, rather stylish wallpaper. Donald winds through it all and I follow, towards two other doors. 'That's the bedroom,' he says, but doesn't offer me the opportunity to go in. I get a glimpse of a huge iron bed, extravagantly covered in blankets and embroidered cushions, the sunlight streaming in through a small window, a black-and-white photo on the mantelpiece of two men in beautiful 1950s suits, their arms around each other's shoulders, cigarettes in hand.

'This is where Giles kept most of his old things,' he says when he opens the door to a guest bedroom. The first thing I see is a wall lined from floor to ceiling with heavy wooden shelves. It's as though I'm back in Will's workshop, because here are the assembled innards of dozens of old wirelesses, all lined up amid transistor radios, hi-fi oddities and even 1980s home computers, many stacked haphazardly on top of each other like a crazed museum. Stuffed into small gaps are the little boxes filled with screws, wires and valves that Will also kept. There is even the same musty smell of grease and metal in the air. On the opposite side of the room, a small wooden wardrobe stands beside a writing desk which has a beautiful articulated reading lamp on it.

I wander along the shelves, peeking behind the larger wireless cases, hoping to catch a glimpse of a case. There are some magazines, a few books, a bundle of 78 rpm records, tied together with twine. I find two photo albums, and wonder if I'll get lucky and chance upon a photo of Elsa, but they're all in colour, and seemingly from the 1960s onward. Parties, business conventions, images of Giles and Jeremy on holiday – outside a Parisian restaurant or grim-faced next to a Punch and Judy stand, knotted hankies on heads. At the end of the shelves, in a dark corner, there is a wooden box with ANDERSON'S stamped on it, and I get excited until I open it and discover another radio, bedded in wisps of old straw. I turn and go through the desk drawers, then look under the desk itself. Nothing. When I get to the wardrobe, I know this is it, the final remaining hiding place. But when I open the doors, it's all clothes, musty and reeking of mothballs, some hanging along the rail others piled at the base. Donald must register my disappointment.

'Nothing?' he says.

I shake my head.

'I did try to warn you,' he says. 'Come on.'

He heads out and I glumly follow, but when I pass the bedroom door I stop. He stops too.

'No,' he says.

'Please. Just one look.'

'My father wouldn't have any clutter in there, it was his rule.'

'I know,' I say. 'But maybe it wasn't clutter. Maybe it was more important. Giles had really strong feelings for Will. Did he ever tell you that? Maybe your dad understood it? Maybe he knew that the past . . . you can't bury it. You need it.'

He shakes his head, but more out of exasperation than denial.

'One look,' he says. 'Then I would really like to get back to running my shop.'

At that moment, his mobile phone starts ringing and he backs away, shooing me toward the bedroom.

Inside, there's just the bed, a huge mirror on one wall with a wildly extravagant frame and two neat Deco bedside tables. If there were cupboards or wardrobes in here, they're gone now. All gone. The reality of it hits me. This is the end. I slump back and sit down on the high bed, bewildered by the disappointment of it. Outside, through the window, I hear the sound of the music coming up from the store below. I turn to it forlornly, trying to work out what it is; it sounds so familiar. And then the back of my foot knocks against something hard under the bed.

Chapter Thirty-Seven

There are four suitcases underneath. I look up to check that Donald is still busy on the phone, then I begin to pull them out and open them. Two are empty, another is full of crisp white bed sheets. The one I bumped my foot against is the oldest, constructed from brown leather, padded at the corners, the handle sewn to the face with thick stitching, a label tied to it. I take the label in my hand and turn it round. Written in faded ink is one single word. WILL.

Carefully, I pull the case out and place it on the bed. The handle is warm in my trembling fingers. It seems to throb as though carrying some sort of electric current. There is a sudden weird intensity in everything. The music downstairs fades away and the silence is as loud as anything I've ever heard. There are two latches keeping the case closed and they are dotted red with rust. I grapple with them, aware that I promised not to break anything. One gives almost straightaway, but the other seems stuck fast. 'Come on,' I whisper. 'Come on, open.' I'm almost clawing at the thing, trying to get my fingertips under it to give me more purchase. 'Open up!'

I seethe, feeling a surge of anger, feeling months of frustration flooding through me. Months of it, years of it. 'Come on!'

I get four fingers under the clasp and pull. I feel two nails break and almost scream with the pain of it. And then click. Snap. It opens. Breathing heavily, I lift the lid.

The start is not promising. A woollen scarf, a pair of leather gloves, mosaiced with cracks. But then, taking them out reveals the next layer; a family photograph in a carved wooden frame – two parents, two young boys in matching suits, all grim-faced. The next layer, a leather wallet, containing three old banknotes and some sort of medal, triangular in shape, bearing the words *República Española*. A leaflet about Civil Defence work. Then a coin, a two-shilling coin, dated 1938. I lift it up into the sunlight and I think, is this the one? Is this the coin Will said he'd tossed to decide on whether or not to call Elsa? I toss it myself and it comes up tails. That's when I see it. Below everything else, a hardback book with a dark green cover. I take it out carefully, slowly, and open it. Inside the blank first page there is a stamp that says BATH CENTRAL LIBRARY. The next page has the title.

Art Now by Herbert Read.

My breath goes. I feel my heart begin to hammer. I can see Will, I can see him so clearly, telling me about this book – the book that Elsa led him to. I hear a growing buzz, as though the air itself is expectant. Can it be? Can it be? I flick through, past images of paintings and artists, the smell of old paper, the yellow-tinged pages damp against my fingertips. The buzz in the air.

I don't know why, but I'm not scared. I'm not freaking out. Now that I am here, it feels like this was always going to happen.

Turning through the last few pages, I'm almost at the end when something falls out. Dumbstruck, I watch it drift to the floor like a feather.

It's a piece of paper. I lean down and I can see there's writing on it. In a woman's slightly scrawled handwriting are the words:

So here you are! Please let me know what you think of the book.
1 Bloomfield Crescent, Bath 2950.
Elsa.

In the corner, a small drawing of a cow.
Elsa.
I cover my mouth as the full weight of the discovery finally hits me. I feel the scorch of tears in my eyes.
It happened. They met.

Chapter Thirty-Eight

I feel my legs giving way so I sit down on the bed next to the case and let myself cry – with relief, with hope. They met, they talked and there is no way the Will I know, the Will I talked with and cared for ... there's no way he would have let her get away. Something happened the night of the bombing that tore them apart, something I haven't understood properly. All the other evidence, the evidence that separates them, the news of her imprisonment, her escape, her death, it's all wrong somehow – I just need to look at it from a different angle. I thought I was ill, I thought I was crazy, but I wasn't. The world is.

Then I hear the sound of someone clearing their throat and I look up to see Donald waiting for me in the doorway. I don't know how long he has been there watching me sitting on his father's bed, clutching this old book to my chest, my eyes swollen with tears. I don't know what he sees in my expression or if he understands what I've found. All I know is, after a few more seconds of silence, he says simply, 'Take it. It's yours.'

We walk back down the rickety stairs and out to the shop, and I am in a daze, the book wrapped in my arms.

'Giles did talk about Will,' says Donald. 'He was clearly an unrequited love. Giles visited him for several years, but then I think it all got too painful for him, and my father didn't like it. I remember once, Giles said, "Poor Will, he was in the wrong place at the wrong time" and when my father asked about the night of the Bath Blitz, Giles said, "No, not the bombing, after that. His whole life after that."'

I nod and thank him for his time and his patience. Then I walk out across the shop. The assistant stops me.

'You never called,' he says.

'I'm not really on the lookout for expensive speakers.'

'It wasn't about the shop. I wanted to ask if you'd like to go for a drink. Or something.'

I'm too confused to process what he is saying.

'I don't think so.'

The way I put it comes out wrong, it's too harsh. I itch with the awkwardness of this unexpected side-plot to the day. The fabric of my dress feels prickly. My glasses are really heavy all of a sudden. This is what it's like, I think, to be noticed.

'I'm not really in that place right now,' I say. 'But thank you. I really mean that. Thank you.'

On the train home, rumbling west through muddy fields, my mind is on fire. I feel like I have only a fraction of a larger puzzle. I have the past, but what of the present and the future? Even if Will and Elsa met and fell in love, what does this mean for us now? What am I supposed to do?

When I get home there is an answerphone message for me. It's Valerie.

'I have just had a very unexpected telephone call from Donald Menzies in London. It seems his father was much more than a business partner to my brother. He'd like to meet – he thinks we have stories to share. I should have realised about Giles and Jeremy, but it was you who found it out. I owe you a debt of gratitude.' There is a slight pause.

'Laura, when you came to see me, I called you fragile. Never let anyone call you fragile again.'

Chapter Thirty-Nine

'I made a mistake. A huge mistake. I don't think Will has dementia or any sort of mental illness. I want to retract the report. I think he needs to be re-assessed.'

It's mid-morning and the office is quiet. One of the carers I used to work with was just leaving as I arrived and she barely registered me as we squeezed past each other on the stairway. I made such a great impression here.

Inside, the care agency is just as it always was – ageing PCs on cheap desks, the walls covered in calendars and work rotas, grubby windows looking out over the clustered rooftops to the rear of Union Street. When I walked in, the smell of the place – the mix of cleaning products and whatever was last warmed up in the microwave – gives me a potent hit of the anxiety I always used to feel here. My heart thudding, my insides churning, the pressure on my chest like an immovable weight.

Jane is at her desk, looking harassed and tired. Her eyes betray a complete inability to process what I'm doing here or what I'm saying.

'Laura,' she says, clearly trying to maintain control. 'You don't work here anymore. You don't have to worry about it. I don't understand ...'

' ... I found something. In London. It's something that backs up Will's story about his life. I think he is mentally capable.'

My words are tumbling out, falling over each other to be free. I know I sound manic.

'Come on, calm down.' She gestures at the seat on the other side of her desk and I take it, trying to inwardly slow my breath, my brain. 'Whatever you've found, Will Emerson was exhibiting a range of behaviours that suggested he was not capable of making important decisions about his ongoing care. That whole incident with the boy down the road, his accident, the squalor he was living in, how aggressive he was with you at the end.'

'He was frustrated – with himself, with me. He's been holding onto this all his life. The past has haunted him, it's dragged at him, but he's never been able to deal with it. He's alone and lost. I know what that's like, Jane! I know what it does to you.'

She closes her eyes and sighs, then looks at me for a few moments.

'Do you not think, perhaps this is what it has always been about,' she says. 'It's about you and your life, and your dad and how he treated you. I think this whole thing with Will has been a way of dealing with that.'

'Please don't patronise me.'

'I'm not. I'm just trying to figure out why you're here when the very best that we can do for Will, is make sure he gets really good care for the last years of his life. He'll get that at the residential nursing home. And that is why, tomorrow afternoon ... '

'It's not the best for Will!' I burst in, really yelling now. 'It's for everyone else's convenience! He's a person, with feelings and hopes and history. He doesn't want to leave that house and I know why now.'

'The decision has been made, Laura! Even if I accepted what you're telling me. Even if I called social services and submitted a new report, it wouldn't make any difference. Will's solicitor has power of attorney and it's up to them. They've sold the house to the construction firm and that is completing soon. There's nothing we can do. You have to let it go, for your own sake.'

There's something in her tone that infuriates me – that cloying, sympathetic wilt. The verbal pat on the hand that says 'there, there'.

'This is wrong,' I mutter.

'Oh, for heaven's sake, have you been to see him recently? He's utterly non-verbal and unresponsive. We've found a care home. I've been trying to tell you! I am going over tomorrow afternoon with some of the staff and we're transferring him. It has all been arranged. He's not really Will anymore, Laura. I doubt anyone can reach him now.'

Chapter Forty

I use the key and step cautiously into the house. The art book, with its precious note tucked inside the pages, feels warm in my hands, like a life. The hall is still and silent, as though everything is normal, but as I pass, I see the rooms have been cleaned ahead of the sale. The furniture and rugs are gone from the parlour, and in the kitchen, the cupboards and fridge have been emptied of food. It is like a film set. In a few hours, Jane will come with some staff from the care home and they'll take Will away for ever. The house is being demolished. This is my last chance to reach him – and through him, Elsa.

So let's pretend Will's story is true. Let's pretend everything I've experienced in this house is real. What does Elsa want me to do?

I walk through the hall and on to the stairs, heading to Will's room, and I don't see his carer coming down in the opposite direction carrying a load of bedding until we almost bump into each other.

'Jesus,' she hisses. 'You scared the shit out of me!'

'I'm sorry.'

'This house is creepy enough as it is, without you jumping out at me. What are you doing here anyway? He's going to the home today.'

'I know, I just wanted to see him off.'

'That's fine, but he's not upstairs, we've moved him down to the library.'

I nod and turn back.

This room hasn't been touched. The books, the newspapers, the radiogram and piano, all still here. Will is in his chair and it is a shock when I see him. He is deathly white and ancient, like some desiccated body discovered in an ancient tomb. He is half sitting up, half slouching, a plain blanket over his skeletal body. His deep-set eyes are watery, staring somewhere very distant. I pull up another chair and sit down next to him, putting the backpack on the floor, but he doesn't acknowledge me at all.

'Will,' I say. 'It's me. It's Laura. How are you doing?'

Nothing. Beyond us there is the bustle of the street outside. The growl of engines, the distance hammering of electric tools on the building site. A world away.

I go back and sit with him.

'I know you said you didn't want to see me again,' I say. 'But I've found something.' I slide the book onto his lap. He doesn't move or look at it.

'Will,' I say, trying to sound friendly and bright, as though we are talking in his kitchen or a café, or a dance hall. 'It's the note from Elsa. The one she left for you in the library. I found it.'

I lift open the book cover and remove the piece of paper. When I hold it up to him, nothing registers in his expression. I have to keep it together.

'Would you like me to read the note to you?'

311

Nothing. His eyes are glassy and cold.

'It says, *So here you are! Please let me know what you think of the book. One Bloomfield Crescent, Bath 2950. Elsa.* And in the corner there is the little picture she drew for you – of the cow. It's a little faded, but it's still there, Will . . . Will?'

Autumn 1938, the Victoria Art Gallery. The two of them circling the room, tuning in to a shared wavelength, amplifying each other. It is clear to me, they were always going to meet. They had to. The sound of it is still in the air.

'Please,' I say, I take the two-shilling coin out of my pocket and place it with the other things. I feel tears gathering. 'Please, Will, it's the book you took out of the old lending library. It's the note from Elsa. You sat at work and didn't know whether to call her, but Smithy tossed this coin, and it was tails. It was the start of everything. Do you remember, Will? You have to remember.'

I'm leaning over him, my arm across his chest, the note in my hand, but there's no movement. His heart is a light stutter. I spent the last seven years drifting through other people's lives, trying not to connect, trying to keep moving; now I am here, stationary, and I don't want to lose him. He used to glare at me, his face furrowed, his expression impatient and unmoving. I was always getting something wrong. But he noticed me, he trusted me. Why did I betray him? I should have looked beyond the obvious explanations. I should have tried to understand what was happening.

An idea strikes me. It was always music that he reacted to, so that's what I need now. I quickly check through the records in the study, but just as I expected, the one I want is not there. But there's somewhere else it could be – I remember. I find a stepladder in the lean-to outside and bring it through the kitchen, lowering it carefully into the cellar, through the skeleton of the rotten staircase. After switching the light bulb on, I climb down gingerly, recalling what happened before – the sound of the typewriter keys, the message on the paper. This time, I know what I'm looking for. On the shelving unit against the rear wall, amid all the household detritus, Will hid one 78 record down here – perhaps he couldn't bring himself to throw it away completely. I pull out the portable gramophone player, and there it is, hidden away in a tattered mildewy sleeve. The disc is dusty and scratched, but seemingly still playable.

'Someday I'll Find You'.

Back in the study, I walk over and pull up the lid of the radiogram. Power on, volume up, not too loud, but loud enough. Deep breath. Place the record on the turntable. Gently, gently, lower the needle. The crackling is alarmingly loud and I hear the bumps as the needle skips. But then the sound softens out, and to my relief, the opening notes begin. With the curtains half drawn, speckles of light hit the walls like beams from a mirror ball. And what I want is for him to recall that first night in the Pavilion. The girl in the daring dress. The words of the song swirling above and around them; the lover waiting in the dreamy moonlight. He hasn't heard this song since they danced together in the garden all those years ago. It woke something in him then – can it now?

'I'm sorry,' I say, my head bowed because I can't look at him. 'I'm so sorry I let you down. It's just that no one ever needed me before.'

The music plays, the voice soaring above the whimsical melody; a voice from half a century ago, but here now. I sit hunched over, my face hidden in my hair, feeling the tears as they drop onto my jeans. Perhaps there are no second chances, not this far along. I want to call my mum. If I had a phone I'd call her and beg her to come.

In the background, the music plays on. The old song, a faint voice crooning over a dance band. The lovers reunited beneath a celestial light. I think to myself, if it fades and ends, then I'm lost.

I'm alone. The sound is so sweet, so lulling, I almost don't feel something grazing against my finger. The slightest touch. I daren't look. Then I can feel the note gently slipping from my grasp. But it is not slipping, it is being taken. There is a strained whisper, as light as organza.

'Elsa?'

Chapter Forty-One

His voice is so distant, I have to look up to make sure I'm not hearing things. He is slowly shuffling upright in the chair, holding the note, the faintest flush of colour in his gaunt cheeks.

'How?' he says. 'Where?'

'It was in a suitcase at Giles's flat in London. It was with some other things from your office.'

His wheezing breath quickens with the effort of thinking, of being again.

'You found it and brought it back for me?'

'Yes.'

'And it's real.'

'It's real.'

He looks up at me and finally makes eye contact, and the spark of him is there. He studies the note, tracing his finger along the lines of her writing. Then he picks up the book and flicks through it.

'There will be a hell of a fine on this,' he says.

He starts laughing, then coughing, and I put my hand on his back.

'Water,' he says. The carer comes in, roused by the noise.

'Can he have water?' I ask. She looks surprised, but nods and hurries away.

When she comes back with a glass, she says, 'You've got him talking? He hasn't made a peep for over a fortnight.'

'Can we be alone?' I ask.

She looks slightly insulted, but then slips away again.

'I dreamed of Giles and Smithy,' says Will. I hand him the water. 'They came to visit me, but somehow we were all young. Giles was giggling as always. I told them I wanted to go home, I wanted to see Elsa and asked them if I could. Smithy took a coin from his pocket and flipped it. He said, "Let the universe decide."'

The glass is shaking in his hand.

'There's something else,' I tell him, unsure of how much to say, trying to gauge how he'll react to the existential crisis I'm about to impart upon him. 'I think ... I think Elsa really *was* trying to contact us – she is in this house, or a different version of this house. Sometimes I've been in your workshop alone and the transmitter has switched on. I thought it was a warning, but now I think ... she was trying to talk to me.'

'I taught her how to use it,' he says.

'I was looking through my notes ...' I take my organiser out of my pocket and flip through the pages with a sort of maniacal zeal. 'And you mentioned that you had given Elsa one of your QSL cards. You said you'd written down your contact information, including the frequency you were transmitting on at the time. Will, what was the frequency? Because I think we have to get back to your transceiver and tune into that.'

He looks at me with an expression that hovers between hope and horror.

'I . . . I don't remember. It was so long ago, and my transmission frequency was always changing.'

'Just think, just picture the card you gave her.'

'I'm trying! All I see is a jumble of numbers.'

'Can't we just switch it on and scroll through the dial, listening? We might get lucky?'

'It's not that simple, the tuning is very fine. If Smithy were here he could . . .'

He stops.

'What?' I say. 'Smithy could what?'

But he is deep in thought, his haggard face crumpled in concentration.

'I once wrote one out for Smithy too. I was showing off my new card designs and I wanted to impress him.'

'But I've not been able to find Smithy!'

'It doesn't matter,' he says. 'Smithy wouldn't take it. He said to me, "Keep it, you might need this information one day." The card is still downstairs in the workshop.'

'Can you walk?'

Slowly and with audible creaks and cracks, he lifts himself forward. Then he stops and looks at me. 'Perhaps we are both mad.'

'Let's find out.'

He smiles weakly at me. 'You've changed,' he says. 'You were terrified of everything when I first met you. Now here you are, determined to drag me to the radio because you think Elsa is there waiting for me.' He looks at the note again, seemingly unable to believe it is here. 'I had given up.'

'Me too. But we can't. All I've ever done is give up and it's never worked out for me.'

I help him as he levers himself off the chair.

'I keep getting an image in my head,' I tell him as we shuffle

317

out. 'That photo taken outside Bath Central Police Station. Those women, dragged from their homes in the middle of the night, all looking scared and exhausted. Except the one at the end. The one with the wild red hair, staring straight into the camera like she's daring history to forget her. But I'm not going to.'

He nods slowly.

'Do you really think Elsa is out there somewhere? I can't allow myself to believe it. Even if I get it working, even if we find the frequency, we don't know if and when she is transmitting.'

'All we can do is go out there and listen.'

We walk through the kitchen, down the garden toward the workshop, and I am relieved to see through the little window that the radios haven't been taken away. Before opening the door, I pause for a moment and feel the pressure in the air that is always here in the garden, pushing out from a central point. The sky above us seems to hum with expectation.

Will takes the lead now, opening the workshop door and heading in. He goes straight to the transceiver station, sits at the chair and begins rifling through the drawers, pulling out papers and notebooks, all mildewed and almost rotten. Some of it falls apart in his hands, becoming confetti in the stale air.

Then he finds a small tin box and clasps at it greedily.

'This is where I kept my cards,' he says. He prises it open, sending dozens of cream-coloured cards spewing across the desk and floor, all of them displaying the same line drawing of the Royal Crescent. One lands right in front of Will and it is filled in, the ink faint and brownish. He takes it carefully.

'This is it,' he says.

'And the frequency?'

He looks up at me with an odd expression.

'It's 3.44Mhz.'

3.44

The clocks.

She was trying to tell me the whole time. I scramble to look at my watch, and while I do, I have this intense feeling that I am inside a machine, a mechanism, the interconnected cogs all fitting into each other.

'It is 3.30,' I say.

Will begins checking wires and connections, flicking switches, his fingers fast and agile. Another drawer contains spare valves, which he carefully removes and lays out on the desk. As I watch from a distance, he operates on the equipment like a surgeon, screwing off panels to reveal the dusty innards, then careful extracting and replacing components. He works silently, my presence seemingly forgotten – to such an extent that when he finally stands up from his work and says, 'Let's switch it all on,' I'm almost shocked. He shows me where to plug in the two sets, just beneath the desk where he can't get to. He checks the microphone. Then we are ready.

We stand quietly without moving, as though at a wake, and I wonder if he is praying, because his eyes are tightly shut. What must he be thinking? How can he prepare himself?

'This hasn't worked for years,' he says, more to himself than me. 'Who knows if . . .'

He hits two switches and I'm braced for nothing, for the whole thing to be an anti-climax, but there is a faint fuzz of static sound and the front of the transmitter begins to glow a warm orange. Will turns the tuning knob and the action is almost painfully slow, the sounds alternating between dead fuzz and static squeals. Not long ago, I thought I was losing my mind in here. Was I? What if they really were just withdrawal symptoms?

'3.44Mhz,' says Will.

Static. A couple of times I think I hear distant voices, but they slip away. A sudden whirling sound dissolves once again into the wash of white noise.

'This is madness,' says Will. 'We have had sixty-six years of silence.'

Sound fades almost entirely for a few seconds, enough for me to once again hear the construction vehicles on the site opposite, as though they are closing in. The air in here has never been so still – it almost looks as though the dust particles are frozen in the air like stars.

It's 3.44 p.m. Who knows if this is the right time? It's just a hunch.

Will sits at the desk and pushes a button on the base of the mic.

'Elsa?' he says.

Seconds tick by, then minutes. I don't dare look at my watch. Something in my head tells me it's okay if this doesn't work, because it would mean the world, the universe – they function in the same way they always did; it would mean we didn't live in a reality where voices of the long dead or long disappeared could come to us from somewhere else.

'Elsa,' he says. 'Are you reading me, Elsa?'

If we were meant to meet at 3.44 p.m., she's late. But what is a few minutes between lovers? Between worlds?

Will has his elbows on the desk, and he slowly moves the microphone away and puts his head in his hands. 'This is ridiculous.'

'Hold on.'

'What were we thinking?' he says.

'Hold on.'

'Hold on to *what*?' he says and almost laughs at the stupidity of

320

it all. 'I haven't seen or felt anything from her in 60 years, then all of a sudden, you come along and ...'

'Will, stop it! You haven't *let* yourself feel anything. You never moved on from the night of the bombing. You're trapped there. But this isn't about the past, it's about now. If you want to hear her, you have to let go.'

'But I ...'

'You have to trust her.'

Without saying anything more, he turns away from the radio, releases his grip on the microphone and closes his eyes.

'Elsa,' he whispers. 'Come in, Elsa.'

There is a curious quality to the air around us. It has the intensity of a gathering storm. I feel the hairs on my neck and arms prick up. Then, out of the dim darkness of the workshop interior, there's a shift in pressure behind us.

'You're right,' Will says to me. I put my hand up to shush him, but he doesn't see. 'Elsa couldn't reach me because I was never really here. But I'm here now. I'm here.'

'Will ... she's here too.'

There is a wild screech on the receiver, loud and almost ear-splitting, and it disorientates me so much I barely hear what follows – a woman's voice unbelievably faint and distant, awash in static. 'Will?' she says. The accent is unmistakably Germanic. 'Is that you?'

Will stands up, his chair tipping backwards onto the floor with a loud clatter.

'Elsa?' His voice is thick with emotion. The words all strangulated by years of grief. 'Elsa, where are you?'

The hissing, crackling noise seems to be all around us, and there are sounds buried underneath it all that could be a voice, although they are impossible to decipher. ' ... Lodge ... I am ... Smithy said ... Forever ... Buried ... Where are ... ' Snatches of words fade in and out, tantalisingly close, then very far, the voice of a swimmer on a raging ocean. But when I look at Will, he is listening and he is smiling. Can he hear her?

'I'm home,' he says, but not to me. 'At Avon Lodge. I've always been here.' But his voice, too, is fading beneath the interference, his words becoming fragments. What I am certain I see in this moment is an image of Elsa herself, stepping out of the dust and darkness toward Will. I am transfixed. I can't process what I am seeing or what it means for them, for me, for time and connection. The electricity in the air is so intense, I feel it on my skin and in my mouth. I don't know whether I really see her or whether it is the shape of the sound, the emotion in the room, the frequency of her.

And then, in the distant background, there is a noise from the house, and when I look out of the window, I see people in the kitchen, clearly heading to the garden. It is Jane with a social worker I recognise and two women in care home uniforms. The sight of them brings reality crashing back in.

'Will,' I say. 'They're here, they're coming.'

I don't know whether he takes this in through the howling noise of the radio receiver. The small group is in the garden now, Jane walking resolutely towards us – they must have noticed the door to the workshop was ajar and guessed where he would be. Will turns to me, finally aware again of my presence.

'Something happened here that night, some terrible cataclysm,' he says. 'I'm in the wrong place. But there is still a link between us. There is a way back, the fault can be fixed. But we must ... '

He tries to listen again. The group bundles in, all four of them. 'Mr Emerson,' says Jane, heading for him, 'you're not well enough to be out here.'

Will steps back but stumbles on the overturned chair. One of the carers goes to support him, accidentally slamming into the transmitter. From inside there is a faint pop then a fizz, and silence.

'She's gone,' he says.

'We'll get her back. We'll fix the radio.'

He turns slowly and looks at me, his eyes glistening. 'There are no more valves. It could take weeks to source another. It's over.'

'No.'

'They've sold the house. This will all be demolished.'

'It's okay,' I whisper. 'We'll figure it out. The important thing is, all the things you shared with me, they really happened – they weren't stories, they were memories.'

Chapter Forty-Two

Tupman's Solicitors is tucked away on one of the narrow streets south of the Abbey, around a corner from Sally Lunn's Tea Shop. The only evidence of the company is a small brass plaque next to the door of a narrow Georgian building, and I walk past several times before I finally spot it. I get a similar feeling to when I stood outside the British Library – that I'm out of my depth, that this is not somewhere I really ought to be. Every experience these days comes with a fresh set of fears and new parameters of both failure and possibility. I still feel the cold jet stream of anxiety through my body; I still feel the heavy nausea and dread writhe in my stomach like a pit of snakes. But I have to be here, because of the report I wrote and the disaster it set in motion; because Will is now in a tiny room in a care home and it's my fault. I am desperate now. Time is running out.

I phoned ahead yesterday. I spoke to a receptionist and tried to explain who I was and what I wanted – that I cared for Will and assessed him for social services, and that I needed to speak to them about the firm's decisions on his behalf. I was put on hold for a long time, and eventually a voice came back on the line telling me to pop in for a discussion. The tone was polite but strained. I was clearly an annoyance. That's one thing I *am* getting used to.

I push open the door and walk hesitantly through into a lush reception area, with two long leather sofas and a huge flatscreen TV on the wall showing the local news. A woman sitting at a desk in the corner peers at me from above her computer monitor. She is wearing a pink cashmere sweater and her hair is in a neat bun. I feel like I have walked into a glossy legal drama.

'I'm Laura James,' I say. 'I have an appointment with . . .' I stop there because I have no idea, and she hangs on the sentence. 'With someone.'

'Let me check,' she says, efficiently tapping at her keyboard. 'Oh yes, you're seeing Charles Whittaker. Just head on to the meeting room through the hall on the left and I'll let him know you've arrived.'

The meeting room has a large rectangular conference table with ten chairs and I have no idea where I'm supposed to sit, so I go for a place in the middle and try to adopt a position that makes me appear at ease. I'm wearing a skirt I haven't tried on for months and I can't cross my legs in it. My shirt is itchy. On the wall is a framed street map of Bath, which looks very old and I am studying it when the door opens and a man bustles in quickly, bringing with him a waft of unfamiliar but expensive-seeming cologne. Charles is very tall and narrow, with wavy greying hair and a three-piece suit that makes him look like a millionaire stock market trader. He walks past me and sits at the head of the table, putting down a large leather notebook and some cardboard folders in front of himself on the table.

'You're Laura James,' he says to me. It's a statement not a

question. 'And you're here about our client Will Emerson for whom you provided home care.'

'Yes, that is all correct.'

I am aware he is taking control of the meeting and that I have to stand up for myself if I'm going to avoid ending up outside in tears in three minutes flat.

'So how can I help you?'

'It's about the report I wrote . . . . the assessment of Will's mental faculties. I'm afraid I made a mistake. I thought he was suffering from dementia, but that's not the case. I'm sure he is capable of making his own decisions and I think he can live at home. I want to ask you to . . .'

'He can't live at home.' His voice is certain and absolute. A fact ticked off and closed.

'But he . . .'

'He can't live at home. We are very close to selling it. We're completing on Monday.'

The whole thing is falling away.

Charles sits back and looks at me, his arms folded across his chest.

'We need more time, there is something—'

'I'm sorry, but I was under the impression that you no longer have a duty of care over Mr Emerson. I'm not sure why this is a matter of concern for you.'

'We're friends. We've become friends. And there is something he needs to do in the house, something very important to him.'

'The social workers have told me he is unresponsive.'

'He was. Until I visited him. He is improving.'

Now, I stare back at him, trying to feign confidence, remembering my encounter with Jane, using the frustration and anger of that. And beyond it, I see my dad, who would sit in the same way with the same expression, glaring across the kitchen table at me when I'd failed my Maths or Physics homework, the books scattered between us. The whole through line of it, coming to an end point.

'Are you asking me to withdraw the house from sale?'

'Yes, just so we can ... '

'I am not going to do that. We have been given lasting power of attorney and our role is to make the best decisions for him.'

'But I don't think this is the best decision.'

'I very much disagree. Did you know Will's family have been a client of this firm for over a hundred and fifty years? His grandparents, his parents, him. This is not something we take lightly.'

'If you give social services a little more time, they can reassess his mental health and Will can go back home – then maybe with more intense, specialist care, he can—'

'You don't seem to be listening. Will Emerson cannot live at home.'

'But, with care ... '

'He can't live at home because it is unfit for habitation. After reading your report we had a full building survey completed. You were right – there is major subsidence, with considerable distress and deterioration in all the exterior and interior load-bearing walls. The house is effectively collapsing into its own cellar.'

'Could it not be repaired?'

'That would cost many thousands of pounds and there would be months of building work. He is eighty-seven years old.'

'Then can we just postpone the sale – for a few weeks, even?'

'No. I'm afraid that's out of the question. We're selling to the construction firm on the understanding everything will go through quickly. There's no chance they will agree to a delay. Besides, Will needs his finances in order for the care home.'

He gathers his folders together and stands up, clearly satisfied that the meeting is over. 'We'll exchange and complete on Monday. Until then, Mr Emerson obviously still has access to the house. If there is something you or he needs to do there, I suggest you do it right away. Now, if you'll forgive me, I have an important phone call at eleven.'

He is up and reaching for the door.

'The construction company,' I say suddenly, standing too. 'They'll demolish the house, won't they?'

'Yes, I'm afraid that's their intention.'

'Have you been there?'

'Not personally.'

'You should go – while you have the chance. It's right on the brow of the hill, overlooking the city. On a clear day, you see it all – the church spires, the Abbey, you can see Beecham Cliff in the distance. The street was bombed during the raid on Bath, a few houses either side were destroyed, but Avon Lodge survived. It's all Will has ever had or known. Don't you care? You're just going to let them pull it down? I suppose it's all business to you, none of this matters.'

Charles hesitates at the door then turns.

'I was working here in the 1970s, you know. Back then, they'd started bulldozing whole rows of buildings at this end of town. They pulled down Southgate Street, Philip Street, St James Street South. Shops, homes, cinemas, all gone in the name of modernisation – you could see them falling from this window. I'd walk home past the building sites and the grit would get in your mouth and eyes. I remember thinking it was astonishing, people going about their business as though nothing had happened, so many memories wiped away. I felt as though the streets were full of ghosts. I've never forgotten it. So please, don't tell me

what I think about this. I know it's sad. We'll do our best for Mr
Emerson and his house. You must use the time you have – that's
all anyone can ever do. Now, I really have to get on with my day.
I'll show you out.'

Chapter Forty-Three

The care home is called Lansdown Manor. It's a converted Georgian mansion set within a vast, neat lawn, barely half a mile up the road from Avon Lodge. The building is surrounded by pretty flower beds, and through the downstairs windows I can see a big communal room, dotted with armchairs where tea is being served by smiling staff. It's like walking into a TV advert for quality residential care. Jane and the solicitor clearly did the best they could with Will's savings. I am here because I feel I should see where Will has ended up. I should know how the story ended. This is where we are now. This is reality.

I leave my bike outside the main entrance and the doors slide open for me, welcoming me into a large reception area, all marble floors and huge potted plants, like a spa hotel. A smartly dressed woman at a glass-topped desk looks up at me as soon as I'm inside.

'Can I help you?' she asks.

'I'm here to see Will Emerson.'

'Are we expecting you?'

Who is 'we'? I think to myself. Everything feels surreal and creepily theatrical, as though I'm involved in some sort of sinister dream sequence. This is not how it is supposed to end. As she waits for me to answer, her expression fades into a sort of confused grimace.

'Yes. Yes, I phoned ahead.'

The efficient smile returns.

'I'll get someone to take you up,' she says brightly.

I'm guided along a wide sunlit corridor and into a lift by a carer in a smart, light blue dress, which is clearly the home's uniform. 'He's in his room,' she says with a blank professional smile. The lift moves very slowly and the air feels dense and hot. When the doors open she says, 'Follow me.' It's another wide corridor, lined with overly pretty watercolour paintings of the Abbey and Royal Crescent. I walk slowly because I'm scared of what I'll find; I'm scared he will be strapped into a gurney, drugged up to his eyeballs. Everything about this visit feels rife with dreadful possibilities. I suddenly wish I'd listened to him when he said to me in the hospital, let's say goodbye and never meet again. But then I remember Elsa, the radio transmission, the possibility they could reconnect – the possibility that now seems doomed. I shouldn't be here – that's why I feel so weird. I should have just got out when I had the chance. Now I'm stuck in a horrible limbo between hope and hopelessness. And I have to see him, because I know there hasn't been closure and if I don't see him, he'll haunt me for ever.

The carer knocks on his door, then thrusts it open.

'Mr Emerson,' she shouts. 'You have a visitor.' Then she turns to me. 'Go in.'

The interior reveals itself as I push forward, a neat, empty little room with an oatmeal-coloured carpet, a little coffee table, a large window looking out over the front lawn – and there in an oversized armchair, looking outside toward the Bath skyline, is Will, dwarfed in the seat like a sickly, withered child. The sorrow of it almost makes me choke.

'I saw you ride in,' he says.

I look around the room, trying to think of something positive to say, anything apart from, 'Tomorrow your home will be sold and then demolished and whatever Elsa wanted us to find will be lost for ever.' The room is so warm, but I am shaking.

'You don't have any of your things here.'

'They say they will collect anything I want from the house.'

'What about one of the wireless sets. The transmitter? It could still ...'

'It's blown,' he says it with a soft almost indulgent smile. 'The parts can't be replaced.'

'Another one then? We could buy a new one. We could make contact again.'

'It had to be that one.'

'How do you know?'

'I just do.'

'Maybe ... maybe we could figure it out ourselves. She said there was a way back. The answer is in the house somewhere, it must be.'

'The house will be a pile of rubble next week.'

There is some sort of electrical hum, a heater perhaps. It is a dead noise, a flatline.

'We got so close, so close,' says Will, looking around the tiny room. 'But I'm in the wrong place now.'

And really, hasn't that been the story all along?

I don't remember leaving the care home. I don't remember how I got outside, if I found my own way or if one of the staff spirited me away. But seemingly in the blink of an eye, I'm outside, clambering onto my bike, pedalling fast and erratically in my desperation to get away, my eyes blurry with tears. I veer onto Lansdown Road and a van swerves and beeps at me; a man leans out the passenger window and yells, 'Watch where you're fucking going!' I cycle fast down the hill, and don't want to look at Avon Lodge as I pass, I just need to get away from that place and everything about it. But I do look, and then I skid to a halt, swerving the rear wheel round so I don't go straight over the handlebars. Florence, Will's elderly neighbour, is standing outside the house looking up at it like a lost child. I've never seen her outside before, and something about the image is unsettling.

I wheel back toward her.

'Florence?' I say.

'Hello,' she replies, not looking away from the building.

'You've heard?' I don't have to say anything else. She turns momentarily toward the property development, the huge glass and steel building emerging from behind the tall plywood hoardings that enclose the site.

'They've been after Avon Lodge for years,' she says. 'Another relic of the past to be quietly euthanised. They don't understand – some things are outside of their control. There is still something to be done.'

'But it's all set,' I say. 'Avon Lodge is going to be bought and knocked down.'

For the first time she looks away from the building and toward me.

'We'll see,' she says. And this time, she's smiling.

I get home, exhausted and bewildered, and I can't find my keys so I have to knock and hope Mum is in. She opens the door almost immediately, a mini vacuum cleaner in her hand.

'I'm dusting,' she says. 'You look terrible. Come in, I'll make some tea.'

I'm halfway up the stairs when I hear her yelling from the kitchen. 'Oh I almost forgot. You got a phone call from Will's solicitor.' I stop on the stair and turn back. Mum comes through and looks up at me. 'He said to call him. He said you ought to call him right away.'

Chapter Forty-Four

'There's been a ... development.'

I'm on the phone in my bedroom, cross-legged on the bed. The receptionist answered on the second ring, but I was on hold for an age before Charles finally picked up.

'What?' I say. 'What's happened?'

'Just before we were about to exchange, I got a call from a local property developer. He'd heard about the sale to the construction company and wanted to put in an offer: ten thousand pounds above the asking price – in cash. He said he wanted to save the house, renovate it. Morally, I should have turned him down immediately. Gazumping is not illegal, but it's pretty dirty.'

'What did you do?'

'I thought about our little conversation.'

I almost daren't ask. 'And ... ?'

'Morality is an ambiguous concept, is it not?'

Florence must have already known the building was safe when I saw her outside. She wasn't saying goodbye to Avon Lodge, she was revelling in her success. Her son Matthew will not be demolishing the house, but according to Charles, he will have to get started immediately on a massive refurbishment in order to save it. The interior will be gutted, the workshop pulled down and the garden dug up to provide foundations for an extension. Charles also told me that Matthew is happy for me and Will to pop in and out if we need anything – although time is short; the house, the garden – they will soon be unrecognisable.

A week later, I sit in the Society Café on Kingsmead Square, watching the crowds wander past, a group of homeless men on one of the benches, sharing a bottle of cider. I still feel dizzy with the pace of recent events. The house isn't being demolished. There's still a chance to discover its secret. Is this the end we were always meant to be heading for?

The news has lifted Will. Over the past two days, he's started making trips out of his room and making unreasonable demands of the staff – a heart-warming development. One of the carers said to me, 'No one is really meant to start getting better at eighty-seven.'

But if we're going to find something, we have to do it soon – the building work has already begun. Now, sitting here in this café, one question lurks at the back of my mind like a spectre. Really, truthfully, how am I ever going to understand how Will and Elsa can be together? I can't structure my questions into coherent thoughts, or my thoughts into questions. I spend hours reading through the notes in my organiser, following meagre leads, the pages filled with notes and diagrams, the connections I have drawn and imagined between things, the patterns I've seen. Smithy's obsession with science and the experiments he spoke of send me to Google, my mind wandering through wormholes and multiverse theories. If there are parallel realities, can we travel between them? Does the fabric of spacetime sometimes tear? Could a bomb do that? If you fall through, how do you go back to where you are meant to be?

You can figure this out, I think. Somewhere in the house, there's a way back. We have everything we need, we just have to put it together.

I have the timeline I displayed on my bedroom wall and I roll it out along the table in front of me. I trace my finger along from 1938 to 1942. And there is a vague memory nagging at me. It involves something Will told me about the immediate aftermath of the bombing. In my head, I journey back to the night. Will came round, he was injured; presumably the little boy, David, was dead. What happened next?

I bundle my organiser back into my bag, finish my coffee and scramble for the exit. I have to go back. To see the garden again before it is churned up beyond recognition. I have a gut feeling the answer lies in knowing exactly what happened that night. Maybe then I'll know what to do.

Chapter Forty-Five

When I get to the house, the garden wall has been demolished and there is a large yellow skip in the front yard. Two sections of fencing have been taken down on the right-hand side, so that work vehicles can be driven in and out of the back garden. I walk over and peer through. The place is a mess. A digger has been driven over the lawn and parked at the far side, churning up all the grass. There is a large pile of wooden planks outside the workshop – the shelves that used to hold the radios. Everywhere, discarded tools and buckets lie about.

'Looks like a bomb site, doesn't it?' says a voice from beside me. It's Matthew, with his smooth confident face, wearing spotless work trousers, green wellington boots and his purple scarf. We look out over the mess of the garden. A few workmen are removing tiles from the roof of the workshop, passing them down to the ground below.

'Thank you,' I say. 'For saving the house.'

'I don't think Mother would have forgiven me if I hadn't. She's seen so much of this area being destroyed. It's our chance to save something. I have big plans. Big, but sympathetic to the old place. We're just about to start digging the foundations for an extension.'

I'm only half listening though, watching the builders near the workshop. One comes out from inside, his face grubby, yelling something at the men on the roof.

'What a mess,' I say quietly. I am glad Will isn't here to see this.

Matt looks in the direction I'm staring.

'It's got to come down,' he says. 'The joists are rotten and the walls are all slanted and buckling, like they've been hit by a truck or something. I'm surprised it's still standing at all. It must be difficult, though – to see this?'

'Do you mind if I go into the garden? I won't get in the way.'

'Be my guest,' he says. 'This house ... it has a real atmosphere to it, doesn't it? Gave me goosebumps when we first looked round. We have to work fast though, the whole thing really is on the verge of collapsing.'

Standing in the middle of the garden, the noise of the construction work, the landscape scarred, piles of debris lying about, I try to picture that night – the night of the bombing. Will woke up, the boy gone, presumably dead. Then what? A few men came to help him. I look around me at the churned-up grass, broken pieces of furniture from the workshop, bricks half buried ... a breeze whips up around me – in it swirl what look like flakes of ash. The workmen are arguing about something, their voices raised. A man had grabbed Will's arm. He yelled something ... 'You saw it, didn't you? You saw it!' ... Will said he had looked terrified. He had witnessed something inexplicable in the garden; Florence, too, had seen a weird light above Avon Lodge, but her bedroom overlooked the street – she couldn't have seen the source of it. Not like that man did. But no one believed him.

A spark of déjà vu. Something half remembered and groggy. I've

339

been here before. A rescue, a voice. Somebody blacked out, and when they came round, there were people trying to help. Is this Will? Is this his memory?

Somebody fetch her some water.

No, it's mine. The art gallery. I fainted and the curator came to help me. I didn't make a damn note because I was out of it. We talked about the war exhibition, about the video recordings of the survivors, the witnesses ... 'We couldn't use them all,' she said. 'Some of them were very strange.' I've been following the strands, tying up loose ends, feeling certain that I was on the only route through the chaos. But I was leaving stuff behind. There was a thread waiting, begging to be pulled. It was those interviews from the Victoria art gallery exhibition. Some have never been shown to the public. Did the man in the garden take part? Have they been kept somewhere?

What did he see?

Chapter Forty-Six

I arrange to meet the curator in the little rotunda area next to the upstairs gallery. There are low leather chairs in a circle and behind them three large marble sculptures of women in flowing robes, giving the small space a sense of grandeur. The curator is already here – when I phoned she seemed very happy to chat. On the table in front of her there's a brochure with the word BLITZED in dramatic letters on the cover, and a battered A5 notebook. She spots me and smiles, beckoning me over. 'There's a coffee machine,' she says, gesturing behind her, 'I'm not sure I'd wholly recommend it.' But I don't want any stimulants right now – I feel edgy enough as it is. I still get that rise of tension and alienation with new people, as though I'm play-acting a version of myself that I'm not familiar with.

'So you're interested in our 1995 exhibition?' she says. 'It was one of the first I worked on. We showed lots of local artists of the era, people like Leslie Atkinson and Clifford Ellis, and we had photos and diaries – we even had the weathervane salvaged from the ruins of St James's Church. But it was the interviews you want to know about?'

'Yes, that day you helped me in the gallery, you said there were some you couldn't use in the exhibition?'

'Quite a few in the end,' she says. 'Lots of them repeated similar stories. We did collate them and shared the archive with the council, but some we didn't keep.'

'Why?'

She pauses for a second, clearly struggling over how to phrase her reply.

'I think I mentioned it last time, but a couple of the interview subjects were ... a little eccentric. The things they remembered didn't really make a lot of sense. I wonder if perhaps their tales had become embellished or they had misremembered or got confused. We thought it best not to use or archive those.'

'Did you keep them anywhere?'

'I think so, but I'll have to dig them out. Was there anything specific you were looking for?'

'I'm hoping you may have spoken to a particular witness. I think he was a firewatcher or air raid warden, stationed up on Lansdown Road. There's a chance his story would be ...'

She holds her hand up in an excited gesture of recognition.

'The bright light guy,' she says. I stare at her. 'One of the strangest interviews we did. A firewatcher who'd been stationed up on Lansdown.'

'Yes!' I say. I need to remain professional. 'Do you have that interview?'

She sits back in her chair, deflated.

'No, we don't, I'm afraid. When the project started, we hired this really experienced local videographer to handle the interviews – he'd been recommended to us and it all seemed fine. But then after a week's filming, he suddenly left the project. Not only that, but he took that day's footage with him – and when we asked for it back he became very angry and abusive. The Lansdown interview was the last one he filmed. We were able to get another cameraman to take on the job, but it wasn't the best start.'

A local filmmaker. Angry. Abusive. I get a horrible cold feeling, like being lowered into icy water. I don't want to ask, but I have to.

'Do you . . .' I take a breath and swallow. 'Do you remember his name – the first videographer?'

'I have it written down somewhere,' she says, picking up the notebook from the low table. She flicks through the pages for what seems like an hour. I sit back, trying to be calm.

'Here it is,' she says. It can't be him. There must be hundreds of freelance camera operators in the South-West. And yet, I feel a horrible, dawning sense of inevitability – like a tired animal finally caught in a trap by a ceaseless predator. 'His name is Michael James.'

Chapter Forty-Seven

The sound of his name hits me like a punch in the gut. It's him, it's Dad. The impact of it takes my breath away and the room starts to spin, the sculptures looming over us. The curator leans across and puts her hand on my shoulder.

'Are you okay?' she asks. She must think I am prone to fainting spells.

'Yes. It's just that I know him. I mean, I *knew* him. A long time ago.'

How did this happen? How were we both drawn to the same place, for the same reason, a decade apart? And then another realisation hits me.

'When ...' I have to struggle to get the words out. 'When was this? When did he do the filming?'

'It would have been the January before the exhibition started.' She goes through her notes again. 'Yes, here it is. His last day of filming was January fourteenth.'

January fourteenth, 1995 – the day he came home, packed a bag and disappeared from our lives. Surely the two things can't be connected? What the hell happened in that interview? Whatever it was, I need to know, because there may be a clue on there about Avon Lodge that night. And there's only one way I will ever get to see that footage.

I spent years trying to get away from Dad, moving on every time he made contact, getting rid of my mobile phone, all my social media accounts, staying off-grid as much as possible. But it didn't matter, it was all for nothing. We both seem to be cogs in the same machine, clicking slowly and inevitably into place.

But he'll be in his seventies now. Is he even alive?

Mum gets home from work just before six and I am sitting waiting for her in the living room, trying to look relaxed. For the past hour I've been rehearsing what to say and how to broach it with her. We have avoided talking about Dad at all costs; a decade of tiptoeing around the subject while the trauma of him hung in every room like a noxious smell. But this can't wait. Avon Lodge is being torn apart – if there is some way back to Elsa, we need to find it now. I need to know what the firewatcher saw.

She bundles into the room carrying two shopping bags, making straight for the kitchen without even seeing me. I get up and follow her – my plans already falling apart. She is cheerfully transporting tins of soup from one bag to the cupboard.

'Hi, Mum.' Something in my voice makes her tense up straight away.

'What is it?' she says. 'What's happened?' Her ability to read me has become uncanny. Or maybe it's just that my life is a constant drama. I have to come straight out with it.

'I need to see Dad.' For a few moments her only response is to slowly close the cupboard door. 'Do you know where he is?'

She leans heavily against the kitchen work surface.

'Why?' she says. 'Why now?'

'It's about Will.'

At first she looks confused and then cross.

'What on earth has your dad got to do with Will? And you're not even working there anymore!'

She turns back to the bag and delves in for another can, clearly hoping this is all just going to go away.

'I've been visiting Will, trying to help him come to terms with things.'

'What things?'

'What happened to him during the war.'

'He's eighty-seven, Laura! Isn't it a bit late for therapy?'

'It's more complicated than that.'

'But why *you*? Why do *you* have to do this?'

'Because I'm the only one who cares or believes him.'

'And what help do you think your father is going to be?'

'He filmed some interviews with Bath Blitz survivors and I need to see the footage. I think one of them was a neighbour of Will's.'

'But Laura, the last thing you need is to see him again.'

'I know.'

'I don't understand what is happening with you.'

'Mum, neither do I. But I need to do this.'

She edges toward me and puts a hand on mine.

'I ... I can't,' she says. 'I can't let him be near you again. It was my fault – what he put you through. All that pain and damage. It was my job to protect you and I didn't. I was afraid and I failed. So no, I can't put you back in touch with him. I can't do it.'

I look at her and I see the colour has drained from her face. It's so easy for me to forget sometimes, that I'm not the only victim in this house.

'It's *his* fault,' I say. 'His.'

She doesn't answer, but almost imperceptibly, she shakes her head.

'Mum, remember that time he came home pissed out of his head from some work function – I was eight or nine, and you took me to a restaurant in town and let me have ice cream for starters, and main course and pudding because that's what I needed? Remember when I was thirteen and I was trying to choose my GCSE options and Dad told me I didn't have what it took for the careers I wanted? You sat with me and got me to write down all the jobs I dreamed of doing, and then you wrote down next to them all the skills I had that matched them?'

'I don't. I don't remember.'

'I do, Mum. I do. That's how you protected me. You listened to me and you knew me – you knew what I needed. That's how I got through. But I need something else now. I need to know where he is. Can you help me?'

Chapter Forty-Eight

I'm going to visit my father. Those words sound utterly unreal. We've spent the last few months rooting around in Will's sad and desperate past – now it's time to face mine. He is old and weak, but I didn't sleep last night thinking about it, my heart pounding, sweat soaking through my T-shirt. I wasted my twenties hiding from this man. But still, I have to do this. Yesterday, I called Will to tell him what I had discovered at the gallery. He didn't want me to see my father either.

'Even if this man was interviewed by the gallery, even if your father still has that footage, how can it help us?' he said.

'If we know what happened that night, it might lead us to Elsa.'

'How?'

'I just have a feeling the answer is there. Besides, we're running out of time. They're demolishing the workshop, they're starting work on the house. We need something now.'

'Do you have to travel far?'

Slough. After he left us, Dad headed back to the town where he grew up. According to Mum, he has a flat there. She is desperate for me not to go, but she has lent me her car so I don't have to deal with trains and taxis. I sit in the living room, looking out of the window summoning the courage to leave, reassuring myself that Dad might not even be there. I haven't phoned ahead – I didn't want to hear his voice. Not until I see him. I want all the shock at once, like ripping off a plaster.

I'm just leaving the house, when I see a taxi pull up. The driver gets out and quickly runs round to the passenger door, opening it and bending almost all the way inside to help someone out. That someone is Will. He's wearing an overcoat and a flat cap, clearly dressed for an outing.

'What are you doing here?'

'I'm coming with you. To your father's house.'

We stare at each other across the pavement as the taxi pulls away.

'How did you get out?'

'It's a residential care home not a prison. And they've realised the reports of my senility have been greatly exaggerated.'

'But you're only just back on your feet. This is going to be stressful.'

'I've survived everything else,' he says indignantly. 'I *shall* be accompanying you.'

A woman walking a tiny Yorkshire terrier barges between us amid our impasse.

'Why?' I say to him.

'Because you need a friend.'

The two-hour drive passes in awkward silence, both of us lost in our thoughts. Dad's flat is in a small block named Steel Court, a 1960s red brick edifice, three storeys high, the walls dotted with broken satellite dishes and CCTV cameras with the wires hanging out. When we pull into the car park, there are kids cycling around and one stops to stick his fingers up at us.

349

'Nice,' I say quietly.

'Shouldn't they be at school?' asks Will.

I park up and sit at the wheel staring through the windscreen.

'I think I should go in alone,' I say. 'Just to begin with.'

I can feel Will looking at me, starting to say something then deciding against it.

'There is a nice little coffee place over the road,' he says, pointing to what looks like a derelict building with a sign saying RON'S CAFÉ above a large, grimy window. 'You can come and get me when you're ready.'

'Thank you.'

I'm still not moving.

'Are you sure about this?' he says.

'No.'

'You don't have to do it – not for me.'

'It's for me. I have to do it for me.'

He smiles and puts his hand on my arm.

'Then go get him,' he says.

At the main entrance there is a large wooden door with a cracked wire-mesh glass panel and beside it an intercom with two rows of buttons. Deep breaths. Focus on the task. I am here for a reason. I tap the button next to Dad's flat number. While I wait, I contemplate getting back in the car and driving away for ever. Then a sudden burst of noise.

'Who is it?' a voice says.

'It's Laura.'

In the long silence that follows, I wonder what is going through his mind. Perhaps he thinks I have finally seen his emails or listened to his phone messages. Perhaps he thinks I am here to let him apologise and explain, to forgive him.

350

'Come in,' he says at last. 'Take a left and I'm second on the right.'

There's a loud buzzing noise from the door, and I push it open. Before I can step in, I have to wait for a few seconds to let a wave of nausea wash over me. Inside, there is a smell of cheap institutional cleaning products; the floor tiles are glossy grey like a prison, the walls are hospital green and smeared with dirt. As soon as I take the left turn and look down the long corridor, I see my father standing wraith-like outside his door. The sight is utterly shocking. He looks so old, leaning heavily on a walking stick, his thin frame bent forward. He is wearing a creased shirt tucked into a pair of elasticated trousers, and his grey hair is thinning to nothing. He looks up at me like a beaten dog.

'Laura,' he says. 'You don't look like your mother. You don't look like either of us.'

Ah yes, this is what I remember. Oblique comments, delivered in a dry monotone – I hardly ever knew if they were compliments or crushing insults, and he never clarified. The hours I'd spent feeling hurt and upset but not knowing if I should be, which was worse. My whole life I've been unable to accept positive comments – I've distrusted people who are nice to me. This is what you did, Dad. I'm standing in the corridor trying not to cry, wiping my eyes with the tips of my fingers, hoping my mascara won't smudge. Maybe a year ago, I would have run, but not now. I'm not here for his apology or his approval. Fuck him. I just want the footage.

I follow him inside his little flat, through a narrow hallway into the living room. It looks like what I guess it is – an alcoholic's doss house. There is a threadbare 1970s sofa, a torn filthy carpet and an electric fire with burn marks on the woodchip wallpaper above it. That's it. There's one photo on the wall of me, Mum and him on holiday in Italy in 1990 – the World Cup year. We're sitting by the pool in a cheap holiday resort. My expression is guarded. A miserable smile. He sees me looking at it.

'Happy memories,' he says hopefully.

I don't even nod.

'Can I get you a drink? A tea?' he says.

'I'm fine.'

'It's no trouble.'

'I'm fine.'

'I'll make one anyway.'

He disappears into a little kitchen. As I walk further into the room, I see a cabinet in the corner, crammed with bottles – supermarket vodka and gin – most of them almost empty.

'How is your mother?' he calls. I hear a kettle being filled and cups being clanked down on a work surface. I don't want to make small talk, I don't want any friendly gesture to be mistaken for forgiveness.

'She's fine.'

He leans into the room.

'You look well,' he says. 'You're looking after yourself?'

'Yes.'

He hasn't asked why I'm here, but I sense he's holding off on that – trying to elongate this period of polite chat so he can get the measure of me. A sick sense of anticipation bubbles in my stomach. It is the ghost of my childhood, waiting for an outburst, certain the next thing I said would be the thing to set it off. But standing here, now, in his wretched little room, I also feel something else: a sense of control, of sympathy even. It's not just that he is a pathetic shadow of the man he was, it's that I have more of myself to call on.

He emerges from the kitchen holding two mugs. I take one, noticing the yellow tinge of his skin. Outside the window, the traffic buzzes past relentlessly. I can see the café where Will is sitting alone.

'So,' he says. 'How have you been?'

I almost burst out laughing. 'You think we can just pick up again like that?'

There is a brief hint of darkness across his face, a tinge of impatience, anger even. I can still spot it. Something deep down inside me, something uncontrollable and instinctive, is coming to the surface.

'You made it very hard for me to contact you,' he says. 'And now here you are.'

'I didn't want you to contact me.'

'I understand. I know I wasn't the best father, but I ...'

That's it. The trigger I've been waiting for.

'No!' I say. The word comes out with such force he almost jumps. 'You don't get to finish that sentence. There's no "but". I don't want to hear excuses.'

'I just want to try to explain!' His voice is a desperate plea.

'I don't want to hear it.'

'Things were very difficult for me. There are things I couldn't bring myself to tell you about my past. My parents were killed in the war, I was taken far away. I grew up in a children's home – a brutal place. I never felt that I belonged anywhere, and then I—'

'Stop.' I want to put my hands over my ears. I can feel adrenaline coursing through me – a thudding energy that now needs somewhere to go.

'... My job, it was so stressful – the pressure, the long hours, I couldn't cope, and then, the commission at the art gallery, I—'

'I said, STOP!' My voice reverberates around the empty room. 'It's always about you! It always has been! My whole childhood was about accommodating you, making you feel better, not annoying

353

you, not interrupting you, not asking you for anything when you were busy or tired, and you were *always* busy and tired. We did everything we could for you. But what about me? I grew up thinking I was in the way – how could I ever get over that? And then sometimes, you were the nicest dad in the world. And that – *that* – is what made it so fucking cruel – because I lived for those moments. So I don't want to hear you explain everything away. You ruined me, Dad. You ruined my life.'

To his credit, he does not look away. I rub at my eyes with my palm. Too late to worry about mascara now.

'I know,' he says softly. 'I should have got help. You deserved better.'

My throat is hurting so much from trying not to cry. I don't want to give him that. I don't want him to think he's been able to apologise. Instead, I storm over to the table and put the mug of tea down.

'I'm here because I need your help,' I say. 'That's all.'

'Anything,' he says.

'The footage you took from the Victoria Art Gallery. I need it.'

He puts his tea down too.

'What? Why ever for?' A pause, as a realisation seems to come to him. 'Laura, do you know something about . . .'

'For God's sake, do you have it?'

He visibly flinches.

'Yes . . . Come with me.'

I follow him back to the hallway and into another small room. 'My office,' he says. It is chaos. On one side, there is a narrow oak desk with a surprisingly up-to-date computer and monitor, buried amid camera equipment, dirty plates and newspapers. Above the desk is a large cork board, absolutely covered in pieces of paper and Post-it notes pinned in huge clusters, and along the opposite wall is a row of five identical filing cabinets, some drawers half open, bulging with cables and camera equipment. It looks like the sort of place you'd find a shadowy hacker in a Hollywood spy movie.

'This is what's left of a lifetime's work,' he says, ushering me in. He pulls out the chair next to the desk and slowly lowers himself onto it, grasping the computer mouse. The display pings into life.

'What do you do now? Your mother hasn't told me anything.'

He is busy going through files on his computer, but I know he is listening intently. This is the way he always asked me about my day, about school, about my life: short questions, while doing something else. I don't want to give him anything, but I don't want him to decide not to help. I have to play at being his daughter.

'I am – I *was* – a carer. I've been looking after—'

'How did you find out about this footage?'

His voice is becoming strangely agitated.

'The gallery told me you had it.'

'Did you read one of my letters? My email messages?'

'No.'

He looks at me in agonised confusion. This is clearly not the way he was expecting things to go.

'If you haven't read my letters, why were you looking for it?'

I can't understand what his emails and messages have to do with this.

'It's for someone I was looking after. We're trying to find out about something that happened to him.'

'I thought you were here for me. For us.'

'What do you mean? This has got nothing to do with you.'

Dad is clicking on menus, scrolling through windows, his hand shaking on the mouse, making it reverberate against the desk. He turns to me. There is an emotion on his face that I've never seen.

'But you're wrong, Laura. You're wrong.' He clicks on an icon. A window opens on the PC showing what looks like television static.

A video starts playing on the screen. It is a sharply dressed old man with a warm smile, sitting on a chair in what looks to be a corner of the Victoria Art Gallery. A voice asks where he lived during the war, but Dad skips through the footage. I see silent segments of other interviews, but he buzzes through those too. Then he pauses the video.

'I'm interested,' he says, not looking away from the screen. His tone is slightly quizzical, as though trying to understand or recall something. It feels as though he is trying to regain some control over the situation. 'Did your mother never tell you? I was born in Bath.'

He starts the footage again. There is a man in his late seventies talking about being a firewatcher during the bombings, but it's not clear yet if this is the witness I need. While I'm watching, there is an invasive train of thought that won't go away. Dad was born in Bath? What year? I'm working backwards, doing the maths. He was a child during the war. He'd have seen the bombing. He'd have been there.

'I had an excellent view of Bath from my rooftop,' the man says. 'I was up on Lansdown Road, you see.'

'This is it,' I say, moving closer to the screen.

Dad turns slowly to look at me, his withered face slack and questioning. He is watching me, waiting for me to work something out.

'What are you really doing here?' he says.

He starts to lift himself from his chair, leaning heavily on the desk. As soon as he's up, he backs away from me, further into the room.

'I don't know what you mean.'

'You do! You must!' He shakes his head incredulously. Then looks at me again. 'Who is your client? Who are you here for?'

'The second night was chaos,' says the man in the video, his voice high and weak, like a child's. *'There was no organisation, a lot of the volunteers didn't show up, you see. Some were injured, some were exhausted, others had fled with their families. I was spotting sticks of incendiaries dropping all over the area, but I had a devil of a job reporting it in.'*

'Dad, what is it?'

He can't talk, I think for a few moments that he's having a stroke. In the background the video keeps playing.

'I saw the Assembly Rooms go up,' says the man. *'Oh, it was terrible. A terrible thing to see. And then Lansdown Road itself was bombed, three in a row, all down the street –* boom, boom, boom, *the explosions came closer and closer. I was in a bloody panic, I'll tell you that.'*

'Who is the man you're caring for?' demands my father. 'What is his name?'

'What happened next?' asks the interviewer on the screen.

'His name is Will,' I say to Dad. 'Will Emerson.'

Dad looks as though I have physically struck him. 'My God,' he says. He shuffles backwards and leans heavily on the window sill. 'It can't be.'

'Did you know him? He's here. He came with me. He's in the café over the road.'

'No,' he says. 'It's not possible. Is this a joke? Are you ... is this your revenge on me?'

'Dad, do you know him?'

The man on the video pauses for a moment, shaking his head. *'And then I saw the strangest thing. I was looking down over the roof, following the line of bombs, waiting for another explosion, I was sure the next one would hit the house at the end of our row, Avon Lodge it was called ... and instead, there's this blinding white light around the house – a dome of light. I can't explain it. But there was no sound, nothing. It seemed like all the sound in the world had stopped. And when the light faded, there were two bodies lying in the garden. It was as though something had brought them and left them there. And I recognise 'em. It's Will Emerson, and then it was the little lad from up the road. Oh, what was his name again?'*

My mind is whirring. Dad was six in 1942. He lived in Bath. He has no recollection of his family. He would never tell us about his childhood. The man is still talking on the screen. *'Later on, the boy and Will were taken away. Will came home eventually, I'm sure of it, but I never found out what happened to that child.'*

Dad stops the video. He is looking at me, but also at some point beyond me, to something else. 'They took me away in an ambulance,' he says. 'I told them about the light in the sky – how we fell through it. They said it was shock. My whole life I knew I was in the wrong place. When I heard that man talk about it ... it confirmed everything.'

Finally, the cogs click into place.

'You're him,' I say. 'You're the boy. You're David.'

But Dad has his face in his hands and he is weeping. I hear a sound behind us and turn round to find Will standing there, looking at us, his mouth open in shock.

Chapter Forty-Nine

28 April 1942

I know what the sirens mean. The bombing planes are here. Everyone said they would fly over us and go to Bristol. Mummy told me Bath wouldn't be bombed because it's not important. Daddy once said that if the German men did drop their bombs here, someone would tell him on the radio, and he would shoot them down. He is in the RAF and he flies a Hurricane. He has already shot down some German planes. I wish he was here now, but they told me he is missing in action. Everybody is missing in action.

The planes did come, even though people said they wouldn't. On the first night, Mummy woke us up and we had to go to the cellar and stay there all night. When it was the morning, we went outside and it was all smoky everywhere, all over the city. Mrs Dyson came and said her church had been blown up. She was crying and Mummy made her tea. Why did they blow up a church, though? I wanted to go into town to look but Mummy said no. I asked her why Daddy hadn't shot down the planes and she said it was a big war and he had other planes to shoot at. I asked if I could go and see Will and Elsa and she said yes.

Will and Elsa are my favourite neighbours. They live three houses away. Will has got lots of wireless sets and he has shown me how to work them. I help him fix them and change the valves. Once we did Morse code with someone in Holland. Sometimes, he lets me listen to *Children's Hour* with him, and we sit in the workshop. Elsa brings us cake. Elsa is teaching me to play the piano. I can do 'The Grand Old Duke of York' and 'Baa Baa Black Sheep'. She comes from another country and Hitler made her leave. I am glad she is here. She's funny and tells good stories. She knows a lot about pictures and music. Will and Elsa are in love a lot. You can tell because they always look at each other in a kind way.

On Saturday night, it was very late and the bombers came back. This time, the booms were much closer and my sister was very scared and cried but I didn't cry. Mummy shouted at the planes, and this made my sister even more scared. We went down to the cellar again, but the bangs were so close that Mummy said we might have to leave the house and go to a shelter. She went upstairs to look and was gone for a long time. My sister was crying. I had an idea. I thought if I could go on Will's radio, I could do Morse code to my daddy and he could come and shoot the planes. Even if he was very busy in France, he would come if he knew they were bombing our house now.

I left my sister and went up the stairs. There was no sign of Mummy, but the back door was open, so I ran out. I ran through the back gate and along the alley. The sky was all black and red, like a picture of Hell that they showed us at Sunday School. I had to keep running. The noise was loud. Sirens and planes and shouting. I put my hands over my ears and kept running until I got to Will and Elsa's house. I knew they wouldn't mind if I went to the workshop to call Daddy because I had a mission. So I climbed over the fence and went in. It sounded like there was a monster outside coming closer and closer. I couldn't remember how to use the radio, so I pushed the buttons over and over again. I pushed all of them. I was saying, 'Daddy, Daddy, come and help us. Daddy, I don't know where Mummy is.'

And then Will was at the door and he said we had to go. I could see bits of fire all around him and I was scared. He picked me up and tried to take me back to his house. I could see Elsa and she was in the doorway. She looked very frightened.

That was when I saw the light. It was very white and all around us, but only me and Will were in it, everything else was gone. There was a bomb floating down, but very slowly. I didn't know whether it would land or explode. Will said, 'Hold tight,' and we fell away. When I woke up I was lying on the ground and people were helping me. They said Will was gone. They put me on a stretcher. I was crying. I asked for my mummy and my sister. One man asked me where I lived, I told him the house number. I saw another man look at him and shake his head. I tried to stop crying because Daddy said, 'Always be brave, you're the man of the house when I am away.' I didn't recognise anyone who was coming to help me, and there was something strange about everything. I asked someone where I was, and they said, 'You're in Bath, lad, you're safe.' But no one understood. They said I'd had a shock and I had to be brave. Everyone told me how brave I would have to be.

When I woke up in hospital, it was night-time and nobody was with me. I remembered what Mummy told me when I got lost on holiday. We were shopping and I ran off to look at something, and when I looked round, I couldn't find Mummy. It was so busy and there were lots of ways to go. I wandered about and I thought I'd never see her again. Then a lady leaned down to me and she said, 'I think your mummy is in that shop,' and she pointed. As soon as I went in, I found Mummy – she was asking everyone if they had seen me. She hugged me very tight and let me cry. When I felt better, she said, 'Next time, remember that the universe likes to be neat. When things get lost or out of order, it will make sure the pieces find their way back together. You just have to say "I'm lost, I'm not where I'm supposed to be" and listen out for the answers. Someone will come.'

In the morning, a woman came to see me in the hospital. She had a clipboard and a form and she wrote a lot of things down. She said, 'You are going to live with a lovely family in Bathford for a while, and then we will find you a place to stay with lots of children like you.' I said, 'What about my sister, will she come? She gets very worried without me.' The lady went back to her notes. She was trying to write something but she had to stop to wipe her eyes. I told her I was learning to play 'Baa Baa Black Sheep' on the piano and Elsa was teaching me. She asked who Elsa was. Then she said, 'David, we're going to do our best to take care of you.' I told her the secret that I like my middle name best. She said, 'What is your middle name?' and I said, 'Michael.' She smiled and said in a whisper, 'Well, we shall call you Michael from now on. How would you like that? After all, Michael James is a very handsome name.'

Just when she was supposed to go, I held on to her hand and I said to her, 'Something's gone wrong. When the light came, we fell through a door that wasn't there. I don't think I am where I am supposed to be.' She smiled again but then she walked out. I waited for someone, I waited for the universe to tidy up. But no one came.

Chapter Fifty

2008

'Will?'

The voice is Dad's. He is standing now, the two men facing each other for the first time in over sixty years. With considerable trepidation they move closer, their shuffling feet noisy on the laminate flooring. I stand up too, trying to comprehend the fact that my life is caving in on itself, the different parts of it fusing together like a nuclear reaction. I thought I was here to help Will, I thought I was outside of his story, an observer – but I'm in it too. I was in it when I first stood outside that house, I was in it from birth.

'Dad?' I say. But I can't even begin to think of what my question is. He is not looking at me, anyway. He is looking at Will. Time passes as slowly as an orbiting moon, and it is me who has been eclipsed.

'What happened to us?' says Will.

My father goes to reply, but instead his mouth hangs open, gaping and silent, the necessary words seemingly irretrievable.

Will shakes his head. I look at him as he tries to make sense of it all, as he casts his mind backwards through the decades toward the things he lost, or simply blocked out.

'Smithy,' he says, almost entirely to himself. 'Smithy knew. It is coming back to me now.'

'What was it?' I say. 'What did Smithy know?'

'The place we woke up after the bomb blast, it wasn't the place we were in before. He said a tear was opened, a fault line. We fell through. A timeline like ours but not ours.'

My dad nods. 'I was a child, but I could tell even then. The world seemed different. There were little things that weren't the same. People missing, buildings gone. They weren't bombed, they were just never there.'

'Or they were somewhere else ...'

'... Because different decisions had been made, different outcomes emerged.'

'The coin toss,' I say. I open my bag and drag out the time-line, rolling it out onto the desk. 'You met Elsa at the Pavilion, she wrote the note for you in the library, but then you couldn't decide to ask her out, so Smithy tossed the coin. That's where everything diverges. You woke up in a world where the coin had come up heads.'

There is a look of shock and realisation on Will's face. 'Giles and Smithy, they came to me in hospital. I told them about Elsa. We tried to work it out together.'

'The newspapers,' I say.

'Cooperton collected them for me. He brought them to the hospital. We were highlighting the stories that differed from the events as I remembered them. He helped me write the journals.'

Concussed and traumatised, Will had been working through it all – it wasn't just that Elsa had gone, his whole past had changed.

Everyone thought he was insane – including himself – but he wasn't a madman, he was an immigrant, a stranger in a strange land.

Will collapses onto one of the chairs. 'This can't be.'

'But you must know it's true,' my father says. 'I never felt like I belonged here, I struggled for years to understand why. As soon as I heard this man's story, I knew what it meant.'

'That's why you left,' I say. 'That's why you left us.'

'It wasn't because I didn't love you, it was because I'd always, always felt like an intruder – and when I heard that man speak, it confirmed everything. And I know, oh Laura, I know I spent your whole life making you feel like an intruder too. I wanted to explain, but you wouldn't listen, you ran away.'

'It was too late by then!'

We're silent for a moment, all trying to figure out our roles in the world unfolding before us. I want to get up and leave – I want to be out of there, far away from Dad, from Will, from the bomb that followed me through time and detonated in my life.

'Does the witness say anything else?' asks Will.

My dad pauses. 'Yes, but, I don't think ... '

'I need to know.'

I glare at Dad, willing him to answer. He looks at us warily.

'After the bright white light, he said ... he said he saw the bomb land in the garden. But it didn't explode – it just sent a lot of earth flying. He climbed down off the roof and ran over to the house, and he found us there in the garden. He claimed that when the rescue squad finally turned up, he told them everything he'd seen but no one believed him. They thought he was in shock. According to him, the bomb disposal team never investigated it, but he was adamant in the interview: a bomb did land in the garden.'

'We were sent from one timeline where a bomb exploded to another where it didn't?' says Will. 'So it's still there?'

'If it really did land, yes, I expect so – buried deep under your lawn. Bath is probably filled with unexploded ordinance. I doubt it's dangerous if it's not disturbed.'

Will and I look at each other, our faces mirroring each other's alarm.

'The building work,' I say. 'They're digging a trench right through the garden.'

Chapter Fifty-One

The drive back seems to take an age, Will dozing beside me, exhausted by the day's events. I'd asked Dad if he wanted to come with us. He told me no. 'I am where I deserve to be,' he said. As we approach Bath I'm half expecting to see a mushroom cloud rising above the rooftops. 'Should we call the police?' Will had asked before we left. But what would we tell them? That we had footage of an eccentric old guy who vaguely recalled seeing a bomb landing in a garden over sixty years ago – just after witnessing a mysterious dome of light? As soon as we're on the A46, I tune the radio to the Bath station, and listen out for the news. To my relief, the first bulletin is all about the completion of the new shopping centre in Southgate. So is the next one. I put my foot down and keep driving.

I am thinking of my dad as the city becomes visible in the distance and I half hear the next news bulletin beginning. So many things about him make sense now – the darkness that hung over us all for so long. I remember how lost he always looked, how bewildered. I have to make sense of this new reality. Somewhere in the background, there's the newsreader's voice. '*An area of Bath has been cordoned off by emergency services this evening . . .*'

I am still thinking of Dad and Will and Elsa as we pass Beckford's Tower.

'*Eyewitnesses say police arrived at a house on Lansdown Road . . .*'

'Laura,' says Will, rousing himself. He turns the radio up.

The tyres slip beneath us.

'*Builders may have disturbed an unexploded Second World War bomb . . .*'

There is already a cordon across Lansdown Road as we arrive. A couple of officers are directing the cars ahead of us to turn around and go back, but I swerve into a parking space.

'Stay here,' I say to Will, trying to control my growing sense of panic.

I climb out of the car and walk as calmly as I can over to another officer who's being shouted at by a hassled-looking woman.

'She is a pedigree cat, I am not leaving her,' the woman says.

'You can't go back to your home,' the officer tells her. 'You have to wait for the all-clear.'

The woman storms off. He turns to me wearily.

'Is everyone out?' I ask. 'There were lots of builders working at Avon Lodge.'

'Yeah, it's clear. We're just waiting for the bomb disposal team. To be honest, it's unlikely to be a bomb, they just dug a trench and hit something metal. It's probably just a bloody pipe. You should stay back, though.'

It's okay. Everyone is safe. I feel a rush of relief, and start walking back to where I parked, keen to get the news to Will. But as I look through the windscreen I stop in my tracks.

He's not in the car.

I look around desperately, but he's not among the small group of residents gathering behind the police cars and he's not further down the street. Then it dawns on me with horrible certainty where he has gone.

As the police officers deal with the increasingly frustrated home-owners, it is easy to creep unseen along the houses, then behind the trucks outside the property development. Heart thudding, breathing fast. When I get to Avon Lodge the front door is wide open. In the hallway a strange breeze tingles on my face. The hairs on my arms stand up. Forwards, past the parlour and the study, both empty and quiet. Somewhere, a distant humming begins. I can see myself, just ahead, walking down this hall many weeks ago for the first time, drenched from the rain, my shoulders hunched. I can see Elsa in a blue cotton dress, her hand lazily tracing along the wall. It feels as though everything is existing here at once, thrumming against time, and this can't go on. Something has to give.

I step through the doorway into the kitchen and it feels like I'm wading in water, like when you try to run in a dream and your legs are useless. I know what I'm going to find and I don't want to find it. The hum has become a rumble, as though being generated by something of incredible, unearthly power. The back door is open, and I go to it and walk through. Then I stop.

Will is standing in the middle of the garden, his back to me, right on the edge of the long deep trench. I make a gasping noise, even though I knew I'd see him – where else would he be? But I don't want it to be true.

'Will?'

I walk up to him very slowly, hearing my own breathing, then

369

stand beside him. I look down into the chasm and I see what he's staring at: a metal object half submerged in mud and rusted to the colour of dried blood.

'It's a five-hundred-kilogram high-explosive bomb,' he says calmly. 'Probably on a timer or pressure fuse that failed to trigger. It's strange, isn't it – all this time, the answer has been buried here, waiting for someone to find it. Now all it requires is a nudge. You need to go,' he says without looking at me. 'You need to go right now.'

'Will, please.'

He turns. I realise that beneath his coat he is wearing his smartest clothes; the cloth trousers with the high waist, checked shirt and a tie. His hair is neatly brushed. He's smiling. In his hand, he has a shovel.

'Laura, it's okay.'

'Please, Will,' I put out my hand. 'Please come with me.'

He's still smiling but he shakes his head.

'This is what we've been leading to the whole time.' His voice is so quiet and calm.

'It isn't,' I say, and there's a lump in my throat so I have to force the words out. 'There's another way. We just have to think. We have to think about it together.'

'It's over, Laura. This is how we correct the error.'

'What are you saying?'

'You know, my friend. You know.'

'You can't. Please. Please, Will. Come with me now.'

'This is where I belong, not in that bloody old folks' home.' He looks up again. 'It's almost here. You can feel it in the air, can't you?'

I can. I hear it. The hum in the distant sky.

'I don't want you to go.'

'I know.'

'I need to take care of you.'

'Not anymore. You saved me months ago. I was lost for years, for decades, before you arrived. It's all right now.'

'I don't have anything else. I don't have anyone. I got everything else wrong. I've wasted all the time. It's gone.'

'It isn't gone. It's inside you. You have to go. You can't come with me. If you stay in the light, you'll be lost for ever. You've got to live.'

The humming is louder, louder, I feel it pushing me aside, as though trying to expel me from the garden, from the house. I wipe my tears away and stand against it.

'You told me once . . .' I stop, my breath catching. 'You told me once that not everyone will find love, that it's rare.'

'I did.'

'I don't think I'll ever have it.'

Will shuffles closer to me, and lifts his hand to my face.

'Oh, Laura, I was wrong,' he says, his face impossibly young. 'I was wrong the whole time. That's why I couldn't hear her – because I closed myself off for all those years. I was asleep while life happened around me. But you, you're wide awake.' The sound is rumbling through the ground, I feel it in my bones. 'Now I'm awake too.'

He looks up at the sky. 'They're here,' he says.

As the wail of sirens begins, there is a scent around me of violets and I sense someone nearby, just at my shoulder. A voice whispers, 'Laura.' Her voice is calm and kind. 'Go back.'

Even though I can't feel it, my legs are moving. I don't realise until I'm in the kitchen, and then through the hall, that I am running fast. It feels like the walls are closing behind me, as though the house is unpacking itself. All the years of the place are seeping out. The cobwebs are falling from the ceilings, there is a speckled

371

light on the walls, like fresh floral wallpaper. When I burst outside and look back, the gate closes on its hinges. The walls are sooty.

I'm out onto the road when the sky cracks open.

It doesn't sound like a bomb blast, it's like time itself is suffering some horrible fracture. A darkness billows out above the house like a black wave, the force of it lifting me off my feet and throwing me across the asphalt like a ragdoll. I lie there, clutching at my ears, screaming through the fury as dark objects pass across the sky above me.

But there is no noise. There is utter silence.

Cautiously, I open my eyes and find my glasses beside me, miraculously unbroken. There is blood dripping from my nose, and my ankle is horribly twisted. The pain is sudden and massive. But I have to get up. Slowly, I drag myself to my feet, and I see it – a weird curve of light around me refracting at the edges of my vision like lens flare. It's as though the space is encapsulated in a gigantic dome, a ghostly half-moon. I look at Avon Lodge and there are houses either side of it and all the way up the street where the development site should be. I look back toward town and I see firemen in old-time outfits – a man in a tin hat with ARP stamped on the front is gesturing toward them in silent slow motion. People in blackened clothes. An old motor car swerves through. I have to get out. I can't be inside the light when it fades. I can't be taken. I attempt a single step and it's agony. Another step, and it feels like my bones are crumbling. I want to cry and drop to my knees. But then up in the window of the house a few doors down I see a pale little girl staring out at me, her hair in two long neat plaits. I know she has been watching me, urging me on. She raises her hand and waves very slowly. I've got to go. Two more shuffling steps. My future is out there, I will need all my strength to reach it. My hand breaks through the light, but it is already starting to

372

shift and shimmer. *Laura, please, it's inside you and you can do it. If you're going to live, you have to move.* I lift my leg. One step, but God, the pain. Please. I'm seeing stars; I'm a little girl in the planetarium with my dad, thinking the whole universe is out there waiting for me.

And for her, for her, I drag myself forward and through and free.

I turn back to Avon Lodge and call out, 'Will!' Then in an instant the bubble bursts, the light closes into the house, and then it's gone and I feel certain that reality is collapsing in on itself and I am gone too.

Chapter Fifty-Two

26 April 1942

I hear a muffled voice, some distance away, calling my name. There is a ringing noise in my ears, which grows more insistent by the second, and I can sense flashing lights nearby. My body feels as though every tendon is stretched to breaking point.

When I finally summon the strength and bravery to open my eyes, it takes several seconds to comprehend where I am.

I am in my bed, in Avon Lodge. Everything is simultaneously recognisable and alien – the furniture, the wallpaper, the door to the hallway, opposite me. But as my senses realign, emerging from shock and silence, I understand that everything is utterly different. The walls are lined with prints, which have been carefully cut from magazines, there is a dress hanging on the wardrobe door, and as I move my head in the direction of the window, I see that it is blocked by a heavy fabric, pinned to the wall. Blackout blinds.

The surge of adrenaline is instant. I sit up in the bed and the speed and painlessness of the movement confirms the instinct dawning on me somehow from deep inside. I am not eighty-seven. The ringing in my ears is an air raid siren. I am back.

In a single movement, I am out of the bed and at the window, tearing aside the blind. The sky is on fire. I can hear the throbbing whine of the bombers coming in from the north for another run. I have to remind myself to breathe, and for a second I almost faint where I stand, but I clutch on to the window ledge and screw up my eyes, trying to clear my mind of the sensory bombardment. What is it Laura used to do when she was anxious? Grounding, she called it. Telling herself where she was and what she was there for. I am at home, it is 1942. What am I here for? And then it hits me.

Elsa. Where is she?

If I am back, then why isn't she in bed? Is this a kind of purgatory? Or hell? So close but yet . . . David. David is in the workshop. I look through the window again and this time what I see is almost too much to comprehend. Amid the flashes of the bombs, and the haunting light of flares, I see a figure running across the garden, wearing a man's trenchcoat over a nightdress. It is unmistakably Elsa, the sense and shape of her returning immediately to me as though the previous decades had never passed. Elsa. Running to the workshop. This time, she is going for David herself.

Without thinking, I am out of the room, scorching down the stairs, processing little snippets of my surroundings on the way. The hall carpets new and clean, the walls freshly papered. The sounds of the aircraft, coming in now, lower than before and gaining in volume, and I know these are the ones. This is where the future comes from. I leap the last few stairs, confident all of a sudden that such a physical endeavour is possible – and I'm right; rebounding against the wall, I ricochet into the kitchen, still running – and the dark room is lit up orange with the fires from the city below. I have to stop her, or save her, or save both of them. By the time I reach the kitchen door, she is nearing the workshop, and I yell at her, 'Elsa! Elsa come back!' And for the first time, she turns and I see her face, and all of time melts away. It's her as she was, as I remember – and in that instant I understand that years of memory did not add anything to her, I did not idealise her at all. She is what I always saw: beautiful and determined – her physical presence utterly unavoidable, almost transcendent amid the darkness and noise. She looks at me, raises her hand and shouts in return.

'Go back!'

The words reach me through the cacophony of engines and explosions, and the other noise I had forgotten about but now fills me with chilling familiarity: falling masonry. Go back. That short command has haunted me through time, I have heard it almost every night in my dreams. Only now the roles are reversed. Elsa has gone for David, instead of me. She is trying to change history.

Just as she is prising open the workshop door, I go to follow her – all my senses and emotions are yelling at me to do one thing – to go after her, to bring her back to the house. To get her to what I feel is safety. But she looks up again, and with greater force and urgency this time, she screams, 'Go back, Will. Listen to me!'

And this time I stop.

Despite instinct, despite love and urgency, I stop.

Because last time this happened, I got it wrong. I ran when I should have waited. I ignored her when I should have listened. Now the line of aircraft is almost overhead and I know the bomb doors are opening so that their cargo can be delivered onto our street. Elsa shoulder barges the workshop door and she is inside, I see her moving into the room and saying something. There is a high-pitched scream from above. The payload has been dropped. The future is coming. I look up but can see nothing through the darkness and swirling ash. When I jerk my head back toward the workshop, the door is closed. Has she run out? Is she coming across the garden? There is grit and smoke in my eyes. I step back into the house, wiping at my face, almost falling backwards onto the floor. Despite myself, despite my instinct to go out there and run for her, I step backwards, backwards, like she said, toward the cellar door. In the same moment, there is a massive blast in the garden, the force wrenching me from my feet, hurling me down into blackness. They say you don't hear the bomb that comes for you. They're always right.

This time I am not unconscious. I am lying at a crazed angle on the stairs, my head toward the cellar floor, half buried amongst bricks and shards of wood; thick smoke is billowing everywhere, filling the air around me like flood water. Struggling on to my hands and knees, I have to claw my way upwards through the rubble – from the kitchen there is an eerie red glow and a thought hits me that the whole of the house is on fire. But I'm not thinking of Avon Lodge, I'm thinking of Elsa.

My hands are sticky with something as I wrench my way up and it's only when I reach the top of the stairs that I realise it's blood. I have been tearing myself to pieces on broken glass. The kitchen is apocalyptic, the whole rear wall blown out, little fires burning around what's left of the room. Through the drifting smoke I see glimpses of the garden, a churned mass of mud and burning shrapnel. And there in a split second of clear air I see the workshop, collapsed in on itself, flames shooting from the crushed window, far up into the sky.

'Elsa!' I yell.

I try to stand up and step forward but the agonising pain and angle of my foot tell me my ankle is broken. There are sirens in the distance, but they are so far from us. It's too late. Somewhere deep

377

inside me, a voice says with quiet confidence that Elsa couldn't have survived. If she ran from the workshop, she would have been caught in the blast. But if she stayed . . .

I'm crawling forward now, out through the wreckage of the house and into what's left of the garden. The noise from above is receding. The bombers are leaving. Now, the sounds of aftermath: the screams of the injured and bereaved, motor cars carrying nurses and rescue squads. I keep crawling forwards toward the workshop, knowing it's hopeless, summoning the last of my courage to greet what is waiting for me in there. Amid the ruin, I can just make out the remains of the radio transmitter, burned out and broken; the armchair where Elsa used to sit, lying on its side. On my knees sobbing, I watch as the smoke clears.

And somehow, beneath the weight of the fallen roof and walls, the sturdy work table is still standing intact, the door leaning against it like the entrance to a child's den. I try to see underneath but a bank of thick black smoke wafts in from the houses up the street and for several seconds I can see nothing, my eyes streaming with tears. I rub at them, rubbing and rubbing, my chest convulsing with coughs. Then at last, I look up again.

Through the last of the smoke, I see her. Walking steadily towards me, stepping over twisted metal and chunks of fallen masonry, her face bloody, hair caked in mud, the trenchcoat blackened. She is carrying the boy in her arms, his body white against the horror like an angel. She stayed where she was. She got under the table, the sturdiest thing in there and she waited it out. Go back, she had shouted to me. She was right.

Slowly, painfully, like a punch-drunk boxer, I rise to my feet and stagger towards her, as she moves towards me. Then she is there, and we are together, and we look at each other for the first time in six decades.

'It's you,' I cry. I lift my hand to her face. 'Oh God, Elsa, are we really here?'

David stirs, but she seems unable to put him down. I move in closer and put my arms around them both. Finally, through the shock and disbelief, I let myself feel something, an unstoppable flood of emotion and images. The moments of us together, the moments I collected all through my life and couldn't let go of. It didn't matter that it had been more than sixty years – what difference does time make? It's meaningless. The real distance between people is love. If you have that, there are no miles, or hours or days or centuries.

'I love you,' I say. It is so quiet, like a whisper. She couldn't possibly hear over the noise of flames and chaos.

'I love you too,' she says. 'I held on. For my whole life, I held on.'

'I'm so sorry. I couldn't hear you.'

'You just needed help. You needed help to listen. You always did. You remember the art gallery? I followed you there. I was waiting for you to talk to me, but instead you stood staring at that ridiculous painting.'

'The cows?'

'The cows.'

'I happen to think it's a very fine painting.'

'I see I still have a lot to teach you about art.'

'It brought us together at least.'

'You still have it? My sketch?'

'It was lost for a long time. Like me. Laura found it. I couldn't have done this if it wasn't for . . .'

And we both look back at the house and say at the same time. 'Laura.'

Chapter Fifty-Three

2008

Everything is dark and I feel weightless, as though gravity has abandoned me. Then a shaft of bright white light shines directly into my eyes. I can see shapes moving in closer. Is this it? Is this the afterlife?

'Can you hear me?' a voice says. 'What's your name, love?'

It's a thick Somerset accent, which is not what I was expecting.

'Laura,' I say. 'I'm Laura.'

'Laura? We just need to check that you're okay. Can you tell us what happened?'

This is not the afterlife. I'm lying on the road and there are two paramedics leaning over me – the man with the kind voice, and a woman speaking into a walkie-talkie, her eyes on me. The blue lights from the ambulance reflect on the damp tarmac like flashing neon.

'I'm fine,' I say and I try to sit up, but they're holding me.

'We're going to get you to hospital; just to be safe. Were you in an accident?'

Everything is woozy and unclear, and their voices echo as I'm lifted upwards and onto something soft.

'Have you found anyone else?' I say.

The two of them look at each other.

'Let's get you in the ambulance.'

I can barely speak. There are straps being placed around me on the stretcher.

'There was a man in the garden,' I say.

'It's okay, Laura. Just relax.'

There are busy sounds of people working, bustling about; I can smell disinfectant. When I open my eyes, I know that I am in the RUH and when I turn my head, I see Mum on the chair beside my bed. She is holding my hand.

'You're nothing but trouble,' she says.

She smiles and leans forward, brushing a hair away from my eyes.

'Will ...' I say.

She puts her finger to her mouth in a shushing motion. 'You need to rest.'

'But Will ... he was in the garden.'

She shakes her head. 'Get some sleep.'

She leans across and kisses me on the forehead. I am caught out by the feeling of it – of being cared for so closely. It is something she hasn't done since I was a child. I feel as though I am being protected from something.

'I have to know,' I say. 'What's happened?'

'We don't know, love. It looks like you may have been in a hit and run accident outside Avon Lodge. What were you doing there?

I know that house is precious to you, but darling, they've been gone for years.'

'I was there with a man. I took him there.'

A brief look of concern flashes across her face.

'What man?'

'He was my . . .' I start, but then I try to picture him and I can't. My mind is fogging over. 'I was looking after him, I think.'

Almost invisibly, she shakes her head.

'You were looking after him? I don't know what you mean.'

'My job.'

'You don't have a job.'

'Mum, I'm scared. I can't remember . . .'

'You're exhausted. The doctors think you might have concussion.'

'There was a bright light. All around me.'

'You really need to sleep.'

'Mum, what's happened to me?'

'You've been in an accident and you're in hospital.'

'No. Before that.'

She smiles a warm, concerned, indulgent smile.

'You were travelling for a long time, and then you came home.'

When I wake up later, Mum is gone and the ward is dark and quiet. I try to think back to before the accident but the details are blurry and inconsistent. I feel as though everything is in flux, as though the past is being rewritten. Memories move in and out like theatre sets. Instinctively, I look at the little table next to the bed, but can't recall what I'm searching for. Then I realise it's my mobile phone. Does Mum have it? Do I own a phone? I carry something with me wherever I go. A memory hits me. I am standing outside Avon Lodge and it's pouring with rain. An old man answers the door. Granddad?

'Are you okay?' a nurse asks as she passes.

A clear thought emerges from the fog. They have left something there for me. A voice tells me, go back. Go back.

Chapter Fifty-Four

1942

The walk is very different in the early summer. Instead of barren fields and bare trees, we're surrounded along the lanes by cow parsley and cuckooflowers and the air is buzzing with insects. We're holding hands, Elsa and I, almost gripping each other – a few days after our return, we're still afraid to let go. Everything is strange and bewildering, like shock or love.

'We're almost there,' I say, and for a while I just walk and look at her, and she looks back at me, and there are no words for what we're feeling. She is wearing a tea dress printed with tiny flowers, the skirt billowing in the warm breeze. Her hair is loose. The walk is steep, but I'm finding the strength in my legs again, the ghost of old age slowly departing.

'I see it,' Elsa cries, pointing. And there, around a little cove of trees, is Sham Castle, its ridiculous semi-grandeur just as impressive and farcical as we remembered from all those years ago. We traipse through the long grass and toward the brow of the hill, and the view over Bath. And all the memories flood back to me, of the first time we were here. I was so wild for her, she was all I could think about; this girl who fought her way across Europe; this girl who taught me about art and music. Our first kiss in the cold outside her aunt's house; the morning after her arrest, when she pushed me against the table with her hips. The feeling of her haunted me for decades.

How do you tell someone that? How do you really tell someone how you feel when you love them with everything you have? I stop for a second, feeling utterly overcome, feeling dizzy with it. Elsa stops too and walks back to me, smiling.

'Are you okay?' she says.

'I'm just ... I can't ... it's too much to take on.'

'Come here,' she says. She takes my face in her hands. 'It's okay. It's okay to be afraid and to be happy. This is what I've always tried to explain to you, through everything. It is okay to feel. You can just let go. I'm here, Will. I'll hold you up.'

The city is a mess. Buildings gone or half gone, the piles of rubble like giant graves, church spires that ruled the skyline for decades, now lost. But the workmen are here, the houses being slowly repaired. Our own has been carefully bolstered and will survive. Perhaps I'll rebuild the workshop.

'It's still beautiful,' says Elsa. 'Even after everything.'

'It's strange isn't it, to know what is coming; to see all the buildings that survived but will one day be knocked down anyway. Perhaps things will be different this time.'

I take her hand again.

'I am certain they will be,' she says.

The city will be rebuilt, it will prosper. Forty years from now, a new generation of residents will come in from London, along the intercity train lines; they'll buy up the houses on the Circus and the Crescents; they'll scrub the faces of the buildings until the honeyed stone is returned to its former glory.

And in the summer evenings, the sun will come in low over the rooftops bathing every wall in a delicate pink light, like cherry blossom. Perhaps Elsa and I will climb up here to watch it, or we'll sit in a café in Kingsmead Square or on a picnic blanket in the park. Her head is close to mine and her hair whips into my face, the smell of violets about her – I wonder if this will ever stop making me tearful with joy.

'There is just one question I have for you,' I say as we start our way back, along the paths and quiet roads. 'What did you do for all those years when we were apart, while I slept and stewed at home?'

She smiles to herself and links her arm into mine.

'I don't mind ...' I continue. 'I understand if ... if your life was ... more full.'

She leans in and kisses me on the cheek.

'It's a long story,' she says. 'I might even tell you one day. That's if I remember. I'm beginning to forget the things that happened before.'

'Me too.'

'Perhaps we will lose it all. I think perhaps we have to.'

Back at home, we open the front door to laughter. Michael whips out of the parlour followed by Florence, both of them being pursued by Aunt Josephine wielding a newspaper. 'I must swat these damned flies,' she yells, as the children scream and pelt into the kitchen, toward the garden. 'Come on,' she shouts. 'We have set a picnic up. The light is beautiful.'

I glance into the parlour, at the olive sofa and the rugs, vibrant

386

with colour. And a memory hits me, so clear it is almost painful. I see her here, the young woman who came to help me – so unsure of herself, so anxious, her hands drawn up into her sleeves. I can almost see her.

'Are you all right?' asks Elsa from the hall. She comes over and looks into the room.

'There was someone who came to care for me. I was terribly rude to her, but she kept coming. She was so brave. How terrible, I can't remember . . .'

'Laura,' says Elsa.

'That's it! I saw her there for a second, but I can barely remember what she looked like.'

'There was something about her that was open. I figured out a way to communicate with her through machines – the clocks, the radios. We're here because of her.'

In the kitchen, the walls still smell of wet paint. Elsa chose the colour, a lovely pale blue. We used the money from the government to repair and rebuild the rear wall – I did a lot of the work myself. Cooperton dropped by to give his advice on the interiors.

'Come on,' Auntie Jo shouts again.

Elsa takes my hand and we walk out into the sun. I have moved what's left of my wireless collection into the cellar until I decide whether or not to rebuild the workshop, and Michael and I have more or less taken up residence down there, making repairs, setting up a new antenna. I think it's good for the boy – he lost his family and his home. He is still in a state of shock. The authorities will have to decide what happens next. If we are to adopt, we will need to be married, but we'd like him to stay with us.

I turn to Elsa urgently.

'Will Laura come back? If we change her father's life, will we take her away?'

'No,' Elsa says. 'She has to come. She was a part of this from the beginning; she will get her turn at happiness too.'

I feel a swell of relief.

'We need to put something aside for her,' I say. 'Even if we forget everything, even if we are long gone, I want her to know that we were thankful.'

Elsa looks around for a second, then watches Florence running past, laughing. 'I know what to do,' she says.

'Where is everyone?' shouts Auntie.

All through these days, Elsa and I keep pausing and looking at each other and saying over and over again, 'I missed you, I missed you.' Auntie Jo finds this hilarious and melodramatic. 'You've barely been apart,' she cries. These are the things we have to keep remembering. We were ghosts for a long time. We're not ghosts anymore.

Chapter Fifty-Five

2008

The sky is clear and bright and a warm breeze helps to push me up Lansdown Road as I pedal. Arriving outside the decrepit house in the early summer sun, I am struck with the certain knowledge that I'm in exactly the right place.

I check my watch. It is 9.47 a.m. I feel strangely content and alive.

Leaning my mountain bike against the garden wall, I push my glasses back up then look again at the large, dark Victorian house in front of me.

It is grubby, but beautiful. Bath stone, bulging bay windows, two ornamental turrets above the attic rooms, to give it a sort of fairytale grandeur. It is clear that some cracks in the stonework around the windows have been filled in. There are new glass panes in the front door. It is set back from the road, separate from both a smart row of houses on one side and a vast construction site on the other, but Avon Lodge looks as though it is comfortable in its own company.

I am here just to look, hoping perhaps that it will jog some memories. I've been out of hospital for two days, and I still feel like a stranger in a strange land. Everything is familiar and yet slightly off – and I have memories that don't match the city I'm in, as though the components of Bath have been shuffled and put back slightly differently. On my ride this morning, I cycled up the Parade, toward the Empire Hotel, and passed the beautiful Royal Literary and Science Institute on the Orange Grove – I had to call Mum and ask, 'Has that building always been there?'

The last few days have made me think a lot about what it is that connects us to the world and the people we know. Would I recognise my mother wherever I saw her, in whatever context? One thing I now understand for certain is that I am not where I was. I am somewhere else. I woke up this morning and knew I felt different, that a massive weight had been lifted from me, a weight that had been there for years. After an hour or so I worked out what was missing. Dread. Someone once told me that in quantum theory there is a concept called the observer effect: merely viewing a phenomenon inevitably changes the phenomenon itself. Perhaps it also changes the observer too. I can't talk to Mum about this yet because frankly I'm beginning to scare her. Whoever she is.

'Inspecting the workmanship?' a voice says from behind me.

It is a kindly-looking middle-aged man in a tweed jacket and a purple scarf.

'No, I was just . . .'

'It's all right, Laura, I know this house is important to you. I'm Matthew. Remember me? My mother Florence lives just there.' Instinctively, I look toward the house a few doors down. An old woman is watching us from an upstairs window. The man looks too. 'She's always been a little eccentric, but she is getting frail and confused these days. She has lots of lovely memories of your grandparents, but her stories don't always make sense.'

Grandparents?

'I'm sure your mother told you, but I bought Avon Lodge a few weeks ago – we're renovating it. Am I right in thinking you were here the other day? One of the workmen said you were involved in an accident. Are you all right?'

'I'm fine.'

'I haven't seen you since you were a child. Will and Elsa were a lovely couple, weren't they?'

The mention of their names sends a spark of recognition through my brain. I see them dancing somewhere, I see them walking along the Bath skyline together, I see him as an old man, alone ...

'Sixty years they lived here together,' Matt continues. 'That's when they weren't galivanting off around the world. Anyway, I'd better get back to it. We're just digging out the foundations in the garden. It's a bit of a mess out there. Lord knows what we'll unearth.'

He laughs indulgently then waves, pushes open the gate, and walks up the path to the door. I lift my bike from the wall and begin to walk it away, too distracted to get on and ride. Something happened here, I think. Something happened.

A few houses down from Avon Lodge I hear a front door opening, and I turn to see the old lady from the window. She is wearing a flowing white nightdress and a thin satin gown that rides up and around her in the breeze.

'Wait,' she calls. 'I have something for you.'

I stop, but I'm thinking about what the man said, that she is not quite with it anymore; that she won't make any sense. I will have to be patient – somehow, I know how to deal with this kind of situation.

'You're back,' she says. 'I didn't think I would see you again.'

'You've seen me before?'

She gives me a puzzled look, but then smiles warmly.

'Yes, of course. I knew you as a child. And I knew you in the time before.'

'The time before?'

A breeze is catching up, sending an old cola can scuttling along the pavement beside me.

'The time before this. When you looked after Will.'

'I don't know what you mean.'

There are clouds gathering at the edges of the horizon – how did I not see them until now? They are dark and high, like vast airships coming in.

'You came here almost every day to look after Will. I saw you. From the window. He was alone then, he was alone for so many years.'

There is a sound in the air, or is it a feeling? Something like an electric charge, the hum of a distant engine. For the first time in ages, I begin to feel tense and anxious and those emotions seem utterly unnatural.

'I should go,' I say. *She's old and confused. Her stories don't make sense.* I climb onto the saddle and I'm just about to push away when ...

'I have something for you!' she repeats. This time she holds something out to me. It is a tin box. The buzzing, I now realise, is the sound of a detuned radio, but I have no idea where it is coming from. The voices flow in and out as though it is not quite at the correct frequency.

'Will and Elsa gave it to me to pass on to you. But they had very specific instructions. They told me I was only to give it to you after 26 April 2008. I have been waiting. I've been looking out for you.'

392

I open the box and inside, there is a book. It has a green cover and the title is embossed in gold writing on the spine. *Art Now* by Herbert Read. As soon as I touch it, it is like electricity again. I see them, the two of them. Happy together.

'Be careful,' she says. 'I think there is a note inside. You don't want to lose it.'

'I won't,' I say. 'I'll read it later.'

Carefully, I put the book into my backpack, and get ready to cycle away for the last time.

'You should visit them,' she says. 'I can tell you where they're buried. Although, of course, that's not really where they are.'

I did go to see them that afternoon. And the next. Holcombe Cemetery is a sprawling patchwork of meadows separated by tree-lined pathways, its hundreds of gravestones lined neatly amid the lawns and wild flowers. It was here they buried the victims of the Bath bombings. The quiet of the place, the solitude; it was what I needed to try and get my head straight – or as straight as it could be.

And on the third afternoon, when I go to the grave, there is someone else standing by it.

I see them from quite a distance away. It is a young woman in a tea dress – her long red hair catching in the breeze. She has her back to me and she's looking at the gravestone, then she lays down a small bouquet of pretty purple flowers. I almost can't move when I see her. I know it is their grave she is standing at.

I walk slowly along the path toward her, she doesn't turn. She doesn't move. When I am close enough to reach out and touch her, she turns.

She is about the same age as me, kind of beautiful but not conventionally, her face somehow too bold and sculpted. I am very sure that I recognise her.

'Elsa?' I say. That name again. I step up beside her as birds sing and the scent of her perfume hangs about us.

'Yes. And you're Laura? Michael's daughter?'

'. . . Yes.'

'Hi! At last! It's crazy we've never met properly. But then we're such a scattered clan, no one has kept in touch.'

She notices my bewildered expression. 'Okay, I'm getting ahead of myself here,' she says. 'So, my mum is Will and Elsa's first daughter. And I'm Elsa, named after my grandmother, just to make things extra confusing. Your dad was adopted by Will and Elsa, right?' She shakes her head incredulously. 'I mean, I know you and me are not actually related, but . . . I don't know, I always really wanted to meet you. It's so lovely to bump into you here!'

I gulp almost audibly. A shiver passes over me. We both turn to the grave.

'You've heard their story, right?' she says. 'They met at a dance at the Pavilion and then Grandma Elsa left a note for Will in the library asking him out on a date, which was pretty forward for the time. His friend made him toss a coin to decide whether to call her, and he did, and they were together for the rest of their lives. Isn't that incredible? How one tiny action can have these gigantic consequences? It's so weird to me.'

'It is,' I say slowly. 'It is weird.'

There's a silence.

'I like the flowers you brought,' I tell her.

'Violets, naturally. Grandma loved them,' she says. 'I'm going out to Vienna in a few weeks. I really want to see where she came from – get a feel for the family history and all that. I'm catching the Eurostar over to Brussels then the sleeper train from there. So, what are you doing now?'

'I'm just staying here in the cemetery for a bit, I think.'

394

'No,' she laughs. 'I mean in life.'

'Oh … well, I'm sort of between lives at the moment.'

'I know that feeling.' She is quiet for a few seconds. 'Have you seen your dad recently?'

'No … I … no.'

'I guess it's tough with him filming all over the world? Anyway, I'd better go. It was nice to meet you, Laura.'

'And you. Really nice.'

She wanders away and immediately I regret not saying more, not asking more, not arranging something. Then she stops.

'I have a dumb idea,' she calls. 'You should come! You should come to Vienna! It would be really nice to get to know you. I feel like we should know each other. We can catch up, tell each other our life stories and … No, sorry, that's idiotic. Sorry. You can't just drop everything and go to Europe.'

'I don't really have anything to drop.'

She smiles again and walks toward me, grabbing a notebook from her bag. When she's close to me, she scribbles something down, rips out the page and puts it into my hand. 'It's my phone number,' she says. 'Just in case.' I look down at the paper, and beneath her number she has sketched a flower.

When she's gone, I lean down to the gravestone and follow the engraved letters with my finger.

IN LOVING MEMORY OF
WILL AND ELSA KLEIN-EMERSON.

ALWAYS TOGETHER,
IN THIS LIFE AND THE NEXT.

In this life and the next.

395

Looking down at Elsa's note, I weigh things up. I've been thinking about applying for research jobs, maybe studying part-time. But there's no rush. I can go with her if I want. All possibilities are there to be explored.

I realise it will take me weeks, maybe even months to piece together what has happened to me. Maybe I'll never know. Maybe this is just how it is. How do we really know what to expect when we wake in the morning, or when we stand outside a stranger's house, waiting to be let in?

But Will is not a stranger – I know that. And neither is Elsa. We have a connection, it buzzes in the air between us like a signal. Time passes, the universe expands, pathways close and open, but there are links between us that don't fade.

Life is a radio dial; we travel along it from left to right, and on the way we discover stations that we fall in love with and cherish – then we move on and lose them. But those stations aren't gone. They're still transmitting. If you listen very closely, you hear their ghosts amid the static. The people we've loved and think we have lost, the things that moved us, they are always there, they are bright and alive, somewhere on the dial.

You just have to listen.

Acknowledgements

While researching and writing this novel, I discovered there were three subjects I needed to know a lot more about: Bath during the 1930s, vintage radio technology, and multiverse theory. Thank you to Bath historians Cathryn Spence and David McLaughlin for meeting me on several occasions to talk about the city and its past – what fascinating conversations! Thank you to Stephen Clews, manager of the Roman Baths, for showing me around the Pump Rooms, and to Fleur Johnson from Bath Fashion Museum who took an afternoon out of her schedule to show me beautiful 1930s dresses. Also, the historian Daniel Snowman provided me with invaluable advice and information about the experience of Jewish émigrés from Germany and Austria and the lives of upper-class Jewish families in Vienna in the 1930s.

For sharing their incredible knowledge of vintage communications, I'd like to thank Elizabeth Bruton of the Science Museum, Giles Read and Elaine Richards of the Radio Society of Great Britain, David Higginson of the British Vintage Wireless Society and Ian Brothwell of the Radio Amateur Old Timers' Association. Thanks also to Phil Booth, and to Neil Wilson, owner of the

Washford Radio Museum, who walked me around his vast collection of vintage wireless sets even though it was in the middle of being relocated.

Thank you to Sam Green and Liz Wilson for talking to me about physics, and especially to Professor Jonathan Butterworth from the physics and astronomy department at UCL, for letting me come to his office, drink his tea and chat about multiverse concepts – particularly brane theory.

A huge thank you to my friend Rob Lomax, a senior lecturer at UWE, who answered many questions about social work and social policy, usually sent to him in frantic Saturday afternoon emails. Thank you to Jenny Atkins at Bluebird Care in Frome for talking to me about the home care sector.

Several people generously agreed to read this novel in various states of incompletion. Thank you to my pals Jordan Erica Webber, Eva Field and Christian Donlan for their time and feedback – I couldn't have finished this book without them. On this note, a special thank you to Rosanna Forte at Little, Brown, for spotting several pan-dimensional continuity errors that would have flummoxed even Marty McFly and Doc Brown. Thank you to the many successful authors I have met online and at literary festivals, and then complained to about the writing process – these include Ian Rankin, Chris Brookmyre, Louise Jensen, Amy McCulloch and Sandhya Menon.

I want to thank everyone at Sphere and Little, Brown for their help, support and guidance during the two years it took to write this novel – especially my long-suffering editor Ed Wood, whose instinctive understanding of what makes stories work (even stories about multidimensional love affairs) continues to astonish me. Thank you to Clara Diaz, Andy Hine, Kate Hibbert, Laura Vile and Catherine Burke. Thank you to the world's most patient and understanding desk editor, Thalia Proctor, and my brilliant agent and invaluable ally, Eugenie Furniss.

Thank you to the staff at the Bath Record Office and the team at Frome Library where I wrote most of this book.

A very special thank you to Kate Gray and Holly Nielsen who provided extremely important advice regarding the character of Laura James. I can't tell you how much I appreciated your trust and help very early in this process.

Thank you to my friends Simon Attfield, Will Porter, Simon Parkin, Joao Sanches, Caspar Field, Keza MacDonald and Chella Ramanan. Thank you to my sons Zac and Albie for inspiring me, for testing me and for joining me in many restorative video game sessions (which reminds me, thank you Respawn Entertainment for Apex Legends!). Thank you to mum, Catherine and Nina. Thank you to Morag, the absolute love of my life.

Keith Stuart is an author and journalist. His heartwarming debut novel, *A Boy Made of Blocks*, was a Richard and Judy Book Club pick and a major bestseller, and was inspired by Keith's real-life relationship with his autistic son. Keith has written for publications including *Empire*, *Red* and *Esquire*, and is the former games editor of the *Guardian*. He lives with his wife and two sons in Frome, Somerset.

Help us make the next generation of readers

We – both author and publisher – hope you enjoyed this book.
We believe that you can become a reader at any time in your life,
but we'd love your help to give the next generation a head start.

Did you know that 9% of children don't have a book of their
own in their home, rising to 12% in disadvantaged families*?
We'd like to try to change that by asking you to consider the role
you could play in helping to build readers of the future.

We'd love you to think of sharing, borrowing, reading, buying or talking
about a book with a child in your life and spreading the love of reading.
We want to make sure the next generation continue to have access
to books, wherever they come from.

And if you would like to consider donating to charities that help
fund literacy projects, find out more at www.literacytrust.org.uk
and www.booktrust.org.uk.

Thank you.

hachette
CHILDREN'S GROUP

little, brown
BOOK GROUP

*As reported by the National Literacy Trust